EISENHOWER

The Inside Story

By Robert J. Donovan

THE ASSASSINS

BY ROBERT J. DONOVAN

HARPER & BROTHERS, PUBLISHERS

New York

EISENHOWER

The Inside Story

ILLUSTRATED

EISENHOWER: THE INSIDE STORY

About one fourth of the material in this book was first published in the New York Herald Tribune under the title EISENHOWER IN THE WHITE HOUSE

Library of Congress catalog card number: 56-9653

To

AMY, PATRICIA *and* PETER

CONTENTS

Contents

and Passes a Lonely Vigil with the President – Eisenhower Is Taken to the Hospital – Nixon's Busy Night – How the Government Ran – The Cabinet Discusses Procedures for Carrying On in the President's Absence – Convalescence

A section of photographs will be found
following page 74

PREFACE

In portraying President Eisenhower and his associates in action in the first Republican administration in twenty years, I have assembled a great deal of material which ordinarily does not come to light until long after a President has left office and which in certain respects is unique. This includes a wealth of unpublished information, as well as numerous interviews with the Cabinet officers and other key men involved in the shaping of historic events. Although it is too early to write a definitive record of the administration, I am hopeful that the quality of this material may make the book, within its limits, a durable history of the President's first three years in office.

It is to the best of my ability a reporter's book, straightforward and objective. What did the President do? What was his attitude? Whom did he talk to? What did he say? What did others say? Did something please the President or did it anger him? Was there any humor or pathos in the incident? What entered into the President's thinking? Why did he do what he did? These questions, applied to the many different situations and problems, are what this book is mostly about.

My purpose has not been to praise or blame or make a critical appraisal, but to tell a story. I have tried to give an intimate picture of the varied and critical scenes of the President's life in the White House, in his office, at Cabinet meetings, in private conferences, in the making of high policy—and in some of his lighter moments, painting, playing golf or cooking steaks on the roof.

In doing so I have been sparing in my own observations, but not to such a rigorous extent as to omit comment when the story requires it.

Needless to say, there is nothing official about this volume. I have set down the facts as I have understood them. No one in the

White House, or in any way connected with the President or with the government, read any part of it before publication. The only exceptions were certain pages, containing national security material, submitted for the standard technical clearance.

No quotations, direct or indirect, originating in private meetings and conferences, have been "manufactured" by the author.

R. J. D.

Chevy Chase, Maryland

ACKNOWLEDGMENTS

This book would scarcely have been possible without the encouragement in the first place and the generous help and support throughout which came to me from Roscoe Drummond.

I also have good reason to be grateful for the active and unstinted support and understanding I have received from Ogden Reid, president and publisher of the New York *Herald Tribune*.

I am indebted beyond expression for the help of various members and former members of the administration in reconstructing many of the scenes of the last three years. Their names I cannot very well mention because of the confidence I owe them as "news sources." Certain of them provided me a great deal of information which they had taken pains to assemble and which, in some cases, they might have used instead in their own future writings.

I am grateful for the editorial help I have received from John Appleton, of Harper & Brothers, and for the continuous criticism and correction of the manuscript by my friend Donald Irwin of the *Herald Tribune*. I am indebted also to two other *Herald Tribune* colleagues, Robert S. Bird and Marcus Duffield, who pitched in and helped when the going was tough. I owe much to Vera R. Glaser, who worked with me on research from beginning to end.

EISENHOWER

The Inside Story

CHAPTER 1

From the Commodore
to the White House

The Cabinet Meeting at the Commodore – Eisenhower Previews His Inaugural Address – Of Parades and Homburgs – The President-elect and Wilson Debate East-West Trade – Interregnum at the Commodore – The Truman-Eisenhower Meeting – The President-elect Visits Korea – Strategy Talks Aboard the Helena – Admiral Radford and the American Military Position in Asia – The Inauguration

I

The private luncheon in the South Room of the Hotel Commodore in New York on January 12, 1953, was drawing to a close when the President-elect, Dwight D. Eisenhower, arose to address his future Cabinet and White House advisers.

"I am going to read you now what I have prepared," he told them, taking up the latest draft of his inaugural address.

With the inauguration only eight days off, the President-elect had summoned his Cabinet and staff to a two-day session which opened with this luncheon after a prayer by the Secretary of Agriculture-designate, Ezra Taft Benson, who was, and is, a member of the Council of Twelve of the Church of Jesus Christ of Latter-day Saints. Situated at the Lexington Avenue end of the lobby floor of the Commodore, the South Room has walls of gray and a green carpet with a geometric figure. Three ceiling-high casement windows are draped in gold cloth. Eisenhower and his guests sat in green leather arm chairs at a U-shaped table covered with pale green linen and decorated with green and gold flowers.

1

The President-elect, of course, was at the head of the table. On his right sat the new Vice-President, Richard M. Nixon. John Foster Dulles, the Secretary of State-designate, was at Eisenhower's left.

The session, without parallel in American history, had been called to discuss some of the fiscal and other problems for which these men, many of them new to public life, would soon be responsible. The war in Korea was heading into its thirty-second month. A budget deficit of nearly ten billion dollars threatened in the next fiscal year. Stalin's Russia was stockpiling atom bombs at an unpleasant rate. All around the world, in Europe, in Iran, in Indo-China, serious troubles beset the Western allies.

A new President, however, cannot think only of such things as his time for taking office approaches. He has to weigh the problem of what kind of hat he will wear at the inauguration and of which of two socially equal inaugural balls he will attend first. What hour the inaugural parade begins, how much time he will have to gulp down his first Presidential lunch before falling into the march down Pennsylvania Avenue, what the feelings of the last units in line will be if they don't pass the White House before dark—all these matters have to be considered very seriously.

On this first day of the session, therefore, the main business was to come to grips with such questions and to give the Cabinet an opportunity to hear and, if it chose, to criticize the inaugural address.

When the President-elect read it through after lunch, applause resounded through the room.

"I read it far more for your blue pencils than I did for your applause," Eisenhower reminded his listeners, "because at first, in our attempt to state a philosophy of government and of intent, we were not close enough down to our daily living. So we have been gradually rewriting it, but it is very difficult to abandon in your own thinking and your own writing an original conception. One reason I wanted to read it now is so that you can think it over and be ready to tear it to pieces."

The first to respond was Charles E. Wilson, the white-haired former president of General Motors, who was to become, after some difficulties with the Senate over his ownership of General Motors stock, the fifth Secretary of Defense.

"I think it is wonderful," Wilson said. "I am in favor of flying the flag pretty high."

"I am, too," Eisenhower replied. "I would get out and shout it out loud, but you have also got to bring basic principles down to living because here is this thing going out to probably one of the greatest audiences that has ever heard a speech. It is going in the papers. Here are thousands out in front of us. You want every person there to carry home with him a conviction that he can do something."

At sixty-two the President-elect was a ruddy, partly bald, good-looking man of strong spirit and abounding physical energy. He stood five feet and ten inches tall and weighed a hundred and seventy-eight pounds, which was only six pounds more than his weight as a West Point cadet forty years before. His long career as an Army officer had left him with an upright and dignified bearing. His large hands were becoming slightly gnarled, and his tenseness was revealed now and then in the way he would squeeze his right fist around in the palm of his left hand. His eyes were a luminous blue, intensely expressive of warmth, coldness, anger, mirth, or whatever his mood at the moment happened to be. His most striking characteristic was, and still is, a leaping and effortless smile that seems the warmer for the sternness or impassivity from which it springs. Eisenhower is a man of pronounced and changing moods, but as he met unofficially with his Cabinet for the first time that day his spirit was one of cheerfulness and relish for his new role.

"I had in here in one place," he muttered, rummaging through his manuscript, "that peace rests squarely on, among other things, productivity, and I am pointing out that everybody can help in productivity. That is one of the factors of peace because it relieves pressures in the world that are favorable to Communism. I think it is still in here a little bit, but in my work at midnight I have gotten confused."

Turning to Emmet Hughes, the former articles editor of *Life*, who was then his chief speech writer, he said that he would like to restore some of the references to the merits of productivity.

"You remember we have talked about it a half-dozen times, and it always eludes us," he said. "We must point out something that is very important and where every man feels he can do a part. That is the reason for the preacher and the teacher and the mother in the home, but workmen can help to produce something more to allay this starvation and distress in the world. Now if you will take this and make any of those editorial changes we are talking about, I will appreciate it."

"I have one little thing on productivity," Wilson said. "It is the urge and continuing effort to accomplish more with the same human effort. That is the basis of the thing. Sometimes people think productivity is sweating the boys more. That is not the thing."

"That is one reason," Eisenhower remarked, "we were afraid that anything we would say would leave the impression that we were preaching going back to the forty-eight-hour week, or something like that. It does not mean that, but it does mean that when a fellow is working at his maximum capacity and efficiency he is doing something not just for his pocketbook or the profit of the country, but the world."

"A free society stimulates the efficiency of the millions," Wilson said. "We should urge that we accomplish more with the same effort for the good of all."

"It is on a high plane and for the occasion it is very good," Ezra Benson said. "I think it is wonderful."

"After you go home," the President-elect said, glancing around the table, "if you happen to think of something that should go in, we would be delighted. We still have a few days."

"We want to keep it largely on a high spiritual plane with exhortation," he added, "but at the same time trying to relate it to our everyday living."

"I did not see anything I would want to change," Wilson assured him. "When you started to talk about productivity being left out, you gave me this other idea."

"We can get in something on that," Eisenhower said. "I don't know how far we can explain it, but we can get over the idea that everybody who is contributing something to satisfy the basic human needs in this great world is doing something to promote peace. I think that the man at a lathe ought to feel just as much satisfaction in doing his part and just as much responsibility for doing his part as a Senator."

The President-elect then turned the attention of the meeting to plans for the inaugural festivities.

"Some of you gentlemen were here with me," he said, "when we agreed we would start a fashion where there was a little bit more flexibility for men's dress, and we would appear, those of us who were here agreed, in striped trousers, but we would have short coats or cutaways, as we pleased, and we would all wear dark Homburgs and dark overcoats. We got a bit of a blink from some of the Congressional delegations, saying they must wear silk hats."

"They are going to be the silk-hat boys," he quipped, "and we will wear dark Homburgs."

Whether Eisenhower realized it or not, the public announcement that he would wear a Homburg also got a bit of a blink from the White House. Silk hats had been in vogue at inaugurations since Franklin Pierce took office exactly one hundred years before. Harry S. Truman's associates said indignantly that since Truman was still President, it was for *him* to set the style and for Eisenhower to follow it as a courtesy. In the end, however, Truman turned out in a Homburg, as did all the other dignitaries with the exception of Senator Carl Hayden, Democrat, of Arizona, a member of the Joint Congressional Inaugural Committee, who did his stubborn best to keep the old tradition alive with a silk hat.

"Tradition is not involved," Eisenhower insisted at the luncheon. "If we were going back to tradition, we would wear tricornered hats and knee britches. We will not do that, so we will do as we please otherwise."

After examining this point from several angles, Robert Cutler, the brisk, pungent president of the Old Colony Trust Company, in Boston, who had been designated as Special Assistant to the President for National Security Affairs, made his comment.

"If Mrs. Hobby comes in knee britches," he said, "I want to be in the front row."

One of the unexpected consequences of the Homburg decision was that several members of the Cabinet had to make quick trips to a haberdasher because they owned silk hats but not Homburgs.

The program for January 20 was then detailed by Joseph C. McGarraghy, chairman of the Inaugural Committee.

The day would begin, he explained, with a special service for the President-elect and his family at the National Presbyterian Church in Washington. Eisenhower had joined the church, which had been the place of worship of Presidents Jackson, Pierce, Polk, Buchanan, Grant, Cleveland and Benjamin Harrison.

"May I interrupt a second?" Eisenhower asked. "I forgot to say that everybody here, with his wife or his family, is invited to that."

McGarraghy outlined plans for the inaugural parade, which would not, he said, get completely past the White House until about five o'clock.

"Let me ask you another question," the President-elect broke in. "Will the head of that parade be organized sufficiently ahead of time so that we can cut this luncheon hour even shorter, and it will be ready to start? Speaking as one who has marched in one of the blankety-blank things and had to wait an hour on Pennsylvania Avenue while someone went up to lunch, I would very much like to help out several thousand people who will be waiting in the cold."

Not receiving a direct answer, Eisenhower returned to the subject later, saying, "If that Congressional Committee can seat us quickly, I don't see why we can't have a bite to eat in fifteen minutes, because the poor devils who march in that parade are going to have nothing to eat at all."

McGarraghy said he hoped the parade would be moving at one-thirty.

"I would like to start it a little sooner if we could," Eisenhower replied.

McGarraghy checked off the names of some of those who would sit in the reviewing stand in front of the White House.

"How about Mr. Hoover?" Eisenhower inquired.

"I beg your pardon," McGarraghy replied, "Mr. Hoover will be there."

Eisenhower observed that he had invited the former President personally.

Two simultaneous inaugural balls, one in the National Guard Armory and the other in McDonough Gymnasium at Georgetown

University, had been arranged because of the heavy demand for twelve-dollar tickets and three-hundred-dollar boxes. Eisenhower told McGarraghy that if one of the balls was to enjoy a higher social standing than the other, then he wanted to spend more time at the one that was less eminent. McGarraghy assured him that no distinction was intended.

"As far as you are concerned," Eisenhower said, "you have tried to make them absolutely equal."

McGarraghy said that he had.

The President-elect said that he had not intended to put pressure on any member of the Cabinet to attend the service at the National Presbyterian Church. It was just an invitation, he said. Others were free to attend whatever church they wished.

"I must tell you one thing," he smiled. "Mrs. Eisenhower and I got a nice invitation to the inaugural ball, saying R.S.V.P., and I told her to answer it and say we had another engagement."

J. Mark Trice, executive secretary of the Joint Congressional Inaugural Committee, then reviewed the plans for the luncheon at the Capitol after the Inauguration, and Eisenhower brought up the parade again, saying he did not see why it could not start pretty close to one o'clock.

"It depends on how fast you eat," Trice said.

"It gets very dark," the President-elect warned. "Let me tell you something: I know more about this parade business than most people. You put all those people there all day long, standing in the cold, and finally they march past the reviewing stand when darkness has hit us, and particularly if it is a cloudy day. They see all their preparation and work is gone, and you have made some enemies. If we have allowed them to be there, we ought to get them past in daylight hours if we possibly could. To my mind it is a little too bad we didn't start this thing at eleven instead of twelve. But I will tell you what I will guarantee—that my wife and I will swallow our lunch in a hurry to be ready."

"Of course, you couldn't start at eleven," said the Constitutionally-minded Trice, "because you have to wait until the stroke of twelve to get the ceremony started because the Presidential oath goes up to twelve noon on January 20."

Well, Eisenhower replied, people had been guilty of setting the clock back or forward in the past.

(His fear that darkness would overtake the parade, which that year featured among other exhibits an atomic artillery piece, later proved well founded. It was nearly seven before the last marcher passed the White House, and it was not until two minutes after seven that the Eisenhowers entered their new home.)

"While I have interrupted," Eisenhower said to Trice, "let me say one more thing. Somebody very kindly ordered my son home from Korea, so to whatever party you have add one major of infantry, will you?"

"That has already been done," Trice said.

Major John S. D. Eisenhower, the President-elect's son, had been ordered home from the front lines by Truman to attend his father's inauguration.

The talk next turned to the time and place for the swearing in of the Cabinet. Some of the group were not sure of precedent.

"After all," Eisenhower observed, "there has not been a change in administrations for a long time."

The late Martin P. Durkin, Secretary of Labor-designate, said that in 1933 Franklin D. Roosevelt had sworn in his Cabinet and he favored having Eisenhower do likewise.

"I would be in favor of just going right over with our wives after the parade and getting it done," said George M. Humphrey, the new Secretary of the Treasury.

"I would say to bring any immediate members of your family," Eisenhower told them, "and as far as I am concerned, that could include brothers and sisters and your own children. Certainly, we can handle that many in the White House. Bring your own children and their wives. I wouldn't want to start off by starting a family row around here."

"In my own behalf," he said, "maybe I had better extend that to grandchildren. Mine is only five years old, but I am certainly not going to exclude him."

Young Dwight David Eisenhower (called David) and his three younger sisters, Barbara Anne, Susan, and Mary Jean, are the children of Major Eisenhower and Barbara Jean Thompson Eisenhower. The

daughter of an Army colonel, Miss Thompson had met young Eisenhower while he was stationed in Vienna after World War II.

With the inaugural plans finally decided, the discussion returned
to the inaugural address. Eisenhower told the Cabinet: "I think
if you are going to institute and make progress on what you might call
a spiritual crusade of any kind, you have got to identify the follower
with the leader, and if we here identify ourselves collectively as the
leader, we have got to identify the fellow plowing a row of corn or
driving a taxi. We have got to identify him with it. I think all the
way through we must seek to do that."

Eisenhower cautioned against having the speech sound like a
political talk at a whistle stop. He did not want to talk like a
schoolteacher, yet, on the other hand, he felt that an inaugural
address must have dignity.

"I personally am a little bit reluctant," he explained, "ever to
talk in terms that look like we are running a school. I do believe
in this particular one—Lincoln himself didn't say, 'Eighty-seven
years ago.' He said, 'fourscore and seven years ago.' He instantly,
on the opening of that speech, established a certain stateliness.

"He didn't use the language that he knew better than anybody
else—if you will read some of the stories that he told. I am open
to argument on this, but in this speech I deliberately tried to stay
in the level of talk that would make as good reading as possible at
the Quai d'Orsay or No. 10 Downing, but I particularly tried to
make the words that would sound good to the fellow digging the
ditch in Kansas."

"You flew the flag!" Wilson exclaimed. "It was wonderful!"

Dulles expressed his own concern that too much emphasis in the
address was placed upon economics.

"But we must remember also today," Eisenhower countered, "that
unless we can put things in the hands of people who are starving
to death, we can never lick Communism."

A picture he got of China, he said, was one of claws reaching out
to grab anyone who looked as though he had five cents.

"I am convinced that we have got to do something about production," he said. "Maybe I am wrong."

"In India today," Dulles pointed out, "the great peril of Communism comes from intellectual centers."

The next to express his views was former Senator Henry Cabot Lodge, Jr., who was to become the chief of the United States Mission to the United Nations and who would, in that capacity, regularly attend meetings of the Cabinet. He objected to a reference to Moscow in the current draft as having been the center of autocracy and as being presently the center of revolution. Lodge felt that this implied that autocracy no longer reigned in Moscow, and beside, he said, lots of downtrodden people in the world would like to have a revolution.

"Despotism?" the President suggested. "You are right."

"If you gave us a flip from autocracy to despotism," Wilson told Hughes, "it would be better."

Finally, the passage was flipped out of the address altogether.

The President-elect talked about a reaffirmation of faith on inauguration day. "I am not an ordained minister," he said, but he added that the first thing to be remembered was that the Government of the United States was founded on religious faith.

A number of subjects came up during the afternoon. Eisenhower gave his views on the role of the Cabinet and the National Security Council. And even though he had not yet taken office himself, he spoke with concern about the 1954 Congressional elections, then twenty-two months away. The Republicans, who had won Congress by a slight margin on the day he was elected by a landslide, would have "to do a real job" to win again in 1954, he said.

Before the meeting broke up for the day the President-elect and Wilson got into a small argument on a subject that was to pose a large problem for Eisenhower in the months ahead—the matter of trade between East and West, particularly trade in products of a military value.

"I am a little old-fashioned," Wilson said. "I don't like to sell firearms to the Indians."

"Remember this," Eisenhower retorted. "You are trying to set up out of Moscow what you might call a series of centrifugal forces. The last thing you can do is to begin to do things that force all these peripheral countries—the Baltic States, Poland, Czechoslovakia and the rest of them—to depend on Moscow for the rest of their lives.

"How are you going to keep them interested in you? If you trade with them, Charlie, you have got something pulling their interest your way. You see, you immediately jump to guns and ammunition. I am not talking in those terms. It must be selective. You are not going to keep them looking toward us and trying to get out from under that umbrella unless you give something in the way of inducement to come out. You just can't preach abstraction to a man who has to turn for his daily living in some other direction."

Wilson said that he was a good compromiser when he understood the facts.

"But I think," he added, "I am going to be on the tough side of this one."

"Charlie," the President-elect replied, "I am talking common sense."

On the second day, the Cabinet discussed the problem of ending the wage and price controls that had been imposed early in the Korean war and the gloomy outlook for achieving in the near future the Republicans' cherished goal of a tax cut and a balanced budget.

On the subject of jobs in the new administration the President-elect laid down a rule which he was to restate periodically throughout his administration. Friendship with Eisenhower, he told the Cabinet, was not to be regarded as a qualification for office. On the contrary, he said, anyone who advanced a claim of friendship was forthwith to be denied consideration for any position. (At a meeting of the Cabinet on October 30, 1953, Eisenhower noted that he had seldom attempted to influence Cabinet officers in appointments made to high posts in their departments. One of the rare exceptions, he said, was the case of Walter Bedell Smith, his chief of staff in Europe in World War II, who became Under Secretary of State in the new administration.)

II

The end of the two-day session brought the period at the Commodore near to its close. The American people had never seen anything quite like this preparation of a new administration for taking over the duties of the old. In the two months between the election and the inauguration the new White House staff, or a considerable part of it, worked together day and night under Sherman Adams, the tireless former Governor of New Hampshire, who had been designated as the Assistant to the President in the new administration.

This was the period also in which relations between the new Administration and the Republicans in Congress began to take form. A good deal of political maneuvering went on between Forty-second Street and Capitol Hill. The Commodore group, for instance, would have preferred to have Republicans in Congress postpone legislation for a new Hoover Commission to give the Eisenhower administration a chance to do its own housecleaning in Washington and decide for itself what needed to be reorganized. This wish, of course, was not to be realized. On the other hand, Senator John Bricker, Republican, of Ohio, was already seeking early in January the support of the President-elect and Dulles for the Constitutional amendment on treaties which was to give those gentlemen so much misery in the months ahead. Senator Bricker didn't get his wish, either.

At times the confusion at the Commodore was so profuse that some members of the new Administration asked themselves wryly whether the country would be in safe hands when they took over. Still it was better to be confused in the Commodore than in the White House, and there can be little doubt that this experience helped facilitate the transition that occurred on January 20.

President Truman did his part to bring about an orderly change also. He did so not only by inviting the President-elect to the White House for a conference and briefing but by directing his department heads to confer with the Republicans who were to succeed them. Twenty years earlier President Hoover had invited President-elect Roosevelt to the White House to discuss the war debts and a second meeting was held at Roosevelt's request for a review of the foreign situation. However, the conferences among lower officials of the departing and new administrations, starting with the attendance of Budget Director-designate Joseph M. Dodge at the meetings on the new budget being prepared by Truman, had no exact precedent.

Eisenhower was at the Augusta National Golf Club resting up

for a couple of weeks after the campaign when he received Truman's invitation to a conference at the White House. He accepted readily, but, like Roosevelt, he was unwilling to consider entering into any commitments before taking office.

For example, in one of the letters he exchanged with Truman at that time Eisenhower wrote:

> Augusta, Ga.,
> November 7, 1952.

Dear Mr. President:

Because I believe so firmly in true bipartisan approach to our foreign problems, I am especially appreciative of your letter of November 6 suggesting that I have a representative sit in on discussions involving a number of impending decisions in this field. However, because I have had no opportunity to accumulate a staff of advisers and assistants, it will take me a little time to designate anyone who could participate profitably in this kind of conference. I shall give priority attention to the matter and I will communicate with you further no later than Monday next, November 10.

In your letter you use the word "authoritative" by which I take it you mean that my representative will be able accurately to reflect my views. This he will be able to do, but quite naturally this will likewise be the limit of his authority since I myself can have none under current conditions.

> Respectfully,
> Dwight D. Eisenhower

On November 18 the President-elect flew from Augusta to Washington for the conference. At the White House, Eisenhower first went into Truman's office to talk to the President personally. The bitterness of the campaign having shattered the friendly relationship that had once existed between the two, their meeting was somber and tense. Truman did most of the talking, giving his reasons why he had invited Eisenhower to discuss the turnover of the government and reviewing some of the problems confronting the new President in several fields, including atomic energy. After they had been alone together for twenty minutes, they went to the Cabinet room for a briefing which Truman had arranged.

Their respective advisers were grouped around the Cabinet table awaiting them. On Eisenhower's side were Dodge and Lodge. While Dodge had been named to represent the President-elect at the Budget Bureau, Lodge had been appointed as Eisenhower's personal liaison with other departments. Truman's group included Secretary of State Dean Acheson, Secretary of the Treasury John Snyder, Secretary of Defense Robert A. Lovett and W. Averell Harriman, Director of Mutual Security.

Eisenhower and Truman entered the room serious and distant. Truman took the President's chair on the east side of the table. Eisenhower sat opposite him, at the place now occupied by Vice-President Nixon, with Lodge on his right and Dodge on his left. Truman began by distributing copies of a memorandum which had been prepared for him by the Treasury Department. The only parts of it that were not an entirely perfunctory explanation of Treasury functions were:

2. Taxation—In the tax field the immediate problem will relate to a number of defense tax increases, including the excess profits tax, which are due to expire between June 30, 1953, and March 31, 1954. The new Administration will have to formulate a tax program for recommendation to the Congress to meet this situation. The importance of the tax problem is indicated by the fact that the government is operating at a deficit and the scheduled tax expiration would reduce revenues by about $2 billion in the fiscal year 1954 and by about $8 billion a year when the reductions reach their full revenue effect.

3. Debt Management—In the field of debt mangement, there is a $267,000,000,000 national debt created largely as a result of World War II. Some of this debt will require refunding during 1953. There will be new money to raise to finance the Government deficit, if there is one in the calendar year 1953, and to provide for seasonal cash requirements during periods in which expenditures temporarily exceed receipts. . . .

After glancing at it, Eisenhower informed Truman that he expected soon to name his Secretary and Under Secretary of the Treasury.

Truman said that he had called the conference to demonstrate to the world that national unity prevailed in the United States. The purpose of the meeting, he said, was to preserve respect for the United States in the eyes of the world and to frustrate any hopes the

Kremlin might have for exploiting the change in administrations to divide the Western Alliance.

It was his purpose, Truman continued, to do everything possible to facilitate the orderly transfer of the powers of government and to give the incoming administration all the information it desired.

He said that he had no intention of trying to shift to Eisenhower any responsibility which the law placed on the administration still in office, nor of trying to commit or bind Eisenhower to anything. On the other hand, he said, there were certain questions upon which Eisenhower might speak out with great benefit to the country. But that, he made it clear, was Eisenhower's own concern. After this preface he introduced Acheson.

With great solemnity the Secretary of State reviewed some of the troubles confronting the United States, beginning with the Korean problem. In the United Nations, he said, a very serious situation was developing over the India truce plan, which had been presented the day before. Acheson objected that this plan would circumvent the principle, upon which the United States had insisted throughout the truce negotiations, that no prisoners of war should be forced to return home against their will.

The India proposal was subsequently modified to embrace the principle of nonforcible repatriation, but at the time of the White House conference there was no assurance of any such outcome. Indeed that very day expressions of sympathy for the original proposal had come from most members of the U.N. subcommittee with jurisdiction over it, including Great Britain, France and Canada. Acheson spoke with deep concern about this threatened split in Allied unity. Since our allies might be in doubt as to Eisenhower's views, he said, the President-elect could help defeat the plan by speaking out against it. He suggested a draft of a simple statement by the President-elect to this effect.

"Call Eden tonight," Eisenhower jotted on a scratch pad.

Acheson turned gloomily to the situation in Iran where Premier Mohammed Mossadegh's government had broken off relations with the British in the dispute over oil. The Secretary of State said that both sides were being unreasonable. He revealed that he was planning to prod the British to hasten a settlement and commented that this action might cause some ill feeling in London. This was something, he added, that the incoming administration ought to be aware of.

Eisenhower said that he expected to see Sir Anthony Eden, then British Foreign Secretary, on the following Thursday. Acheson replied that he hoped that the President-elect would impress upon Eden the importance of preventing British and American objectives in the Korean negotiations from becoming crossed.

Acheson deplored the lack of progress of the European Defense Community proposal. In fact, he said, the whole effort was in danger of slipping backward. Among other things, he told Eisenhower, the treaty was being used in France as a weapon against Foreign Minister Robert Schuman by his foes. That very day, Acheson added, the government of Chancellor Konrad Adenauer in West Germany had suffered at least a temporary setback on the E.D.C. in Parliament.

Looking at Southeast Asia, Acheson said that a big question was whether the French had the will to carry on the fight in Indo-China against the Communists. A strong feeling was running in France to call the whole thing off, he reported, and most of the native population seemed undecided in its loyalties.

Acheson said that the economic base of the NATO alliance was proving to be much too weak. Noting that the Reciprocal Trade Agreements Act would expire the following June, he said that the new administration would have to take urgent action in the field of foreign economic policy.

Acheson's statement concluded the briefing. As the President-elect was getting ready to leave for further discussions in the Pentagon, Truman produced a draft of a joint statement to be issued after the White House conference. At the suggestion of Lodge certain sentences were stricken out, including one that read, "We both agree that it is of the utmost importance to preserve the principle that prisoners of war shall not be forcibly repatriated."

Eisenhower and Lodge shared Truman and Acheson's feelings about the issue of nonforcible repatriation. When he became President, Eisenhower insisted on this principle as strongly as Truman had. Lodge did not believe, however, that at that time Eisenhower should be committed to a statement of views on it prepared by the outgoing administration. Lodge had strong reservations about Acheson's handling of the prisoner issue in the U.N. and he wanted Eisenhower to be left completely free to word his own statement at a later date.

With the deletions agreed to, Truman and Eisenhower issued a statement saying that important international problems had been discussed and that the meeting and the arrangements for liaison between the old and new administrations "furnish additional proof of the ability of the people of this country to manage their affairs with a sense of continuity and with responsibility."

III

In a campaign speech in Detroit on October 24 Eisenhower had said:

> Where will a new administration begin? It will begin with its President taking a simple, firm resolution. That resolution will be: to forego the diversions of politics and to concentrate on the job of ending the Korean war—until that job is honorably done.
> That job requires a personal trip to Korea. I shall make that trip. Only in that way could I learn how best to serve the American people in the cause of peace. I shall go to Korea.

Eleven days after his meeting with Truman he took off from Mitchel Field, Long Island, for a tour of inspection of the snowy Korean battlefields.

The trip was a very significant one in some respects. The view Eisenhower got of the dour life of the American combat soldiers and the dissipation of American resources in a remote, indecisive struggle intensified his determination to obtain a settlement one way or another. Furthermore the talks on strategy which he held with his advisers aboard the cruiser *Helena* and at Honolulu on the return trip crystallized the thinking that was to underlie the military policies of the new administration.

The problem the President-elect posed in these discussions was how to solve what he called "the great equation" of maintaining indefinitely a strong military force without bankrupting the country in the process. Both Dulles and Admiral Arthur W. Radford, then

Commander-in-Chief, Pacific, offered ideas that became part of the concept of strategy that Eisenhower was working out.

Radford, who had joined the group at Iwo Jima on the way to Korea, felt that the United States was engaged in assorted uncoordinated holding operations in Asia without a really effective long-term, comprehensive strategic plan.

His view was that American military power was overextended, with too many forces committed, notably in Asia, to positions in which the Communists could pin them down. Instead of such scattered deployment, Radford favored concentrating American power in a strategic reserve in or near North America. Under this arrangement the main reliance for holding the front lines would rest on the indigenous forces being built up in non-Communist countries while the mobile power of the United States remained poised to strike at strategic enemy positions in case of war.

In line with this Dulles pressed the view he had been expounding for more than two years on the creation of a massive striking power calculated to deter the Communists from war. He argued that the United States could not possibly mount an adequate static defense all around the vast perimeter from which the Communists might attack. Rather than trying to spread our defenses thinly everywhere, he said, the United States should concentrate on deterring attack by maintaining tremendous retaliatory power capable of striking back swiftly at the sources of aggression. This phase of the discussion foreshadowed the policy of "massive retaliation."

Both Radford and Charles E. Wilson felt that in the future Asia would be the pivot in the cold war. While acknowledging the importance of Asia, Eisenhower said the West could not solve the problems that faced it in Asia until Europe became strong. Once Western Europe had the power to sustain and defend itself and make its influence felt around the world again, he argued, the Asian problem would come into manageable proportions.

The Korean trip had a decisive bearing on the ultimate selection of Radford as the new chairman of the Joint Chiefs of Staff. While the President-elect had known Radford in the service, Wilson had never met him before, and Eisenhower wanted the Secretary of Defense's recommendation for a successor to General of the Army

Omar N. Bradley, whose second term as chairman of the J.C.S. would expire the following August. Eisenhower felt that the new chairman should be an officer who was in sympathy with the notion of a broadened strategy in Asia, which Radford surely was. Another consideration facing the President-elect in this matter was that the Republicans had been charging for years that the Roosevelt and Truman administrations had concentrated too much on Europe and too little on Asia, and Eisenhower was looking for a chairman of the J.C.S. whose record would indicate an urgent interest in the Far East. Nothing was more in evidence in Radford's record than this. Finally, Eisenhower and Wilson were greatly impressed by Radford's performance on the Korean trip.

Illustrative of the new President's respect for Radford was a remark he made at a meeting of the Cabinet on the following April 10, nearly a month before he nominated him as chairman. In reference to a controversy over whether the Sands Point Naval Station at Seattle should be closed, he noted that Governor Arthur B. Langlie, of Washington, had quoted Radford to the effect that such a step would be folly. Eisenhower remarked that he had more confidence in the judgment of Radford than of many others.

While aboard the *Helena* Eisenhower learned that on December 5, in a speech before a meeting of the National Association of Manufacturers in New York, General of the Army Douglas MacArthur had announced that he had "a clear and definite solution to the Korean conflict," involving no "increased danger of provoking universal conflict." MacArthur would not say publicly what his plan was but offered to reveal it to Eisenhower if the President-elect was interested. On the *Helena* this was taken with a grain of salt by some of Eisenhower's advisers, who questioned whether the President-elect should involve himself at this juncture with MacArthur.

Why not? Eisenhower asked. After all, he said, MacArthur was a great soldier, and although he and the former Far East commander had differed on some things, he could see no harm in consulting him.

That settled, some of the Eisenhower group still felt that any message to MacArthur should be kept secret, but the President-elect again demurred. Why, he asked, should he not heed MacArthur's offer? If anyone had any good ideas, he said, characteristically, he was willing to listen. He radioed MacArthur, saying, in part:

I appreciate your announced readiness to discuss these matters with me and assure you I am looking forward to informal meetings in which my associates and I may obtain the full benefit of your thinking and experience.

On December 9 Eisenhower's press secretary, James C. Hagerty, released this message and the reply, in which MacArthur expressed his thanks and added:

This is especially so because, despite my intimate personal and professional concern therewith, this is the first time that the slightest official interest in my counsel has been evidenced since my return.

When the exchange of messages appeared in the newspapers, one of those who read them—and hit the ceiling—was President Truman. The morning papers had been put aboard Truman's train in West Virginia while the President was returning to Washington from his mother-in-law's funeral in Independence, Missouri. Through his press secretary, Roger W. Tubby, he issued a statement saying that if MacArthur had a reasonable plan for ending the war without starting a greater one, he should present it to the proper authorities —meaning the President—at once. Still smoldering, Truman sailed into both MacArthur and Eisenhower at his press conference the next day. He doubted, he said, that MacArthur had a feasible plan for ending the war. And as for Eisenhower, Truman declared, the trip to Korea had been a piece of demagoguery undertaken merely to carry out a campaign pledge. This remark infuriated Eisenhower.

The President-elect and MacArthur met after Eisenhower's return to New York, but the details of MacArthur's proposal were not disclosed.

The President-elect and Mrs. Eisenhower, accompanied by Major Eisenhower and his wife, left New York for Washington on Sunday afternoon, January 18, their six-car special train pulling out of Pennsylvania Station an hour late because Eisenhower was still revising the inaugural address. The Eisenhowers journeyed to Washington in the Pennsylvania Railroad's Business Car No. 90, the same one in which General Eisenhower had traveled on his triumphant return from Europe in 1945. He had asked that the Presidential railroad car *Ferdinand Magellan* be put at the disposal of the Trumans for their trip home to Independence after the inauguration. The Eisenhowers' train rolled into Washington on a siding half a block east of Union Station because the concourse of the station had been plowed up three days before by a runaway train. The family went directly to the Presidential suite, No. 1240, at the Statler Hotel, where the President-elect had stayed numerous times.

"This and the suite at the Brown Palace in Denver," he once remarked afterward, "are the only hotel rooms in which I really feel at home."

After twenty years out of power a jubilee had dawned for the Republicans. The Washington newspapers called the inaugural festivities the most lavish in history. In the fervor even the Republican National Committeeman from Rhode Island wrote an Eisenhower song.

"The beauty parlors," reported the *New York Times*, "were doing their best to meet demand for the 'Mamie bang' at $2 a hair-do if you curled your own and from $10 to $17.50 if you used store hair." The hotels were jammed, and it was noted that the capital had rarely, if ever, seen so many mink coats, a circumstance that may or may not have attracted the attention of Republican orators who had so recently wrested votes from the Democrats over the so-called mink-coat scandals of the Truman administration.

The sun shone on inauguration day, and it was unseasonably mild. In a strained atmosphere the President-elect and his wife picked up the Trumans at the White House at eleven-thirty in the morning for the traditional drive to the Capitol. The Eisenhowers did not go inside the White House; the meeting took place outside on the north portico.

The oath of office was administered on the Capitol steps by Eisenhower's old friend, the late Chief Justice Fred M. Vinson. The President swore on two Bibles—the historic Bible used by George Washington and the Bible Dwight Eisenhower had had at West Point. His Bible was opened at II Chronicles 7:14: "If my people, which are called by my name, shall humble themselves, and pray, and seek my face, and turn from their wicked ways; then will I hear from heaven, and will forgive their sin, and will heal their land. . . ." The Washington Bible was open at Psalms 127:1: "Except the Lord build the house, they labor in vain that build it: except the Lord keep the city, the watchman waketh but in vain."

President Eisenhower, deeply preoccupied all that morning, was tense and solemn when he appeared on the rostrum and took the oath, but as he turned to deliver his address, his seriousness evaporated in a vivid smile, and he flung his arms up in his familiar V-sign —a reminder of the earlier career that had already stamped him as one of the famous men of his time. "The world and we," he said, "have passed the midway point of a century of continuing challenge. We sense with all our faculties that forces of good and evil are massed and armed and opposed as rarely before in history. This fact defines the meaning of this day."

It defined indeed the condition that was to underlie and influence almost all that he was to do in his years as President.

His words seemed to be directed more particularly to peoples abroad than to Americans at home, as he pleaded for peace—but peace not gained through "appeasement." He made it clear that the United States would not withdraw from its accepted role in international affairs. But he also let it be known that he expected this country's allies to do more than they had been doing to carry "their full and just burdens in the common defense of freedom" and, especially in Europe, to achieve a greater degree of unity. He said: "Only as free Europe unitedly marshals its strength can it effectively safeguard, even with our help, its spiritual and cultural heritage."

Two days later he wrote to William H. Draper, Jr., United States Special Representative in Europe, saying that he thought his address might be satisfactory to those Europeans wise enough to see that they must begin to produce if America was to maintain its enthusiasm for assisting Europe.

The inaugural address was too much a product of staff work to be eloquent. Virtually the only thing remembered about it today is the one touch that was Eisenhower's personally—the prayer with which he prefaced it. He wrote the prayer that morning while sitting on the couch in his Statler suite after his return from the service at church. It read:

Almighty God, as we stand here at this moment, my future associates in the executive branch of government join me in beseeching that Thou will make full and complete our dedication to the service of the people in this throng and their fellow citizens everywhere.

Give us, we pray, the power to discern clearly right from wrong, and allow all our words and actions to be governed thereby, and by the laws of this land. Especially we pray that our concern shall be for all the people regardless of station, race or calling.

May cooperation be permitted and be the mutual aim of those who, under the concepts of our Constitution, hold to differing political faiths, so that all may work for the good of our beloved country and Thy glory. Amen.

In the crowd that was massed along Pennsylvania Avenue to watch the inaugural parade was a souvenir dealer named Louis, whose stand, at Eleventh Street, featured G.O.P. elephants, pennants and similar trinkets. Conspicuous among his wares were buttons, some of which read I LIKE EVERYBODY and others I HATE EVERYBODY. When Louis paused to take stock during the afternoon, he made a discovery which not only caught something of the spirit of that day but which foreshadowed perhaps the most important of Eisenhower's achievements as President—his guidance of the people away from the hatred, the suspicions, the bickering, the lies, the bitterness, the savagery even that had defiled American public life since the end of World War II and particularly since the start of the Korean war.

"Most people like everybody today," Louis observed. "We're not movin' the 'hate' ones except to kids."

CHAPTER 2

The Republicans Take Over

The Troubles over Wilson's Nomination – The State of the Union Message – The Seventh Fleet Order – Removal of Wage and Price Controls – Prayer in the Cabinet – Eisenhower Receives Walter Reuther – The President's Feelings about the "Business Administration" Label

Three days after the inauguration the President met officially with the Cabinet in the White House for the first time, and the discussion soon turned to Charles E. Wilson's nomination, which had been approved only that day by the Senate Armed Services Committee but still awaited confirmation by the Senate.

The President assured the Cabinet that Wilson, who was not present, was a man of great integrity. He could not conceive, Eisenhower said, of Wilson's favoring General Motors while conducting the affairs of the Defense Department. Undoubtedly, he continued, Wilson intended to act with such rigid firmness in the government's dealings with General Motors that a question of favoritism on his part never would arise.

In this connection the President observed that it would be an excellent policy for all members of the Cabinet to be alert to cases in which they might be accused of favoritism. He bade them lean over backward to avoid giving cause for any such charge. They should not hesitate, he told them, to disqualify themselves in doubtful cases.

Wilson's nomination had hit a snag in the Senate committee before the inauguration when Wilson testified that while he had ended all other connections with General Motors, he still retained $2,500,000

24

worth of G.M. stock and more than $600,000 in bonuses and other rights. Because of the heavy taxes he would have to pay, he had been unwilling up to that time to sell these securities.

Wilson's continued stock ownership, however, looked unsatisfactory to Senators because it seemed to transgress the conflict-of-interest statutes, which were to cause the administration more and more trouble as time went by. The statutes make it illegal for a government official "directly or indirectly interested in the pecuniary profits" of a corporation to deal with that corporation "as an officer or agent" of the United States. Since General Motors held about 7.8 per cent of the dollar volume of the Defense Department's contracts, Senators did not see how Wilson could avoid technical violation of the law if he was at one and the same time Secretary of Defense and a large General Motors stockholder.

The issue caused the new administration considerable embarrassment, and when the record of the hearings was published, it gave the Democrats their first fun since the election as a result of this exchange:

Sen. Hendrickson—Mr. Wilson, you have told the committee, I think, more than once this morning that you see no area of conflict between your interest in the General Motors Corporation, or the other companies, as a stockholder and the position you are about to assume. Well, now, I am interested to know whether, if a situation did arise where you had to make a decision which was extremely adverse to the interests of your stock and General Motors Corporation, or any of these other companies, or extremely adverse to the company, in the interests of the United States Government, could you make that decision?

Mr. Wilson—Yes, sir, I could. I cannot conceive of one because for years I thought what was good for our country was good for General Motors, and vice versa. The difference did not exist. Our country is too big. It goes with the welfare of the country. Our contribution to the nation is considerable.

As was to be the case with more than one of Wilson's utterances, this made a nice conversation piece for critics of the administration for months, especially when, as was often the case, Wilson was quoted erroneously as having said, "What's good for General Motors is good for the country."

The issue never came to a showdown, which might very well have gone against Wilson. During the inaugural parade Eisenhower and Nixon sat down together at a foot-warmer in the stand in front of the White House.

"Well, you will be glad to know," the President said, "that Charlie Wilson has finally agreed to sell his stock."

Wilson's promise to dispose of all his General Motors holdings by April 1 and to give no more than from 10 to 20 per cent of them to his children resulted within a few days in confirmation of his nomination by the Senate by a vote of seventy-seven to six. Sherman Adams told the White House staff that Eisenhower regarded the Wilson case as the first test of the administration's ability to distinguish right from wrong.

The new Secretary was not alone among the men appointed to high positions in the Pentagon who had to get rid of stock holdings before the Senate would confirm their nomination. Roger M. Kyes, the new Under Secretary of Defense, and Robert T. Stevens, the Secretary of the Army, had to sell theirs. So also did Harold E. Talbott, the Secretary of the Air Force, who thus got by the conflict-of-interest statutes this time only to trip over them with a crash two and a half years later.

During his first week in office the President had to busy himself with preparation of his first State of the Union message, to be delivered on February 2. At the first official Cabinet meeting in the White House on January 23 he expressed some concern that the message might not have enough to it to warrant bringing Congress into a joint session to hear him. As the days passed, the message was put together principally in small conferences among Eisenhower, Emmet Hughes and officials concerned with the particular section under consideration. The section on labor, for example, was agreed upon on the 23rd at a meeting of the President, Hughes, Secretary Durkin and Senator H. Alexander Smith, Republican, of New Jersey, chairman of the Senate Committee on Labor and Public Welfare. While deferring specific recommendations until after further study, it said that experience had shown that the Taft-Hartley Act stood in need of "some corrective action" and should be amended promptly, which, as things turned out, it never was.

By the second meeting of the Cabinet in the White House on

January 30 the draft of the State of the Union message was far enough advanced for the President to read parts of it and to invite suggestions for improvement. Ambassador Lodge recommended that the passage on Social Security be strengthened to conform to Eisenhower's campaign speech in Boise, Idaho, the previous August. That was the speech in which, espousing "the middle way," Eisenhower said that this course "assumes that all Americans of all parties have now accepted and will forever support what we call social gains, the security that people are entitled to in their old age. . . . We accept as part of these social gains the fact that Americans must have adequate insurance against disaster." This thought was incorporated in the message.

Mrs. Oveta Culp Hobby, who was then administrator of the Federal Security Agency but who was to become the first Secretary of Health, Education and Welfare after that department was established on April 11, 1953, was dubious about some of the wording of the passage on Korea.

She felt that the phrase "neither emergency nor peace," as it appeared in the draft, conveyed the impression that the President did not regard the Korean situation as an emergency of any kind. To express his meaning more exactly he agreed to change the wording so that the paragraph read:

We are, of course, living in an international situation that is neither an emergency demanding full mobilization, nor is it peace. No one can know how long this condition will persist. Consequently, we are forced to learn many new things as we go along—clinging to what works, discarding what does not.

During the review Eisenhower declared that he wanted to work into the message a strong passage about free enterprise which would help counteract the tendency, as he said, of newspaper columnists to regard it as something opposed to humanitarianism and inimical to labor. No passage corresponding to this exact prescription ever did turn up in the final draft. However, in declaring his intention to end wage and price controls the President extolled the "atmosphere of freedom" in which American economic strength had developed. And in a final word of praise for individual freedom he observed that one form it took was the right of workers to strike.

Along with the statement that wage and price controls were to be ended, the most interesting part of Eisenhower's first State of the Union message was his declaration of policy on the mission of the U.S. Seventh Fleet in the Formosa (Taiwan) Strait. He said:

In June, 1950, following the aggressive attack on the Republic of Korea, the United States Seventh Fleet was instructed both to prevent attack upon Formosa and also to insure that Formosa should not be used as a base of operations against the Chinese Communist mainland.

This has meant, in effect, that the United States Navy was required to serve as a defensive arm of Communist China. Regardless of the situation in 1950, since the date of that order the Chinese Communists have invaded Korea to attack the United Nations forces there. They have consistently rejected the proposals of the United Nations Command for an armistice. They recently joined with Soviet Russia in rejecting the armistice proposal sponsored in the United Nations by the Government of India. This proposal has been accepted by the United States and fifty-three other nations.

Consequently, there is no longer any logic or sense in a condition that required the United States Navy to assume defensive responsibilities on behalf of the Chinese Communists, thus permitting those Communists, with greater impunity, to kill our soldiers and those of our United Nations allies in Korea.

I am, therefore, issuing instructions that the Seventh Fleet no longer be employed to shield Communist China. Permit me to make crystal clear this order implies no aggressive intent on our part. But we certainly have no obligation to protect a nation fighting us in Korea.

The Joint Chiefs of Staff dispatched the order, which, omitting the classified prefatory references to other directives, read as follows:

2 FEB 53

OPERATIONAL IMMEDIATE
TO: CINCPAC PEARL HARBOR TH
INFO: CINCFE TOKYO JAPAN

THAT PORTION UR CURRENT DIRECTIVE WHICH REQUIRES YOU INSURE THAT FORMOSA AND PESCADORES WILL NOT RPT NOT BE USED AS BASES OPNS AGAINST CHI MAINLAND BY CHI NATS IS RESCINDED.

The statement in the State of the Union message had been drafted by Dulles in Washington before the inauguration as a result of a decision that he and Eisenhower had reached together. They acted with little or no recourse to military advisers because they regarded it primarily as a political matter. Nevertheless the President brought it up before the Cabinet on January 30, and after he had read the passage, Wilson raised a question which was soon to be echoed all over the world. Did the order, he asked, contain any implications bearing on American relations with Chiang Kai-shek? The President replied that there were no implications at all in the impending action. The statement meant what it said and nothing more, he assured the Cabinet. It certainly did not imply, Eisenhower added, any intention on the part of the United States to commit aggression.

The statement to this effect in the final draft of the State of the Union message said, simply, "This order implies no aggressive intent on our part." Two days before he delivered the message news of his decision on the Seventh Fleet was leaked to the press through Congressional sources, so by the time the President went to the Capitol serious doubts already had been aroused as to its meaning. In reading the message to Congress the President tried at the last minute to re-emphasize nonbelligerency by changing the sentence to, "Permit me to make crystal clear this order implies no aggressive intent on our part."

Some there were, however, to whom it did not seem to be crystal clear. The day after the message was delivered Anthony Eden told the House of Commons that London had protested to the United States, warning that the act might "have very unfortunate political repercussions without compensating military advantages." Prime Minister Jawaharlal Nehru, of India, said that it intensified "the fear psychosis of the world."

The order had, as it was intended to have, more psychological than direct military effect. Almost as soon as Communist China entered the Korean war in 1950 the Seventh Fleet had in fact dropped the "shield" of protection of the Communist coast. From that time on Chinese Nationalist parties had periodically poked at the mainland without restraint by the Fleet. Indeed, there were reports, which were never denied by the Pentagon, that at times the American Navy had given the Nationalists a hand to help them maintain contact with guerrillas on the continent. In a sense, therefore, the new order merely legalized a condition that had existed for some two years, and the statement that the Navy had been serving in effect as a defensive arm of Red China was putting the case pretty strongly.

Neither Eisenhower nor Dulles expected or intended that the order would lead to the invasion of the mainland by Chiang. Nevertheless the President and the Secretary of State had resolved that the stalemate in Korea must be ended, and the idea behind the Seventh Fleet order was to give the Chinese Communists forebodings that Formosa might yet be used by the United States as a base of operations against them if they did not agree to a Korean truce. Eisenhower and Dulles felt very strongly that if the Chinese Communists were convinced that the alternative to stalemate was powerful American attacks against them on two or three other fronts, they would come to terms in Korea. Another purpose was to put pressure on the Communists to station along the coastline opposite Formosa troops that might otherwise have been employed in Korea.

Militarily the order was the least risky of a number of courses that might have been adopted to put new pressure on the Chinese Communists, and politically it gave the young administration a look in the eyes of its sympathizers of having some good cards up its sleeve for the game with the Reds. "Unleashing Chiang," some called it, with more hope than understanding of the situation. The phrase was not one used by the President.

Even now a difference of opinion persists within the government as to the value of the order. Some still regard it as a bit of psychological tomfoolery that did more harm than good. Others, especially those around Dulles, believe it had a much sharper impact on the Chinese Communists than was realized in the United States and that the Reds took it seriously for what it was meant to be—a token of this country's determination to broaden the war against China if the Korean stalemate continued.

When the President returned to the White House after delivering the State of the Union message, he took up directly the business of ending controls. That same afternoon he met with Arthur S. Flemming, Director of Defense Mobilization, Flemming's special consultant, Harold S. Vance, and others to prepare for early issuance of the necessary executive orders.

The administration had come to power generally committed to end wage and price controls. The main question before Eisenhower and his advisers was one of timing. Serious discussion of the problem began aboard the *Helena* in December, with the debate centering on whether controls should be ended immediately after Eisenhower took office or on April 30, when they would have expired by law, or whether they should be terminated sometime between these dates.

Advisers like George Humphrey, Emmet Hughes and General Lucius D. Clay, chairman of the board of the Continental Can Company, favored decontrol immediately after the inauguration. Eisenhower and Dodge were apprehensive about moving too fast; both had reservations about ending controls before April 30. After all, no one could be altogether certain what decontrol would do to the economy. The labor unions were worried, and the Democrats sounded grave warnings about the inflation that might result. Among others, Senator Herbert H. Lehman, Democrat, of New York, and George Meany, president of the American Federation of Labor, cried danger. In January before the inauguration Michael V. DiSalle, head of the Office of Price Administration under Truman, warned some of Eisenhower's representatives that removal of controls would prove a dreadful mistake and one that would cost the country billions of dollars. Even many Republicans were apprehensive over the possible inflationary effects of immediate decontrol.

Aboard the *Helena* Eisenhower spoke very strongly in favor of the principle of an economy free of controls. He recalled that in Germany immediately after the war he had ordered a start in the removal of economic controls and said the effect had been good. He was sure that decontrol would be beneficial to the American economy also; it was the timing that troubled him. Before departing from New York he had created a small advisory committee on the subject, and now that his designation of Sinclair Weeks as Secretary of Commerce had been announced, he radioed Weeks to put the committee to work to prepare recommendations. On January 6 the group submitted a report calling for a prompt end of controls.

When the problem was presented to the Cabinet on the second

day of the preinaugural session in the Commodore, Humphrey, Wilson and Weeks spoke up for quick termination, but the President-elect, along with Lodge and Harold E. Stassen, Director of Foreign Operations, continued to be more cautious. Eisenhower was reluctant to strip his administration too quickly of authority, and in any case he decided to defer action until after his State of the Union message.

Throughout the talks at the Commodore, as well as in the White House, Eisenhower insisted that there must be no doctrinaire approach to the matter, an attitude he was to adopt many times with respect to many subjects during his years as President. The decision on controls, he said, must be made on the basis of what was best for the country and not what was best for some particular economic theory.

In the discussions he laid down two rules. One was that the decision on the timing of decontrol must not be a hasty one. The other was that the administration must be ready to try some new control if serious inflation should follow the termination of existing controls.

As late as the first of the weekly meetings with Republican leaders of Congress on January 26 the President left open the date on which controls would be removed, though he assured the leaders that he would not ask for extension of the law beyond April 30. Meanwhile he was coming under increasing pressure to act soon. The livestock industry, for example, was in some trouble at the moment and had persuaded Secretary Benson to add his voice to the chorus for repeal. By the time of the second Cabinet meeting in the White House on January 30 the President was ready with a draft of his State of the Union message, in which he promised early steps "to eliminate controls in an orderly manner."

On February 6 Eisenhower ordered an immediate end to wage controls and immediate removal of controls on the prices of a wide range of consumer goods, including meat, furniture, clothing, meals in restaurants and almost all of the thousands of items sold in retail stores. The action, first of a series extending over a period of weeks, was approved by the Cabinet that morning.

This was the meeting, incidentally, which the President opened with an announcement that thenceforth all Cabinet sessions would begin with a few moments of silent prayer. Before the first meeting in New York Benson had raised with Eisenhower the question of starting with a prayer, and Eisenhower approved. When after the inauguration the Cabinet first met in the White House, the prayer was omitted, and Benson wrote a note to the President recalling their talk in New York. He said that his note was just a reminder, that he would not press the matter and would never mention it again. The President sounded out the other members. Each of them agreed when he put the suggestion to them, and in establishing the new practice on February 6, the President said that the weekly prayer would be a silent one unless on particular occasions some member desired an oral prayer.

From that time on, the procedure seldom varied. Cabinet members who happened to be seated when the President entered rose until he had taken his chair. Then all would sit around the coffin-shaped mahogany table and bow their heads until the President ended the brief silence with, "Thank you."

This same February 6 was a busy day for the new President. In the afternoon his callers were Walter P. Reuther, then president of the Congress of Industrial Organizations, and David J. McDonald, head of the United Steelworkers, who came to discuss the role of labor in America. Eisenhower was very curious to know more about the kind of man Reuther was, and he listened with great interest as the C.I.O. president expressed his views on how labor-management relations could contribute to the cause of peace in the world.

Reuther told the President that labor was willing to co-operate in seeking a settlement of issues long in dispute. He suggested that such a settlement might be reached if the President would appoint a commission representing labor, management, the administration and Congress to study these issues.

Afterward the President informed his associates that he had been very much impressed by Reuther. In particular he mentioned the labor leader's moderation and sincerity. Reuther's air was so co-operative, he said, that any fair-minded person would give the most serious attention to whatever he proposed. The President remarked that he had detected none of the socialistic views he had heard attributed to Reuther.

Nevertheless Reuther's proposal did not take root. For one thing the Republican leaders of Congress were cool to it. For another an attempt by Durkin to get a meeting of minds among business, labor and government representatives on amendments to the Taft-Hartley Act fell so flat that it sapped enthusiasm in the White House for another try.

With the decision to end wage and price controls out of the way—an action which, happily, proved quite painless to the economy—the question of whether the administration should ask Congress to enact certain standby controls in case of emergency still troubled the President. Some of his private discussions on consumer-credit controls—regulations for the financial terms of installment buying—shed an interesting light on his feelings at the time, particularly on his sensitivity to Democratic charges that the administration was dominated by big business.

Eisenhower was not concerned whether Congress did or did not enact standby controls on wages and prices. He declined to support Senator Homer E. Capehart's bill for such controls, though he was willing to accept them if Congress passed such legislation, which it did not. He viewed standby controls on consumer credit, however, in a different light. Whereas economists regarded these as direct controls, the President had the habit of considering them indirect, and he told the Cabinet on March 13 that he felt he had implied in the campaign that the administration would use indirect controls, such as, he said, controls on credit, to prevent excessive fluctuations in the economy. Obviously disturbed at the thought of being left without adequate weapons to combat inflation, he told the Cabinet that prudence dictated that such power should be available to him.

Secretary Humphrey argued the point. He said, among other things, that the extremely controversial nature of credit controls made it undesirable for the President to ask for standby powers. He strongly urged him not to do so, but the President was not persuaded.

At the weekly legislative conference on March 16 he took up the subject again, declaring that the administration must not be indifferent to the interests of the public. He thought it would be prudent to have standby controls on consumer credit as a sign that the administration did not intend to be caught empty-handed in the event of an emergency. Application of these controls at the proper time, if such action ever became necessary, he said, might even head off the need for new wage and price controls.

Neither at this meeting nor subsequently, however, did the President succeed in winning the support of the Republican Congressional leaders for his view. At the meeting on the 16th the late Senator Robert A. Taft, of Ohio, opposed standby controls on consumer credit on the grounds that they were of direct rather than indirect nature. Such powers as regulation of bank loans and housing credit, Taft argued, were of much more fundamental importance to the economy.

Though he was destined to be disappointed in the matter, the President again brought it up very forthrightly at the meeting of the Cabinet on March 20. He conceded that there were many arguments for and against standby consumer-credit controls and said that a clear decision based solely on the merits of the case evidently was not possible. He maintained, however, that authority to impose these controls ought to be established as evidence of the interest of the administration in the ordinary citizen.

The President observed that "business administration" had become the standard epithet for its critics to hurl at the Republicans. The administration, he said, should take pride in the phrase as being one that meant that it was devoted to a businesslike approach to the problems of government. Nevertheless, he cautioned, willing acceptance of the label made it absolutely necessary for the administration to be humane and to manifest its humaneness for all to see. Be businesslike, yes, the President said, but let the administration never fail in the slightest degree to show its concern for "the little man." The President was emphatic in urging the Cabinet not to allow "demagogues" in the Democratic Party to grab off the claim of being sole champions of the people.

Time and again as the months passed he was to warn his fellow Republicans in private that the "business administration" label placed them under a heavy obligation to attend to the interests of the little fellow. And time and again he was to rankle at Democratic claims that Democrats were interested in the people whereas the Republicans were concerned only with big business.

When the Cabinet on June 4, 1954, approved a program for group hospitalization and other benefits for Federal employees, he remarked dryly, "Everyone will find some way of calling it a 'rich man's bill.'"

CHAPTER 3

Stalin's Death
and the Rosenberg Case

The Strain of the First Weeks – Eisenhower Paints Lincoln – The President Discusses His Favorite Predecessors – The President's First Trip – "Have You Heard the News?" – No Clemency for the Rosenbergs – An Ugly Demonstration – The Enslavement Resolution

Like other Presidents before him, Dwight Eisenhower found his first weeks in the White House a heavy strain. Even though his purpose was gradual change rather than abrupt change, he experienced great difficulty in giving affairs the new turn in direction to which he aspired.

The war in Korea was dragging on with no assurance of a quick settlement. The task of cutting expenditures looked more formidable the closer the administration came to grips with it. Although the economy took the ending of controls in stride, neither the President nor anyone else could be certain in advance that it would. On February 12, six days after the President's order, Budget Director Dodge told a meeting of the Cabinet that some rises in prices were to be expected as a result of decontrol and that these would inevitably increase the cost of national defense. On top of this, Dulles warned that the international situation was very serious and that it might take a grave turn that could create a situation requiring reimposition of controls. A more hopeful word came from the Secretary of the Treasury. The economic picture would not be serious,

Humphrey said, if the administration carried out the President's policy of reducing government expenditures. The President told the Cabinet very emphatically that the United States had been living too long on a high plateau of tension. The American people, he said, simply could not go on all their lives under emergency measures.

On Capitol Hill, Senator Joseph R. McCarthy had begun his showy investigation of the Voice of America, one of many McCarthy incursions that were to give the President a deep feeling of harassment and frustration and to give his young administration a look of being unable to cope with Congressional encroachment. At a meeting of the Cabinet on January 30 Attorney General Herbert Brownell, Jr., called attention to the many investigations already in progress. At that moment, he reported, there were ten separate investigations of the State Department alone. Of them all, the White House regarded the investigation of the Voice of America as the most unwelcome, because the President had set up several groups of his own to look into the operations of the Voice. Eisenhower thought that in this instance, as in others, the administration should first be allowed to investigate itself. Only if this self-inspection failed to correct abuses, he believed, would Congress be warranted in stepping in with its own inquiry.

The wearisome and, Eisenhower came to feel, dangerous pressure on the White House to consent to amendment of the Constitution as proposed by Senator Bricker had commenced. Few issues, if any, during his years in the White House were to exhaust the President's patience to the extent that the interminable haggling over the Bricker amendment did.

The honeymoon with Congress which traditionally is supposed to ease a new President through his early days never seemed to materialize for Eisenhower, who tried more than many Presidents have done to co-operate with the legislative branch.

In the preliminary picture-taking at one of his early press conferences photographers asked him to say something so they could get an action shot.

"I know of nothing more difficult than to think of something witty to say to you fellows," he remarked.

"Say something serious, sir," a photographer told him.

"Everything is serious these days," the President replied.

In those first weeks the unique confinement of the White House got its grip on Eisenhower. He fretted under it and under the heavy schedule of callers and ceremonies and the endless intrusion of one small detail after another.

"When does a man get a chance to think around here?" he asked his staff. He used to inquire whether there was not some room where he could go off by himself and concentrate on important problems. To be sure there were such rooms, but, of course, he never got around to using them.

It was during these early weeks that Eisenhower to take his mind off his troubles at night began painting a portrait of Lincoln after Alexander Gardner's photograph, which hung in the white-walled Cabinet room. As one might expect of a political traditionalist like Eisenhower, Lincoln and Washington were his favorite predecessors, and while in the White House he has given a good deal of thought to why they were successful Presidents.

In talking this over with friends, he has said that the quality which made Washington and Lincoln great leaders was their singleness of purpose. Instead of rushing hither and yon ordering people about, he points out, each of them moved relentlessly toward one goal: the founding of the nation in the case of Washington and preservation of the union in the case of Lincoln.

Eisenhower has related with great admiration incidents which he thought illustrated Lincoln's singleness of purpose. He tells the familiar story of how Lincoln, on November 13, 1861, was snubbed by General George B. McClellan, commander of the Army of the Potomac, who went to bed while Lincoln waited in the general's house to see him. And of how, on the afternoon of the day Lincoln was shot, Secretary of War Edwin M. Stanton had refused Lincoln's personal request that Major Thomas T. Eckert, chief of the Telegraph Office of the War Department, be allowed to accompany him to Ford's Theater that night as a bodyguard. What impresses Eisenhower about these incidents is that Lincoln's drive toward his goal was seemingly so great that he never allowed himself to be deflected by such things as slights by subordinates.

As was often the case, Eisenhower had difficulty with his colors in painting Lincoln's face.

"You've given him a ruddy complexion! Lincoln's face was *sallow!*" Thomas E. Stephens, the artist from Gramercy Park, in New York, told the President when he saw the painting. Stephens, who has done many portraits of the Eisenhower family, including the portrait of the President that will hang in the White House permanently, often coaches him in painting.

Eisenhower used to lament at the time that he knew nothing about the chemistry of paints and next to nothing about anatomy. Mechanical drawing, he recalled, was the one subject that nearly got him "busted out" of West Point in his second year. Whenever anyone brought up the comparison between his painting and Sir Winston Churchill's, Eisenhower would laugh. There was no comparison, he would say, informing his friends that an eminent painter had once told him that if Sir Winston had devoted his life to painting as assiduously as he had to politics, he would have become one of the world's greatest contemporary painters. Besides, the President would say, Sir Winston, whose talents have earned him the title of Honorary Academician Extraordinary of the Royal Academy of Arts, had much more time to practice than Eisenhower did and was able to devote whole vacations to painting.

Late in February, 1953, the President was looking forward with relief to his first brief trip since the inauguration. He was going to fly to Augusta on the 26th for four days of golf. The day before he left he held his second press conference, during which a reporter noted that Stalin had been quoted a few weeks earlier to the effect that he would look favorably on a meeting with Eisenhower.

"Do you think anything could be accomplished at this time," the reporter asked, "and would you be willing to go out of this country to meet Mr. Stalin?"

Well, the President replied, this was asking him in advance to express whether he thought there was or was not a good chance of such a meeting. He said that he would meet anybody anywhere if he thought there was the slightest chance of doing any good. What he meant, he explained, was that he would go to any suitable spot— say, halfway between the United States and Russia—to talk with anyone so long as this country's allies were fully informed of the matters under discussion. Defending freedom, he observed, was a big job and not just the business of one nation.

On March 2, the day after his return from Augusta, the President received Prince Faisal Al Saud, Foreign Minister of Saudi Arabia. He promised the prince that he would try to correct a "deterioration of relations" between the United States and the Arab countries. The following night, March 3, Eisenhower retired unaware that a momentous event was occurring in the Kremlin.

An hour and a half after midnight the telephone rang in the H Street residence of Presidential assistant Robert Cutler. Waking from a sound sleep, he answered and heard the voice of Allen W. Dulles, Director of Central Intelligence.

"Have you heard the news?" Dulles asked.

"What news?" Cutler demanded.

Stalin had suffered a stroke and was believed to be dying, Dulles replied.

Because of his position Dulles has immediate access to the President at any time, day or night. He asked Cutler whether he thought he should go to the President's bedroom with the news. Cutler was inclined against it and suggested instead that they meet in the President's office at seven o'clock before Eisenhower got there. Dulles, who is the brother of the Secretary of State, agreed. After he hung up Cutler was so excited he was unable to go back to sleep. At three o'clock he telephoned C. D. Jackson, Special Assistant to the President and Eisenhower's chief adviser on psychological strategy. Cutler told him the news and the plan for the early-morning meeting. Then at four o'clock Cutler called Hagerty.

"I know what you're going to say," Hagerty answered sleepily. "Three people have called me already."

Cutler asked Hagerty if he would join him, Jackson and Dulles in the President's office at seven.

"Let's meet in my office first," said Hagerty, who felt that they should get together some ideas for the President's consideration before seeing him.

Cutler agreed, and he himself began drafting a few sentences of a prospective Presidential statement, one of which was to the effect that the Almighty watches over people of all nations.

When the group gathered in Hagerty's office in the west wing of the White House, Cutler telephoned an usher in the mansion proper to inquire for the President.

"The President hasn't waked up yet," the usher replied.

Eisenhower learned of Stalin's death when he awoke. It was a raw morning, and when the President sauntered into his office at twenty minutes to eight, he was wearing a tan polo coat and a brown hat with the brim snapped far down over his forehead.

"Well," he said rather tartly, eyeing Cutler, Dulles, Hagerty and Jackson, who had moved in from the press secretary's office, "what do you think we can do about *this?*"

That started a discussion which lasted for some two hours, with Jackson, who was on leave of absence as publisher of *Fortune*, striding, long-legged, up and down the President's office sending out a shower of ideas. Drafts of a statement were dictated and revised and then begun anew. During the morning the group went into a regular meeting of the National Security Council which had been scheduled for that day. Even before the meeting had ended the statement was issued to the press. It said:

At this moment in history when multitudes of Russians are anxiously concerned because of the illness of the Soviet ruler the thoughts of the American people go out to all the people of the U.S.S.R.—the men and women, the boys and girls—in the villages, cities, farms and factories of their homeland.

They are the children of the same God who is the Father of all peoples everywhere. And like all peoples, Russia's millions share our longing for a friendly and peaceful world.

Regardless of the identity of government personalities the prayer of us Americans continues to be that the Almighty will watch over the people of that vast country and bring them, in His wisdom, opportunity to live their lives in a world where all men and women and children dwell in peace and comradeship.

The statement, in effect, was an appeal to the new rulers of Russia, whoever they might be, to keep the peace.

The President was at dinner with Mrs. Eisenhower on the evening of March 5 when Hagerty telephoned him about the latest announcement on the Moscow radio:

The heart of the comrade and inspired continuer of Lenin's will, the wise leader and teacher of the Communist Party and the Soviet people—Josef Vissarionovich Stalin—has stopped beating.

Hagerty suggested that the President direct a formal message to the Kremlin, which he did, omitting expressions of praise and sympathy. The message said:

The Government of the United States tenders its official condolences to the Government of the Union of Soviet Socialist Republics on the death of Generalissimo Josef Stalin, Prime Minister of the Soviet Union.

Like everyone else, the President could only wonder and wait to see what changes would now occur in Russia. Without jumping to conclusions, he voiced hope in confidential talks with his advisers that a new era would open in relations between Russia and the West.

On March 6 the dictator's death was discussed briefly in the Cabinet. Lodge reported that Soviet officials at the U.N. seemed nervous. He urged a cautious attitude on the part of the United States. The President said that since 1946 officials of the State Department and the Psychological Strategy Board had been speculating on what would happen when the Soviet government changed hands. But now that it had occurred, he complained, he had looked in vain for any plans or studies that might have been worked out in advance so that the government would be ready to react. This lack of planning, he commented, was a fresh indication of the necessity for such work as was then being done by Jackson and Cutler.

Psychological warfare, a term the President dislikes, came up in the Cabinet for discussion at this period in connection with another of the endless facets of the Communist problem—the Rosenberg espionage case. At the meeting of February 25 Jackson, discussing the work of a commission the President had appointed to study psychological strategy, said that an opportunity had been missed by not having the Voice of America radio among the first organs to announce Eisenhower's refusal to commute the death sentences of Julius and Ethel Rosenberg. Left-wing groups all over the world were doing their utmost to distort the facts about the President's action and to arouse hostility toward the United States in consequence of it.

Jackson said that with better planning the Voice might have presented the President's viewpoint to the world before unfriendly organizations had an opportunity to spread their version. Not the least mischievous aspect of their version was that this was a case of official anti-Semitism in the United States—an American Dreyfus affair.

The Rosenberg case was one of the disagreeable responsibilities which the President found awaiting him when he took office. The Rosenbergs, parents of two young boys, had been convicted and sentenced to death for having conspired and confederated with Harry Gold, David and Ruth Greenglass and others in the late 1940's to deliver to Russia through Soviet agents sketches of secret atomic experiments conducted at the Atomic Energy Commission laboratory at Los Alamos, New Mexico.

The Rosenbergs had appealed for Presidential clemency while Truman was still in office, but their plea did not reach the White House until February. On February 11 Eisenhower denied the appeal. In a public statement he said, in part:

. . . By their act these two individuals have in fact betrayed the cause of freedom for which free men are fighting and dying at this very hour. . . .

I have made a careful examination into this case and am satisfied that the two individuals have been accorded their full measure of justice.

There has been neither new evidence nor have there been mitigating circumstances which would justify altering this decision, and I have determined that it is my duty, in the interest of the people of the United States, not to set aside the verdict of their representatives.

The next day, Lincoln's Birthday, the Cabinet met, and the President explained in detail why he had not granted the Rosenbergs' petition.

In reaching the decision, he said, he had asked himself four questions, and he enumerated to the Cabinet both the questions and the answers he had arrived at, as follows:

1. *Q. Was there in the entire record of the trial any disagreement among duly constituted officials?*

A. There was none. The decision of all who heard the case was unanimous that the Rosenbergs were guilty of the charges against them.

2. *Q. Was there any advantage to be gained for the United States by commuting the death sentence?*

A. Possibly if the Rosenbergs were allowed to live, they might furnish valuable evidence against other conspirators. Notwithstanding, such a procedure was better adapted to a police state than to a democracy, and the President could not bring himself to decide the case on the basis of such a consideration.

3. *Q. Was there sufficient substance to the crime to warrant the death penalty?*

A. In the President's judgment there was.

4. *Q. What would the psychological effect throughout the world be if the executive branch of the United States Government reversed the decision of the judiciary in this case?*

A. There would be a significant adverse reaction. The impression abroad, the President felt, would be that American democracy was unable to take a definite action in a clear-cut case.

The President notified the members of the Cabinet that he would be willing to reopen the case at any time before the executions if any one of them believed that to do so would serve the best interests of the United States.

This was not to be the end of the matter for Eisenhower. On the day before the spies were scheduled to be electrocuted at Sing Sing Prison on June 18, Associate Justice William O. Douglas unexpectedly issued a stay in the Supreme Court. It was based on a previously unargued technical question as to whether the Espionage Act of 1917, under which they had been convicted, had been superseded by the Atomic Energy Act of 1946. On June 19 the Supreme Court, in a six-to-two decision, vacated the order, and the execution was rescheduled for that evening.

When the Cabinet met on the morning of the same June 19 the President said after the silent prayer that the last forty-eight hours had been a particularly trying period for him. In Korea, he said,

Syngman Rhee's release of North Korean prisoners of war had put the truce negotiations in jeopardy. And now, as a result of Justice Douglas's stay, the Rosenberg case was at a new crisis. From all over the world the President had been besieged by many scientists, clergymen, statesmen and Communist and non-Communist organizations alike to grant clemency. Even Pope Pius XII, without making any personal plea, had passed on to the Department of Justice appeals the Vatican had received on behalf of the Rosenbergs. Letters about the case had swelled the President's mail to the highest crest since he took office.

He never remembered a time in his life, the President told the Cabinet, when he felt more in need of help from someone much more powerful than he.

As if all these other troubles were not enough, he said, he deemed it his duty to notify the Cabinet that he had been advised the night before—he did not say by whom or for what reason—that he should stop wearing double-breasted suits.

He asked the Attorney General to discuss the Rosenberg case. Brownell reviewed the status of the case which, at that hour, was still before the Supreme Court, and emphasized that the issue was purely technical and that the Douglas stay seemed to be without foundation because the Atomic Energy Act had not been passed until after the commission of the Rosenbergs' crimes.

The President then expressed his own concern that the new development may have confused the public and obscured the fact that there was no question involved as to the guilt of the defendants. As for granting clemency, he said it was his opinion that any intervention by him could be justified only where "statecraft" dictated in the interests of American public opinion or of the reputation of the United States Government in the eyes of the world.

Lodge and Jackson deplored the flood of propaganda instead of factual information about the case. The Attorney General said that information which corroborated the guilt of the Rosenbergs was in possession of the government but that it could not have been used in the trial.

The Cabinet agreed that the President should issue a second

statement emphasizing that the free world had an interest in the proper handling of the case.

Within an hour after the Supreme Court vacated the stay the President's second statement was made public. It said, in part:

I am convinced that the only conclusion to be drawn from the history of this case is that the Rosenbergs have received the benefit of every safeguard which American justice can provide. There is no question in my mind that their original trial and the long series of appeals constitute the fullest measure of justice and due process of law. . . .

Accordingly, only most extraordinary circumstances would warrant executive intervention in the case.

I am not unmindful of the fact that this case has aroused grave concern both here and abroad in the minds of serious people, aside from the considerations of law. In this connection I can only say that, by immeasurably increasing the chances of atomic war, the Rosenbergs may have condemned to death tens of millions of innocent people all over the world. The execution of two human beings is a grave matter. But even graver is the thought of the millions of dead whose deaths may be directly attributable to what these spies have done.

When democracy's enemies have been judged guilty of a crime as horrible as that of which the Rosenbergs were convicted; when the legal processes of democracy have been marshalled to their maximum strength to protect the lives of convicted spies; when in their most solemn judgment the tribunals of the United States have adjudged them guilty and the sentence just, I will not intervene in this matter.

All that evening, while President and Mrs. Eisenhower were in their quarters on the second floor, a hideous demonstration clattered outside on Pennsylvania Avenue beyond the White House fence. An attorney for the Rosenbergs stood at the very gate of the White House and in so many words accused the President of the United States of murder. Hundreds of Rosenberg sympathizers paraded in the moonlight along the sidewalk in front of the White House, and from time to time women fell out of line to sob and pray at the fence. Meanwhile thousands who were greedy for news of the executions stood across the street in Lafayette Park (police kept the opposing groups separate) and jeered and howled at the pickets. Tying up traffic in the worst jam since the inauguration, scores of hot-rods and teen-agers, rich in the culture they were absorbing in these young years, drove gleefully back and forth in Pennsylvania

Avenue, jibing at the pickets and waving placards inscribed with such statements as TWO FRIED ROSENBERGERS COMING RIGHT UP. It was from the loud radios in their cars that news of the electrocutions reached the crowd, bringing wails from the pickets and shouts of exultation from Lafayette Park.

In these months the President had troubles with still another kind of psychological problem involving Communism—the so-called enslavement resolution.

At the Chicago convention the previous summer the Republicans had been anxious to exploit politically the lingering resentment in the country over the Yalta and Potsdam agreements. As a result the foreign-policy plank in their platform, which Dulles had a major part drafting, contained this statement:

The Government of the United States, under Republican leadership, will repudiate all commitments contained in secret understandings such as those of Yalta which aid Communist enslavements. It will be made clear, on the highest authority of the President and the Congress, that United States policy, as one of its peaceful purposes, looks happily forward to the genuine independence of those captive peoples.

During the campaign some Republican speakers were carried so far in their enthusiasm as to hold out the prospect of liberation of satellite peoples. In his first speech as Secretary of State, Dulles told the enslaved peoples, "You can count upon us." But he had in mind, he made it clear, only peaceful measures. The notion of liberation, stamped as it inevitably was with the image of military adventure by the United States, never got a foothold in the policy of the new administration. With stress upon "peaceful methods and devices," the President said in his State of the Union message:

We shall never acquiesce in the enslavement of any people in order to purchase fancied gain for ourselves. I shall ask the Congress at a later date to join in an appropriate resolution making clear that this government recognizes no kind of commitment contained in secret understandings of the past with foreign governments which permit this kind of enslavement.

These words were cheered by Republican members, some of whom seemed to jump to the conclusion that one of the first acts of the Eisenhower administration would be the repudiation of the

Yalta agreement, with all that this would imply in the way of condemnation of Franklin Roosevelt. Their hopes were to be disappointed.

After working closely with Dulles on the wording, the President on February 20 sent up a resolution proposing that Congress join him in rejecting "any interpretations or applications" of secret agreements "which have been perverted to bring about the subjugation of free peoples." The resolution proclaimed "the hope that the people who have been subjugated to the captivity of the Soviet despotism shall again enjoy the right of self-determination within a framework which will sustain peace."

Four days earlier Eisenhower had unveiled the resolution to Republican leaders at a White House conference, and their reaction was chilly. One of the Senators immediately called attention to the discrepancy between outright repudiation of Yalta promised at Chicago and the mere rejection of "interpretations" proposed by the President. While it was clear which agreements the President's proposal referred to, nowhere was Yalta or Potsdam even mentioned in the resolution, nor was there any denunciation of Roosevelt and the Democrats, just the Russians.

As William S. White has pointed out in *The Taft Story*, the administration was confronted with

certain unpleasant realities, the principal one of which was the simple fact that President Eisenhower on foreign policy in no sense controlled the Republican part of Congress, whereas President Eisenhower on foreign policy had the willing support of the vast majority of the Democrats there. The Democrats put the word about that while they would be very unhappy to part with the President on a world issue . . . they would not find it in their hearts to support any manifesto that disparaged Franklin Roosevelt.

The President felt, as he said later at a press conference, that the resolution would be worthless unless it had overwhelming bipartisan support. At the Republican leaders' meeting on February 16 he intimated that he would like to call in the Democrats on the resolution also, but the Republican chieftains were opposed because they did not see how any further meeting of minds could be achieved by bringing in Democratic leaders.

When the resolution was introduced, the Democrats were pleased with it and the Republicans were irked, the more so because of the Democrats' satisfaction. At the weekly legislative conference in the White House on February 23 Taft told the President that the support of Republicans in Congress would be very much limited unless the resolution was so revised that it in no way indicated approval of the Yalta agreement. Otherwise, he said, it could be interpreted as being exactly contrary to the feeling of many Republicans toward Yalta.

Dulles was opposed to change. The resolution, he argued, approved nothing, and he warned that if the change which Taft suggested was made, the resolution would be open to countless amendments. Obviously reflecting the President's point of view, the Secretary of State maintained that if the amendments went too far, the resolution might repudiate certain agreements, only to boomerang against the United States. His point was that once the process of repudiation had set in, the way would be cleared for Russia to repudiate agreements that were advantageous to the West. Any language that opened the door to repudiation of such agreements, Dulles cautioned, would be a matter of serious concern to America's allies because they would be the first to suffer from Soviet repudiations.

The President carried this argument forward at a press conference two days later. The West, he warned, could be put in a very awkward position in places like Berlin and Vienna if the United States repudiated all agreements made during the war.

So strong was the traditional Republican hostility toward Yalta, however, that he was unable to hold the Senate leaders in line against amendment of the resolution. With Taft voting with the majority, the Senate Foreign Relations Committee agreed to incorporate an amendment stipulating that the resolution "does not constitute any determination by Congress as to the validity or invalidity of any provisions" of agreements between the United States and Russia. *Invalidity*, reflecting on Roosevelt's right to negotiate as he had done with the Russians, hit the Democrats exactly the way it was supposed to and with the inevitable result. The Senate Democratic Policy Committee rejected the new wording, thereby squelching such hope as there was for bipartisan support. At the Republicans' legislative conference in the White House on March 9 the leaders told the President that with no solution to the controversy in sight they had decided to postpone action on the resolution. The decision was one to which the President readily assented. The next day the resolution was dropped for good.

One of the lessons of this affair was that old warmed-over issues like Yalta, which still galvanized the die-hards of his party in the Senate, had no deep hold on Eisenhower. The President was much too preoccupied with the present and the future to be absorbed in past quarrels, and he saw, in any case, no appreciable political gains to be won by flogging these old nags to death, especially when it disturbed current international relations.

CHAPTER 4

Conservatism and
the Military "New Look"

*The President Orders a Review of Basic Security Policies – Eisenhower's
View of the Soviet Menace – A Middle Road to National Security – No
Fixed D-Day – The New Policy – Row over Air Force Cuts – Cabinet
Discussions on Reducing Government Spending – Eisenhower vs. Dan
Reed on Tax Cuts – The President's Irritation with the N.A.M. and the
Chamber of Commerce*

I

One of the President's early acts was to order a "new look" at the
basic security policies of the United States and their cost.

The Communist aggression in Korea in 1950 on the heels of the
explosion of the first Soviet atomic bomb had driven the Truman
administration into a vast program of building up American armed
strength. Then as the Korean war settled into a stalemate and evidence accumulated that a world war was not impending, the Truman
administration itself began to retard this scheduled build-up. But
without a truce in Korea and with Stalin's intentions suspect, the
goals of the Truman program remained uncertain and changeable.
Meanwhile military expenditures and authorizations for new spending
on national security kept piling up, causing large budget deficits year
after year.

As Eisenhower viewed the situation after taking office, the possible menace of the Soviet Union took two forms. One was
the external threat of Soviet military might. The other was

internal—in the sense that the existence of this power, coupled with Communist adventures around the fringes of the free world, might drive the United States into weakening and eventually destroying its own economy through the indefinite expense of preparedness.

What he proposed, therefore, was that the United States should strive for a middle road between the security of a great mobilization achieved at crushing cost and a dangerous insecurity resulting from failure to spend enough money for national security.

To cope with the external threat the President proposed to maintain a military establishment sufficient to make the United States reasonably secure against attack and which could help defend other vital areas of the free world, like Western Europe. As for the internal threat Eisenhower sought at least a beginning of the end of heavy budgetary deficits, and that spring he approved a substantial lowering of expenditures for national defense, including a highly controversial five-billion-dollar cut in new funds for the Air Force. Notwithstanding, the Eisenhower program made air power the supreme arm of American military might. Even with the cut, the Air Force received more than 40 per cent of all military funds in the budget that went into effect on July 1, 1953.

In April, 1953, the President gave his approval to a new policy which veered away from a military build-up for meeting major aggression by any particular D-Day. Eisenhower felt that the concept of preparing for a particular time of crisis, which might or might not occur, overlooked or ignored the problem of what to do with such an expanded military establishment once it had been created.

The cost of maintaining it year after year, he knew, would be very great, yet chopping it down suddenly after a period of crisis had passed could precipitate a depression and cause the national military power to deteriorate. Hence the new policy aimed at leveling out the peaks and valleys of military preparedness, as the saying went. Based on the concept of a floating D-Day, it called for maintenance of a level of forces and material which could be paid for without staggering the economy and which could be borne for an indefinite period of years.

This new policy placed less emphasis than before on expanding

American and NATO forces to the maximum levels authorized, but heightened the emphasis on continental defense.

His arguments carried the weight of authority of one who had been a distinguished professional soldier. Perhaps no single act during his years in the White House, however, caused more apprehension and sincere differences of opinion than the cuts in military spending, approved though they were by Congress and welcomed by the taxpayer. In view of Russia's progress in production of jet planes and guided missiles, to say nothing of atomic and hydrogen bombs, the argument was not simply whether expenditures should have been left where they were but whether indeed they should not have been materially increased. Some of the President's highest military advisers believe that in 1956 the country's defenses are stronger than they were when Eisenhower took office. Fundamentally their explanation is that the United States has more and better atomic weapons and more planes capable of delivering them than it had in 1953, although, of course, other factors enter into the picture also. A more difficult question and one still much in dispute is whether the United States is stronger *in relation to the Soviet Union* in 1956 than it was in 1953.

Democrats and Air Force officials fought the President's cut in Air Force funds. Representative Samuel W. Yorty, of California, demanded that Wilson resign. Representative Melvin Price of Illinois, posed in a speech in the House a question that Eisenhower's critics were to re-echo through the next three years: Was strategy determining the budget, or was the Republican desire for a balanced budget determining strategy?

At his conference with the legislative leaders on May 12 and May 19 the President replied to this criticism, making three main points about the Air Force cuts.

First, he said that the Air Force had been getting appropriations and letting contracts too far in advance of delivery of planes and thus was operating on excessive "lead time."

Second, he explained that the Air Force had been obtaining new planes before it had either the personnel to fly and service them or the bases to accommodate the planes. The consequence of this was that the number of effective air wings was well below the level suggested by the number of available planes—"paper wings," he called them. The administration would concentrate, Eisenhower said, on providing these other essentials to increase the number of "real" wings.

Third, the President said he distrusted build-up "targets" and "target" dates. The 143 wing goal of the Truman administration, even if it were within reach, Eisenhower said, would not necessarily provide adequate security, nor would a smaller number necessarily doom the country to insecurity.

One of the reasons the United States became involved in the Korean war and now had to bear the financial burden of it, the President said, was that it had lacked a program which it could maintain consistently over the years and which was open to progressive improvement.

In the end the President won his fight in Congress over the cuts. This was only the beginning of the evolution of military policy under Eisenhower. As we shall see, the evolution, which picked up speed after the Korean truce, was to continue through the next three years.

In steering his administration to a new military policy the President was dealing with the field he knew best, but it irked him to be accused of approaching it with a military mind. Such a charge had been made in connection with his reorganization plan for the Defense Department, which Congress approved, increasing the authority of the chairman of the Joint Chiefs of Staff, among other things.

When the plan came up for discussion in a White House staff conference on June 22, 1953, Eisenhower was angered by recent allegations that the reorganization plan would create a Prussian-type general staff. In particular he resented a statement known to have been made by a member of Congress that the plan was the result of having a "military man" in the White House. What hurt the President was that this man had worked with the Eisenhower headquarters during his campaign and knew the President well. Eisenhower told his staff that it exasperated him to have "to defend myself against the charge of being a military man." He felt that his conduct over the years was ample evidence that he was not afflicted with the so-called military mind.

II

When Jackson was starting to draft the State of the Union message aboard the *Helena* in December, Eisenhower gave him a memorandum in longhand, outlining in the rough the approach the new administration would take to fiscal and budgetary policies. The memorandum said:

There will be an immediate & radical revision in the objectives of the fiscal policy of the Gov. However, our economic machinery is so delicately balanced that the accomplishment of these new objectives will proceed cautiously and slowly, making progress over an extended period, taking only a short step at a time.

Like a heavy truck racing down an icy hill, the brakes must be lightly and expertly applied to avoid a wreck and slowly come to a stop before turning off in the right direction.

The inheritance from the outgoing administration of not only an enormous debt but plus a generally unappreciated tremendous amount of present commitments for future payments upon past obligations further seriously complicates any rapid accomplishment of the revisions required.

Throughout the spring of 1953 the administration labored to make the turn off the icy road. Controls had been removed. Military spending was being reduced. Great efforts were made to economize. With the approval of the President, Dodge ordered all departments on February 3 temporarily to curb construction work and limit the hiring of new employees. His directive stated further:

It is the policy to operate at a minimum level of cost and expenditures. This policy requires that the necessity for all work be questioned and that action be taken to eliminate unnecessary programs and to hold the remainder to minimum levels. Each department and agency head is therefore directed to:

a. Permit no increases over the January rate of obligations except on complete justification and specific approval, unless such increases are clearly necessary to meet requirements fixed by law.

b. Initiate an immediate review within his department or agency calling for recommendations on the downward adjustment of program levels and for information as to the probable effect of such adjustments on Government services.

The results of these reviews should be used wherever possible in the 1954 Budget revision procedure and in the preparation of submissions for the 1955 Budget.

You are expected to translate these guides into proposals for specific revisions of the budget figures for your department or agency. . . .

In time Eisenhower was able to announce that the administration was reducing Truman's request for new money by $8,500,000,000 and that it intended in the following year to spend $4,500,000,000 less than had been planned.

The greater part of these savings was made possible by the ending of the Korean war. The significant cuts in the budget necessarily went hand in hand with the reduction in military spending. Practically, there was nowhere else where reductions of such magnitude could have been realized. Even before the Eisenhower administration took office, the trend in spending authority had started downward from the peak of the Korean war, but it was a painfully slow trend—the proposed 1954 budget left over by Truman still showed an estimated deficit of nearly $10,000,000,000. Moreover as Eisenhower's *Helena* memo had indicated, the new administration had inherited an estimated $80,000,000,000 of spending authorizations, which had been approved by Congress since the start of the Korean war but which current revenues did not provide for.

"The bills for the payment of nearly all of the $80,000,000,000 of obligations," Eisenhower said in his State of the Union message, "will be presented during the next four years. These bills, added to the current costs of government we must meet, make a formidable burden."

More than three years were to pass before the administration completed the transformation from an annual deficit to a balanced budget. In the beginning the pace was cruelly disappointing to conservative Republicans, especially in Congress. The President's unwillingness to place a balanced budget above all other considerations was to lead him into sharp differences with the Old Guard of his party. In almost no other field, however, did the administration apply its energies more forcefully. If it moved slowly, it nevertheless moved steadily, powerfully propelled by George Humphrey and aided by the high prosperity which yielded bumper taxes. Time and again the problem was to occupy the attention of the Cabinet. Discussions during this first spring illustrate Eisenhower's and his Cabinet's attitude.

Cabinet, March 6, 1953

Dodge reported that forty-five government agencies had submitted revised estimates for the 1954 budget but that economies were not great. It might be necessary, he said, for the President to direct further reductions.

Cabinet, April 17, 1953

Dodge lamented the difficulty of putting through budget cuts which collided with the local interests of members of Congress, particularly when these cuts affected social welfare, veterans benefits and public works. He complained of the unwillingness of Congress in such cases to allow cuts to stand. The Vice-President commented that the importance of local issues in Congressional elections is exaggerated. He observed that such elections are decided on one or two major issues. In the case of government spending, Nixon suggested, the issue would be support of Presidential leadership by individual members of Congress.

Cabinet, May 1, 1953

The President observed that he never had promised tax reduction until the budget could be balanced. To cut taxes first, he cautioned, would bring inflation, with the result that lower taxes would be self-defeating.

Cabinet, May 22, 1953

Secretary Humphrey warned that unless there were extensive cuts in expenditures, going well beyond those already achieved, the fiscal year 1955—starting fourteen months hence—might find the government with a deficit approaching $14,000,000,000. Deficits were in prospect year after year, Humphrey said, if the administration did not make major revisions in government programs. He proposed that the administration set as its goal a $60,000,000,000 budget for the year beginning July 1, 1954. (At the height of the election campaign Eisenhower had said in Peoria, Illinois, on October 2, 1952: "My goal, assuming that the cold war gets no worse, is to cut Federal spending to something like $60,000,000,000 within four years." Humphrey's suggestion would have meant reducing it to that figure in Eisenhower's second year. How steep such a reduction would have been is evident when the figure is compared with the $78,000,000,000 budget for the fiscal year 1954, which Truman had proposed in January but which Eisenhower scaled down.)

Humphrey told the cabinet that drastic action would be necessary if the Republicans were to vote a tax-reduction bill of their own in 1954.

When the Secretary of the Treasury had finished speaking, Wilson said that he interpreted it to mean that nearly $10,000,000,000 more would have to be cut from the Defense Department budget. With the Korean war continuing, he said, this would be next to impossible.

At this point the President moved into the discussion. He observed that major reductions in the budget seemed almost unattainable in the face of the prevailing psychology of the country, which, he noted, not only favored heavy expenditures for defense but at the same time insisted on continued spending of large sums on undertakings and obligations entered into in times of peace. He commented with irony that Wilson was at that very moment being forced to defend himself against serious attacks in Congress for what he was not spending rather than for what he was.

In a more serious tone Eisenhower said that he was very much disturbed by suggestions of additional heavy cuts in the defense program. As for talk that the outcome of the 1954 elections would depend on whether the Republicans could balance the budget and reduce taxes, Eisenhower insisted that the administration had no right to jeopardize the security of the United States by cutting expenditures too precipitately within one year.

The administration, he said, should be entirely honest with the American people about the considerations involved in attaining a balanced budget and reducing taxes. It should do so, he said, even at the cost, if that is what it had to be, of being voted out of office for not balancing the budget. He said he thought that the people would realize that national security must not be endangered just for the sake of a balanced budget and that more than one year might be required to obtain that balance.

The President then proceeded in so many words to pose this question: If balancing the budget was everything, why should only the military programs on which the security of the country depended be sacrificed? Why shouldn't the sacrifice be spread through veterans' benefits, the farm program and grants-in-aid to the states—obligations, he said, which had been assumed at a time when the country was not under compulsion to spend heavy sums for security?

Eisenhower made it very clear to the Cabinet that he was not suggesting abolition of such programs. The point he was making was that if great reductions had to be effected, it would be better to institute them almost anywhere else than where they would strike vitally at national security.

(This part of the discussion was academic because the President never seriously entertained the idea of reductions on such a scale.)

The President reminded his associates of the unceasing efforts that must be made to inform and educate the people. He said that he was appalled at the evidence in his mail of the "almost complete lack of information the American people have on subjects we have talked about time and again."

The metropolitan newspapers, of course, were so full of this information that it was old stuff to government officials, and they got bored reading it, he said. But he reminded the Cabinet that in the vast non-metropolitan areas there was no such volume of news and the public was not so well informed.

When Eisenhower took office, he was convinced that taxes were too high, but he feared that reducing them before cutting expenditures would cheapen the dollar. He was determined that spending must drop first, and this led him into one of his first big controversies. His antagonist was the new chairman of the House Ways and Means Committee, Representative Daniel A. Reed, Republican, of New York, an octogenarian, who was a former football coach at Cornell and still looked the part.

Insisting that Republicans had promised to cut taxes, Reed introduced H.R.1 to advance the date when the income-tax rate would drop. The reduction which would have come about on January 1, 1954, under the law as passed by a Democratic Congress would, under the terms of Reed's bill, have taken effect on July 1, 1953. This would have thrown the budget all the more out of balance, and in the State of the Union message, the President took a stand against an early tax cut. Reed went right ahead with his plans nevertheless and so persistently that by the time Eisenhower met Republican legislative leaders on February 9 he was apprehensive that the public would come to expect a tax cut that year.

He restated his opinion that a balanced budget must come first, and the leaders agreed that they would oppose Reed.

Notwithstanding, the Ways and Means Committee reported the bill on February 16. At the leaders' meeting that same day, therefore, the President said that he would take advantage of his first Presidential press conference scheduled for the next morning to present his views on the subject publicly.

Before the 294 reporters who turned out for the occasion he said that despite some of the things he had seen in the newspapers in the last nine months, he had never promised to cut taxes. While tax reduction was an absolutely essential objective, he said, it must come in the proper order of things, and that meant not until a balanced budget was in sight.

His views were dully reported but without much effect on Dan Reed. "When I fight, I fight," Reed said after leaving a meeting in the White House a few months later. Reed not only fought to cut income taxes in July but he fought even more strenuously a subsequent proposal by the President to extend the excess profits tax, which was to expire on July 1, for another six months. While the President disliked this tax, he needed the revenue. Also, the more astute Republicans were reluctant to allow a tax on business to drop before taxes came down for individuals. Politically it was wiser to have both reductions occur simultaneously.

That is the way it finally happened, even though Eisenhower could not prevail on Dan Reed personally. The administration had to do battle with Reed over both the income-tax cut and the excess-profits tax extension, and it beat him in both fights. Through the House Rules Committee it blocked H.R.1 from the floor. And when Reed retaliated by refusing to call the Ways and Means Committee into session to report out the excess-profits tax extension, administration forces got through the Rules Committee, a resolution to bring the measure to the floor regardless of Reed's committee. Before this came to a test, however, Reed was overruled by his own group.

Dan Reed and Syngman Rhee gave the President some of his worst headaches that first spring. Commenting at a meeting of the Cabinet on June 26 on the twin problems—a standing joke at the time was to refer to them jointly as Syngman Reed—Eisenhower waxed philosophical and said that in the face of such troubles he found there was great value in maintaining one's confidence and good spirits. These good spirits were justified because when the tax fight had ended in victory for the President, the strain between Eisenhower and Reed wore off and they became friends.

Following the silent prayer at the meeting of the Cabinet on June 5, the President remarked that he needed spiritual help to preserve his disposition. Not only had he been hounded by the old cry for more patronage, he said, but it had come to his attention that the National Association of Manufacturers and the United States Chamber of Commerce had opposed extension of the excess-profits tax. These business organizations, in the President's opinion, did not seem to realize that the middle-of-the-road course he was pursuing was the only one that gave them any chance of having a fair share of legitimate influence with the government. If a Republican administration was to make a go of it, he felt, the right wing would have to make certain concessions from its traditions. Taking a practical political view, both Lodge and Benson observed that no stand taken by the Chamber or the N.A.M. could do Eisenhower much harm.

This was not the first time nor the last that the President fretted over the unyielding attitude of conservatives in his party.

When, for example, at a legislative leaders' conference on February 8, 1954, mention was made of the line being taken on a certain issue by the Americans for Democratic Action and "left-wing" Democrats, the President recalled a conversation he had had with a friend who was a member of the boards of directors of many companies. His friend told him, Eisenhower said, that he was repeatedly beset by complaints of associates that the new administration was not moving fast enough to undo the work of Roosevelt and Truman.

His friend told the President that he himself believed his business associates not only failed to comprehend the immense cost of providing for national security but were in need of education on the problems of government.

To this the President added his own comment to the leaders that if persons who ought to know better criticized the administration, despite its efforts to prevent left-wing extremism, they would succeed only in tossing the whole country into the arms of the left wing.

On February 16, 1954, Eisenhower regaled the Cabinet with the story of a citizen who had sent a letter to Republican National Chairman Leonard W. Hall, with a carbon copy to Mrs. John S. Doud, the President's mother-in-law, denouncing in disgust the "New Dealers" in the administration. The worst social reformers of the whole lot, the writer grumbled, were Dwight Eisenhower and George Humphrey.

At the legislative leaders' conference on March 1, 1954, the President, plainly annoyed, mentioned complaints he had been receiving from certain very conservative Republicans. Some of them, he said, were threatening to withhold contributions to the party in the future because they thought the administration was acting too much like the New Deal. The President said he thought that this kind of criticism was particularly out of place in the midst of the business recession that had then descended on the country.

Such complaints were occasioned by the great central problem the Eisenhower administration has had to deal with: striking a proper balance between the costly requirements of national security and the other needs and wants of the people. The Cabinet discussed this problem on June 5, 1953.

Secretary Dulles gave an interpretation of the elements of national security. On the one hand, he pointed to the potential dangers of Soviet aggression. On the other hand, he reviewed some of the principal instruments for combatting these dangers: a global system of air bases, economic aid to allies, the defenses of NATO, and strengthening of the forces of free countries to cope with local wars.

Economically, Dulles said, it was impossible to accept the concept of Fortress America—the United States hunched up in armed isolation in which its trade with foreign countries was stifled.

Warning that Communist successes in Indo-China would have far-reaching implications, he summarized the minimum military and economic measures that would have to be taken by the United States in the face of the prevailing international situation.

The President then spoke of the difficulties of maintaining even the minimum security measures in a democracy. The fundamental struggle going on in the world, he said, was between the totalitarian state, which could compel its subjects to shoulder the burdens of military security, and the democratic free state, which must persuade its citizens to accept sacrifice in order to maintain that freedom.

"It is a struggle of men to rule themselves," he said.

CHAPTER 5

The New Order
in the White House

Some Early Milestones – Changes in Cabinet and National Security Council Procedures – The Staff System in the White House – Sherman Adams – Eisenhower's Foreign Policy Speech to the Editors – The St. Lawrence Seaway – Niagara Power – Steps to Eliminate Corruption from Government

I

During a discussion in the Cabinet on May 29, 1953, on the possibility of cutting Federal expenditures by reducing or eliminating certain grants to the states, Ambassador Lodge threw in, rather at random it seems, the question of whether grants for highway construction could be lowered. The President at once opposed any such step, saying that his own opinion was that the Federal government should be spending more rather than less for highways.

"I withdraw," Lodge said.

Eisenhower took him up quickly on this remark, reminding him that just because the President disagreed did not mean that further discussion was foreclosed.

"I have given way on a number of personal opinions to this gang," he told Lodge.

This was one way of saying that from the outset Eisenhower regarded the Cabinet and the National Security Council as bodies for very candid discussion and debate. His efforts to improve and

64

strengthen the organization of the Cabinet and the N.S.C. were among the early milestones of his Presidency.

That first spring was a time when other milestones were beginning to appear along the way also. The pioneering of the staff system in the White House. The emergence of Vice-President Nixon as an important and not just a ceremonial figure in the administration. The President's speech on foreign policy before the American Society of Newspaper Editors. The break in the generation-old roadblock holding up the St. Lawrence Seaway project. The creation of the Department of Health, Education and Welfare. "Tidelands" oil—the Federal quitclaim to the coastal states of the submerged offshore oil lands, which Eisenhower had indorsed in the campaign. Measures to eliminate corruption from the government. Executive Order No. 10450, which altered the Employee Security Program but did not alter it enough to prevent such future fiascos as the Ladejinsky and Chasanow cases.

In the Cabinet and the N.S.C. Eisenhower established a greater formality of procedure than had been adhered to in the past. In the case of the Cabinet the President felt that under his predecessors that venerable body had functioned with too little precision, and he instituted reforms which were intended, among other things, to reduce to a minimum aimless, unpremeditated discussion of matters that happened to pop up in meetings without notice in advance or preparation. Increasingly, he has used the Cabinet as a medium for obtaining the adherence of all department heads to the policies of the government, not only for the sake of efficiency but to prevent feuds like the Ickes-Wallace affair between members of his own administration.

(I don't believe that Eisenhower has ever used the expression "my administration" or "my Cabinet." If so, he has done it seldom. He speaks of *the* Cabinet or *the* administration.)

The President broadened the regular attendance at Cabinet meetings to include officials who, though not heads of Cabinet departments, hold positions specially qualifying them to participate. For example: Lodge, Stassen and Philip Young, chairman of the Civil Service Commission. Another reform he promoted was a mechanism to insure that policies made in the Cabinet room would take root in the departments and not just fade away with the echoes of the voices around the Cabinet table.

To give more cohesion to its work Eisenhower created the position of Secretary to the Cabinet and to it appointed Maxwell M. Rabb, a shrewd, amiable, conscientious lawyer from Boston, who had been an assistant to Sherman Adams in the beginning. As a means of getting away from random discussions in the Cabinet, Rabb draws up each week a formal agenda, something that the Cabinet had not had in the past.

On Wednesdays, generally, he reviews the agenda with the President and briefs him whenever necessary on trouble spots and recent developments in particular fields to be discussed. Often he gives him memorandums prepared specially for the President's understanding of specific problems before the Cabinet.

Well in advance of the meetings of the Cabinet, which are held on Friday mornings and usually last about three hours, Rabb circulates the agenda among the members, along with position papers of the respective departments which initiated the items on it. All this is done, of course, to try to insure informed discussion by familiarizing the members with the subjects that will be brought up on Friday.

Almost as soon as the Cabinet rises each week, Rabb meets with a group of sub-Cabinet officers. One of two sub-Cabinet bodies organized during the Eisenhower administration, this particular group, composed of executive assistants to Secretaries or Assistant Secretaries, is charged with seeing to it that decisions made in the Cabinet are followed up by the departments. Rabb reviews in detail what has taken place in the Cabinet meeting and informs the group of new decisions which the respective departments will have to carry out. When the individuals then go back to their departments, they are responsible for keeping track of what is being done to this end.

Both in the Cabinet and the N.S.C. Eisenhower has encouraged debate and has seemed to take a keen pleasure in the clash of minds around him. While the Cabinet deals more with domestic policy and the N.S.C. with foreign and military policy, the President has encouraged members of the Cabinet to express their opinions on foreign affairs also. He did so, for instance, at a meeting of the Cabinet on November 12, 1953.

Secretary Dulles gave a review of Eric A. Johnston's mission to the Near East to pacify the Arabs and the Israelis and, as a step in that direction, to promote a project similar to the Tennessee Valley Authority on the Jordan River for the benefit of both sides. After Dulles had spoken, the President said that since foreign policy so often involves domestic policy as well, he was eager to have the Cabinet talk about it. The best policy at home, he said, was to do the right thing abroad even though this might temporarily alienate extremists in the United States. He cautioned the Cabinet against "playing politics" with foreign affairs. Obviously referring to Israel, which Dulles had just mentioned, the President said that he had been told of one case in which the Truman administration had used foreign policy for domestic political advantage.

Eisenhower has been very deliberate in obtaining final agreement by the Cabinet on questions before it, and this agreement becomes, when the President approves it, the policy of the administration. In summing up a discussion, the President will say, "I guess we will all get behind this thing then unless I hear something to the contrary"— or words to that effect. A Cabinet member may be opposed to a certain course of action, but as a general rule Eisenhower wants such opposition argued before the Cabinet and not before him personally. He has conducted the Cabinet on the principle that since all are free to participate, the ultimate decision is binding upon all. And under these terms it would be bad medicine for one Cabinet member to go off and start feuding with another over a policy that had been settled upon in the Cabinet. One of the conspicuous traits of the Eisenhower administration, especially in contrast with the two preceding administrations, has been the lack of public vendettas among its high officials. This is not to say, of course, that serious differences of opinion and conflicts of personalities, as between, for example, Nelson A. Rockefeller, former Special Assistant to the President, and Under Secretary of State Herbert Hoover, Jr., have not smoldered behind the scenes from time to time.

In the management of their own departments the President has allowed members of the Cabinet a great deal of freedom—more indeed than some members of his own administration have thought best at times. For Eisenhower to dictate to a Cabinet officer would be a rarity. He relies on persuasion, and does not always succeed in persuading, either.

After Secretary Benson had announced on February 15, 1954, that the government support price for dairy products would be reduced from 90 per cent of parity to 75 per cent on the following April 1, Eisenhower argued with him that this was too sharp a drop to come all at once. It would be better, the President maintained, to make the 15 per cent reduction in two stages. He argued in vain. On April 1 the support went down to 75 per cent.

The President has repeatedly defended the right of department heads to latitude of conduct. He did so, for example, when Brownell leaked to a few newspapers the news that Governor Earl Warren, of California, had been selected by the President as Chief Justice, which caused resentment among papers not privy to the news. (Soon after this episode the Cabinet, on October 2, 1953, was discussing the removal of controls on nickel, and on the question of timing there was talk as to possible ways of enlisting the support of those groups favoring decontrol. The Attorney General, jokingly offering his services, said, "I could leak.")

Another typical example of Eisenhower's attitude toward the rights of Cabinet officers was his reply to a question at a press conference about a letter written to Congress by James P. Mitchell, who had succeeded Durkin as Secretary of Labor, indorsing the Ives equal-employment-opportunity bill, which granted enforcement powers to the Federal government.

The President said his own opinion was that certain things were best not handled by punitive or compulsory Federal law. However, he added, Mitchell, as well as every other Cabinet officer, was allowed to hold his own personal views on certain details of government activity, even if these differed from the President's, and was authorized to express them. He did not, he explained, consider Mitchell's letter an act of disloyalty to him. He said that he respected Mitchell's personal views and that he did not want a bunch of yes-men around him.

Eisenhower has placed great stress on strengthening the N.S.C.

by expanding and intensifying its staff work and by encouraging long, frank, argumentative discussions to get away from any evanescent quality its deliberations may have had in the past. On his own staff, as was mentioned, he created the position of Special Assistant to the President for National Security Affairs, which was occupied first by Cutler and now by Dillon Anderson, a conservative lawyer from Houston, whose avocation is writing fiction (and getting it published). This assistant is the President's chief liaison with the Council and is chairman of the N.S.C. Planning Board. He keeps in intimate contact with the President on problems of national security and regularly gives him thorough briefings on the business of the Council.

During these briefings, which constitute one of the important fonts of the President's information on current affairs, Eisenhower sometimes will pace up and down his pleasant office, now pausing to listen, now smacking his fist into the palm of his hand to drive home a point of his own as he thrashes out an idea with his assistant. At other times he will slump back in his chair to listen, doodling, writing his initials, chewing on the rims of his spectacles or holding the spectacles at an arm's length, upside down and backward, sighting a picture or some other distant object through jiggling lenses. (The President must have a dozen or more pairs of bifocals, which he leaves scattered about so he will always have a pair on hand when he needs them. All during his long convalescence in Fitzsimons General Hospital in the fall of 1955 one pair of spectacles lay where he had left them on his desk at Lowry Air Force Base, in Denver, and another on his desk in the White House.)

Along with the procedural changes in the Cabinet and the N.S.C., Eisenhower made important changes designed to bring a greater orderliness into White House business. Most notably, he imported from the Army a form of the staff system, in which all functions and responsibilities flow in a more or less fixed order and sequence from the President on down. For all practical purposes the main difference between this and the previous operation of the White House staff lies in the immense but unwritten authority vested in Sherman Adams as the Assistant to the President. This office had existed under Truman, but it never carried such responsibility and power as Adams has wielded. With great exertion Adams has handled a considerable amount of the work that in past administrations has been done by the President himself.

Although not a direct descendant of John Adams and John Quincy Adams, the slight, gray-haired former Governor of New Hampshire is a member of the family that gave the United States its second and sixth Presidents. Prints of them and of other early Presidents hang on the walls of his office. A liberal Republican, Adams was Eisenhower's floor manager at the Chicago convention and his chief of staff during the campaign. One day after the election Eisenhower told him, "I have been thinking this over. You had better come down with me to the White House. You be down there at my right hand." At Eisenhower's right hand, where he has been ever since, Adams has been the chief of staff in the White House and the overseer of the work of the executive branch of the government. While it has not been an inflexible rule, it has been the general practice that almost everything of importance in the White House bearing on domestic and political policy clears through Adams. He has been the pivot of political maneuver in the White House. He is the channel through which many of the most important projects in domestic affairs reach the President. What has been even more significant in fixing his influence is the fact that by the time many of these projects have reached the President they have already been shaped in part by Adams himself.

Time and again when a caller or official springs an idea on Eisenhower, the President will tell him, "Take it up with Sherman." Almost invariably before Eisenhower signs his approval to a paper, he will glance over it for the familiar notation, "OK, S.A." If it is missing the President will ask, "Has Governor Adams approved this?" And if the clerk who presents the paper wants it signed then and there, the answer had better be, "Yes, sir."

Adams has a remarkable ability for interpreting and articulating to others the thinking and the feelings of the President. Indeed this is an important part of his function and no small source of his influence. He has the blunt manner of a man who makes decisions like a machine, but there are warmth, humor and an authentic charm beneath it. His well-publicized severity has mellowed greatly since the first hard months in the White House when he had more than official business to worry him.

Illustrative of the part that Adams, with the President's backing, plays in the government was a case in which the heads of two departments were at odds over the appointment of a chairman to a board that works closely with both departments.

"Either make up your minds," Adams told them, "or else tell me and I will do it. We must not bother the President with this. He is trying to keep the world from war."

The principal ingredients of Adams's role were all present in this instance. First he brought the departments together to reach an agreement. Next he was prepared to step in and provide a solution himself if they could not agree. Finally he kept the burden of the problem off the President to leave him free for other things.

This was no isolated case. It is the kind of thing which goes on in Adams's office hour after hour and which, though nominally he is not a policy-making official, has left his imprint on a great deal of domestic policy. Foreign policy is a field in which he takes little active part, although he attends meetings of the N.S.C. as well as of the Cabinet.

Adams has been a whipping-boy for extreme right-wing Republicans who dislike the direction in which Eisenhower is taking the party but who have found it safer to hit Adams with blows intended for the President. To them Adams has been a symbol of what they profess to believe is a small clique of men who have insulated the President from the Republican organization—the "palace guard," as McCarthy once called it in attacking Adams.

Republican grousing about Adams has irritated Eisenhower to the point where one day he said angrily to an associate, "The trouble with these people is they don't recognize integrity."

"The one person who really knows what I am trying to do," Eisenhower has said, "is Sherman Adams."

"The President," a White House official once revealed, "has great faith in Adams and has told me many, many times that with Adams as his assistant he can sleep better at night. He finds it a great relief to have Adams around—to know that no one is going to come knocking at the door to make a deal."

An example of the kind of thing the President may have had in mind occurred early in the administration when a group of Republican businessmen whose industry was affected by a case then pending before a Federal commission blithely called on Adams to ask that the White House intervene in their interest. Adams heard them out and then read them an almost savage lecture on ethics in government, which sent them away empty-handed and furious.

II

Stalin's death in March renewed the quest by high officials of the administration for a way to improve relations with Russia and relax the tensions of the cold war. The administration was somewhat encouraged by Malenkov's indorsement, in his oration at Stalin's funeral, of the principle of peaceful "coexistence and competition" between the Communist and capitalist nations. This hopefulness, tempered though it was by caution and old suspicions, increased when Malenkov, in his own inaugural address, declared that "there is not one disputed or undecided question that cannot be decided by peaceful means on the basis of mutual understanding of interested countries." For good measure the Supreme Soviet had cheered when Malenkov added, "This is our attitude toward all states, among them the U.S.A."

Early in March, discussions were held in the White House on the advisability of the President's making a foreign-policy address of extraordinary importance. As the idea took shape, the speech would attempt not only to give new vigor to America's lagging leadership in international affairs but to impress upon the world in general and the new Soviet leaders in particular this country's determination to work for peace. Now that the harshness of Stalin's rule was beginning to thaw a bit and Russia was showing signs of a "peace offensive," the time was approaching, it was thought, for the United States to specify for all the world to hear some of the things the Soviets must do if the two countries were to meet halfway in settling their differences.

The President informed the Cabinet on March 27 that he had begun work on such a speech; the occasion chosen for its delivery was the annual meeting of the American Society of Newspaper Editors in the Statler in Washington on April 16.

Eisenhower went to Augusta for his annual spring golfing vacation early in April and worked over the final draft of his speech there. When he flew to Washington on April 16, he was wretchedly ill of what was diagnosed as food poisoning. He began his televised speech in the Presidential room of the Statler bravely enough but with almost every page he grew paler and weaker. Perspiration trickled from his temples, and he gripped the rostrum to steady himself. By the time he came to the last page he was jumbling some of his sentences together in a shaky voice. He said afterward that the last few paragraphs swam illegibly before his eyes. Few of the speeches he has made as President, however, received such acclaim.

The world knows [he said] that an era ended with the death of Josef Stalin. The extraordinary thirty-year span of his rule saw the Soviet Empire expand to reach from the Baltic Sea to the Sea of Japan, finally to dominate some 800,000,000 souls.

The Soviet system shaped by Stalin and his predecessors was born of one World War. It survived with stubborn and often amazing courage a second World War. It has lived to threaten a third.

Now a new leadership has assumed power in the Soviet Union. Its links to the past, however strong, cannot bind it completely. Its future is, in great part, its own to make.

The President spoke of the unity and strength of the free world and its willingness to respect the rights and interests of Russia.

So the new Soviet leadership [he continued] now has a precious opportunity to awaken, with the rest of the world, to the point of peril reached and to help turn the tide of history.

Will it do this?

We do not yet know. Recent statements and gestures of Soviet leaders give some evidence that they may recognize this critical moment.

We welcome every honest act of peace.

We care nothing for mere rhetoric.

We are only for sincerity of peaceful purpose attested by deeds. The opportunities for such deeds are many. The performance of a great number of them waits upon no complex protocol but upon the simple will to do them. Even a few such clear and specific acts, such as the Soviet Union's signature upon an Austrian treaty or its release of thousands of prisoners still held from World War II, would be impressive signs of sincere intent . . .

With all who will work in good faith toward such peace, we are ready with renewed resolve, to strive to redeem the near-lost hopes of our day.

The first great step along this way must be the conclusion of an honorable armistice in Korea. This means the immediate cessation of hostilities and the prompt initiation of political discussions leading to the holding of free elections in a united Korea.

It should mean, no less importantly, an end to the direct and indirect attacks upon the security of Indo-China and Malaya. For any armistice in Korea that merely released aggressive armies to attack elsewhere would be a fraud.

We seek, throughout Asia as throughout the world, a peace that is true and total.

Out of this can grow a still wider task—the achieving of just political settlements for the other serious and specific issues between the free world and the Soviet Union . . .

We are ready not only to press forward with the present plans for closer unity of the nations of Western Europe, but also, upon that foundation to strive to foster a broader European community . . . This community would include a free and united Germany, with a government based upon free and secret elections.

This free community and the full independence of the East European nations could mean the end of the present unnatural division of Europe.

In conclusion the President urged disarmament and international control of atomic energy, with a system of inspection under the U.N., and said:

This government is ready to ask its people to join with all nations in devoting a substantial percentage of the savings achieved by disarmament to a fund for world aid and reconstruction . . .

The monuments . . . would be these: roads and schools, hospitals and homes, food and health.

"The President's speech," wrote Richard H. Rovere in *The New Yorker,* "scored an immense triumph with both world and American opinion; it firmly established his leadership in America and reestablished American leadership in the world. . . ."

As Rovere also pointed out, the speech carried timely and welcome reassurance to this country's allies that, contrary to some growing fears abroad, the Eisenhower administration was not

The famous meeting at Morningside Heights, September 12, 1952.
After a battle at the Chicago convention, Senator Taft was ready
to campaign for Eisenhower, but first obtained "full approval" at
this conference for a statement of political beliefs written by Taft.
(*Wide World Photos*)

After his election Eisenhower had this visit with outgoing President Truman to work out a smooth change-over between the old
and the incoming administrations. The atmosphere was strained.
(*Wide World Photos*)

One of the first shifts in policy—the substitution of Homburgs for top hats at the inauguration. "Tradition is not involved," the President said. "If we were going back to tradition, we would wear tricornered hats and knee britches." (*Wide World Photos*)

The first picture of the President, his Cabinet and members of his staff. Clockwise around the table: Henry Cabot Lodge, Douglas McKay, George M. Humphrey, Richard Nixon, Herbert Brownell, Sinclair Weeks, Oveta Culp Hobby, Sherman Adams, Joseph M. Dodge, Arthur S. Flemming, Martin P. Durkin, Arthur E. Summerfield, John Foster Dulles, the President, Charles E. Wilson, Ezra Taft Benson. Standing: Philip Young (left) and Robert Cutler (right). (*Wide World Photos*)

The President's painting of Lincoln, done from a photograph by Alexander Gardner. Each member of the White House staff received a color print of the portrait. (*Wide World Photos*)

The summit meeting at Geneva. The President sits with Soviet Prime Minister Bulganin at left and Edgar Faure of France and Anthony Eden of Great Britain at right. Although Eisenhower scored a personal victory at this conference, "the spirit of Geneva", proved too fragile to make a permanent improvement in East-West relations. (Wide World Photos)

In December, 1955, the President met with Congressional leaders of both parties to review the foreign and defense programs. Pictured above leaving the White House are Sen. Harry Byrd (D. Va.), Sen. William Knowland (R. Cal.), Speaker Sam Rayburn (D. Tex.), Rep. Jere Cooper (D. Tenn.), Sen. Lyndon Johnson (D. Tex.), Rep. Clarence Cannon (D. Mo.), with hat, and Rep. Joseph Martin (R. Mass.). (*Wide World Photos*)

A momentous decision is announced on February 29, 1956, to a record gathering of newsmen as the President makes known his willingness to run for a second term. (*Wide World Photos*)

The President, Mrs. Eisenhower, Mrs. Barbara Eisenhower, and Colonel Gordon Moore, Mrs. Eisenhower's brother-in-law, relax after the conclusion of the President's television and radio broadcast to the nation at which he discussed his decision to seek office again. (*Wide World Photos*)

proposing any sudden and fundamental changes in the familiar course of United States foreign policy.

The President's insistence on certain positive actions by the Soviet Union as an earnest of its desire for a settlement remained, right up until his trip to the Big Four Conference in Geneva in July, 1955, a precondition to any agreement by him to meet the Russians.

At the period of this speech the administration's zeal for psychological warfare was at its zenith, and C. D. Jackson and his warriors had prepared for weeks to scatter the President's words and ideas around the world. The address was broadcast live to Great Britain. Texts were sent by radio and pouch to American diplomatic missions abroad, and chiefs of mission were instructed to give prime ministers and foreign ministers a copy and to call their attention personally to particular points made by the President.

The State Department sent texts by radio to sixty information centers abroad and by commercial telegraph to thirty-four more. More than three million pamphlets containing the speech in full or in part were prepared for distribution in Europe and Latin America alone. And in New Delhi, India, for example, 105,000 handbills in eight different languages were distributed. In Germany texts were distributed among 921 newspapers and magazines. The address was displayed in the windows of the United States Legation in Budapest, prompting more than a thousand persons, it was reported, to go and get copies in the first week. Films of the President delivering the speech were prepared for distribution, and kinescopes were flown abroad for televising from stations on three continents. Broadcasts to Iron Curtain countries were repeated again and again.

Labor union officials in this country were given copies. New York businessmen were notified in advance that something big was coming, and some of them, in turn, spread the word by telephone. One of them said he believed that through his own efforts he alerted a thousand other men. The diplomatic corps in Moscow was reported enthusiastic, and Sir Winston not only praised the speech, but had the British Ambassador in Moscow personally hand a copy of his own statement to this effect to Soviet Foreign Minister V. M.

Molotov. State Department cables even noted reports from Budapest that Hungarian officials (not, unfortunately, at high levels of government) wept and prayed as they listened to a broadcast of the President's speech in translation.

Among the domestic issues that were engaging the President's attention at this time was the St. Lawrence Seaway. The question came up in the Cabinet on March 13, and before seeking opinions around the table the President observed that because of the cost he had never been among the enthusiasts for the project. Up to this time he had not taken an official position on it. During the discussion Secretary Humphrey and Adams made a very favorable case for the seaway. As the former chairman of the board of the M. A. Hanna Company, of Cleveland, Humphrey explained that he was predisposed toward it because the steel industry favored the seaway for the access it would provide to Canadian ore.

Humphrey, with the backing of Brownell, recommended that the administration take a strong stand for the Wiley bill to establish a St. Lawrence Seaway Development Corporation to build the American section with the proceeds of self-liquidating bonds.

One of the factors that forced the issue was Canada's threat to construct the seaway alone if the United States continued to procrastinate. The President said at a press conference on March 19 that he would be distressed to see Canada go ahead without the United States because in time Americans might have reason to regret being frozen out of a share in control of the seaway. And in the Cabinet on March 27 the President, Nixon, Wilson, Brownell, Adams, Stassen and Secretary of the Interior Douglas McKay all spoke in favor of having the United States participate rather than stand aside and give Canada exclusive control.

The matter came before the Cabinet again on April 3. It was one of those meetings which the President occasionally opens with some casual remark he has made a mental note of. He said that he would like to see something done to "glamorize" the work of the foreign service. The worth of foreign-service officers was not receiving the recognition it deserved, he commented. He indicated that a motion-picture company was interested in making a film about the foreign service, and he requested the co-operation of the Cabinet.

The President made it plain that he was still troubled over the merits of the St. Lawrence project. He desired that all sides should receive a fair hearing in the Senate to take some of the heat out of controversy. As an example of the opposition arguments he was hearing he circulated among the Cabinet a memorandum from the Chicago Chamber of Commerce purporting to show the comparatively high cost of transportation on the seaway. The issue, he intimated, was more complex than he had anticipated. The President said, however, that the administration could not always be on the defensive and would have to support the project sooner or later. But before a stand was taken, he wished to have more of the opposition views presented at the forthcoming Senate hearings.

In the Cabinet on April 10 Dulles said that the State Department was not yet certain what position it should take in the hearings. Enumerating his reasons for delay, Eisenhower said that the Cabinet had never heard in full the arguments against the seaway, which had been presented to him recently by the presidents of several railroads. Eisenhower and Humphrey discussed these arguments across the Cabinet table.

Humphrey maintained that access to Labrador ore deposits made the inland waterway necessary to national security. He emphasized that the Mesabi Range in Minnesota no longer offered hope of rapidly expanding yields, whereas the Labrador deposits had the potential for the kind of expansion once possible in the Mesabi. He told the President that the arguments about high costs of transportation on the seaway were based on differentials in railroad rates, which could be misleadingly interpreted. Even at the end of this meeting, however, the President and the Cabinet decided that the administration would not at that time support the Wiley bill. There was still strong opposition among the Republican leaders of Congress, and the President, in this as on other occasions, was anxious not to provoke a split in the party unnecessarily.

The impasse was finally broken when the President announced at a press conference on April 23 that the National Security Council had found it advantageous to the security of the United States that the seaway should be built, and built with American participation. The next day he wrote encouragingly to Senator Alexander Wiley, Republican, of Wisconsin, chairman of the Senate Foreign Relations Committee and sponsor of the seaway bill, saying that he approved the recommendation of the N.S.C. that "early initiation and completion . . . is in the interest of national security."

The Cabinet gave its approval on May 8 after Secretary Weeks read a report of a Cabinet subcommittee unanimously favoring American participation. Weeks said, parenthetically, that the administration could expect soon to feel pressure for financial help in developing harbors to accommodate seagoing vessels. More than a year later, on July 16, 1954, Dulles commented at a meeting of the Cabinet that there would be some merit to such requests. The President pondered this for a moment and then remarked that Duck Island, in Lake Ontario, where the Secretary of State has a summer home, must need a new harbor.

Congress finally passed the St. Lawrence bill on May 7, 1954. His earlier reservations now swept aside, the President took considerable pride in the fact that a project favored by every administration since Wilson's had come to fruition under his. When he was signing the bill, he suddenly paused to ask, "What is the date?" Eisenhower has a habit of fixing the dates of Sundays in his mind and calculating the dates of other days from them, but on this occasion the system broke down momentarily. He remarked afterward that others must have had just as bad a lapse because it took thirty seconds for someone to remind him that it was May 13.

Off and on during these months the President was confronted with the question of whether public or private utilities should operate new electric power facilities at Niagara Falls, a project entirely separate from the St. Lawrence. The conversations illuminate Eisenhower's thinking on the relations between states and the Federal government.

In the meeting of the Cabinet on May 8, 1953, the discussion turned to the Miller bill to authorize development of Niagara power by five private utilities, which was contrary to the traditional policy of both parties in New York. The President told the Cabinet that he felt that the question lay within the jurisdiction of the state. The Federal government, he said, should not presume to decide it.

Four times he broke into the discussion, each time more insistently than before. First he asked, "Isn't this for New York to decide?" Next he interrupted to say that he could not see why the administration had to resolve the question. It was simply not in keeping with its philosophy to do so, he insisted. When McKay said that his department would have to take a stand on the Miller bill, the President told him, "You can be against a law about this. Let New York decide." Later he said again, "We can't tell the state. If we do, we will be just as doctrinaire as others have been."

There is probably no issue on which Eisenhower has said more often that he deplores a doctrinaire attitude than on the issue of public *versus* private power.

When the Miller bill was discussed at the weekly legislative leaders' conference on the following July 20, the President was concerned with who should make the decision on Niagara power and not with what the decision was to be. He pointed out that it was an intrastate matter and hence lay outside the jurisdiction of the Federal government.

"I am neither a public nor a private power man," he told the leaders. "I merely want to see that a state has rights which legitimately belong to it. I believe in the cooperation of all three." (Meaning the Federal government, the state government and local private interests.)

Again the President told the leaders during the three-day conference in December, 1953, that the Niagara power issue should be left to the state to decide. While as a general rule he favored private power development, he said, he believed that this questioned turned on the matter of a state's rights.

Partly no doubt because of his own campaign in 1952 against the Democratic scandals in Washington, there was no subject on which Eisenhower was more sensitive when he took office than corruption in government. At the sixth meeting of the Cabinet on February 25, 1953, he urged the heads of departments to be alert to conditions that might breed scandal and to be quick about calling on the Department of Justice to investigate dubious situations. He told the Cabinet of reports he had received that the Truman administration had sometimes delayed investigation, and he was emphatic in saying that the new administration must take positive action to prevent corruption.

Whenever this subject has come up, Eisenhower has almost automatically made a point of citing the principle that employment by the government is a privilege and not a right—a rule he applies in the cases of security risks also. When the selection of high officials of his administration began before the inauguration, he made it clear that those chosen must have records of conduct beyond reproach. He let it be known to them that they must expect a systematic inquiry into their backgrounds, and even members of the Cabinet were subjected to full field investigation by the Federal Bureau of Investigation.

Early in the administration the Attorney General instituted a number of reforms to root out questionable practices of the past. All new United States Attorneys were required to give up their own law practices upon taking office. Too many instances had come to light where attorneys were not devoting their full time to government responsibilities, and there had been some cases, according to Brownell, in which attorneys had committed the ultimate in conflict of interest by representing both sides to a dispute. An end was put to secrecy in the granting of pardons, and civil cases were made a matter of record in the Department of Justice. This applies not only to civil cases in the tax field but to all civil cases in which the government is a claimant or defendant.

The power of decision as to whether a defendant is physically and mentally able to stand trial was taken out of the hands of the Department and given to the courts. A great many tax-dodgers and others accused of crimes against the government, it seems, develop heart attacks or mental illness when the trial approaches. Previously someone in the Department of Justice could decide whether to let individuals off on this ground, which, of course, opened the door to abuses of favoritism. Now the courts decide.

During 1953 the Department of Justice prosecuted several Republican officials, and the attitude of the administration was that these cases stood as a warning of its intention not to tolerate corruption.

Representative Ernest K. Bramblett, of California, was indicted and later pleaded guilty to charges that he had lied in denying that he had taken salary "kickbacks" from two employees. Warren L. Stephenson, the executive secretary of the Eisenhower Inaugural Committee, was indicted for perjury in his testimony before a House subcommittee about his role in obtaining a Navy contract for a California firm. Stephenson, who had traveled on Eisenhower's campaign train—the same one from which the candidate denounced the "5 per centers" of the Truman administration—was accused of having made a "4 per center" deal on the contract.

In Georgia the chairmen of the Republican Committee of Pierce County and of the Republican Committee of the Eighth Congressional District were indicted for soliciting money for post office jobs. A cost accountant in York, Pennsylvania, who offered to contribute a thousand dollars to the Republican Party in return for appointment as local postmaster was indicted. In Minnesota the Republican chairman of the township of Rome and a Republican precinct captain in the village of Frost pleaded guilty and were fined in criminal proceedings for accepting political contributions in return for promises of influence in the obtaining of Federal jobs.

In 1954 the administration discovered that in connection with insured loans of the Federal Housing Administration fraudulent profiteering had been going on for years. Once the matter reached the White House prompt action was taken to deal with it. The President accepted the resignation of Guy T. O. Hollyday, commissioner of the F.H.A. There was, however, no shadow of wrongdoing associated with his name, only a feeling that he had not been tough enough in dealing with the situation.

At a Cabinet meeting on March 4, 1955, the Attorney General gave a report on conviction in the "windfall" cases—the cases in which builders of apartments had obtained government-insured loans for more than the construction cost and pocketed the difference. The President inquired what kind of sentences these profiteers were being given. Brownell replied that in his opinion the sentences were too lenient, whereupon Eisenhower observed that he would like to see full justice done in such cases.

Some months after the discovery of the F.H.A. scandals the Budget Bureau directed all government departments and agencies to review and tighten up their procedures for keeping tabs on the conduct of their employees. The directive stressed checks on the conduct of those government employees who handle large amounts of cash or who are engaged in procurement or in making or insuring loans, granting licenses or certificates or in handling economic regulation or law enforcement, "which may substantially affect the material fortunes of private interests."

In the first three years the administration has had trouble, as has been mentioned, with conflict-of-interest cases. There have been political accusations of favoritism toward big business in the regulatory agencies under the Republicans—"giveaways" is the Democratic label. While the acreage of the National Parks has increased under the Republicans, private interests have made some inroads into National Forests and National Wildlife Refuges. But the record on known and proved corruption—fraud, the sale of influence and favors and similar crimes by politicians and officeholders—has been a very clean one.

At a meeting of the Cabinet on April 1, 1955, the Attorney General called attention to the conviction that day of Henry W. (The Dutchman) Grunewald, a lobbyist, for conspiracy to "fix" tax claims. The Attorney General also recalled the earlier convictions of Joseph D. Nunan, Jr., Commissioner of Internal Revenue from 1944 to 1947, and Daniel A. Bolich, former Assistant Commissioner of Internal Revenue. Proof had now been established in court, Brownell said, that great corruption flourished in the Internal Revenue Service under the Democrats.

He told the Cabinet that the bribery to the tune of a quarter of a million dollars which had been proved in the recent cases was the biggest scandal of its kind in history, with the payments exceeding even those of Teapot Dome. (In the Teapot Dome scandal of the Harding administration Secretary of the Interior Albert B. Fall received some $260,000 in Liberty bonds from Harry F. Sinclair and a non-interest-bearing "loan" of $100,000 from Edward L. Doheny after Fall had secretly leased government oil reserves to Sinclair's Mammoth Oil Company and Doheny's Pan-American Oil Company.)

The President remarked that it was ironical that the Democratic tax scandals received, as he put it, such small headlines in comparison with those of the Republican Teapot Dome affair.

CHAPTER 6

The President and Congress

Eisenhower's Concern over Congressional Relations – Beginnings of Trouble with the Right Wing – Velde – The Bohlen Case – "Don't Join the Book-Burners" – The J. B. Matthews Affair – The Election of Leonard W. Hall – Eisenhower's Woes over Patronage

I

After Election Day when Eisenhower regarded the task ahead of him on January 20 he was not overly troubled by the problem of managing the executive branch of the government. He felt that with the help of capable men and with his own extensive background in Washington, including his experience as Army Chief of Staff, he could handle this part of the responsibility of the Presidency more or less to his satisfaction. Of much greater concern to him then and after he had moved into the White House was his relationship with Congress.

From his own experiences in testifying before committees he knew a good deal about Congressional processes and Congressional hazards. The difficulties between Truman and Congress in recent years had been only too pressing a reminder of the frustrations that can mire a President if he is unable to win Congressional support.

Eisenhower brought to the White House a genuine respect for Congress and a traditionalist's conception of the separation of powers. In talks with associates he has referred to himself more than once as a "Constitutional President."

Although the Republicans had won control of both houses in the election of 1952, the victory had been a narrow one, and, unlike Roosevelt in 1933, for example, Eisenhower took office without a dependable majority in Congress. When the Eighty-third Congress convened in January, 1953, the line-up of parties was:

SENATE

Republicans	48
Democrats	47
Independent	1

HOUSE

Republicans	221
Democrats	211
Independent	1

To make matters more difficult for the President much of the Republican power in Congress was still lodged with those Old Guard elements who had favored Taft rather than Eisenhower for the nomination. Taft himself was now the Republican leader in the Senate.

In the preinaugural meeting of the Cabinet in the Commodore, Eisenhower announced that he intended to co-operate very closely with Congress. He spoke at some length of his hopes and his expectations that the Republicans in Congress would soon get out of the frame of mind of being in the opposition, an attitude firmly molded by twenty years of Democratic rule, and would get into the spirit of helping the new administration.

In the early meetings of the Cabinet a good deal of discussion was devoted to the problem of creating amicable relations with Congress. At the very first Cabinet meeting in the White House on January 23 the President, in referring to liaison with Capitol Hill, declared that the administration must recognize the great responsibility of Congress and the necessity for co-operating with the members.

At the meeting on January 30 he told the Cabinet that the best approach to Congress in the face of some of the early difficulties that were cropping up was to maintain a silence "of confidence." For he expected, he said, that these early troubles would work themselves out if fuel was not added to the fires of controversy. He expressed his own confidence that Republicans in Congress would not be long in realizing that they were the majority party now and that the continuance of this majority after the 1954 elections would depend on proving to the voters that the Republican Party was capable of effective teamwork.

He said that he wished to do all that he personally could to bring about harmony and that to this end he was preparing to invite the Congressional committee chairmen to the White House for luncheon. Soon he invited all members of the House and Senate— a total of more than five hundred men and women—to a series of luncheons. Nothing like it had ever been done before. Many members, including a sizable number of Democrats, had never before seen the private quarters of the White House.

These luncheons were purely social affairs in which the President sought to cultivate the friendship of individual legislators and to give them a feeling that he was interested in the problems of them all, Republicans and Democrats alike. After attending one of the luncheons, a Democrat, Representative Michael J. Kirwan, of Ohio, wrote the President, saying that his hospitality was fostering "a feeling of friendliness which will do more to bring about co-operation of members of Congress than all the testimonies presented to Congressional committees."

To all appearances the President did engender a feeling of friendliness and respect by these luncheons and by other manifestations of his esteem for Congress. In the nature of politics, however, there are limits to what such amenities can accomplish, and even in the midst of them the gap between the President and the extreme right-wing Republicans not only persisted but began to widen ominously.

At the meeting of January 30 the question of Congressional investigations came before the Cabinet for the first time, and here again Eisenhower urged co-operation. After Brownell had mentioned the ten separate investigations of the State Department then in progress, consuming, he noted, the time of its officials, the President said that the administration should take a sympathetic attitude toward those investigations already being conducted. They were in reality, he said, investigations of the Truman administration and might furnish helpful guides for the new administration's efforts to eliminate waste and inefficiency.

Eisenhower suggested that department heads could help reduce the interference of investigations with current business by conferring with the chairmen of the investigating committees and explaining what measures were now being initiated to correct abuses, so that inquiry might be restricted to other areas. The President viewed this approach as one that would benefit both the administration and Congress and produce co-operation between the two. At least, he felt, this way of handling the matter would serve to distinguish between "constructive" investigations and those aimed simply at headlines.

The President and Lodge both spoke of the need for self-investigation by the executive branch. Lodge and Brownell noted that while this would not prevent Congressional investigations, it would take some of the steam out of them.

In the Cabinet on February 20 the President asked that as a means of strengthening confidence in the efficiency of the new administration, all department heads give Congress complete information on the reduction of government personnel under their jurisdiction.

On March 13 a discussion in the Cabinet turned once more to the problem being raised for the administration by continuing Congressional investigations. Weeks observed that soon these investigations would reflect Eisenhower's administration instead of Truman's. Once again the President replied that Congress and the administration must co-operate in making a creditable record by 1954 or else run the risk of losing control of Congress.

The President's air was determined, but disillusionment was setting in.

The pressure for the Bricker amendment was intensifying. On March 13 Dulles warned the Cabinet of the possibility of a head-on clash between the administration and Bricker's numerous and powerful supporters. Representative Harold H. Velde, Republican, of Illinois, the new chairman of the House Un-American Activities Committee, who was to cause the President more than one excruciating embarrassment, said on a radio program that religion offered a possible field for investigation by his Red-hunting group and that an inquiry very likely would extend to "individual members of the cloth, including some who seem to have devoted more time to politics than . . . to the ministry."

"Are you in favor of the Federal government, through the Congress

of the United States, investigating Communism in the churches?"
the President was asked at his press conference on March 19.

The President smiled and rubbed his chin with his fingers. Well,
he replied, he believed that if the churches, which certainly should
be the most formidable foes of Communism, needed investigation,
then the country had better take a new look at the whole business and
go far beyond investigating Communism. He based this statement,
he said, on the belief that the churches, with their testimony to the
existence of an almighty God, were the last institutions that would
be teaching or tolerating Communism. Therefore, he concluded, he
could see no possible good to be achieved by questioning the loyalty
of the churches on that issue. Others also joined in squelching
Velde's inspiration, and nothing came of it finally.

Far more serious and disconcerting to the President was the fight in
the Senate in March over his nomination of Charles E. Bohlen as
Ambassador to the Soviet Union. As a career foreign-service officer
Bohlen had attended the Yalta conference in 1945 as a Russian-
language interpreter for Roosevelt. As if that were not enough to
damn him in the eyes of the right-wing extremists in the Senate, he
had refused in an appearance before the Senate Foreign Relations
Committee when his nomination was under consideration to join
the chorus of condemnation of Yalta. On the contrary, he defended
the arrangements made there as having been in the best interests
of the United States at that time. While the cold-war-ridden world
looked on and the prestige of the new President and Secretary of
State was heavily involved in the outcome, the late Senator Pat
McCarran, Democrat, of Nevada, and his Republican ally, McCarthy,
not content with the Yalta issue, gave the fight a still uglier turn by
raising a question as to Bohlen's loyalty.

On March 20 McCarran charged in the Senate that R. W. Scott
McLeod, the State Department security officer, had been "unable
to clear" Bohlen "on the basis of information received from the
F.B.I.", but that McLeod had been "summarily overridden" by Dulles.
The Secretary of State immediately denied this. Later that same day
McCarthy said that Dulles's statement "appears to be completely
untrue" and he suggested that the Foreign Relations Committee
question Dulles under oath. McCarthy said that he had known for

years what was in Bohlen's file and that calling him a "security risk" was "putting it too weak."

Contrary to some reports at the time, McLeod did not see Eisenhower about the controversy. What happened was that the next day, Saturday, March 21, McLeod asked to see General Wilton B. Persons, then Special Assistant and later Deputy Assistant to the President. McLeod told Persons that he was unhappy over the things that were happening and over the charges of a dispute between Dulles and himself. In the circumstances, he said, he felt that the proper thing for him to do would be to submit his resignation. Persons replied that he did not think resignation was necessary. Persons's advice was to let the situation between McLeod and Dulles work itself out. McLeod, of course, did not resign.

Dulles had assured the Foreign Relations Committee that an F.B.I. investigation had left "no doubt" that Bohlen was loyal and was not a security risk. The Secretary explained that McLeod had passed the Bohlen report to him with a note saying that because it contained derogatory information, it was not a case which he, McLeod, could approve automatically. This was the usual procedure, Dulles testified.

Still, McCarthy and McCarran had stirred up such a tempest that on March 23 Taft and Senator John J. Sparkman, of Alabama, the 1952 Democratic Vice-Presidential nominee, agreed to act as a sort of two-man Senate jury and read the F.B.I. summary of the Bohlen file. Two days later Taft told the Senate:

There was no suggestion anywhere by anyone reflecting on the loyalty of Mr. Bohlen in any way or any association by him with Communism or support of Communism or even tolerance of Communism . . . There was not any suggestion that would in my opinion create even a prima facie case or a prima facie charge of any ill doing on the part of Mr. Bohlen.

On March 26 the President told his press conference that he was very deeply and personally concerned in the Bohlen case. Bohlen's record, he said, showed dedication to the United States. The President said that he had known Bohlen for years and had been a guest in his home, had met his very charming family, to use Eisenhower's words, and had played golf with him. He said that he had listened to Bohlen expound his philosophy. So far as he could see, Eisenhower said, Bohlen was the best-qualified man that he could find for the Moscow post and that was why his name had been sent to the Senate and why it was going to stay there. McCarthy had said that it would be a serious mistake for the President not to withdraw the nomination.

Taft threw his great weight in the Senate to Eisenhower's side, not because he was happy over the nomination, which he was not, but because he felt that a President should be permitted to appoint men of his own choice and because he knew that a defeat on the issue would be an unseemly blow to the new President's prestige. With his help, therefore, the nomination was confirmed by a vote of seventy-four to thirteen. Afterward, according to his biographer, White, Taft passed the word on to the White House, "No more Bohlens!" There were those in the White House, it must be added, who felt the same way and who were shy of anything that would arouse another intraparty fight like the Bohlen case.

The case was not only a scar but an omen. The shadow of coming events could be seen in McCarthy's charges that Eisenhower had broken his campaign promises to "get rid of all Acheson's architects of disaster" and "clean up the mess in Washington" and in the countercharges of the President's friends in the Senate that McCarthy was using the Bohlen case to mask an attack on the President and Dulles.

Throughout this first spring in office when Eisenhower had hoped that public attention might be concentrated on his approach to the great problems of foreign and domestic policy the headlines were dominated by quarrels over investigations, book-burnings and McCarthy's antics.

For months a controversy, which finally involved the President, flared over McCarthy's investigation of the State Department's International Information Administration (later replaced by the United States Information Agency), including the Voice of America and overseas libraries maintained by the government to disseminate information about the United States. This inquiry had a particularly gaudy quality, replete with resignations, dismissals, authors on the witness stand, scurrying by the State Department to satisfy McCarthy, and the noisy debut of Roy M. Cohn and G. David Schine, who a year later were to spurt through evanescent stardom in the McCarthy-Army hearings. As assistants to McCarthy they toured Europe in April to investigate alleged inefficiency and cases of doubtful loyalty in the information service, and their trip aroused a storm of criticism and ridicule abroad.

The most serious aspect of the long controversy, however, concerned books by left-wing writers in American overseas libraries.

Under the Truman administration the International Information Administration had authorized in January, 1953, the use of pro-American material by Communist or other left-wing authors on the grounds that it might "be given a special credibility among selected key audiences," who would be likely to sympathize with such writers. This directive became a target for McCarthy, and in February the State Department revoked it and ordered removal from the libraries overseas of the writings of Howard Fast, an American novelist, who later in the year was awarded a Stalin Peace Prize.

This was the beginning of a series of revisions by the Department in its policy on books in overseas libraries. On March 18 it authorized the Voice and other overseas information agencies to use Communist material to "expose Communist propaganda or refute Communist lies," but it excluded "the works of all Communist authors" and "any publication which continuously publishes Communist propaganda." McCarthy called this a "good, sensible order" and complimented Dulles on it, but the matter did not end there.

The issue raised the question of just where the United States stood on the subject of free expression of thought, and the question became very acute indeed when the news broke that some books had been burned in American libraries overseas—a disheartening spectacle only too reminiscent of the Nazi book purge of the 1930's.

In June the President visited Calvin Coolidge's old haunts in Custer State Park in the Black Hills of South Dakota and with a dry fly and Colorado spinner fished in the same French Creek where Coolidge had caught trout with worms, thereby scandalizing the sporting world and even causing reverberations in Congress. On the way back to Washington, Eisenhower visited Sherman Adams's alma mater, Dartmouth College, and on June 14 made a speech on the campus in which he said:

It is not enough merely to say "I love America" and to salute the flag and take off your hat as it goes by and to help sing "The Star-Spangled Banner." Wonderful! We love to do them, and our hearts swell with pride because those who went before you worked to give us today, standing here, this pride. And this is a pride in an institution that we think has brought great happiness, and we know has brought great contentment and freedom of soul to many people. But it is not yet done. You must add to it.

Don't join the book-burners! Don't think you are going to conceal faults by concealing evidence that they ever existed. Don't be afraid to go in your library and read every book as long as that document does not offend your own ideas of decency. That should be the only censorship.

In answering questions at his press conference on June 17 the President expanded on his Dartmouth speech, though not with the sting that some of his friends would have liked (he refused to say whether he had intended criticism of McCarthy) nor always with sufficient clarity of language.

The instance I have in mind was an answer in which he said that if State Department personnel burned a book which appealed to readers to become Communists, then that was something that fell outside the limits he was setting, and State Department people could do as they pleased to get rid of such books. On the basis of these words some straightforward newspaper stories reported that the President had said that book-burning was all right in the case of certain books. Eisenhower himself was much put out at his next press conference by the mere suggestion that he had expressed his approval of burning books under any circumstances.

In any case the essence of his remarks was clear. He was opposed to suppression of ideas. He believed, however, that the United States should not pay for books to be put on shelves abroad which advocated a system of government that would destroy the United States. Books advocating Communism, he felt, should be excluded from American overseas libraries. But other controversial books, even those depicting America's bad points, should be allowed, as should nonpolitical books by left-wing authors, such as Dashiell Hammett's mystery stories.

On June 26 the subject came before the Cabinet. Dulles said that the book-burnings had been independent acts by librarians, moved either by fear of or out of hatred for McCarthy. (The implication of the latter, presumably, is that some librarians may have burned books for the deliberate purpose of discrediting McCarthy.)

The Secretary of State told the Cabinet that abroad great importance was attached to McCarthy's position and to his activities.

As for books, Dulles said that the law establishing the overseas libraries provided that to be included they must be descriptive of American life or must be concerned with American foreign policy and that literal interpretation of the statute would exclude Shakespeare, the Bible and Edward Gibbon's *The Decline and Fall of the Roman Empire.* The President asked for a policy statement on books by the next Cabinet meeting.

On July 8 the administration made public through Dr. Robert L. Johnson, president of Temple University and the then Administrator of the International Information Administration, the statement, the principal points of which were:

1. The government was under no obligation to place in special-purpose libraries any books directly or indirectly advocating destruction of American freedom and institutions.

2. Books must not be excluded as Communistic because they criticize American institutions and policies.

3. The yardstick for selection should be the usefulness of a particular book in meeting the needs of a particular area.

4. Conceivably, books by Communists or Communist sympathizers may be included in special instances if these authors have written something "which affirmatively serves the ends of democracy." So also may books of humor or mystery by such authors.

5. Controversial books were acceptable.

6. Responsibility for recommending the selection of books should be entrusted to carefully chosen advisory committees composed of persons of unimpeachable reputation who are experts in their respective fields.

7. "Under no circumstances should any book be burned . . . The burning of a book is a wicked symbolic act. There is no place for book-

burnings in an American library, let alone a library operated by our government. We don't deal with ideas we dislike by imitating the totalitarian techniques we despise. The burning of a book is not an act against that book alone; it is an act against free institutions."

Earlier, Johnson had revealed that on orders from Washington about three hundred books by eighteen authors had been removed from overseas libraries. The day before the policy statement was issued, however, the State Department said that it had ordered many of them to be restored to the shelves.

The matter was discussed in the Cabinet again on July 10. Dulles referred to the policy statement and emphasized that the solution to the problem lay in wise handling of the information program administratively.

Wilson suggested that possibly the government should get out of the business of maintaining libraries abroad, but Dulles and Stassen promptly took the opposite view. They urged that overseas libraries should be allowed to have any books deemed suitable for libraries in the United States, except that public funds should not be spent for books alien to the purpose of overseas libraries.

Humphrey and Mrs. Hobby proposed limiting the function of overseas libraries to the presentation of Americana. The Vice-President told the Cabinet that Congress would never vote funds for general-purpose libraries overseas.

C. D. Jackson wound up the discussion by observing that the Johnson statement seemed to offer the most practicable solution to the problem. For one thing, he said, it provided that books should be selected in the future in accordance with the existing law and, for another, it avoided ordering a screening of books already on the shelves, an act, Jackson said, which would have been damaging to American prestige.

On July 9 Eisenhower received the following telegram:

The President
The White House

The sweeping attack on the loyalty of Protestant clergymen and the charge that they are the largest single group supporting the Communist apparatus is unjustified and deplorable. This is a matter of vital concern to the nation. You are to be congratulated on your recent warning against casting doubt on the loyalty of the churches and synagogues. We fully recognize the right of Congress to investigate the loyalty of any citizen regardless of the office he may occupy, ecclesiastical or otherwise. But destroying trust in the leaders of Protestantism, Catholicism or Judaism by wholesale condemnation is to weaken the greatest American bulwark against atheistic materialism and Communism.

The message was signed by Monsignor John A. O'Brien, of the University of Notre Dame; Rabbi Maurice N. Eisendrath, president of the Union of American Hebrew Congregations, and the Rev. Dr. John Sutherland Bonnell, pastor of the Fifth Avenue Presbyterian Church, in New York, the three being the national co-chairmen of the Commission on Religious Organizations of the National Conference of Christians and Jews.

The occasion for this protestation was an article in the July issue of *The American Mercury* by J. B. Matthews, whom McCarthy on June 22 had appointed staff director of the Senate Permanent Investigations Subcommittee, of which the Wisconsin Senator was chairman. The article began: "The largest single group supporting the Communist apparatus in the United States today is composed of Protestant clergymen."

Matthews, who several years before had been director of research for the House Un-American Activities Committee, alleged that "at least seven thousand" Protestant clergymen had served "the Kremlin conspiracy" and that since 1948 the Communist Party had "placed more and more reliance upon the ranks of the Protestant clergy to provide the party's subversive apparatus with its agents, stooges, dupes, front men and fellow travelers." However, he added: "The vast majority of American Protestant clergymen are loyal to the free institutions of this country."

Three Democrats and one Republican—a majority of the McCarthy sub-committee—attempted on July 7 to compel Matthews to resign, but McCarthy blocked their motion on the ground that he, as chairman, had complete authority over the hiring and dismissal of certain members of the staff.

McCarthy was far off base, and the White House tagged him. There was general agreement that the President should send a strong reply to the clergymen's message. A long meeting was held in Adams's office on the 9th among Adams, Hagerty, Persons and Emmet Hughes, during which they drafted a Presidential telegram. When they showed it to Eisenhower, he had no reservations whatever about issuing it, and late that day Hagerty made it public.

Addressed to the three senders, it said:

I have received your telegram of today's date. I want you to know at once that I fully share the convictions you state. The issues here are clear. Generalized and irresponsible attacks that sweepingly condemn the whole of any group of citizens are alien to America. Such attacks betray contempt for the principles of freedom and decency. And when these attacks—whatever their professed purpose be—comdemn such a vast portion of the churches or clergy as to create doubt in the loyalty of all, the damage to our nation is multiplied.

If there be found any American among us, whatever his calling, guilty of treasonous action against the state, let him legally and properly be convicted and punished. This applies to every person, lay or clergy.

The churches of America are citadels of our faith in individual freedom and human dignity. This faith is the living source of all our spiritual strength. And this strength is our matchless armor in our world-wide struggle against the forces of godless tyranny and oppression.

DWIGHT D. EISENHOWER

The telegram, which was interpreted as a broadside by Eisenhower at McCarthy, created a sensation, and within an hour McCarthy accepted Matthew's resignation.

Coming on top of the Bohlen affair, in which Taft and other influential Republicans had risen up in the strongest party opposition yet to the Senator from Wisconsin, the President's telegram caused one of the first big dips in the long decline that was, however faintly discernible at the moment, stretching ahead of McCarthy. There was irony in this, too, because McCarthy, so far as anyone knows, had nothing whatever to do with Matthews's article. He was simply trapped in a case of guilt by association, which had been his own favorite snare for catching others.

II

A political problem, unconnected with any single faction of the party, which bothered and often exasperated Eisenhower, was patronage. He was well aware, of course, of the political importance of appointments to government jobs by a new administration. But he was unaccustomed to dealing with such matters, and in addition he felt that the President of the United States has more important obligations to attend to. His thoughts on the subject were expressed quite candidly at various meetings in the White House.

Cabinet, April 10, 1953

Following the resignation under fire of C. Wesley Roberts, chairman of the Republican National Committee, the Republicans were preparing to elect a successor. Postmaster General Arthur E. Summerfield, who once held the post himself, said that it would be helpful to the new chairman if he could exert more power over patronage by assuming some of the responsibility held by Adams, now that most of the top posts had been filled. The President replied that the Administration was ready to play the game with the National Committee but that the National Committee for its part must play the game with the administration and recognize that patronage was not going to save the country.

The President observed that the National Committee was divided by factionalism—meaning the Taft and the Eisenhower elements. He feared that there would be some who would try to undermine the new chairman as soon as he had been elected. For this reason, Eisenhower told the Cabinet, he had refused to take a position on the choice of the chairman because he did not wish to be responsible for the latter's being marked as "my man."

Cabinet, May 8, 1953

Leonard Hall, the new chairman, was present. The President asked him to use his influence to minimize the demands of Congress on department heads. Hall then expounded his views on the need for strengthening the Republican organization to win the 1954 elections. He suggested that certain appointments be made and certain administrative actions taken, with particular attention being paid to racial groups, to help insure success in critical election districts. In midterm elections, he noted, it is difficult to throw the mantle of Presidential popularity over Congressional candidates.

Patronage was important in strengthening the party organization and could be dispensed without lowering the standards of government personnel, Hall continued. The administration had set up in the noncompetitive civil service field a Schedule C for policy-making or confidential positions, to which a person could be appointed or removed at will. Hall pointed out that if holdovers from the Truman administration were removed from positions where they could influence the choice of personnel, Schedule C offered a field for appointments by the Eisenhower administration. Alternatively, he suggested that the Civil Service Commission draw up a list of positions which should be in Schedule C and thus open to appointment by the administration. (Schedule C was established because the new administration found it was saddled with Truman appointees in policy-making jobs. In the beginning, for example, Mrs. Hobby discovered that she could appoint only a few persons of her own choice. As the administration moved to correct this situation, the President warned in the Cabinet against any revival of the spoils system. He told the Cabinet that the administration not only must not engage in the spoils system but it must not give the impression of doing so.) The President asked Cabinet officers to keep Hall informed about jobs in their respective departments.

Eisenhower emphasized that he expected Hall in co-ordinating patronage to get rid of some objectionable aspects of the past.

He revealed that a member of the Cabinet had come to him and reported that a certain Republican National Committeeman had approached this Cabinet officer and insisted that a particular person be appointed to a vacant position. Furthermore, Eisenhower said, the National Committeeman had threatened to go to the President over the head of the Cabinet officer if the latter did not make the appointment.

The President said he bitterly resented conduct of this kind.

The new administration had not even begun to approach, in its dispensing of patronage, the ruthlessness of certain previous administrations, he said, and then went on to tell this story about an experience of his own under the Roosevelt administration:

In the early 1930's Eisenhower as an Army officer was put in charge of some activities of the Civilian Conservation Corps in Pennsylvania and in time he had to select some captains and lieuten-

ants to assist him. He sent to Washington a list of names and
waited for approval. Instead of getting approval he was nearly blown
over by a blast of criticism for having named men who were all
Republicans. In selecting his assistants in the C.C.C., he told the
Cabinet, he had paid no attention to political affiliations because he
believed that Army personnel stood outside politics. He recalled that
he was totally amazed to find that anyone should have injected
politics into Army assignments and particularly in a lowly C.C.C.
project in Pennsylvania.

Cabinet, June 5, 1953

The President said that he did not like to have patronage problems
brought to him time after time by individuals in the Republican
Party. He said that Hall was in a position to take care of this matter
and that Hall had his full support in placing well-qualified men in
the government.

Cabinet, June 26, 1953

The President suggested that when vacancies were filled in Schedule
A (a category of jobs for which an examination is impractical) and
the appointive Schedule C, recommendations of Hall should be considered. A greater effort should be made, he urged, to broaden geo-
graphical representation among new government employees. He cited
Tennessee as a state that ought to be borne in mind. He said and
said again, however, that persons recommended by Hall were to be
given only the same consideration accorded others. It was primarily,
he explained, a matter of giving Hall an opportunity to make recommendations. He cited the criticism of the administration's slowness
in handling patronage and observed that it would be worthwhile to
remove the causes of dissatisfaction if in doing so the administration
did not interfere with sound personnel policies.

Dulles reported that the State Department was attempting within
reason to co-operate in patronage matters. He said, however, that his
department could not be run on the basis of patronage. And he
warned that the administration should be careful to avoid alienating
Democratic support in Congress because such support would be
needed if certain Republicans persisted in opposing the administration on foreign-policy measures.

Nixon and Adams noted that it was the policy of the administration to give positions to pro-Eisenhower Democrats.

(There was some weeding out of Democratic appointees by the Eisenhower administration, but no attempt at wholesale removal of Democratic career officials. Certain conservative Democrats have been appointed to important posts—Gordon Gray in the Pentagon and David K. E. Bruce in the State Department, for example. Also in 1953 Governor James F. Byrnes, of South Carolina, was appointed to the American delegation to the U.N. But the Democrats have accused the administration of freezing them out of policy-making positions, such, for example, as Dulles, Warren R. Austin, the late Henry L. Stimson and the late Frank Knox held in the Roosevelt and Truman administrations.)

Staff Conference, July 9, 1953

Adams, who has kept a firm grip on appointments, held that the White House had an inescapable responsibility in the matter of patronage, because constant pressures require not only that control be exercised to prevent the corroding of wise personnel policies but that patronage be used wherever legitimate to bolster the party. White House control over appointments, Adams said, had not been relaxed since the recent establishment of patronage machinery in the National Committee under Hall. Often, he said, the White House had served as the compromiser between the wishes of department heads respecting a particular appointment and the desires of Congressmen. In this role the White House was a buffer to protect the department heads from demands from Capitol Hill, he explained.

Staff Conference, July 17, 1953

Leonard Hall protested that as of that day he could not find six members of Congress who were indebted to the administration for appointments sponsored by them. The policy of the White House, Hall said, had been to appoint people and only later to enlist the support of others in the party on their behalf. Out of forty appointments made so far from New York State, only four had been initiated in the state, he said.

The new chairman said that geographically the Atlantic seaboard dominated the patronage of the Eisenhower administration. He recalled that on a certain day he had been asked by department heads to clear with local political leaders five appointees. All five, he said, were Democrats.

Hall told the White House staff that of five State Department employees who had participated in what he described as a meeting to "kill off" the prestige of Dulles in 1952, four were still in the department, and of these, he added, two had since been promoted.

He said that the clamor for patronage could be muted effectively if twenty-five thousand jobs were made available to Republican officials to distribute.

Cabinet, October 9, 1953

The President, who had had breakfast with Hall the day before, was not in one of his best moods when he reported that the chairman was still concerned about patronage. Hall, he indicated, believed that not enough Republicans had been given jobs in the administration to silence demands at the grass roots. The President quoted Hall as having said that these demands made it difficult for the National Committee to act effectively in other important respects. At this point Eisenhower heatedly gave the Cabinet to understand that he was sick and tired of being bothered about patronage. He had always tried to do what he could about it, he said, but the situation never seemed to improve.

"Everything seems to have been patronage this morning," he grumbled as the meeting ended.

Cabinet, October 30, 1953

The President again reported that Hall felt that his effectiveness was being impaired because he was always being greeted at the grass roots by questions about patronage. Eisenhower repeated a previous suggestion that each department head should name a high assistant to be a liaison man with Hall in handling this problem.

Cabinet, December 11, 1953

The President opened the meeting by recounting a story he had heard about a certain man—he actually named him—who had resigned from the C.I.O. Political Action Committee during the Truman administration to become director of a Federal office in Kansas City. Although, the President said, this man fully expected to be replaced when the Republicans came to power, he was, almost eleven months later, still on the job. Someone had suggested, Eisenhower continued, that his continued presence implied that the administration was on the defensive and this might encourage Democratic holdovers to put up a fight if and when they were replaced by Republicans. The political background of the man was evidence, the President said, that his present job could scarcely be considered a policy-making one in this administration. He concluded that this was a clear-cut case that could be disposed of and was a contrast in that respect to some of the customary nebulous complaints he had been receiving.

(Prompt investigation of this case by responsible officials proved that the problems of patronage are not simple. For one thing, it developed, the Republican state and county chairmen preferred that the man remain in the job to keep him "on ice" and thus deter him from effective campaigning in the next election. For another, the national head of the agency in Washington adjudged him one of the best men in his position in the country. And to top it off, the man's daughter was engaged to the son of one of the most important Republican politicians in the region!)

Cabinet, January 20, 1954

After recounting a recent discussion at a legislative leaders' conference, the President expressed his hope that any Cabinet member whose department still had some patronage problems lying around would give his personal attention to disposing of them once and for all.

(As the President's tone indicated, the pressure for jobs, which naturally was high in the beginning, was now falling rapidly. By the end of 1955 nearly seventy thousand jobs had been processed through the White House patronage machinery.)

Legislative Conference, March 1, 1954

Someone said that the House Agriculture Committee still had much the same staff as it did before the 1952 election when the Democrats were still in control.

"Oh, boy," exclaimed Eisenhower with the gratification of one seeing an uncomfortable shoe put on another foot, "that's the first time I've heard this argument turned around!"

CHAPTER 7

Eisenhower and Taft

The Rivals Become Friends – Chicago – The Morningside Conference – Durkin – The White House Door Is Open – Augusta – Taft Explodes – Taft's Last Days – An Eisenhower Commentary on Taft

One of the sharpest jolts Eisenhower received during his early months in office came when he comprehended fully and finally the zeal of many Republicans for balancing the budget regardless of those requirements which the President deemed essential to national security.

The most dramatic conflict of the two points of view was to occur on April 30, 1953, between Eisenhower and Taft in a blowup at a legislative conference in which Taft came as near to taking the roof off the White House as anyone ever has (except the President himself occasionally) during Eisenhower's tenancy.

Distressing as this was to the President, it was an isolated incident in the relations between the two men who had fought a historic political battle in Chicago in 1952 for the Republican nomination and then, victor and vanquished, become sincere friends and collaborators, one as President and the other as the powerful and respected majority leader of the Senate.

Defeat on the first ballot at Chicago had been a shattering defeat for Taft, snuffing out "Mr. Republican's" third and last chance to follow the footsteps of his father to the White House. Immediately after the balloting Eisenhower left his suite in the Blackstone Hotel and made his way across the street to the Conrad Hilton Hotel to shake hands with Taft. They met by the elevators on the floor where

Taft's headquarters was situated. Many Taft workers were still in tears. The press of a dense crowd around Eisenhower and Taft was suffocating as they stood in front of cameras, both tense and shaken but both struggling for self-control and smiling mechanically.

"I came over to pay a call of friendship on a great American," Eisenhower said. "His willingness to cooperate is absolutely necessary to the success of the Republican Party in the campaign and of the administration to follow."

"I want to congratulate General Eisenhower," Taft said. "I shall do everything possible in the campaign to secure his election and help his administration."

Taft did what he said he would do. He went out and he campaigned strenuously and gave Eisenhower powerful help, particularly in areas like Ohio, Tennessee and the Middle West where the Senator's influence was strongest. But he did so only after one of the most disputed episodes in the campaign—the breakfast meeting between Taft and Eisenhower on September 12, 1952, at 60 Morningside Drive, in New York, which was Eisenhower's residence as president of Columbia University.

The Senator brought to that meeting a long statement, or manifesto, in which he set forth his understanding of Eisenhower's philosophy on a number of issues, and when he departed a couple of hours later, he had won Eisenhower's "full agreement" to it. The statement had a strong, Taftian, right-wing flavor, and Eisenhower's approval of it caused a furor. Adlai Stevenson called it a "great surrender" by the Republican candidate, and even some of Eisenhower's followers were dismayed that he should have approved a statement prepared by Taft and so expressed in words and spirit as to displease many liberal and independent voters whom Eisenhower was wooing.

What strikes one upon reading the statement dispassionately years later, however, is that it *did* coincide, imprecisely perhaps, with many, though of course not all, of Eisenhower's views. The statement had the full aura of Taft's language, which was more extreme, much harsher and far more redolent of the conservative Republican opposition than Eisenhower's language. Eisenhower's own expression of the same principles would have been then—and would be today—

different, more moderate, less narrow and partisan, freer of old associations. But in general the principles themselves were by no means alien to him.

As for foreign policy, the statement acknowledged that differences, though "differences of degree," existed between the two men. At home, Taft had written, the issue was "liberty against creeping socialization." This was a slogan, but it certainly was not out of keeping with Eisenhower's political mood. Nor were some of the other essential parts:

I am convinced that he [Eisenhower] will carry out the pledges of the Republican platform. . . . General Eisenhower emphatically agrees with me in the proposal to reduce drastically over-all expenses. . . . General Eisenhower has also told me that he believes strongly in our system of Constitutional limitations on Government power and that he abhors the left-wing theory that the Executive had unlimited powers. . . . General Eisenhower has also told me that he believes in the basic principles of the Taft-Hartley Law, its protection of the people and the freedom of the union members themselves against the arbitrary use of power by big business or big labor, and is opposed to its repeal. . . .

General Eisenhower agrees that the proper role of the Federal Government beyond its present activities is one of advice, research and assistance to the states, the local communities and the people. . . . General Eisenhower stated without qualification that in the making of appointments at high levels or low levels there will be no discrimination against anyone because he or she has supported me, and that he is determined to maintain the unity of the entire party by taking counsel with all factions and points of view. . . .

These passages are not recalled for the sake of arguing one way or another the wisdom and propriety of Eisenhower's approval of the Morningside statement. They are recalled, rather, to emphasize that there existed, in spite of their differences, many important areas in which the views of Eisenhower and Taft were, if not identical, at least close enough so that with patience and understanding they could be harmonized. This fact was a key to the ultimate relationship between Eisenhower the President and Taft the Senate Republican leader. Another key was the character of the two former rivals. For all his deep disappointment Taft was a big enough man to bury the hatchet completely. Except for one explosion, he displayed no raspiness or jealousy in his dealings with Eisenhower and his staff, some of whom, like Hagerty, had been, as Dewey men, fighting Taft since as far back as 1940. Eisenhower for his part was determined to get along with Taft and to make the Senator his friend and collaborator, and to this task he applied all the genius for harmony that had been so conspicuous in his dealings with allied statesmen and generals in Europe.

When the election was over, Taft was invited to meetings at the Commodore, at which he was treated with great respect. His recommendations for appointments to the Cabinet were received politely by the Eisenhower staff, although only one of the men named on Taft's lists turned up in the Cabinet. This was Benson. Some of the others, however, were eventually given lesser jobs. For instance, Taft had recommended Clarence E. Manion, former dean of Notre Dame Law School, for Attorney General. The post went to Brownell, of course, but Manion was later named chairman of the President's Commission on Inter-Governmental Relations. That was one appointment that did not work out well, and in February, 1954, Adams forced Manion to resign. Manion said that he was ousted because he had contravened administration policy by supporting the Bricker amendment. The fact of the matter was that the White House had had its fill of Manion's extreme right-wing views, and the President was dissatisfied with his conduct of the commission.

Taft appears to have been unhappy over several of Eisenhower's appointments, but the only time he aired his feelings was when Durkin, who was president of the plumbers' union, was selected as Secretary of Labor, a choice which Taft called "incredible." Taft complained in a public statement that Durkin "has always been a partisan Truman Democrat who fought General Eisenhower's election and advocated the repeal of the Taft-Hartley Law." The appointment, he said, denied representation in the Cabinet to "Democrats, North and South, who left the party to support General Eisenhower, and gives representation to their most bitter opponents."

In the end Taft voted to confirm the nomination. Eisenhower had had a reason for appointing a union official to his Cabinet, in which businessmen predominated. He realized that sometime during his term the country might be thrown into a great domestic or foreign crisis. If this ever happened, he wanted to be in a position to have—and to deserve, as his intimates said privately at the time—the sympathetic support and understanding of all elements, including labor, and he hoped that Durkin's presence would encourage such support by the unions.

"Taft's view of the case," says White, "was that Durkin was essentially, and had to be, a partisan over the Taft-Hartley Act, a quite honorable attitude in a labor leader but not one well recommending a man to be the Secretary of Labor. . . ."

In this respect Taft's apprehension proved well founded. After eight months in the Cabinet Durkin resigned because the White House would not go along with his ideas on amending the Taft-Hartley Law.

Two weeks after he had quit, Durkin told the American Federation of Labor convention in St. Louis that the President had personally promised him on August 19, 1953, that he would support nineteen amendments. Then, on September 10, Durkin said, the President changed his mind and said that he could not support them. Durkin carried back to private life a very strong feeling that the White House had let him down. The President's staff always maintained afterward, however, that Durkin was mistaken in thinking that a final commitment had been made on the amendments, and Eisenhower himself made the same point when he said coldly at a press conference that if he had ever broken an agreement, it was one that he did not know had been made.

After one of the first legislative leaders' conferences in the White House following the inauguration, Eisenhower asked Taft to stay behind, and he and the Senator went into the President's office and talked together alone for a few minutes. Taft assured Eisenhower that he could depend upon him to support his program in the Senate. In reply the President told Taft that one thing he wanted the Senator to know about their future relationship was that the door to the White House was always open to him. Whenever Taft wished to see him, even on the spur of the moment, Eisenhower said, he was to walk in, no matter what else might be going on or regardless of whether the President was in his office or in the mansion. It would not even be necessary for Taft to ask for an appointment, the President assured him.

Not long afterward Taft called the White House for an appointment with the President, and when he entered his office, Eisenhower chided him for not having remembered his instruction. He said that in the future Taft should just put on his hat and come over when he felt like it. Their relationship, of course, never became this informal, but the incident was typical of the President's efforts to cultivate Taft.

As the weeks passed, Eisenhower had frequent talks with Taft and listened with care to whatever the Senator had to say. Although Taft was taking a greater interest in foreign policy then than he had in the past, their discussion dealt largely with internal and fiscal affairs. They talked a great deal, naturally, about amendments to the Taft-Hartley Act. Taft told the President that he was agreeable to certain changes in the act, but that he was opposed to any alteration in the essential responsibilities of the contracting parties, as defined in the law as it then stood. He talked to the President about appointments, particularly to agencies like the National Labor Relations Board and the National Mediation Board. He showed special interest in who was to be appointed to the government from the field of labor. In matters like amendments to the Taft-Hartley Law and fiscal policy Eisenhower gave much weight to Taft's views.

Taft is quoted by White as having remarked of the President after a White House call in March, "He is, I think, a man of good will." That meant a great deal to Taft. While the Senator sometimes fumed in private over the way some things were being done in the White House and while he had reservations as to whether the businessmen whom Eisenhower had brought into the government "are going to work out," his respect for Eisenhower grew, and he responded to the President's friendliness.

In March the Senator suspected that Mrs. Eisenhower was not having so good a time as she might because of the burdens of formal engagements, and on the 25th he and Mrs. Taft, who was an invalid in a wheel chair as a result of a stroke in 1950, gave a reception for the President's wife at their home in Georgetown. McCarthy was there, and he and Eisenhower shook hands but spoke only a few words to each other. When McCarthy went over and picked up a drink, Lady Nancy Astor, the seventy-three-old, American-born former Member of Parliament, who was standing nearby, said, "Too bad it isn't poison!" (When he learned of this crack, John Chapple, editor of the Ashland [Wis.] *Daily Press*, called for Lady Nancy's arrest, a suggestion that sent her into whoops of laughter.)

In April Eisenhower invited Taft to Augusta and on an icy spring morning they played golf together in a foursome. The President refused to make the score public afterward, but it was learned that he had shot an eighty-six, many strokes under Taft. On the golf course Taft was in sparkling spirits, the image of a man in superb health. Directly after this visit he began to be troubled by a pain in his left hip. It was the first pang of a fatal cancer.

On April 30 an important conference among the President, some members of his Cabinet and the Republican legislative leaders, including Taft, was held at the White House for presentation of budget estimates and the President's new military policy referred to in Chapter 4. As with other legislative conferences under Eisenhower the meeting was held in the Cabinet room. The President, as usual, took his chair in the center of the table on the east side, with his back to the windows looking out on the rose garden. As the others filed in and took their places, Taft sat down on the west side of the table, facing the President but diagonally to Eisenhower's left.

The President opened the meeting with a statement on foreign affairs and the new military policy. When he had finished, there were explanations of the new budget and national defense by Humphrey, Dodge and Kyes. All three pointed out that although the new administration had been in office barely three months, it was already giving a new direction to Federal spending. A beginning, at least, they said, had been made in reducing Truman's budget estimates.

The full import of their words was nevertheless that heavy military spending would continue, that more deficits lay ahead and that the first Republican budget would be out of balance. When this hit Robert A. Taft, he went off like a bomb.

The sedate discussion was rent by his hard, metallic voice. Fairly shouting and banging his fist on the Cabinet table, Taft declared that all the efforts of the Eisenhower administration to date had merely produced the net result of continued spending on the same scale as the Truman administration. Unless the inconceivable step of raising taxes was taken, he said, the new budget—the budget for the fiscal year 1954—would carry a large deficit. He denounced the budget total as one that exceeded 30 per cent of the national income, a limit Taft thought high enough.

The President was taken aback as Taft barked out a prediction that the first Eisenhower budget would drive a wedge between the administration and economy-minded Republicans in Congress and drag the party to defeat in the 1954 elections.

"The one primary thing we promised the American people," he shouted, "was reduction of expenditures. Now you're taking us right down the same road Truman traveled. It's a repudiation of everything we promised in the campaign."

Taft said that he could see no prospect of future reductions so long as emphasis was placed upon military preparedness for which, he said, funds could be spent without limit.

As he had done on the floor of the Senate in 1951 and 1952, he declared his lack of confidence in the Joint Chiefs of Staff, of which General Bradley was still chairman. Even the members of the National Security Council, he said, depended in the final analysis on the recommendations of the Joint Chiefs. He insisted that it was now necessary to have a complete review of the military program by the best military minds which were not already committed to some particular course.

Taft said that he did not feel that he could again oppose tax reductions for the fiscal year 1955. He did not know the answers to these great issues, he said, but the problems must be studied anew. Otherwise, he said, the Republicans might lose the Presidential election in 1956. He said that it was certain in any case that Republican candidates for the House and Senate would go down to defeat in 1954 if the program was not changed.

For a moment a dead silence filled the tense Cabinet room when Taft had finished. The President was stung by Taft's words. He bent forward, but before he could speak a nervous voice sounded somewhere around the table. Suddenly there was a rattle of small talk and comment. Humphrey had a word to say. Saltonstall and Representative John Taber, Republican, of New York, joined in the conversation. The talk sounded as though the conferees were speaking just to break the tension and give the President a chance to cool off.

When Eisenhower began his reply, he spoke in a low, dispassionate voice. There were, he said, certain essential elements in the global strategy of the United States.

"They are not difficult to understand," he told Taft.

All were agreed, the President said, that Russia must not be allowed to swallow up Western Europe. Since the United States had no desire to take over control of Europe either, he continued, American policy must be based upon making Europe stronger physically and spiritually—a policy necessarily entailing considerable cost.

Turning to the Middle East, Eisenhower said that that region possessed half the known oil resources in the world and must not be allowed to fall into Soviet hands. He called attention to the recent Communist invasion of Laos, in Indo-China, and the peril it held for Southeast Asia.

The President said that the threat of retaliation by bombing did not of itself insure security for the United States. A position of strength must be achieved in all these threatened areas, he continued, to avert the danger of Russia's gradually taking them over without fighting.

He defended the competence of the National Security Council. He reiterated his objective of obtaining security without building up a vast military force by a particular date. He explained, however, that it would take time to accomplish this. To cancel contracts on which work had begun, he pointed out, would be almost as costly as having the contracts fulfilled, so little saving could be realized that way. He described the care which the new administration had taken in preparing its budget estimates. The important thing, he observed, was to arrest the upward trend in expenditures and start it downward, and this the administration had done during its brief span in power.

The President told Taft that he agreed with him that a Democratic victory in 1954 would be undesirable. He said that he did not want to be responsible for the executive branch of the government if the legislative was controlled by the Democrats. But he was convinced, he said, that his proposed budget would not be disastrous to Republican prospects in 1954.

Eisenhower told the conference finally that he could not endanger the security of the United States by agreeing to anything less than an adequate defense program.

Taft said that he was concerned by the implications in Eisenhower's 1954 budget of continued high spending in the future. He asked that hope be held out for a substantial reduction in the 1955 budget.

The President replied that grounds did exist for such hope. Nevertheless he declined to be drawn into any commitment for the fiscal year 1955. He said that he saw no other way to approach the problem than by making an honest effort to reach a solution upon which all could agree.

Although the President did not succeed in reconciling Taft to the 1954 budget, their differences about it never closed the door to their continued co-operation nor did it impair their personal relationship. Months after this incident Eisenhower admitted at a luncheon for Arthur H. Vandenberg, Jr., whose father before his death had shared the Republican pinnacle in the Senate with Taft, that he had been tempted to make a heated reply to Taft's outburst. The intervening small talk enabled him to compose himself.

In retrospect it is not difficult to imagine what a grievous political storm would have broken over the President's head if Taft had walked out of that meeting, denounced the budget on the outside as he had on the inside, and launched a movement against Eisenhower's military and foreign policies.

On the testimony of his closest associates, Eisenhower never resented Taft. On the contrary, they say, he respected him and believed that Taft gave a valuable balance to the political scales in America.

On his trip to the Midwest early in the summer of 1953 the President was leaving Minneapolis for South Dakota on June 10 when reporters told him at the airport that Taft had resigned as Republican leader of the Senate because of his ailment. The President seemed genuinely distressed and surprised, although, of course, he was aware that Taft was ill.

As a young man Taft had lived in the White House when he was in Washington during the years that his father was President. He went there for the last time on June 19. Eisenhower had returned from the Black Hills and a routine conference was to be held on Taft-Hartley amendments. Mortally ill, Taft hobbled into the West Wing on crutches. Before the meeting he made his way into Sherman Adams's office and setting his crutches aside, sank down in a chair to talk to the President's assistant. Adams was deeply touched by Taft's tired and haggard appearance.

"Senator," he said, "I think just to save you from going into the President's office, the President will come in here."

Adams hurried to Eisenhower's office and explained why he thought the meeting should be held in his own office.

"Sure," the President agreed, rising from his chair.

On the morning of July 31 the Cabinet held its weekly meeting in the White House. The President, remarking on Taft's illness, said that no matter what happened it would be impossible for Taft soon to resume his duties in the Senate. Inevitably, therefore, he said, the question of the selection of a Republican leader would confront the Senate. Before Taft had left the Senate on June 10 he had named Senator William F. Knowland, of California, as the leader in his absence, but the appointment was only a temporary one.

The President told the Cabinet that in the selection of a permanent leader, a choice which turned out to be Knowland, the administration would remain on the sidelines absolutely. He hoped, he said, that administration officials would refrain even from expressing their personal hopes as to who would succeed Taft. He said that a fine spirit of co-operation between the White House and the Republican leadership had flourished so far. He mentioned that in recent weeks, for example, Taft and Durkin had sat down together and addressed each other as Bob and Martin. He implied that the co-operation with the leaders had been due in part to the etiquette of the White House in strictly observing the prerogatives of Congress. That was one reason he did not wish the administration to intervene in the selection of Taft's successor.

Taft died in New York Hospital that same morning. Soon after the news reached the White House, President and Mrs. Eisenhower drove to Georgetown to call on Mrs. Taft. As White describes the scene, Eisenhower took Martha Taft's hand in both of his and said, "I don't know what I'll do without him—I don't know what I'll do without him." Publicly the President issued a statement saying:

The passing of Robert A. Taft is a tragic loss to America. The brilliant son of our twenty-seventh President, Senator Taft served the people of Ohio and the Nation with distinction and integrity. He will be greatly missed on Capitol Hill, where his vast knowledge of the business of good government played such an important part in Congressional decisions over many years. The Senate has lost one of its leading members of all time. The American people have lost a truly great citizen, and I have lost a wise counselor and valued friend. . . .

More than a year later, on August 6, 1954, the Postmaster General told a meeting of the Cabinet that he had been receiving suggestions for the issuance of a commemorative stamp to Taft. Dulles said that he was personally favorable to the idea but that such a stamp might cause political repercussions. He suggested that at an appropriate time several commemorative stamps might be issued, including the Taft stamp and one honoring Senator Vandenberg.

Customarily, Summerfield noted, such commemorative issues were limited to Presidents and Secretaries of State. The President said that his first reaction was that a stamp might be issued in honor of Taft. The Roosevelt administration, he said, had not hesitated to act in the reverse direction by changing the name of Hoover Dam to Boulder Dam, where the matter was left until the Republican Eightieth Congress restored the former President's name to the dam in 1947. The question of the stamp was finally referred to the Postmaster General for further consideration.

It was ironical, Eisenhower observed, that many extreme conservatives were now trying to appear as the champions of Taft's memory. The irony of this, he said, lay in the fact that Taft had taken a liberal approach to very many issues.

CHAPTER 8

Truce in Korea

The Alternatives Before the President – The Decision to Seek a Truce – The Threat of Enlarging the War if Stalemate Continued – Cabinet Discussions – No Compromise on the Prisoner Issue – Rhee and the Robertson Mission – Waiting for the News – Eisenhower's Reaction

Public revulsion against the Korean war had been a great factor in sweeping Dwight Eisenhower into office, and the truce that stilled the guns in Korea on July 26, 1953, is one of the landmarks of his Presidency.

The stalemated war had been going on for two years, six months and twenty-six days when Eisenhower entered the White House. Two main alternatives then confronted him. One, which was favored by some of the most headstrong members of his party, was to enlarge the conflict into a great air and sea offensive to defeat Communist China and then to unify Korea by crushing all Red forces south of the Yalu River. This was more or less in line with General MacArthur's celebrated memorandum to the Joint Chiefs of Staff in 1951 in which he proposed: 1. Naval blockade of China, 2. Bombardment of bases and military centers on the mainland, 3. Employment of Chinese Nationalist troops in Korea, and 4. Encouragement of assaults on coastal areas from Taiwan.

The other alternative was in quest of an honorable peace to continue, within the framework that had developed during the Truman administration, the exasperating truce negotiations at Panmunjom.

One of Eisenhower's first major decisions as President was to elect the latter course of seeking a truce between opposing forces in a divided Korea. The President wanted to liquidate the war. He wanted to halt the drain of American power in a peripheral conflict that offered no hope of decision in the struggle against Communism. He believed that the American people wanted an end to the war. As he told the Cabinet in March, 1953, the cost in men and dollars of a large land offensive against the Reds in Korea would have been very great. After all, the once-fluid battle lines had hardened during the year and a half of stalemate since the truce talks had begun at Kaesong on July 10, 1951, and the Communists had seized this opportunity to fortify their side heavily. Furthermore, Eisenhower as a military man was well aware of the momentous yet unpredictable consequences of an attack upon China, which, if launched at all, might well have had to be undertaken without the support of our principal allies, who were opposed to any such venture. As the President explained afterward, at a press conference on January 19, 1956, ". . . we were in a Korean war that, due to the way we were waging it, there was no chance of winning because the crossing of the Yalu River (would have) shocked international opinion."

In deciding to continue to negotiate a truce, however, Eisenhower had resolved that the United States would not accept endless stalemate. In their talks while returning from Korea in December, 1952, he and Dulles had determined to make it clear to the Communists that to delay the truce indefinitely would be to invite the United States to enlarge the war and to strike at China not only in Korea but on two or three other fronts of its own choosing.

The first deliberate hint Eisenhower gave to this effect was the formal statement he issued at La Guardia Field upon his return to New York from Korea on December 14. This statement, on which he and Dulles had worked carefully on the plane flying in from the Pacific, said:

> . . . This journey marks not the end but the beginning of a new effort to conclude honorably this phase of the global struggle. This is not the moment to state more than that resolve. For we face an enemy whom we cannot hope to impress by words, however eloquent, but only by deeds—executed under circumstances of our own choosing.

LATER   Talking informally to reporters at the airport, he said:

Every one of us thinks we have learned something to make this expedition a sort of starting place from where we are going to plan the programs we are going to adopt, and we expect them to be positive programs. Because you know, my friends, just because one side wants peace doesn't make peace. We must go ahead and do things that induce the others to want peace also.

Eisenhower and Dulles concluded that short of actual new military moves, the strongest pressure the United States could exert upon the Chinese Communists to end the stalemate was to keep before them the possibility that the Americans would enlarge the war. With this in view, as was mentioned earlier, they devised the new order to the Seventh Fleet, which Dulles hoped would remind the Communists that Formosa might yet be used as a base for an invasion of the mainland if a truce was not signed.

In his State of the Union message the President said that he was "giving immediate increased attention to the development of additional Republic of Korea forces." In February and again in March the administration authorized increases in the program for raising Korean divisions. In July another Marine division was dispatched to the Korean theater. Meanwhile the United States continued to strengthen its air power in Korea with a program of re-equipping Air Force fighter units with Sabre jets. Other programs begun earlier in the war were beginning to yield more trained American forces and more weapons and supplies. In sum, the U.N. had achieved a position of very considerable military strength from which to negotiate in Korea.

As a warning of what might come if the Communists did not end the stalemate, the United States in the spring moved atomic missiles to Okinawa.

The Korean situation came up in the Cabinet on March 20 during a discussion of the need for standby consumer-credit controls.

Dulles warned the Cabinet not to assume that the crisis was over. If the United States acted on this assumption, he said, then its allies would do likewise, with the result that there would be a general neglect of defenses, which in time would bring on a new crisis. Many vital decisions about the Far East were yet to be made, he said. He reminded the Cabinet that a decision to allow the Korean War to continue in stalemate could cost the administration the support of Congress, endangering the whole legislative program. On the other hand, he said, the alternative of final military victory in Korea would cost a tremendous sum, threatening new inflation and necessitating new economic controls.

The President said that he would not accept these as the only alternatives. There was, he told the Cabinet, a possibility of achieving a limited victory. He said that he would never consent to a course of interminable budgetary deficits.

Some members of the Cabinet then pressed the discussion in terms of Republican campaign promises to end the Korean war, balance the budget, halt inflation and reduce taxes.

The President replied sharply that he never had promised to do all these things immediately and that, on the contrary, he had sounded a warning about the cost of military victory.

Reviewing possible courses of action, he said that to try to end the war by a military drive in Korea would require large new appropriations. But the mere request for these appropriations, he pointed out, would tip off the Communists to American intentions and would give them a chance to take countermeasures. Simply to throw the Reds back beyond the narrow waist of the Korean peninsula, he pointed out, would cost three or four billion dollars. In addition he did not see what justifiable advantage the United States would gain, under these circumstances, in pushing the line up to the waist, a distance of some ninety miles.

As yet there is no way of knowing conclusively what effect the administration's various psychological and military pressures had on the Chinese Communists or, for that matter, what effect, if any, Stalin's death and the new Soviet peace offensive had. Three weeks after Stalin died the truce negotiations suddenly took their first significant turn in months. On March 28 the Communists accepted a U.N. proposal that sick and injured prisoners be exchanged before an armistice. They requested furthermore that the top truce delegations "immediately resume the negotiations in Panmunjom."

Returning from conferences in Moscow following Stalin's funeral

Chou En-lai, the Chinese Communist Premier and Foreign Minister, made a new truce offer on March 30. In words that encouraged American defenders of the principle of nonforcible repatriation of prisoners, which was the last major obstacle to agreement, Chou proposed an exchange after the truce of captives "who insist on repatriation." Those who did not wish to return, he said, could be handed over to a neutral state "to insure a just solution to the question of their repatriation."

At his press conference three days later President Eisenhower reacted by saying that regardless of previous disappointments in dealing with the Communists, he would accept all gestures of peace at face value until they proved false. Agreement on exchange of sick and wounded prisoners was reached at Panmunjom on April 11, and the pathetic pageant of the returning prisoners with their sickening tales of Communist brutality and "brainwashing" began on April 20.

Despite Chou's offer, the issue over exchange of other prisoners after the truce became involved in more weeks of wrangling at Panmunjom, but Eisenhower, like Truman before him, stood firm on the principle of not forcing Communist prisoners who had turned against Communism to return home against their will. Speaking at a dinner of the New York State Republican Committee at the Waldorf-Astoria on May 7, the President said:

People that have become our prisoners cannot by any manner of means be denied the right on which this country was founded . . . the right of political asylum against the kind of political persecution they fear. . . . Consequently, to force those people to go back to a life of terror and persecution is something that would violate every moral standard by which America lives. Therefore, it would be unacceptable in the American code, and it cannot be done.

Beginning on May 22, Dulles had three days of talks with Nehru during a visit to India. Hopeful his words would find their way through diplomatic channels to Chinese ears, he told Nehru that the United States desired an honorable end to the war. But he further informed Nehru, according to his version, that if the stalemate continued, the United States had definitely decided to blast the Communists' sanctuary in Manchuria north of the Yalu.

Throughout the months of negotiations the President and Dulles persisted in the conviction that the Chinese would agree to a truce if they came to fear an attack on two or three other fronts. Later, at a press conference on January 17, 1956, Dulles said that "it is a fair inference" that the United States would have bombed Manchuria if the war had continued. At no time, however, did the President make a formal decision to enlarge the war. Some of those who were closest to him at the time are convinced that he would certainly have done so if the stalemate had dragged on. But his fervent hope was for a truce, and he would have regarded war against China as a dread step to be taken only as a last resort. Thus the course of events then, as in Indo-China later, was influenced not alone by the threat to China of American retaliation in case of continued stalemate but also by the threat posed for United States forces by the Communist military power in Asia. "What has really happened," Walter Lippmann wrote in his column in the New York *Herald Tribune*, "is that both sides and all concerned have been held within a condition of *mutual deterrent*."

On May 25, with South Korea dissenting strongly, the U.N. made what Allied negotiators called the "final" offer, which contained, they said, all the concessions which the Reds could expect. The next day Eisenhower issued a statement in which he said:

There are . . . certain principles inherent in the United Nations Command position which are basic and not subject to change. No prisoners will be repatriated by force. No prisoners will be coerced or intimidated in any way. And there must be a definite limit to the period of their captivity. The procedures used in handling the prisoners must reflect these principles.

In all this our allies are in full accord. These principles accord also with the prevailing view of a representative bipartisan group of Senators and Congressmen who have been consulted.

Finally: These principles on which we stand are the same as those which were formally approved by fifty-four members of the United Nations.

On May 29 the subject of Korea came up again in the Cabinet. Under Secretary of State Smith reviewed the recent progress of the truce talks. He also mentioned a report he had heard from Senator

Bourke B. Hickenlooper, Republican, of Iowa, that "go it alone" sentiment was growing in Congress. Smith told the Cabinet that he believed this resulted from a lack of appreciation in Congress of the serious obligations that would fall upon the United States if it were to act alone against Communism in Asia. Underlying some of the Congressional criticism of the truce talks, he said, was the concern of the members that somehow a truce would land Red China in the U.N.

Even as the outlook for a truce brightened in June, a new cloud sailed over the horizon in the form of strenuous objection by Syngman Rhee to any agreement that would leave Korea divided. The Korean President, an alumnus of Harvard and Princeton, who was then seventy-eight years old, informed the United States that he wanted: (1) An irrevocable promise that the United States would help the Republic of Korea unify Korea by force in the event the international political conference which was to be held ninety days after the truce failed to do so. (2) An agreement that the war would be resumed if the political conference produced no settlement after it had been in session for ninety days.

On June 6 Eisenhower sent Rhee a letter outlining the American position, in which he said:

The moment has now come when we must decide whether to carry on by warfare a struggle for the unification of Korea or whether to pursue this goal by political and other methods.

The enemy has proposed an armistice which involves a clear abandonment of the fruits of aggression. The armistice would leave the Republic of Korea in undisputed possession of substantially the territory which the Republic administered prior to the aggression, indeed this territory will be somewhat enlarged.

The proposed armistice, true to the principle of political asylum, assures that the thousands of North Koreans and Communist Chinese prisoners in our hands, who have seen liberty and who wish to share it, will have the opportunity to do so and will not be forcibly sent back into Communist areas . . .

It is my profound conviction that under these circumstances acceptance of the armistice is required of the United Nations and the Republic of Korea. We would not be justified in prolonging the war with all the misery that it involves in the hope of achieving by force the unification of Korea.

The unification of Korea is an end to which the United States is committed, not once but many times . . . Korea is, unhappily, not the only country which remains divided after World War II. We remain determined to play our part in achieving the political union of all countries so divided.

But we do not intend to employ war as an instrument to accomplish the world-wide political settlements to which we are dedicated . . . It was indeed a crime that those who attacked from the North invoked violence to unite Korea under their rule. Not only as your official friend but as a personal friend I urge that your country not embark upon a similiar course.

The President then offered these commitments:

1. The United States will not renounce its efforts by all peaceful means to effect the unification of Korea . . .

2. I am prepared promptly after the conclusion and acceptance of an armistice to negotiate with you a mutual defense treaty along the lines of the treaties heretofore made between the United States and the Philippines, and the United States and Australia and New Zealand. You may recall that both of these treaties speak of "the development of a more comprehensive system of regional security in the Pacific area." A security pact between the United States and the Republic of Korea would be a further step in that direction . . .

3. The United States Government, subject to requisite Congressional appropriations, will be prepared to continue economic aid to the Republic of Korea which will permit in peace a restoration of its devastated land.

Rhee spurned the armistice terms, saying, "A truce on the present terms simply means death to us. We have consistently demanded that Chinese Communist forces should be driven out of our territory [meaning all of Korea], even if in so doing, we have to fight by ourselves." The South Korean National Assembly voted unanimously against the truce terms, and antitruce demonstrations swept Seoul and other South Korean cities.

With the South Koreans thus bitterly opposed, the Allied and Communist delegates signed on June 8 an agreement on the prisoner issue which had been blocking the truce for so many months. The agreement embodied the principle of nonforcible repatriation.

Through Dulles, Nehru sent the following message to the President:

Please convey to President Eisenhower my congratulations on the signing of the P.O.W. Agreement at Panmunjom. The United States under the leadership of the President has played a wise and generous part in these negotiations which have resulted in an Agreement, and I should like to offer my respectful congratulations to President Eisenhower for his leadership at this critical moment. I earnestly trust that this Agreement will lead to peace not only in the far East but elsewhere.

JAWAHARLAL NEHRU

The President replied:

My dear Mr. Prime Minister:

I thank you for your message received June 9 regarding the prisoner of war agreement reached at Panmunjom. I greatly appreciate your words regarding the part which the United States has played in this matter. It is my earnest hope that this agreement will speedily lead to an armistice and just peace in Korea and to a relaxing of world tensions. India's participation in the work of the Repatriation Commission will mark a further significant contribution toward these ends.

Sincerely yours,
DWIGHT D. EISENHOWER

Allied and Communist officers were putting the last touches to the map of the armistice line on June 18 when, several hours before dawn, the telephone suddenly awakened Dulles in his home near "Embassy Row" in Washington. A State Department watch officer was calling with an urgent radio message from Korea that Rhee was releasing thousands of anti-Communist North Korean prisoners held by the South Koreans. (The total reached more than twenty-seven thousand).

Dulles was dumbfounded by the news. He knew very well that by freeing the prisoners Rhee might succeed in sabotaging the truce negotiations by giving the Communists a pretext for ending all attempts at a settlement. Even though it was about two o'clock in the morning, the Secretary went to the White House telephone which stood beside his private phone and asked the switchboard operator to awaken the President. Shortly, the President picked up the receiver and listened with astonishment to what Dulles had to tell him. The news seemed to upset him greatly.

After the government offices opened in the morning the President and Dulles discussed the release of the prisoners. By now Rhee's act had sent a shock around the world, although both in the United States and abroad there were some who defended and even applauded him for his boldness. During the day Dulles issued a statement saying:

I have been in conference with the President regarding the unilateral action taken by the Republic of Korea to release prematurely North Korean prisoners of war. This action was in violation of the authority of the United Nations Command to which the Republic of Korea had agreed. On behalf of the United Nations we have conducted our negotiations for an armistice in good faith and we have acted and are acting in good faith. President Eisenhower is communicating with President Rhee in this sense.

At the meeting of the Cabinet on June 19 the President, remarking on the trials of the previous forty-eight hours occasioned by Rhee's action and the Rosenberg case, reviewed the difficulties in South Korea.

He bade the Cabinet bear in mind that the principal enemy in Korea was still Communism. He outlined various possible means of conciliating the South Koreans and saving the situation. Finally he remarked that similar problems, though not so pressing at the moment, existed in other parts of the world and that perhaps this experience in Korea should make Americans feel more sympathy for the British in their troubles in Iran.

As was expected, the Communists railed at the release of the prisoners, charged that the U.N. Command had "deliberately connived" at Rhee's action, and demanded that the prisoners be recaptured "immediately," which, of course, was impossible. Nevertheless the Reds did not shut the door to continued negotiations, and in an urgent effort to bring the South Koreans around the President sent Walter S. Robertson, Assistant Secretary of State for Far Eastern Affairs, to Korea to talk to Rhee.

The stubborn South Korean President had the United States of America in a painfully delicate predicament and one that caused Eisenhower great worry. South Korean troops at that time held two thirds of the U.N. line in Korea. If Rhee ordered them to attack, what would have happened to American forces? And what could have been done to stop them, once they had started, from turning the near truce into a full-scale resumption of hostilities? True, the United States could have cut off the Koreans' supply of ammunition, but that would only have meant, if they persisted in an offensive, that their attack would be doomed to collapse without bullets and shells. Then the great danger would arise that a Communist counterattack would overrun the South Koreans and in doing so engulf the American and other U.N. troops holding the remaining one third of the line. A similar danger threatened if, instead of attacking, Rhee simply pulled all his forces out of line.

In the face of the dilemma Robertson, a quiet, debonair, grayhaired man with a Southern accent, met Rhee on June 26. For hour after hour and indeed for day after day Robertson just sat in a room with Rhee and listened sympathetically while the old man poured out his feelings. When at last it became apparent to Robertson that Rhee had about talked himself out, he began patiently pressing the American position. He stressed the willingness of the United States to stand by Korea after the truce and this country's desire to help the Koreans rebuild. He made it very plain to Rhee, too, that under any circumstances the United States was going ahead with the truce. Robertson labored, and evidently with much success, to get around Rhee's fears that the United States would abandon South Korea to its fate at the postarmistice political conference. He assured him that if Rhee would agree to co-operate in the truce, Dulles would visit Korea to discuss the political conference with him.

Robertson told Rhee that the United States would not agree to resume the war automatically if the political conference failed to unify Korea. What the United States would do in such an eventuality was left for determination by the United States.

After two weeks of talks with Robertson, Rhee gave in, promising in writing that he would keep his forces under the U.N. command. On July 11 he wrote Eisenhower that in deference to the President's wishes he would not obstruct in any way the carrying out of the truce. He sent a letter to Dulles the same day saying that although he still questioned the wisdom of the truce terms, he was yielding his convictions to United States policy. While South Korea dissociated itself from the truce, Rhee assured Dulles that his government would abide by it to give the U.N. a chance to unify Korea by political agreement. Dulles told the Cabinet on July 17 that Robertson's mission had succeeded because of Robertson's patient but firm dealing with Rhee.

The Rhee letters brought great relief to Eisenhower. With their assurances he felt that the United States could sign the truce without risk to American forces on the battlefield. On July 14 the Foreign Ministers of Britain, France and the United States issued a statement in Washington declaring that their governments would "again support the restoration of peace and security" by U.N. action if the Communists should "renew their aggression in Korea after an armistice"—a pledge that was echoed three weeks later by all sixteen of the U.N. members who had fought in Korea. The sixteen said that the consequences of such a breach "would be so grave that, in all probability, it would not be possible to confine hostilities" to Korea. The President was prepared to take very strong action against the Chinese Communists if they resumed fighting after the truce. Radford said on January 5, 1955, that this would include "use of atomic weapons, if needed."

During the months when the armistice terms were taking form the criticism encountered by the President and Dulles came not alone from Rhee. There was also criticism at home, especially from the right wing of the Republican Party, which believed passionately that, as the 1952 Republican platform charged, the Democrats had waged the war in Korea "without will to victory . . . and by their hampering orders (had) produced stalemates and ignominious bartering with our enemies. . . ." The attitude of these Republicans, many of whom had favored the MacArthur course, was reflected in an exchange in the Senate between Senators William E. Jenner, of Indiana, and George W. Malone, of Nevada, both of whom professed to regard the impending truce as a victory for Red China.

Malone: Does the distinguished Senator remember any change in State Department policy . . . by Mr. Dulles since he has taken office?
Jenner: I have noticed no change.

When Knowland was asked in a broadcast interview, "Is this a truce with honor that we are about to get?" he replied, "I don't believe so" and ventured the further opinion that under its terms "inevitably we will lose the balance of Asia." Taft said that any settlement which left Korea divided would be "extremely unsatisfactory," creating, he added, "a condition likely to bring war at any moment" and giving the Chinese freedom to attack elsewhere in Southeast Asia. Dissatisfaction was strong also among those who felt, as Hanson W. Baldwin phrased their viewpoint, "that Korea was the right war in the right place at the right time if we wished to stop the spread of Asiatic Communism."

Republican critics were not unmindful of the fact that in certain respects the truce terms were less severe than had been offered originally by the Truman administration. Neither were they deaf to the widespread comment at the time that the reason the terms were acceptable to Congress now was that they were being presented by Eisenhower rather than by Truman and that the very prospect of a Republican uproar had deterred Truman from ever agreeing to such conditions. On June 9 Truman called upon the American people to support Eisenhower on the truce. Apart from specific criticism of the terms a feeling seemed to pervade the country that in spite of the casualties (Americans: 33,629 dead, 103,284 wounded), not much, if anything, had been settled by the fighting in Korea.

A different point of view was expressed by the President and Dulles and shared by many Democrats and pro-Eisenhower Republicans. This was that while the United States had not won the war in Korea in the same sense that the previous war had been won in Europe and the Pacific, the settlement did achieve the original objective, which was to restore peace in South Korea. Furthermore, as Eisenhower told Rhee in his letter of June 6, the Communists were agreeing to terms which abandoned "the fruits of aggression" and which left South Korea in possession of substantially all, and indeed more, of the territory than it had administered before the attack.

Another way of putting it, as Dulles did at a press conference, was that the Korean war had vindicated the principle of collective security.

Above and beyond doubts and criticisms, however, the temper of the country was to agree to the truce, and this, coupled with patient persuasion by Eisenhower, Nixon and Dulles, removed any serious opposition in Congress. Following the President's letter to Rhee, for example, Knowland himself appealed to the South Korean leader to take Eisenhower's advice and avoid any act that would endanger the truce.

After all it was perfectly clear that Eisenhower was not willing to attack Communist China, and those in Congress who might have preferred this course saw little point otherwise in standing up and opposing a truce. Since their only choice, as they saw it, was between stalemate with continued casualties and stalemate with a cease-fire, they logically chose the latter. The Vice-President worked behind the scenes on the doubters. The argument he employed was that since the truce would be welcomed by the people, the Republicans should embrace it as their accomplishment and get the political credit for it.

The truce was to be signed at Panmunjom on the last weekend of July when the President was scheduled to attend Secretary Wilson's first annual Defense Conference at the Marine base at Quantico, Virginia. Last-minute talks with Dulles and Robertson delayed his departure from the White House Friday afternoon and at Quantico that night, seemingly under a strain, he did what, for him, was the unusual thing of staying up until nearly one-thirty talking.

With Hagerty, Cutler, the late Brigadier General Paul T. Carroll, secretary of the White House staff, and Lieutenant General Clifton B. Cates, the commandant at Quantico, he chatted on and on, dwelling on World War II experiences rather than on Korea. He recalled his talks in Berlin after the war with a Soviet general and told how the Russian had described the practice in the Red Army of clearing the way for tanks by marching troops over minefields— a story that offended Eisenhower's sense of human values. In a similar vein he related a conversation in which the general had expressed surprise that Americans should have taken the trouble they did in treating German prisoners humanely. Eisenhower said that he explained to the Russian that ill treatment of German prisoners would have brought retaliation against American prisoners in German hands, whereupon the general inquired why the Americans needed to worry about their soldiers in German prisons since these men no longer were of any military value.

The information the President had was that the truce was to be signed on Sunday morning, and he had asked Cabinet members to attend church with him in Washington at that time. On Saturday afternoon, however, word arrived that the signing had been put off until Sunday night so the attendance of the Cabinet at church was canceled. The slipperiness of the footing in Korea made the President uneasy over the news of the postponement, and that night he again stayed up late talking incessantly with friends.

At Quantico the President had worked on a message which he planned to broadcast when the truce was signed, and on the drive back to Washington on Sunday, July 26, he went over it in the car with Hagerty and Carroll. That afternoon, following their return, he telephoned Hagerty to say that he had just been reading some of Lincoln's speeches and wondered what Hagerty would think if he concluded the Korea message with the passage from Lincoln's second inaugural address, beginning, "With malice toward none; with charity for all. . . ." Hagerty thought it was a good idea, and the President added it to the end of his speech.

Eisenhower is able to lose himself in painting, and that afternoon at the White House, while the hours preceding the signing dragged slowly by, he got out his easel and brushes and painted.

In arranging for the broadcast he had insisted that he would not go on the air until after official word had been received that the truce was signed lest otherwise he announce the truce prematurely and run the risk that some slip in Panmunjom might interrupt the negotiations.

The flash from Panmunjom on the signing reached the White House at 9:38 P.M. and the President prepared to go on the air at ten o'clock. While he was waiting, photographers took his picture as he sat in the broadcast room at the large carved oak desk which had been presented to the White House by Queen Victoria.

"How do you feel?" a photographer inquired.

"The war is over," the President smiled, "and I hope my son is going to come home soon."

His message to the people was a brief one and bespoke his thankfulness over the end of fighting and casualties.

For this nation [he said] the cost of repelling aggression has been high. In thousands of homes it has been incalculable. It has been paid in terms of tragedy. . . .

Soldiers, sailors and airmen of sixteen different countries have stood as partners beside us throughout these long and bitter months. America's thanks go to each. In this struggle we have seen the United Nations meet the challenge of aggression—not with pathetic words of protest, but with deeds of decisive purpose. . . . We have won an armistice on a single battleground—not peace in the world. We may not now relax our guard nor cease our quest. . . . We shall fervently strive to insure that this armistice will in fact bring free peoples one step nearer to their goal of a world at peace.

The next day he sent a special message to Congress asking authority to spend up to two hundred million dollars at that time on Korean rehabilitation—a request speedily granted.

At a meeting of the Cabinet on August 27, with Nixon presiding in the absence of the President, who was in Colorado, Dulles reported on his visit to Rhee after the armistice. The Korean President, he said, had pressed to the last for a commitment from the United States for unification of Korea by whatever means necessary and for material support if the South Koreans should undertake to unify the peninsula by force. Dulles said, however, that the United States retained a free hand in determining its future course in case of new trouble in Korea.

In time the number of American forces in Korea was reduced and the United States and the Republic of Korea entered into a mutual defense treaty. The postarmistice political conference which was held in Geneva ended in failure with the U.N. members charging that the Communists had rejected "every effort to obtain agreement." Like Germany, Korea was left divided with no permanent settlement in sight. In the meantime a stillness fell across the shattered country while to the south the thunder of gunfire rumbled over Indo-China and later over Quemoy and the Matsus.

CHAPTER 9

Eisenhower and Red China

*The Talk About a Naval Blockade – The President Opposes Driving
China Deeper into the Arms of Russia – The Problem of Recognizing
Communist China – Eisenhower Tells His Views to the Congressional
Leaders – The President on Going-It-Alone – Some Cabinet Discussions
on Domestic Problems*

I

During the months when the Korean truce was being negotiated
the President had to deal with conflicts at home over American policy toward Communist China and over the question of
whether, regardless of the wishes of our allies and the U.N., the
United States should pursue a course of its own in Asia.

At the time of the Seventh Fleet order those who had long favored
a bolder course in the Far East revived the proposal for a naval blockade of China. On February 7, for example, Knowland, who was then
chairman of the Senate Republican Policy Committee, gave his
approval to the idea of a blockade by the United States alone if
necessary. The following day Taft said that a blockade would be
"desirable" if it could be undertaken without causing a rift among
the Allies. This would certainly have been impossible. The nations
of Southeast Asia looked with disapproval on talk of a blockade.
The British were thoroughly opposed to the idea, not only because of
the effect of a blockade on their trade with the Chinese but also
because Britain and other Western nations feared that a blockade
would lead to war with China and perhaps ultimately with Russia.

The President himself regarded a blockade as an act of war, and he was never receptive to proposals for blockading China while there was a chance of a truce in Korea. In addition to considering a blockade a belligerent act, he also felt, as he told a meeting of the White House staff on March 2, 1953, that it would be a rather useless one.

At that meeting, as he has done periodically, he reviewed with his staff the things that had been or should be done to live up to commitments he had made in the 1952 campaign. In this talk he placed great emphasis on the importance of foreign trade and said he felt that the administration had not made sufficient progress in encouraging reciprocal trade. He remarked that it was particularly difficult to develop a wise and effective policy on trading between Communists and non-Communist nations.

Then he turned to the question of cutting off all of the free world's trade with China, which would have been a purpose of a blockade. It was naive, he said, to suppose that Red China could be defeated simply by the blocking of this trade. Instead, greatly to the detriment of the free world, he declared, it would compel China to rely to a greater extent on Russia for the products it needed. This, as he saw it, would have the bad effect not only of strengthening the bonds between China and the Soviet Union but at the same time of weakening the economies of free nations which customarily traded with China.

Generally, the President's position has been that since commerce between the free world and the Communist world provides certain advantages for both, the United States should not fasten its gaze solely on that part of the trading that helps the Communists. Rather, he has held that American policy should be guided by consideration of the net advantage in East-West trade. Where such trade in non-strategic goods yields a net advantage to the West, it should be allowed and should be used, if possible, as an instrument for extending Western influence beyond the Communist borders. To say there should be no East-West trade, he once told the Cabinet, would be a fallacy.

When Eisenhower viewed the China problem in those months, he realized that with the Peiping regime behaving as it was, holding and torturing American prisoners and bearing the U.N. brand as an

aggressor in Korea, it was next to impossible from a political standpoint for the United States to grant diplomatic recognition to the
Communist government. He did not believe that at that moment
it should do so. Nevertheless he felt that it was unfortunate that a
climate had developed in which, so it seemed to him, it was looked
upon almost as un-American even to debate the merits of recognition. He sometimes remarked to associates that it might be better if
diplomatic recognition were entirely a matter of acknowledging that
a government was in fact in power in a country. He regretted that
President Wilson had introduced a moral precedent in refusing in
1913 to recognize the revolutionary regime of President Victoriano
Huerta in Mexico.

The President was not convinced that the vital interests of the
United States were best served by prolonged nonrecognition of China.
He had serious doubts as to whether Russia and China were natural
allies. He speculated on whether Soviet interests lay primarily in
Europe and the Middle East rather than in the Orient. Therefore,
he asked, would it not be the best policy in the long run for the
United States to try to pull China away from Russia rather than drive
the Chinese ever deeper into an unnatural alliance unfriendly to the
United States? Likewise the problem of keeping the Japanese
economy alive weighed heavily on him, and he felt that in part at
least its solution must lie ultimately in trade between Japan and
China. The alternative, he feared, would be endles subsidization of
the Japanese economy by the American taxpayer.

Confronted, however, by the hostile conduct of the Chinese
Communists and the intense antipathy to Red China among the
American people, Eisenhower never in the years under consideration
here made any move to change the policy of nonrecognition. To have
done so would undoubtedly have precipitated furious rows in both
parties and particularly among the Republicans, as Knowland made
quite clear on July 1, 1954. He told the Senate that if Red China was
admitted to the U.N. (which probably would have been a con-
comitant of recognition), he would resign as majority leader and
"devote my full efforts" to canceling American membership in and
financial support of the United Nations.

On the other hand, the President strongly and successively resisted being maneuvered into a rigid, uncompromising, unalterable position with respect to future relations with Red China as the Democratic administration had been after the MacArthur hearings in 1951. The President turned a deaf ear, for example, to the appeal by Jenner on May 26, 1953, that he issue a "final statement" that the United States would not recognize the Peiping government or consent to its admission to the U.N. under any circumstances.

One of the most significant expressions by Eisenhower on this matter was at a special meeting he had in the White House on June 2, 1953, with the Republican leaders of Congress. Senator Everett M. Dirksen, Republican, of Illinois, had introduced a rider to an appropriations bill under which American contributions to the U.N. budget would be terminated automatically if Red China was admitted to membership. On May 27 the Senate Appropriations Committee approved it by a vote of twenty to three. At his press conference the next day the President said that he considered this approach to the problem a very grave error. He then had a letter prepared for Senator Styles Bridges, Republican, of New Hampshire, chairman of the Appropriations Committee, urging that the rider be withdrawn. After at least five drafts the letter was finally ready for Eisenhower's signature, but at the last moment he changed his mind and instead of sending it, put in a call for the leaders and asked them to come to the White House.

When they arrived, he told them that he was distressed at the thought that the rider might pass the Senate. He was opposed to it, he said, for two reasons: One was that he did not believe that the United States could properly serve notice on the U.N. in such a manner; the other was that the United States simply could not and dare not live alone in the modern world.

He emphasized that he was not trying to tell the members what their personal convictions should be, but he said that his own conviction was that the rider would seriously impede him in the conduct of foreign affairs.

The United Nations, he said, was the only machinery in existence for bringing together all the countries of the world to discuss international problems, and as such, he added, it represented mankind's hope for an eventual association of nations in which law would replace the battlefield. There had to be such an association, he insisted, because the devastating character of new weapons made global war unthinkable.

Communist China, he pointed out, was not yet in the U.N. But he maintained that it was unwise to commit the United States irrevocably to a situation before it occurred. To illustrate how rapidly situations and outlooks have changed he cited the revolution in the American attitude toward Germany between 1945 and 1953.

The President told the Republican leaders that the situation in which the world found itself demanded patience and courage on the part of the American people and their government to prevent the United States from being overwhelmed by frustrations. If Congress made the mistake of a penny-pinching, dollar-sign approach to the issue of Red China in the U.N., he warned, the effect on world opinion would probably be very bad.

Some of the leaders replied that they had voted for the rider because they were disgusted with the situation then developing. (This may have been a reference to the growing sentiment among many U.N. members for the seating of Red China after a truce.)

One of the Senators explained that he and his colleagues had believed their action would strengthen the hand of the government by setting forth the rules of the game, so to speak, before the issue of China's admission should become critical. They had no desire, he protested, to embarrass the President. Rather, he said, they had considered the rider a legitimate measure to present to the world the attitude of Congress, particularly in view of the Republican position on Red China through the years and the failure of the Democrats, as he put it, to handle the problem.

One of the House leaders said he thought that the President was right and that the rider made no sense. If it ever took effect, he said, it could lead to American withdrawal from the U.N. and the death of the world organization.

The President observed that he did not care how forcefully any-one expressed his opposition to the seating of Red China in the U.N. What concerned him, he said, was not to have the situation foreclosed. Avoidance of war, he continued, depended on constant labor for peace. The structure that had been erected to preserve peace could begin to crumble if the U.N. rider was adopted, he said, and *that* could have no end but disaster.

A Senate leader told the President that the admission of Red China would violate all his fundamental beliefs. The Senate, he remarked, had passed the similar McClellan resolution in 1951. He said he had heard many rumors—and believed them to be true—that Britain would press for admission of China to the U.N. after the Korean armistice. Since, he continued, the United States could not be certain of carrying a U.N. majority with it on this issue, an American position on the subject should now be taken actively and aggressively.

The President firmly disagreed. The rider, he said, was not the right way to register opposition to the seating of China. If a world organization was to be workable at all, he said, every nation must expect to be outvoted at one time or another.

He warned the leaders very solemnly that the destruction of the U.N. would lead to the dissolution of NATO. In that case, he asked, where would the United States be left and how could he possibly discharge his obligations with regard to American security? He wanted to be reasonable and that is why he called his friends in for a talk, he said. Now, he told them, they had to come to an agreement.

The President won. Props began falling out from under the rider when one of the Senate leaders suggested that perhaps another way could be found which would make the attitude of Congress clear but would still be satisfactory to Eisenhower. It might be done, he suggested, through a resolution that would neither be legally binding on the President nor cut off U.N. funds.

The President readily assented to the suggestion of a substitute so long as it did not approach the problem in terms of money. Once it had been passed, he said, he could impress upon foreign governments the feeling of Congress and caution them that if they forced the issue in the U.N., he would not be able to answer for the reaction in the United States. No person in a responsible position had suggested to him, he said, that the United States support admission of Red China. But he reiterated that anything that would completely foreclose freedom of action by the United States in the future would be unsatisfactory.

The Senate was concerned, a leader explained to the President, that if Red China could shoot its way into the U.N., it might then shoot up the U.N.

One of the House leaders suggested that the language of the rider be watered down so that it merely stated Congressional opposition to the admission of China.

The President then reviewed his efforts to improve relations with allied nations. He mentioned the trips of Dulles and Stassen to Europe and Asia, the good-will tour of Latin America by his brother, Dr. Milton S. Eisenhower, president of Pennsylvania State University, and the forthcoming good-will journeys of the Vice-President. The Dirksen rider, he said, would nullify the good effects of these gestures.

One of the Senate leaders thereupon told the President that he and his colleagues on the Appropriations Committee would withdraw the rider.

In reply the President promised that he would immediately set about informing other heads of government about the attitude of Congress on the seating of China in the U.N. In closing the meeting he warned that the budget would have to be increased greatly to provide for American security if this country's allies started to fall away.

"Let's not write off our friends," he concluded.

The next day, Bridges offered a substitute amendment declaring it to be the "sense of Congress" that Red China should be barred from the U.N. The amendment was adopted unanimously by both houses.

While the President did not change the basic position he had stated to the leaders, he was to speak out himself ever more force-fully against admission of Red China, especially after the Communists' performance at the Geneva conference on a Korean settlement.

Even before the meeting with the leaders on the U.N. rider another phase of the controversy over policy in the Far East had been renewed by Taft on May 26 in a speech in which he said; "I believe we might as well forget the United Nations as far as the Korean war is concerned. I think we should do our best now to negotiate this truce, and if we fail, then let England and other Allies know that we are withdrawing from all further peace negotiations in Korea."

Furthermore: "I believe we might as well abandon any idea of working with the United Nations in the East and reserve to ourselves a completely free hand."

Taft's speech was read to a dinner of the National Conference of Christians and Jews in Cincinnati by his son while the Senator was in the hospital.

At a press conference two days later the President commented on this by saying that "if you are going to go it alone in one place, you of course have to go it alone everywhere."* He added:

If you are trying to develop a coalition of understanding based upon decisions, upon ideas of justice . . . then you have got to make compromises, you have got to find that way in between certain complicating local considerations that will serve the best good of all.

Now that is what we are up against today because our whole policy is based on this theory. No single free nation can live alone in the world. We have got to have friends . . . We have to have that unity in basic purpose that comes from recognition of common interests. That is what we are up against.

Now not being a particularly patient man, I share the irritations and the sense of frustration that comes to everybody who is working along in what he believes to be a decent purpose, finds himself balked by what he thinks is sometimes, I say, the ignorance or errors of someone who otherwise is his friend. I understand those things, but I will tell you that only patience, only determination and optimism and only a very deep faith can carry America forward.

In a speech before the national convention of the Junior Chamber of Commerce in Minneapolis on June 10 he rejected as "dangerous" the "fortress theory of defense" in which the United States would have to "stand by itself." This emphasis on maintaining the alliance and cultivating our friends was to remain dominant throughout Eisenhower's future conduct of foreign affairs.

II

While the Korean truce talks and relations with China occupied a great deal of the President's attention early in his first summer in

* Taft later denied he had advocated a go-it-alone course.

the White House, they were not the whole story by any means. The Cabinet met regularly during July, and its discussions, largely on domestic matters, tell some of the other parts of the story.

July 3, 1953 (A breakfast meeting with the President)

Mrs. Hobby complained that a $426,000 cut voted by the House Appropriations Committee in funds for the Office of Education would have a drastic effect on its operations.

The President replied that he was astonished that funds of this magnitude would be taken away from education, which he described as a basic function of government in a democracy. He declared that every liberal—"including myself"—would take exception to this reduction. If the Cabinet did not object, he said, the administration would take forthright action to have the funds restored. The Cabinet agreed.

(When the appropriation came before the Senate, the President wrote to Senator Edward J. Thye, Republican, of Minnesota, a member of the Senate Appropriations Committee, urging reinstatement of the funds. Congress finally restored $300,000 of the cut.)

The Cabinet discussed Latin America briefly. The President observed that because of preoccupation with Europe and Asia in recent years, United States policy toward Latin America was generally unsatisfactory. He mentioned current difficulties in Brazil, Bolivia, Mexico and Panama, and asked all government departments to work closely with the State Department on problems affecting Latin America. Funds invested in Latin America, he said, did not seem to solve economic problems there, with the result that there was always need to deal with the same conditions all over again. He urged that an effective policy be developed for overcoming this situation.

The President said it was important that Latin American countries should try to find private capital in the United States. Walter Bedell Smith noted that the problem was more one of avoiding double taxation than of obtaining guarantees against expropriation of property by Latin American countries. He indicated that there was no difficulty in getting these guarantees.

Eisenhower proposed finally that consideration should be given to the possibility of developing greater economic co-operation among the Latin American countries and greater consolidation of their various economic and industrial resources, such as was being carried forward in Western Europe.

July 10, 1953

The President remarked that he was not in very good spirits this morning because of a particularly disagreeable letter he had read in a letters-to-the-editor column in a newspaper.

(Eisenhower quite regularly read these columns at that time. I do not know which particular letter he was referring to here. A couple of the papers delivered to the White House that day carried letters criticizing, from both directions, the new policy on books in overseas libraries. Also the Washington *Times-Herald* carried a sneering letter about his decision to meet Churchill at Bermuda, implying that the President would be afraid to stand up to Sir Winston.)

Dulles told about the meeting of the Foreign Ministers of Britain, France and the United States, opening in Washington that day, which, as it happened, was the same day Moscow announced that Lavrenti P. Beria had been purged as head of the Soviet secret police. The Secretary of State said that the meeting would be concerned with sizing up the new situation in Russia. It would deal also, he said, with the problems of German unity, Indo-China, Egypt and the European Defense Community.

Humphrey asked what the effect would be on Western Europe of the apparent weakening of the Soviet Union, reflected in the Beria affair. Dulles said that it would tend to decrease the sense of urgency and doubtless would encourage delay in adoption of the E.D.C. The Secretary of the Treasury then mentioned the possibility of taking some forward step at this critical moment.

Allen Dulles reported that the overthrow of Beria had given the Russian people a great shock. Analyzing the development, he said that the Red Army might be augmenting its power. Beria's fall did not necessarily mean, he added, that Malenkov had consolidated his position as Stalin's successor.

Jackson observed that the Beria affair might encourage passive resistance in the satellite states. The time might be appropriate, he suggested, for raising again questions such as slave labor and atrocities in Russia and the Soviet treatment of trade unions. He said he hoped that the Foreign Ministers' meeting would produce a resounding call for free elections in Germany.

July 17, 1953

Secretary Dulles said that the communiqué at the close of the Foreign Ministers' meeting pretty well reflected the substance of the session. (The communiqué said that the Big Three had invited Molotov to a meeting early in the fall to discuss German unification and the Austrian peace treaty. Among other things, it said that "the first steps which should lead to a satisfactory solution of the German problem" would be "organization of free elections" and establishment of a free government for all of Germany. The ministers also discussed "measures to hasten a satisfactory outcome and the restoration of peace in Indo-China.") Dulles emphasized to the Cabinet the unity that prevailed among the Big Three.

The President asked that government departments furnish by October 15 material which they wished to have considered for inclusion in his next State of the Union message. He indicated that if the message became too voluminous, he might not deliver it in person. Nixon agreed that appearances of the President before joint sessions of Congress should be limited to dramatic occasions.

July 31, 1953

Secretary McKay presented a draft of a new statement on power policy, reversing the emphasis of the preceding Democratic administrations on Federal responsibility for building power facilities and placing primary responsibility upon the people of local communities for supplying their power needs. When "economically justified and feasible" the Department of Interior under this policy would plan Federal power projects, especially when they were too big to be financed by local public or private enterprise.

(This departure from a program of public power, which was to have repercussions in the controversies over Dixon-Yates and the administration's assent to private power development in Hell's Canyon in Idaho, was one of the early basic policies which differentiated Eisenhower's administration from Truman's.)

McKay told the Cabinet that his department did not approve of

Federal construction and operation of steam plants to produce electric power.

Wilson voiced his feeling that the policy on T.V.A. should be changed to insure that the rates charged would take into account the costs of operating the vast system.

Many in the Cabinet, including the President, Nixon and Wilson, thought that McKay should indicate publicly that the Federal government planned to undertake certain power projects when the budget permitted. It was also agreed that efforts should be made to enlist the support of Western governors, particularly Governor Warren, of California, for the President's power policy of "partnership" among the Federal government, the states and local private interests.

During the meeting the Cabinet discussed the desirability of having members make information available to the press.

"No one has to shy away from reporters at this point," the President said, "except my brothers."

(The week before, Arthur B. Eisenhower, executive vice-president of the Commerce Trust Company of Kansas City and oldest of the Eisenhower brothers, had kicked up a storm by telling a reporter for the Las Vegas *Sun* that McCarthy was "the most dangerous menace to America" and a "throwback to the Spanish Inquisition." He was further quoted as having said that McCarthy "has never been responsible for the conviction of one . . . Communist.")

Lodge said that it was necessary for the administration to make a complete public presentation of its accomplishments in Congress. He pointed to the need for winning the support of those newspaper columnists who did not seem to recognize yet, he said, that an era of good will was being established under Eisenhower. Columnists, he added, were still trying to play up the differences and underline the conflicts among the Republicans.

"Happy is the country whose annals are brief," said the President.*

* A similar thought seems to have occurred to others. Thomas Carlyle wrote in *Frederick the Great*, "Happy the people whose annals are blank." Thomas Jefferson said, "Blest is that Nation whose silent course of happiness furnishes nothing for history to say." Cesare di Bonesana Beccaria, an Italian writer, said, "Happy is the nation without a history." George Eliot said, "The happiest women, like the happiest nations, have no history."

CHAPTER 10

Low Tide

Discord in the Republican Ranks – The President's Dismay at the Right Wing – Mutual Assistance Funds Are Cut – Republican Coolness to Eisenhower's First Program – The President's Patience Wears Thin – Tired of Being "Kicked in the Shins" – Eisenhower Ponders Founding a New Party

In spite of some relieving events like the Korean truce, the middle months of 1953 were for Eisenhower his unhappiest and most discouraging period in office, except possibly for some of the worst moments of the McCarthy-Army hearings in 1954.

The bitter dissension in the Republican Party in mid-1953 between the pro-Eisenhower moderates and the semi-isolationist, go-it-alone, ultraconservative right wing drove Eisenhower almost to despair of being able to succeed in the Presidency.

His vexation with the powerful right wing reached such extremes in the summer of 1953 that for a time he gave prolonged thought to the idea of a new political party in America—a party to which persons of his own philosophy, regardless of their previous affiliations, might rally.

The deep cut which the Republican-controlled Congress made in his request for mutual security funds was one of the things that brought to a climax the President's chagrin over the attitude of members of his own party. But it was only one in an accumulation of factors, and for a long time before the final vote on mutual security appropriations in August, Eisenhower's disappointment over affairs in Washington had been growing.

The President was annoyed at the way Congress deserted him to cater to the home-town vote. He fretted over concentration on headline-grabbing investigations instead of constructive legislation. His own program that first year was limited enough, with a number of measures deliberately set aside to give the new administration a chance to get its feet on the ground and give them careful study. Modest though it was, however, much of the program failed to pass that summer. Congress either deferred or rejected such administration measures as expansion of social security, amendment of the Taft-Hartley Act, the St. Lawrence Seaway, the Hawaiian statehood bill, the boosting of the $275,000,000,000 debt limit by $15,000,000,-000 and increasing the postal rate. A housing bill was passed only after Congress had chopped down the President's recommendations on new public housing units.

As action on such measures fizzled out, the President's hopes for a strikingly good record with his first Congress went up the chimney. From the very beginning, even in the preinaugural days at the Commodore, Eisenhower had aspired to a display of Republican unity and progress that would commend itself to the voters so strongly that in the 1954 election the Republicans would be returned to control of Congress. Instead of unity he found factionalism and bickering in the party.

After all that Eisenhower felt he had done to get along with Congress, to respect its prerogatives and extend the hospitality of the White House to its members in the long series of luncheons, he was dismayed at what some Congressmen of his own party had to say not only about his program but about the people with whom he had surrounded himself. This sort of thing came as all the greater shock to him because he thought that he had succeeded in creating an atmosphere of trust and confidence. It was almost incomprehensible to him that any Republicans could doubt the sincerity of his own motives and the motives of his assistants.

Roscoe Drummond was striking very close to the President's personal point of view when some months later he wrote in his column in the New York *Herald Tribune* that "there is now another kind of 'mess in Washington.' " Republicans were attacking Republicans, McCarthy was spreading distrust of the Eisenhower administration and Republican feuding was imperiling the President's program, Drummond wrote. Quoting the pro-administration *Business Week* as saying that "it is only natural for people to ask themselves whether Republicans are equal to the responsibilities of power," Drummond wrote:

> What is to be the consequence, what is to be the political harvest of this heedless divisiveness, this feuding, this name-calling, this miasmic preoccupation with bitter negative controversy within the Republican Administration? . . . The effect of this new kind of "mess" is to exhibit the Republican Government as quarrelsome, unproductive and legislatively nearly impotent.
>
> What is at stake is that after 33,000,000 Americans "voted for a change"—voted to experiment with liberal Republicanism as an instrument of government for the first time since the social revolution of the New Deal—a liberal Republican Government faces the prospect of repudiation (in the 1954 Congressional election) and, because of the party's "opposition complex" in Congress, without having had any full opportunity to show its real worthiness and value to the nation. Thus conservative government would be losing, for irrelevant but self-created reasons, its best and long-cherished opportunity.

The patience which the President had shown in his early months in office began to wear noticeably thin in private.

In the Cabinet on May 8 he suggested to Hall that the Republican National Chairman get to work to round up more support for the administration among Republicans in Congress. He said he was tired of having the administration "kicked in the shins" and otherwise set upon by Congressmen who should be supporting it.

During a discussion in the Cabinet on May 22 Wilson said wistfully that he wished that more Republicans would recognize that they no longer were members of an opposition party.

"Brother, I heartily agree," the President replied.

In the same meeting Humphrey cautioned that the national debt might rise above the legal limit.

"Who will have to go to jail if that happens?" Eisenhower inquired.

"We will have to go to Congress," Humphrey said.

"Oh, that's worse!" the President exclaimed.

At the legislative leaders' conference in the White House on May 25 a Senate leader mentioned that the prospects of a certain pending bill were good in spite of the fact that some few Republicans would not support it.

Eisenhower's feelings on this subject being what they were at the time, this comment jarred him.

When, the President demanded, would it be possible to get a piece of legislation worked out on which the Republicans could go before the electorate united instead of always having someone "on our side," in disagreement? The administration was laboring, he said, to co-ordinate its policy with Republicans on the Hill. The newspaper columnists' favorite topic, he continued, was friction between the Republicans, and he protested that these repeated disagreements were just feeding the story for them.

In particular he took exception to Republican members of Congress who criticized the administration over the new military policy. This program, he said, had been devised with great skill. He went on to denounce various other aspects of the criticism of Wilson by Republicans. The very people in Congress who wanted to increase spending for defense, he protested, were the ones who would not stand up for any cuts in other programs, which would provide additional funds for a larger military establishment.

A House leader, pointing to a political phenomenon that was to appear again and again over many different issues, said that critics were not directing their attacks against Eisenhower but were putting the blame on someone else in the administration, in this case Wilson.

"I don't feel neglected," the President replied.

At a meeting of the White House staff on June 22 there was a review of the difficulties besetting the Defense Department reorganization bill in Congress. (This was the same discussion in which the President flared up about the Republican member who had called the bill the product of a "military man" in the White House.) Eisenhower spoke gloomily about his progress in trying to win the support and co-operation of influential Republicans in Congress in spite of the many conferences he had had with them in the White House. He told his staff that he had gone out of his way to develop teamwork between himself and Congress, but that the meetings often seemed to have no effect at all except that sometimes they produced the reverse of what he had sought.

At this staff meeting, incidentally, the President also took umbrage to the tone of newspaper stories about his rehearsals for the unusual television program from the White House on the evening of June 3 in which he, Mrs. Hobby, Brownell and Benson held a round-table discussion of the administration's progress. I am not sure which accounts he was referring to. The Washington *Post*, for example, reported that the rehearsal, coached by an official of the Madison Avenue advertising firm of Batten, Barton, Durstine & Osborn, was held "amid strict secrecy precautions." The *Post* said:

> The White House itself took on something of a Radio City appearance. Television technicians and advertising agency officials scurried through the lobby in a bustle of preparations. . . . White House reporters were barred from the conference room, which has been transformed into a TV studio. . . . Although the White House had indicated the program would be "spontaneous and unrehearsed," as the television trade calls it, "cue cards" containing the first few words of each participant's remarks were set up out of camera range. . . .

The President commented to his staff that the White House was doing the press a service by providing an office for reporters and photographers in the already overcrowded West Wing. This was tantamount to extending the hospitality of the White House to the press, he said, and, therefore, the press should refrain from reporting on "family matters," such as the preparations for the television program. He observed that in this case the press had not played the game.

As for the program itself, the President was fairly pleased with it, but felt that it offered too great a glut of material in thirty minutes.

The President's sense of humor did not desert him during these times of disappointment. On the last day of the fiscal year, June 30, there was the customary rush of legislation to be signed before midnight. Because of errors that necessitated reprinting, however, the housing and defense production bills did not reach the White House until 10:45 P.M. Bernard M. Shanley, who was then special counsel to the President and later his appointment secretary, went to the White House with them only to learn that the President had retired for the night. The bills had to be signed, so Shanley took them, albeit rather apprehensively, to the President's bedroom. Contrary to his expectations, Shanley, who always wears a carnation in his lapel, found Eisenhower in fine spirits. He confessed to the President that there simply had not been time enough for him to check the bills carefully. That was all right, the President said with a laugh. He would sign them then, and if anything untoward was discovered later, they could write "Dis" in front of "Approved."

Eisenhower found nothing to amuse him, however, in the fate of the mutual-security appropriation in Congress that summer. From the early days of the cold war he had been a supporter of the Marshall Plan, and the subsequent military aid for Europe had been the life blood of his work as commander of the NATO forces in 1951 and 1952.

Indicative of his feelings was his later comment at a meeting of the Cabinet on July 8, 1955, on the effectiveness of the Marshall Plan in checking the growth of Communism in Europe after the war. If it had not been for this economic assistance abroad, he said, the American defense program would have required a far greater amount of money than had been spent on it in the postwar years. The United States had realized a high rate of return on the Marshall Plan, he told the Cabinet.

The President would sometimes boil over when people around him referred to mutual security by the old name of foreign aid. The latter, he explained, raised in some minds the notion that the United States was throwing its money around, whereas in fact it was spending in its own vital interests. In the Cabinet on June 26, 1953, Humphrey remarked, in discussing the tight credit situation then affecting the market for Treasury notes, that the government should be very careful before adopting any new measures for "financing the world." The President immediately responded that American assistance was not *that* extensive. Indeed, he observed, the wisest policy might be one of increasing expenditures abroad in order to permit reduced expenditures at home.

That summer, however, few in Congress were thinking in such

terms. Before returning to Independence, Truman had requested an authorization of $7,600,000,000 for the Mutual Security Program. In May, Eisenhower scrapped this figure and asked for some $5,800,-000,000 and shortly revised it to about $5,500,000,000, but there was still a clamor, especially among economy-minded Republicans, for a further cut. This was how matters stood when the Republican legislative leaders held their regular weekly meeting with the President on July 7.

The leaders reported to the President that they were pessimistic about the chances of getting through as large an appropriation as the administration had requested.

Mutual security, the President replied, was one of the most important parts of the entire program. If the appropriation was going to be cut sharply, he said, then the administration might better go back and review the whole range of measures for national security. So effective was the Mutual Security Program, he told the leaders, that if one or two billions of dollars was taken from it, then as a counterbalance it might be necessary to increase other parts of the national security program by seven or eight billions. He said that there could be no hope of reducing defense spending if the heart was to be cut out of the Mutual Security Program.

Eisenhower was not moved when the leaders noted that Congressional criticism was aimed chiefly at economic assistance and thus did not jeopardize support for military programs like NATO. The President replied that economic aid was essential to the whole thing and that cutting it would be like ripping one wheel off a wagon. To confine the program to purely military activities, he said, would be to choose the most expensive way of achieving security.

By this time the President had worked himself into a very emphatic mood. He said that he had been laboring since he took office to save money. Nevertheless, he told the leaders, he wanted to make it very clear that anyone would be making a very dangerous assumption to say, "Now that the Republicans are in power the world is safe, and security programs can be sharply reduced."

The subject was changed, but Eisenhower came back to it again later in the meeting. He could not, he said, overstate his eagerness to do some rethinking of the security problem after action had been completed on the appropriation bills. Some people "ranted and raved," he went on, because the new administration had not "revolutionized" American foreign policy.

It was not going to be revolutionized—he was certain of that, the President said. It could not be revolutionized, he said because the conditions on which it was based do not change radically enough or quickly enough. What could be and was being done, he said, was to change the means and the methods of getting people everywhere to collaborate more earnestly in making a success of anti-Communist alliance. Every day, he said, he was busy communicating with other governments and with friends abroad to impress upon them that if the United States was to continue its assistance, they must make ever greater progress in their own security efforts.

Eleven days after this meeting the House Appropriations Committee under the chairmanship of Representative John Taber, Republican, of New York, who for years had had his axe out for heavy foreign spending, slashed the mutual-security appropriation to $4,433,-678,000, about a billion less than the authorization recommended by Eisenhower. In its report the committee said:

> With the exception of a balanced budget accomplished during the 80th Congress this country has operated on a deficit for so long that, unfortunately, too many individuals are taking it for granted. They have become accustomed to the term. At the risk of seeming academic, the committee must reiterate the thought that only a balanced budget and a sound economy can give us and the other free nations of the world the strength with which to wage a continuing war on Communism. . . .

The committee voted on July 18, and the President had a press conference scheduled for July 22. At a staff meeting beforehand, which he did not attend, the consensus, though the staff was not unanimous, was that the President ought not make a strong statement to the press against the committee's action. The majority of the staff felt that there was logic in some of the points made in the committee's report and that, as the report indicated, a good deal of confusion surrounded the accounting of mutual security funds. The committee had said, for example, that whereas Congress had been told that an unobligated balance of nearly $500,000,000 remained in mutual-security funds, a "more realistic" figure, based on a study by the General Accounting Office, was $2,175,000,000. For all these reasons most of the White House staff felt that the President ought to go slow in publicly opposing the committee.

When this was reported to him at the briefing which Hagerty always holds for the President just before press conferences, Eisenhower immediately took the contrary view. He said that he could not dodge the issue or refuse to go on record as being strongly opposed to the cut.

The question, of course, came up at the press conference, and the President replied in this way. He said that he had been around the fringes of the problem for a long time and had never regarded the Mutual Security Program as a giveaway. The problem was one he viewed, he said, in the light of national self-interest, and this had always led him to the conclusion that the United States must have strong alliances so as to maintain collective security. The way he approached the question of how much to spend on mutual security, he said, was to place the Mutual Security Program "right square alongside our own security program because I think that is exactly where it belongs."

When we go at that program [he said], I don't think merely of how much we are cutting here and there—how we are affecting the security and the position of the United States of America, that is the way I look at it. Now I think—and I have been doing a lot of studying on it— I think that cut is too heavy.

That very same day the House of Representatives turned its back on the President and voted, 289 to 115, for the Taber committee's cut, with only a trifling modification. During the debate Eisenhower's press conference statement was quoted repeatedly on the floor of the House, but to no avail. Representative Thomas E. Martin, Republican, of Iowa, for example, appealed to his colleagues to "bring to an abrupt end this utterly useless and ineffective attempt to buy support and friendship from other nations."

In the privacy of the White House the President stormed over the slash in the mutual-security appropriation. Stupid and short-sighted, he called it. Eisenhower had been involved in one way or another in the cold war since its inception. Some people, he was aware, regarded him as an authority, so to speak, on America's role in this conflict. Why was it then, he asked, that when as President he went to a Congress in control of his own party and laid his judgment before it, he was not given something of this same credit for knowing what he was talking about? He became impatient with people who could not, as it appeared to him, understand the obligations that were involved in American leadership in the world.

It was fully as apparent to the President as it was to political observers at the time that very often his views on vital American policy were closer to those of the Democrats than to many of the Republicans in Congress. "Fifty-eight times," according to *Congressional Quarterly Almanac* for 1953, "Democrats saved the President . . . their votes providing the margin of victory when Republican defections or absences imperiled the happy glow."

This harassed and aggravated Eisenhower. He was incredulous that many people in his own party could not see what to him were the long-range gains toward peace and prosperity inherent in his program. The divisions within the party troubled him deeply, and he gave a great deal of thought to what role he ought to play in trying to heal the breach.

As he turned these questions over in his mind, the President began to ask whether, after all, the Republican Party was represented by men with the vision and the understanding of what was required to lead the United States through the perils of the mid-twentieth century.

In the face of the continuing dissidence and disunity the President sometimes simply exploded with exasperation. What was the use, he demanded to know, of his trying to lead the Republican Party along a course that was progressive and forward-looking but still clung to the middle road?

He began asking his most intimate associates whether he did not have to start thinking about a new party.

As he conceived it, such a party would have been essentially his party. It would have represented those doctrines, international and domestic, which he believed were best for the United States and indeed for the world. It would have attracted those men and women of the older parties who believed as he did and who wanted to promote and preserve enlightened and progressive policies.

The President even went so far as to think of a name for it, but never hit upon one. Nevertheless it was these ruminations, it is said, that produced some of those celebrated phrases of his, like "progressive moderates," which he first used publicly in a press conference on December 8, 1954, and "dynamic conservatism," which he unveiled in a speech before the finance committee of the Republican National Committee, in Washington, on February 17, 1955.

("Dynamic conservatism" was a reversal of the phrase the President originally had in mind. In his office before the speech to the finance committee luncheon he was telling Gabriel Hauge, his Administrative Assistant for economic affairs, that he was going to talk about his conception of "conservative dynamism." Hauge suggested that the expression would have a better ring to it if it was turned around, and the President took his advice. He told the committee:

(I have said we were "progressive moderates." Right at the moment I rather favor the term "dynamic conservatism." I believe we should be conservative. I believe we should conserve on everything that is basic to our system. We should be dynamic in applying it to the problems of the day so that all 165,000,000 Americans will profit from it.)

The more the President pondered the idea of a new party the more he was forced into the realization that it was not the solution to the problem. His own experience in France, with her paralyzing multiplicity of splinter parties, had aroused him to the dangers attending the fragmentation of a great political party. He thought of this now, as he had in the campaign when he had warned in speeches in Wheeling, West Virginia, and Portland, Oregon, against the destruction of the two-party system.

His mind turned moreover to the failure of previous third-party movements in American history, such as those led by Theodore Roosevelt, one of his heroes, and Robert M. La Follette, Sr., and he realized, when he thought it over, that in the United States third parties have tended to lose their focus after the death of their founders. He brought up the case of the Progressive Party which

Roosevelt headed in the Bull Moose campaign of 1912 as an example of how third parties, even though they may serve a useful purpose at the time, are unable to survive.

Thus the idea never progressed beyond the President's thinking and private conversations. After Congress adjourned and the bickering of that first session died away for a while, Eisenhower took a new and calm look at what he was doing and where he was headed. On balance he came to the conclusion that his best hope of attaining his goals was to persevere in trying to give the Republican Party a new viewpoint and a new complexion. He hoped that with patience on his part and through the logic of events and the influx of younger Republicans devoted to his philosophy he could to a considerable extent modernize and unify the party.

The history of his ensuing years in the White House is in part a reflection of his efforts to bring into the ascendancy in the Republican Party a more progressive philosophy and spirit than had dominated it when he took office.

CHAPTER 11

Civil Rights: A High Tide

*The Negro Problem Overlooked in the Rush of the Early Months –
Eisenhower Gets a Jolt – Powell's Telegram – The White House Acts in
a Hurry – Powell Cooperates – More Racial Barriers Collapse – The President's Committee on Government Contracts – Chief Justice Warren
and the School Segregation Case*

After Congress adjourned, the President on the eve of his departure for Denver made a broadcast reviewing in the best light he could the record of the session. Commenting on his speech in an editorial on August 8, the Washington *Post* said, "Perhaps the weakest of the four major areas of action cited by the President is equality of opportunity, on which relatively little has been done."

Maxwell Rabb showed Eisenhower the editorial.

"Mr. President," he said, "someday they will eat their words."

"We'll see," the President replied.

When the administration took office, it was plunged into the whirlpool of Korea, China, the budget, the "new look," the Bricker amendment, relations with the right wing in Congress and a hundred and one other things. Somehow no one gave much thought to the special problems of the Negro, and practically nothing was done about this politically very sensitive matter. True, the President had shown a characteristic spirit of friendliness toward Negroes. From time to time distinguished members of their race were invited to his stag dinners. Mrs. Lois Lippman, of Boston, became, so far as anyone can remember, the first Negro to be appointed to the White House secretarial staff, being assigned first to Adams's office and later to Rockefeller's and others'. (In 1955 E. Frederic Morrow was appointed an administrative officer and thereby became, it appears, the first Negro member of the White House staff in history.) Also in the early months some minor steps were taken, as when the President, after being informed at a press conference on March 19 that segregated schools were still being conducted on some Army posts, jogged the Defense Department to correct the situation. While opposed to compulsory measures, like a Fair Employment Practices Commission, he was committed to the principle that Federal funds should not be spent in support of segregated facilities or institutions.

On the whole, however, the matter of civil rights was let slide in the early months of the administration. Unlike Roosevelt and Truman, Eisenhower had deliberately refrained from assigning anyone on his staff to a more or less full-time job of attending to the problems of minority groups. He wanted these handled as they came along through the regular functioning of the White House staff and not as a special category of political affairs.

At press conferences during the spring Alice A. Dunnigan, a reporter for The Associated Negro Press, took to asking Eisenhower what was happening to the President's Committee on Government Contract Compliance, a group which had been formed by Truman to try to eliminate discrimination from the employment practices of companies holding contracts with the government. Eisenhower had paid scant attention to this committee until her questions began to arouse his curiosity. But with Congress in session, no one was disposed to give any heed to breathing new life into the committee.

This then was about where matters stood on civil rights when, on June 4, copies of the Washington *Evening Star* arrived at the White House with a headline on the front page reading:

HOBBY NOTE FLOUTS
SEGREGATION ORDER,
POWELL CHARGES

No other newspaper story at the time ever caused such commotion in the White House so quickly. The *Star* story shocked the President when it was shown to him, and his vehement reaction shocked his staff, and things began to happen in a hurry.

The story was based on an open telegram which had been sent to

Eisenhower by Representative Adam Clayton Powell, Jr., Democrat, of New York, a Negro who represents a district in Harlem. The telegram began: "The hour has arrived for you to decisively assert your integrity. You cannot continue to stand between two opposite moral poles."

The essence of the communication was that while the President was proclaiming the principle of non-segregation in Federal institutions, his subordinates in the Army, Navy, Veterans Administration and the Department of Health, Education and Welfare were defying his rule in various institutions and installations under their jurisdiction.

The way Mrs. Hobby's name got into it was that Powell said he had information that she had "virtually countermanded" the President's policy on segregation in schools for children on Army posts, which are paid for by the Department of Health, Education and Welfare. Summing up this and other allegations, Powell said:

> This is insubordination. This is not support of you as the Commander in Chief and the President of the United States. This detracts from the dignity, integrity and power of your office. I have faith in you as a man of good insight, decent instincts, and a strong moral character. I beg of you to assert these noble qualities. The free world is looking to you as its last hope. Strong leadership is imperative now; tomorrow may be too late. For fear that this might not reach you, may I have the courtesy of a personal reply?

The President was put out that Powell should have addressed a public complaint of this character to him before taking up the matter in a private communication. But beyond this he was upset by the contents and the charges. Sherman Adams got on the telephone to Mrs. Hobby and Wilson and Vice-Admiral Joel T. Boone (ret.), chief medical officer of the Veterans Administration. Meanwhile in the excitement Presidential aides started drafting letters of reply. One of the half-dozen drafts indignantly accused Powell of utter falsehood. Happily, this draft was discarded. It would have proved very embarrassing to the White House, because to his disgust Adams found out that while Powell may have overstated it, he had a case. Procrastination, indecision and lack of enthusiasm no doubt were retarding desegregation of a number of Federal hospitals, schools and Navy yards.

There was no lack of awareness in the White House now that the administration had been caught off balance on an issue that might very well be exploited by the Democrats, whose supply of issues was rather low at the time. Adams, anxious to straighten it out quickly, called in Rabb—this was while Rabb was still his assistant and before he had become Secretary to the Cabinet—and asked him to see what could be done not only to ward off further criticism but to put into practice the principles which the President had espoused.

Rabb, formerly an assistant to Lodge when Lodge was a Senator, knew his way around the Capitol, and he decided to go to see Powell.

"Adam," he said, addressing the Congressman by his first name, "I'm disappointed in you."

Rabb is a man with an utterly inoffensive manner, and he proceeded as only such a person could have to take Powell to task for what he had done.

Here, he told him, were two men—Powell, who runs stronger than his own party in his district, and Eisenhower, who runs stronger than the Republican Party in the country. Think, he exclaimed, what two such men working together could do for the underdog! But instead of that, he lamented, what had Powell done but blow things sky-high. Perhaps it was true, he conceded, that the administration had not done all that it might have about civil rights. But then, he explained, it had been in power only a few terribly busy months, and, regardless of the shortcomings of others, the President was a man of unquestioned intentions in this matter.

"I'm disappointed in you, Adam," Rabb said solemnly.

"Okay, Max, you win," Powell said. "What do you want me to do?"

Rabb replied that he wanted Powell to give the White House a chance to deal with his complaints. He warned him that this would take a little time and that it could not be done in an atmosphere of recrimination. Powell agreed. Rabb then said that the President would write Powell a conciliatory letter, and he asked if the Congressman would reply in the same spirit. Powell said that he would.

Rabb returned to the White House and started to work on a draft. In its final form this Presidential letter was a model of political artful-dodging. Replying to Powell's resounding accusations, it began:

I have your telegram and I want you to know that I appreciate your kind expression of confidence that I will carry out every pledge I have made with regard to segregation.

The President noted in passing that Powell had "indicated that there is some evidence that the policy I am pursuing against the impairment of equality through segregation has been obstructed in some agencies of the Government." He continued:

I have made inquiries of the officials to whom you refer and learn that they are pursuing the purpose of eliminating segregation in federally controlled and supported institutions.

We have not taken and we shall not take a single backward step. There must be no second-class citizens in this country.

True to his word, Powell answered in a letter beginning:

Your letter . . . completely justified my confidence in you. . . . The most significant statement in your letter, and one which makes it a Magna Carta for minorities and a second Emancipation Proclamation is: "We have not taken and we shall not take a single backward step. There must be no second-class citizens in this country."

Some people in the White House began to breathe a little easier when they read about their Magna Carta and second Emancipation Proclamation.

The problem nevertheless was tackled with conscientiousness and vigor. Rabb was given responsibility for it, and one of his first acts was to deal with the charges in Powell's telegram that segregation was continuing at the Navy yards at Charleston and Norfolk.

Robert B. Anderson, who later became Deputy Secretary of Defense, was then Secretary of the Navy, and Rabb called him and asked if he could drop around to see him. Rabb was not well acquainted with Anderson at the time, but he knew he was a Texan and, therefore, was not altogether sure how he would receive this particular complaint. When Rabb had laid the case before him, Anderson picked up a telephone and summoned Charles S. Thomas, who was then Under Secretary and later Secretary of the Navy, and Rear Admiral George A. Holderness, Jr., chief of the Office of Industrial Relations in the Navy.

"Gentlemen," said Anderson, as his words have since been recalled, "we have a very serious problem. Our directive is to clear out segregation where Federal money is involved."

Without inquiring what other conflicting engagements the two might have had, he requested them to go immediately, Thomas to Norfolk and Holderness to Charleston, to take a look at conditions and give him a report.

Only a couple of days elapsed before Anderson called Rabb and said that the Navy could put an end to segregation at both yards. The ingenuity with which it was done sent the President into an outpouring of praise for Anderson, who was becoming one of his associates whom he most admired. For example, on a weekend when not many sailors were around, the COLORED and WHITE signs over drinking fountains suddenly disappeared and were not replaced. In buildings where similar signs were inscribed over entrances to lavatories the signs themselves were not obliterated. That would have been too obvious. Instead entire corridors were repainted and the signs never restored. Desegregation of the mess halls was more difficult, but gradually it was accomplished.

Segregation was soon abolished in all Navy bases where it was still practiced. Indeed in the months to come the desegregation of all the armed forces, which had begun in the Truman administration, was for all practical purposes completed.

Meanwhile in the White House consideration was given to revitalizing the Committee on Government Contract Compliance. In the end it was decided that an entirely new group with a new name, new authority and a new membership of fourteen representing both the government and the public should be formed. Adams and Rabb worked up a tentative list, and the President went over it with great care. He noticed that the list contained no Southerner and thought that this was a mistake. After mentioning a couple of names, he decided on John Minor Wisdom, a New Orleans attorney and the Republican National Committeeman from Louisiana.

To give the group, which is called the President's Committee on Government Contracts, the maximum prestige Eisenhower named the Vice-President of the United States as its chairman. The vice-chairman was J. Ernest Wilkins, a Chicago attorney, who was later appointed by the President as Assistant Secretary of Labor, the first Negro ever to hold a sub-Cabinet post. (On August 18, 1954, Wilkins became the first member of his race ever to attend a meeting of the Cabinet when he substituted for Secretary Mitchell.)

Along with Wisdom the original list of public members included Reuther, Meany, John A. Roosevelt, son of the late President; Mrs. Helen Rogers Reid, director of the Herald Tribune; John L. McCaffrey, president of the International Harvester Company, and Fred Lazarus, Jr., president of the American Retail Federation.

The committee scored some noteworthy successes in the city of Washington. It persuaded the Capital Transit Company to end its ban on Negro bus drivers and streetcar operators. It also prevailed upon the Chesapeake & Potomac Telephone Company to drop segregation in its business offices. Through its efforts some four hundred Negroes were employed in the Savannah River plant of the Atomic Energy Commission in South Carolina.

In the meantime pressures being exerted from the White House brought great changes in customs in Washington. With the President's approval the Department of Justice filed a strong brief in the Thompson restaurant case, in which the Supreme Court ruled unanimously that restaurants may not draw the color line. This opened the doors of Washington eating places to Negroes. The hotels in the capital were persuaded to accept Negro guests, and the White House, working quietly through local managers and large distributors, swept away the racial barriers in the city's theaters. Segregation was ended also in the city's fire department and other municipal agencies.

Later the Department of Justice filed briefs in the Interstate Commerce Commission cases which resulted in sweeping decrees banning segregation on interstate trains and buses and in terminals. As for the conditions Powell had complained of, every school on military posts was desegregated, and segregation was ended in the forty-seven institutions of the Veterans Administration in which it had been practiced.

In the spring of 1955 the President and Powell had differences over an antidiscrimination amendment which Powell wished to write into the military reserve bill. The President thought that the issue was extraneous to the central question of adequate military reserves and that the amendment was not the proper way to deal with the broad problem of racial relations. Powell sharply criticized the President's position on this, but he told the House in a speech, "No one has done more than the present Chief Executive in the field of civil rights."

The great milestone in this field during the Eisenhower administration, however, was erected not by the executive but by the judicial branch of the government when the Supreme Court on May 17, 1954, ruled unanimously that racial segregation in the public schools of the United States was unconstitutional. In November, 1953, Brownell, acting on behalf of the administration as a friend of the court, filed a strong brief, contending that the Fourteenth Amendment prohibited racial segregation in the public schools and that the Supreme Court had the power to settle the issue. Assistant Attorney General J. Lee Rankin argued the point before the court.

Chief Justice Warren, who read the historic decision, had been nominated by the President following the death of Chief Justice Vinson on September 8, 1953. The appointment was the most important Eisenhower has made, and it was one to which he gave a great deal of thought. He considered a number of persons in and out of the judiciary. One morning, for instance, Dulles came into his office for an appointment and found him looking over a paper with some names on it.

"I see you're running for Chief Justice," the President said as Dulles sat down.

"What?" Dulles exclaimed.

"That's what it says here," the President replied.

The Secretary of State protested that he was doing what he had always wanted to do and what he had been trained for and that he did not wish to do anything else. The President knew this very well, of course; he has always seemed impressed by the background Dulles brought to his post.

"Foster has been studying to be Secretary of State since he was five years old," he once told some friends.

Eisenhower has recommended to associates that for a penetrating insight into Soviet philosophy they ought to have Dulles give them a twenty-minute summary of Stalin's *Problems of Leninism*, something the President once listened to with admiration.

A number of considerations entered into the President's choice of Warren. He was a distinguished and popular Republican, who had been nominated by his party for Vice-President in 1948. Personally the President liked him and felt he possessed an integrity of character that was especially conspicuous in contrast to some of the shoddy ethics that had been on display in Washington. He had had a long and successful public career, having thrice been elected Governor, and at sixty-two, which Eisenhower considered an appropriate age for a new Chief Justice, was in good health. In particular the President was attracted by Warren's positions on certain questions of law and government. Among these, for example, were his opposition to Roosevelt's "court-packing" proposal, his indorsement of the Supreme Court decision in 1952 holding that Truman had exceeded his powers in seizing the strike-threatened steel industry, and his advocacy of state rather than Federal jurisdiction of the offshore oil lands.

The day after the court handed down its decision, the President summoned the Commissioners of the District of Columbia to the White House and told them he hoped that Washington would be a model for the rest of the country in integrating Negro and white children in the public schools. Many who are familiar with what has been done believe that his wish has been well fulfilled.

On April 22, 1955, a year and a half after the President and Rabb had discussed the *Post* editorial criticizing the administration's progress in civil rights, the same paper ran another editorial which made Rabb's prediction come true. Entitled "Discrimination on the Run," the editorial said in part:

Some months back, in reviewing editorially the initial performance of the Eisenhower Administration, this newspaper observed that progress in curbing racial discrimination in public and quasi-public facilities had been disappointing. We are now happy to acknowledge that it has become one of the strongest features of the Eisenhower Administration —and the community and the country are healthier for it.

CHAPTER 12

Storm Signals:
Economic and Political

First Signs of An Economic "Readjustment" – Farm Prices Decline – The President on the Soviet H-Bomb – A Sweeping Proposal for Cutting Government Employment – Norman Thomas's Call on Eisenhower – The Housing and Social Security Extension Programs Take Shape – The Brownell-Truman-Harry Dexter White Affair

On September 19, 1953, the President flew back to Washington from his vacation in Colorado in better health and higher spirits than he had known in months. An eventful period was opening for him.

The atoms-for-peace plan, which he was to announce in a speech to the U.N. General Assembly in December, was finally taking form. In the White House and the government departments the elaborate legislative program to which the President pridefully attached immense importance, was being developed. This was the period also that produced one of the greatest political explosions of Eisenhower's years in office—to be taken up later in this chapter. It was set off by the Attorney General when he told the Executives Club of Chicago in November that the former President of the United States had knowingly promoted "a Russian spy" in the person of Harry Dexter White.

That same fall Eisenhower made three trips out of the country—to Mexico, Ottawa and finally Bermuda for his meeting with Sir

Winston and Premier Joseph Laniel of France. In these months also the President delivered major speeches in New Orleans, Atlantic City, Boston, Kansas City and Hershey, Pennsylvania. In Hershey the Republicans staged a huge birthday party for him, at which he and Mrs. Eisenhower rode in a horse and cart through an arena lighted by thousands of candles. A record of its kind was established during the trip to Boston. On the way the President dropped in at the Eastern States Exposition in West Springfield, Massachusetts, for lunch. A harp ensemble in a tent where the tables were set struck up the traditional "Hail to the Chief," but started it too soon and, as I remember, repeated it twenty times without a stop before the President finally strode in beaming and waving. To the aching ears of the luncheon guests this was the ultimate proof that "Hail to the Chief" was not written for harp.

Distressing symptoms were appearing in many parts of the economy that fall. The drought in the Southwest was having such a serious effect on the livestock industry that the President told the Cabinet on September 25, "If this keeps up, we will soon be grazing cattle on the White House lawn."

Of much greater moment was that which Dr. Arthur F. Burns, chairman of the President's Council of Economic Advisers, had to tell the Cabinet that same day. He reported that a "readjustment" might be on the way if certain indicators meant what they seemed to mean. This was the warning signal of the recession. Burns mentioned: 1. A decline in the stock market, 2. An increase in business failures, 3. A dropping-off in the volume of orders for durable goods, 4. A decline in residential building, 5. A drop in the average length of the work week, 6. Sagging farm prices, and 7. Evidences of excessive inventories.

The problem of falling farm income, which was to dog Eisenhower's footsteps through these years as President, was pressing at an inconvenient time for the Republicans because of several elections scheduled for that fall. In a special election on October 13, for example, the Democrats for the first time in history captured the Congressional seat in the ninth District of Wisconsin, a victory which the defeated Republican candidate ascribed to dissatisfaction over the administration's farm policies.

Two days later the President addressed the Future Farmers of America in Kansas City on the way to Mexico to dedicate Falcon Dam on the Rio Grande River. Eisenhower and his associates got into something of a tug of war over the speech. The President wanted to deliver a purely inspirational type of address to the young farmers. That was what youths would be most interested in, he argued. Benson and members of the White House staff disagreed. They wanted the President to take advantage of this appearance in the middle of the farm belt to put in a strong word for the administration's plans for helping the farmer. The President was stubborn, but they finally persuaded him that young men and women on the farm have a lively interest in government agricultural policies. So he pitched in and defended Benson against his critics and told the Future Farmers that he was calling a White House conference to work out a new program for submission to the next Congress. He made it very emphatic that "the price-support principle must be a part of any future farm program."

The fall of 1953 was the time, too, when the President had to begin living with the realization that the Soviet Union had at last produced a hydrogen bomb. As he told the national assembly of the United Church Women in Atlantic City on October 9, America's "unique physical security has almost totally disappeared before the long-range bomber and the destructive power of a single bomb." Thus, he said, "we are forced to concentrate on building such stores of armaments as can deter . . . attack."

The Atomic Energy Commission had detected an explosion in the U.S.S.R. on August 12 which involved both fission and thermonuclear reactions similar to those in early American H-bomb tests. The Soviet announcement called it "one of a variety of hydrogen bombs." Early in October various high officials of the administration, including Wilson and Arthur Flemming, made statements appraising the new development in such conflicting terms that the President had to step in and order all government officials to refrain from comment on Soviet nuclear capabilities until their statements had been checked by Rear Admiral Lewis L. Strauss (ret.), chairman of the Atomic Energy Commission. On October 8 the President himself read a statement at his press conference, saying:

. . . our government announced that the Soviet produced an atomic explosion in 1949 and two subsequent explosions in 1951. In August of this year we learned through intelligence channels of a Soviet test of an atomic device in which some part of the explosive force was derived from thermonuclear reaction, that is to say, what is popularly known as the H-bomb. . . .

The development did not come as a surprise. We had always estimated that it was within the scientific and technical capabilities of the Soviets to reach this point, and we have been on notice for some years that their own ingenuity has had the material assistance of what they learned of our program through espionage.

The Soviets now possess a stockpile of atomic weapons of conventional types, and we must furthermore conclude that the powerful explosion of August 12 last was produced by a weapon or the forerunner of a weapon of power far in excess of the conventional types.

We, therefore, conclude that the Soviets have the capability of atomic attack on us, and such capability will increase with the passage of time.

Now a word as to our own situation. We do not intend to disclose the details of our strength in atomic weapons of any sort, but it is large and increasing steadily. We have in our arsenals a number of kinds of weapons suited to the special needs of the Army, Navy and Air Force for the specific tasks assigned to each service.

It is my hope, my earnest prayer, that this country will never again be engaged in war. As I said in Atlantic City this week with reference to atomic energy, this titanic force must be reduced to the fruitful service of mankind. . . .

A variety of problems were discussed at meetings of the Cabinet after Eisenhower's return from Denver.

October 2, 1953

The President took note of frequent discussions in high circles of the government about the administration's deficiencies in informing the people about its program. These deficiencies, he said, might spring from the difficulty of defending "the middle road" from attack from both sides. The leaders of the administration, he felt, were left with a tendency to shy away from statements which might cause "sensationalism" in the right or the left. He read a report from Lodge on "grass roots" sentiments, indicating a great deal of criticism or misunderstanding of the administration's program. The President said that while he did not agree with several of the points, he thought the report revealed a need for emphasizing the positive side of the record.

The Cabinet was informed that some 2,500 persons had recently been let out of their jobs at the United States Information Agency. Evidently misunderstanding the reason, or being facetious, the President exclaimed, "If there were 2,500 security risks in one office, I am going to quit."

(A cut in appropriation had forced the U.S.I.A. to reduce its personnel by 2,000 and an additional 500 unfilled positions were abolished.)

Eisenhower and Nixon both emphasized the importance that should be attached to the recommendations of the Commission on Foreign Economic Policy, which was headed by Clarence B. Randall, chairman of the board of the Inland Steel Company, and which was studying the question of foreign trade.

Nixon told the members of the Cabinet that he hoped they would appreciate the strength of the protectionist element in the United States. The President said that he would be disposed to give strong support to whatever the commission might recommend the following January because it was composed of some of the best men in the country. Dulles expressed his concern that the group would not lend sufficient weight to political and diplomatic considerations. The discussion was concluded with the President's asking the Cabinet to give the commission the greatest possible support.

October 23, 1953

The Secretary of State gave a report on the recent meeting of the Big Three Foreign Ministers in London. He said that the course of the war in Indo-China had created a serious danger for the Laniel government in France. Dulles told the Cabinet that the recent American decision to suspend economic aid to Israel resulted not from the new rash of border incidents but from Israeli intransigence in defying a U.N. order to halt work on a hydroelectric project on the Jordan River. (The United States resumed assistance on October 28 after Israel agreed to stop the work.)

Benson reviewed the farm situation. His picture was a hopeful one. He said that the decline in farm prices which had been in progress for two years and the decline in net farm income both seemed to be leveling out, with the result that the farm situation was now nearing stabilization. He said that estimates for the next year were that spending by consumers would remain steady, that exports would continue at about the current volume, that farm income would probably be only slightly below the current level and that cattle prices would remain steady and even recover somewhat. The hardest problem might be that presented by dairy products, he said.

Benson had placed before the Cabinet a draft of a public statement on the farm situation to be issued a few days hence. After listening to the Secretary's oral presentation, however, the President, as well as Brownell, Dulles and Lodge, said that the public statement had too pessimistic a tone. They felt that it should be rewritten to correspond more closely with the picture painted by Benson. The President requested Benson to consult Milton Eisenhower before issuing it.

(The President has often looked to his brother for advice on farm problems. Dr. Eisenhower was an assistant to the Secretary of Agriculture in the Coolidge administration and was the information director of the Department of Agriculture from 1928 on through the New Deal years. He was Land Use Co-ordinator from 1937 to 1942 and then, in 1943, became president of Kansas State College in the heart of the farm belt, where he remained until he went to Penn State in 1950.

(A frequent visitor to the White House, Dr. Eisenhower is one of the President's confidants and has counseled him on other subjects beside farm problems. After his good-will tour of 1953, of course, Latin America became one of them. From the outset he has been a member of the three-man President's Advisory Committee on Government Organization, headed by Nelson Rockefeller. Eisenhower formed this group immediately after the election to advise him on reorganization of the White House staff. It has since had under consideration such problems as reorganization of government agencies, the carrying out of various recommendations of the

Hoover Commission and the Commission on Inter-Government Relations, and—after Eisenhower's heart attack—the lifting of unnecessary burdens from the President.)

On the subject of government employees, Deputy Secretary of Defense Kyes came up with a rather drastic proposal. He said that it was necessary for every department to be given authority to discharge 10 per cent of its personnel without regard to existing regulations so that inefficient employees could be rooted out. He argued that the previous twenty years of Democratic rule had provided an opportunity for overrating employees on efficiency.

Eisenhower squelched this. Defending the sanctity of the Civil Service, he said it would be highly undesirable to create a situation in which the whole body of government employees would get the jitters with every change in administration. Such would be the case, he feared, if 10 per cent could be dismissed without regard to regulations.

The President warned that difficult as personnel problems might seem at the moment, the long step Kyes was suggesting would make them worse. The end, he said, did not justify the means. Kyes replied that his proposal was necessary to protect efficient government employees.

(Nothing ever came of his suggestion.)

October 30, 1953

Eisenhower reported to the Cabinet upon the call that had been paid on him three days previously by Norman Thomas, six-time Socialist candidate for President. The call grew out of an exchange of correspondence in June between Thomas and Scott McLeod. McLeod said that he never would clear a Socialist for a policy-making job in the State Department. Indeed, he said, he would do all he could to remove a Socialist from such a position. Thomas did not have any expectations that a Republican administration would appoint a Socialist to a policy-making post, but he said that McLeod seemed to think that policy-making extended all the way down to office boys.

After the call on October 27 Thomas told reporters that the President had assured him that he had no doubt about the loyalty of Socialists and did not believe that they should be excluded from nonpolicy-making jobs in the government.

Eisenhower substantiated this in the Cabinet. Also he recalled that Thomas had warned about the danger of confusing Socialists with Communists and had urged that government employees should not be dismissed from nonpolicy-making jobs because of adherence to Socialist doctrines. The President told the Cabinet that Thomas had quoted a saying that was current in those days that "McCarthy runs McLeod and McLeod runs Dulles."

Dulles reminded the President that the Socialist Party platform had a plank which, he said, equated capitalism with warmongering.

The President replied that the word "Socialist" had taken on a very broad meaning and that some Socialists were in reality more conservative than some middle-of-the-roaders.

Japanese-American trade was discussed at some length. Humphrey said that unemployment in the United States might make it desirable to exclude certain Japanese products. The President said that in preference to exclusion he would have exporters and importers exercise restraint. Humphrey replied that businessmen had a tendency to take advantage of all opportunities. Perhaps that was the trouble with businessmen, the President remarked.

November 12, 1953

The President said he had decided that he should deliver the next State of the Union message personally. He put great emphasis on the necessity for presenting a program that would refute some of the criticism of the administration and would show clearly the administration's determination to look out for the needs of all Americans, especially the "little fellow" and those in distress. He said that the budget message should contain specific measures in such fields as slum clearance and small business loans so that good intentions could be translated into deeds. The administration must not be known as one which could retrench but which lacked the ability to progress in many vital areas, he told the Cabinet.

Eisenhower took note of charges that the administration was a "millionaires' corporation." (This was probably a reference to the Democratic quip when Durkin was still Secretary of Labor that the

Cabinet consisted of "nine millionaires and a plumber.") He said that in some things like farm price supports the administration had to draw back—meaning turn away from inflexible high supports. But he appealed to his associates to demonstrate unmistakably that the administration was going forward in other fields and was not trying to save money at the expense of little people. He was sick and tired, he said, of the claims of the Democrats that they were the champions of the little fellow.

Wilson said that this spirit of going forward and doing something for people was implicit in his plan for increasing military pay to reverse the decline in morale resulting from inadequate housing for service families and limitations on commissary privileges and family medical services. Eisenhower, drawing on his own experience in the Army, said that it struck him as more important to restore these "fringe benefits" than to raise military pay generally.

November 20, 1953

The Cabinet heard Mrs. Hobby outline the program for expanding Social Security coverage, which her department was preparing for submission at the next session of Congress. The discussion turned to the question of the retirement age, and Secretary Mitchell advocated getting away from an arbitrary age, such as sixty-five, as the norm. Marion B. Folsom, who was then Under Secretary of the Treasury and who was to succeed Mrs. Hobby as Secretary of Health, Education and Welfare, said that some specific age had to be used for purposes of computation but that this did not of itself imply that retirement was compulsory at that age.

The President revealed that Taft had once suggested to him that benefits should be paid to everyone who reaches the age of sixty-five. Taft felt, the President explained, that by doing it this way the program would be simpler to administer. Lodge remarked that this proposal sounded similar to the Townsend Plan.

Humphrey called the Cabinet's attention to Social Security proposals being drawn up by Representatives Dan Reed and Carl T. Curtis, Republican, of Nebraska, and said they wanted to present them to the President. Eisenhower indicated that he would be willing to listen to the Congressmen, but he made it clear that he would refer their plan to Mrs. Hobby for study. He said that he could give them no promises and particularly not the one which he expected them to ask, namely, that he would not oppose their plan.

Mrs. Hobby noted that the Reed-Curtis plan was very similar to one recently put forward by the United States Chamber of Commerce, which she characterized as a "criminal raid on the Social Security Trust Fund."

(The administration plan preserved the basic principles of the Social Security system, notably the principles that it is a contributory system and that the benefits received are related in part to individual earnings. The Chamber of Commerce recommended extending Social Security benefits to all retired workers, whether they had contributed to the program or not, and financing these benefits on a pay-as-you-go basis. It was to be assailed in Congress the following winter as a plan for opening the door for a "raid" by all currently aged persons on the Social Security Trust Fund built up by contributions from workers. Curtis described his bill as similar to this plan.)

Mrs. Hobby told the Cabinet that the Chamber of Commerce plan was politically less attractive than the administration's. Stassen remarked that he hoped the President in front of Reed and Curtis would give strong support to the administration plan and head the Congressmen off from going overboard on theirs. Mrs. Hobby interposed to say that before anyone outside the Cabinet and her department was told of her plan she wished to have a talk with Senator Eugene D. Millikin, Republican, of Colorado, the chairman of the Senate Finance Committee, which would handle the legislation. Nelson Rockefeller, who was then Under Secretary of Health, Education and Welfare, followed this up with a warning that the administration proposal faced the danger of sabotage if its details were revealed outside the Cabinet prematurely.

Mrs. Hobby summarized her program as one that had wide appeal, that was more beneficial to the aged than rival plans and that was economically sound. When she had finished, the Cabinet broke into applause for her presentation, and the President remarked that it looked as though the program was approved. He ended the meeting with a brief, vigorous statement on the necessity of presenting a progressive program. The administration must put through and maintain a moderate program, he concluded, if it was to be justified in the eyes of the people.

December 9, 1953

Albert M. Cole, Housing and Home Finance Administrator, presented the housing proposals which were being prepared for submission to Congress. The plan was in several parts and included a program of "urban renewal" for ripping down slums, rebuilding blighted areas and preventing future blight, all with the help of a broader Federal loan and grant policy and F.H.A.-insured private lending. Also it provided for more housing for low-income families through F.H.A. 100-per-cent long-term loans and some low-rent public housing to meet transitional needs. (All of these provisions would apply only after local governments had attacked their housing problems.) It also included reorganization of the F.H.A. and simplification of its procedures and measures designed to strengthen the mortagage market.

The President said that it was necessary to see to it that low-cost housing provided by the government did not degenerate into slums. Cole replied that a number of recommendations for preventing deterioration were under consideration. He said also that the program would involve little additional cost since funds already authorized were almost sufficient and could be diverted to it. Furthermore, he said, the impact of the program would depend on the initiative of local communities.

The President gave enthusiastic support to the program, which he thought was intelligent, well rounded and potentially beneficial to all parts of the country. Within limits, he said, it should not be blocked by the administration's budgetary goals. He went on to make the point that in a field like housing the Federal government must be active to get done what had to be done, but that the government's program must be intelligent. When the government was drawn into such activity, he added, it must approach it "with jaundiced eye and a good microscope."

On the understanding that further work was necessary on parts of the program dealing with the secondary mortgage market, the procedure for determining interest rates and the number of public housing units, the Cabinet gave its general approval.

December 15, 1953

The Cabinet discussed proposed legislation to legalize as evidence in Federal courts information obtained by wire-tapping and to empower the Attorney General to grant immunity to witnesses. These were aspects of the program the administration was preparing for dealing with subversives. The President mentioned the British Official Secrets Act. He suggested that a similar law might be desirable in the United States, but felt that the climate of American opinion at the time ruled out any attempt to put through such legislation. (The very sweeping British law, for example, makes newspapers liable to prosecution for publication of confidential information. Government employees also are liable if they divulge such information.)

Brownell told the Cabinet that the Truman administration had left the Justice Department files in chaos. During a summer clean-up, he said, the Republicans had come across some twenty thousand documents that had never even been filed. These documents, according to the Attorney General, contained much information that might result in new prosecutions.

The Vice-President started a discussion of outlawing the Communist Party in the United States by mentioning that Australia had such a law. Walter Bedell Smith strongly objected to the idea, warning that to outlaw the party would be to drive it underground. Lodge commented that there was some advantage to the United States in being able to demonstrate to the world that it considered itself strong enough to tolerate the existence of a Communist Party.

Secretary Mitchell read a draft of a proposed Presidential message to Congress in January on amendment of the Taft-Hartley Act.

(The administration suggested a variety of changes in the act, some of which had been proposed by Taft. The suggested amendments, for example, would have liberalized restrictions against secondary boycotts and given an employee an opportunity to vote by secret ballot under government auspices "when he is called on strike." There was an amendment to extend the requirement that union officials sign non-Communist affidavits to cover employers also, or else drop the provision entirely if Congress passed substitute legislation dealing with Communist infiltration. There was also an amendment authorizing fact-finding boards appointed under the national emergency provisions of the act to make recommendations at the request of the President.)

In connection with the last the President asked Mitchell if this was consistent with his—Eisenhower's—efforts to keep the White House out of labor-management disputes to the greatest possible extent. Mitchell replied that fact-finding board recommendations would be made to the White House only in case of a national emergency, in which, the Secretary added, the White House inevitably would have to act anyhow.

The President remarked upon the difficulty of finding any standard government procedure that would be effective in a serious nation-wide strike. He said he did not believe that the country could tolerate a general transportation strike, and he recalled the troubles that had faced Truman in the steel strike of 1952.

In answer to another question by the President, Mitchell said that most of the amendments were designed to meet the objections of labor and that many of them were approved by labor and management.

Lodge said that personally he preferred to have issues such as Taft-Hartley revision, universal military training and excise taxes deferred until 1955. (There was no national election in 1955.) However, he added, if action was required in 1954, he would like to see the Taft-Hartley amendments postponed as long as possible to avoid deadlock. Mitchell said that the question was bound to arise early in the new session in any event, whereupon Lodge suggested that the President's involvement in it should be limited. Mitchell and Adams both pointed out that the President in his messages to the A.F.L. and C.I.O. conventions had given labor reason to expect him to propose amendments. The President leaned toward a suggestion that he treat the subject in very general terms in his State of the Union message in January and allow detailed recommendations to come along later. (That is what was done. Actually, the President played a very slight role in the shaping of the proposed Taft-Hartley amendments.)

The Cabinet approved in principle the substance of the draft but left open for further discussion the manner of submission of the message.

In the meeting of the Cabinet on November 12 the President brought up the matter of the Truman-Brownell-Harry Dexter White controversy, which by then had Democrats and Republicans going at each other with a fury.

From the outset of his term Eisenhower had sought to subdue the conflicts and end the bitterness which had inflamed the American scene for so long and which were causing serious divisions among the people of the United States.

At the second Cabinet meeting on January 30, 1953, he had told his colleagues that he wanted to stay out of controversies concerning the Truman administration and concentrate instead on planning and working to put across constructive programs. There would be times, as in his first State of the Union message, he said, when he would have to refer to problems inherited from the Democratic administration, but he would do so to clarify situations rather than to stir controversy or be vindictive.

At his first Presidential press conference he refused to engage in a dispute with Adlai Stevenson over the latter's statement that the new administration might become the Big Deal because of the predominance of businessmen. His second press conference found him shunning a chance to criticize Truman and Roosevelt, respectively, for the Potsdam and Yalta agreements.

Consistently he has refused to denounce in public either his Democratic or Republican critics—"engage in personalities" is the way he invariably puts it—or publicly to impute false motives to others. Some of his aides once brought him a draft of a Presidential message to Congress which one of them had prepared, containing a number of adjectives implying criticism of Congressional motives. Eisenhower took a pen and crossed out each of these words. Then, removing his glasses and pointing them at his assistants, he said, "Look here, you and I can argue issues all day and it won't affect our friendship, but the minute I question your motives you will never forgive me." This has been a guiding principle of his public utterances.

Never has he taken out after any party or class in the way, for example, that Roosevelt excoriated the "economic royalists" of big business, and he was quick to proclaim his belief in the loyalty of Democrats in disassociating himself from McCarthy's crack that the Roosevelt and Truman administrations represented "twenty years of treason." Eisenhower publicly counseled not only high officials of his own administration but party chieftains like Leonard Hall not to engage in extreme partisanship.

This background of conciliation and pacification, therefore, served to give the attack on Truman and, more particularly, the manner of its staging an impact that was all the more startling.

With the President's general approval the Attorney General went before the Executives Club of Chicago on November 6. He charged that when Truman promoted White from Assistant Secretary of the Treasury to Executive Director of the United States mission to the International Monetary Fund in 1946, he did so knowing that White was "a Russian spy."

Harry Dexter White was a Russian spy [Brownell declared]. He smuggled secret documents to Russian agents for transmission to Moscow. Harry Dexter White was known to be a Communist spy by the very people who appointed him to the most sensitive and most important position he ever held in government service.

Brownell said that on December 4, 1945, an F.B.I. report on the "espionage activities" of White was delivered to Truman at the White House through his military aide, Brigadier General Harry H. Vaughan. The following month nevertheless Truman nominated White to the International Monetary Fund. The F.B.I., according to Brownell, then prepared a second report on White and gave it to Vaughan on February 4, 1946, "for delivery to the President." Copies also were sent to other high officials of the Truman administration. In spite of all this, Brownell said, "the Senate Banking and Currency Committee was permitted to recommend White's appointment on February 5 in ignorance of the report" and "the Senate itself was allowed to confirm White on February 6 without . . . being informed that White was a spy."

A political slugging-match followed Brownell's speech. Stevenson called it "infamous." Democratic National Chairman Stephen A. Mitchell declared that the Republicans were "trying a former President . . . for treason before a luncheon club." Truman himself charged that Brownell had attempted to "make headlines to offset" the effect of Republican losses on November 3 in several elections, notably in New York and New Jersey.

"As soon as we found White was wrong we fired him," Truman said. This was a statement he later had to retract as incorrect—and indeed as highly at variance with Truman's ultimate explanation. White resigned from the Monetary Fund in 1947 and received a letter from Truman expressing "sincere regret and considerable reluctance" at his departure. White died in 1948.

Eisenhower and Brownell had been aware beforehand that the Attorney General's speech would cause an uproar, but they were never prepared for what came four days later. On November 10 Velde, chairman of the House Un-American Affairs Committee, issued a subpoena for the former President, which was served on him at the Waldorf Towers during a visit to New York. This action, for which no one could recall an exact precedent, drew protests from Republicans as well as Democrats. Eisenhower was surprised and upset about it. Throughout the administration it brought concern lest the subpoena arouse public sympathy for Truman and cause Brownell's attack to boomerang.

The former President refused to comply with it, however, on the ground that it violated the Constitutional separation of powers of the legislative and executive branches. Then in a nation-wide broadcast by radio and television from Kansas City he formally answered the Attorney General.

"I have been accused, in effect," he said, "of knowingly betraying the security of the United States. This charge is, of course, a falsehood, and the man who made it had every reason to know it is a falsehood."

Truman explained that he first learned of the accusations against White early in 1947 through an F.B.I. report brought him by

Vaughan and through a warning from James F. Byrnes, then Secretary of State, who also had seen the report. While the matter was
under discussion, White's nomination was confirmed by the Senate.
After consultations with members of his Cabinet, Truman said, he
decided to let the appointment take its normal course. He did so, he
explained, presenting the nub of his case, because any unusual action
might have alerted White to the F.B.I. investigation being made of
himself and others and thus imperiled it. Truman said that it was
"now evident the present administration has fully embraced, for
political advantage, McCarthyism." For this remark McCarthy
demanded and received free time from the television networks to
make a reply to Truman, which will be referred to in a later chapter.

Brownell and F.B.I. Director J. Edgar Hoover subsequently appeared before the Senate Internal Security Subcommittee and testified that Truman's decision to retain White had hampered rather
than helped the F.B.I. investigation. Hoover said that he had
never agreed to it. Brownell complained that sentences had been
lifted out of the context of his speech to make it appear that he
had implied that Truman was "disloyal." All he had meant to
indicate, he said, was "that there was an unwillingness on the part
of Mr. Truman to face the facts and a persistent delusion that
Communist espionage in high places in our government was a 'red
herring.'"

Eisenhower's press conference on November 11 was devoted
almost entirely to the case, and without doubt it was one of the
most ungentle Presidential press conferences in the history of that
institution.

Eisenhower explained that one day—Hagerty placed the date as
November 2, four days before the speech—the Attorney General
reported to him that facts were coming to light in the Justice
Department, adding up to evidence of subversive action of which
high government officials had been aware. Brownell, according to
the President, told him that during the Truman administration
derogatory information about a man named White had gone to the
White House. Then, as the President recalled it, their conversation
went like this:

Brownell: Certainly I am not going to be a party to concealing this.
Eisenhower: You have to follow your own conscience as to your duty.

That was all that Brownell told him, the President said.

"What did you understand was the purpose," a reporter asked, "of bringing information from the files of the F.B.I. before a luncheon group instead of some official body, such as a grand jury or another body of Congress . . . ?"

The President replied that he had not even considered the point. He was told merely, he said, that certain information was going to be made public.

(Hagerty said later that an advance copy of Brownell's speech had been sent to the White House but that the President did not see or approve the text. The words of the President and Hagerty thus added up to this: that the President had approved of Brownell's disclosing the facts of the White case and knew that he intended to do so, but had not specifically approved or disapproved of the Attorney General's text.)

Under questioning Eisenhower said that he never would have subpoenaed Truman.

"Mr. President," a reporter asked, "do you yourself feel that former President Truman knowingly appointed a Communist spy to high office?"

Eisenhower replied: No, it was inconceivable. He did not believe that a President would knowingly damage the United States.

For thirty minutes reporters went after the President hammer and tong on various aspects of the case and the questioning was carried out with an intensity that clearly angered him. Even among the reporters there was disagreement as to whether the press had not stepped too far into the guise of prosecuting attorney—by the manner rather than the purpose of the interrogation.

A point that occurred to me during the conference but which I never saw made afterward was this: If by some remote chance Eisenhower, after leaving office, was put in the position that Truman was then, the same reporters who pressed Eisenhower for information would be driving just as hard at his successor to get the facts which would make a case against Eisenhower stand up fairly or not at all.

The Cabinet met on November 12, the day after the press conference. The President observed that he had seen a comment in the newspapers that he was not supporting his own Attorney General. (The papers, of course, had noted the discrepancy between Brownell's charge that Truman knew White was a spy when he promoted him and Eisenhower's statement that he did not believe that his predecessor had knowingly appointed a spy.)

The President assured the Cabinet that he had conferred with Brownell before saying what he had said at the press conference. He declared that Cabinet members had extensive authority both in their own right and when they were acting for him and that he was determined to stand behind them. He reiterated that except in unusual cases, he would back up the acts of Cabinet officers with all the strength at his command.

Brownell told the Cabinet that in the controversy then raging the point should be stressed that the F.B.I. reports actually went to the White House before White was promoted. He promised to make available to the Cabinet later further information to substantiate his statements in Chicago.

The President observed that at the press conference the real point of Brownell's speech had been missed while the reporters were tending to defend the Truman administration and White. The real point, he said, was whether White was the kind of man who should have been nominated for high office.

CHAPTER 13

Candor, Wheaties, and Atoms for Peace

The Atomic Arms Race Worries Eisenhower – His Talks with Strauss – Operation Candor – The President Gets an Idea – Cutler's Memorandum on an International Pool – Strauss Draws Up a Plan – Churchill's Reaction at Bermuda to the Atomic Proposal – Eisenhower Addresses the U.N.

On a cold winter day in Moscow in the first week of December, 1953, Ambassador Bohlen received a special code message from Secretary of State Dulles, who was in Bermuda for the Big Three conference. At a glance Bohlen knew through prearrangement that the code meant that he was to call upon Molotov without delay. He was to tell the Soviet Foreign Minister that the President of the United States was going to make a serious proposal in person to the U.N. General Assembly in New York and that the proposal would mean exactly what it said. This was to be no propaganda trick.

Neither Bohlen nor Molotov knew what the President intended to say. Eisenhower himself, however, had informed Sir Winston and Laniel at the start of the conference on December 4 at the Mid-Ocean Club in Tucker's Town.

He told them that there was a chance—formal arrangements had not been completed pending his notification of his British and French colleagues—that he would address the General Assembly after leaving Bermuda. His subject, he said, would be the atom.

In preparation the speech had been treated as momentous, a pronouncement intended to echo to the farthest corners of the world. The President told Sir Winston and Laniel he would give them a draft of it for their comment.

The proposal which this speech set forth for an international pool of uranium and fissionable materials for peaceful use had a long, tortuous history whose roots went back to Eisenhower's early days in the White House.

The atomic arms race troubled the President. In the spring of 1953 he discussed it many times with Admiral Strauss, deploring the international stalemate that had existed since the failure of the Baruch inspection plan in the U.N. in 1946. The world, he lamented, was getting nowhere in its quest for disarmament and control of atomic weapons. The only progress being made was in the building of bigger and more terrible weapons. Something must be done. On that he was emphatic. But what he could do puzzled and worried him.

That same spring the President came under considerable pressure to speak frankly to the people about atomic and hydrogen weapons. Some weeks after the inauguration an advisory group, appointed during the Truman administration and headed by Dr. J. Robert Oppenheimer, who was soon to be denied access to government data as a security risk, submitted a top-secret report to Eisenhower on the destructive potentialities of these weapons. The report declared that a renewed search must be made for a way to avert the catastrophe of modern war. Essential to it was wider public discussion based upon wider understanding of the meaning of a nuclear holocaust. This coincided with demands in the press, particularly in the columns of Joseph and Stewart Alsop, that the President acquaint the people more fully with the realities of new super-weapons.

The President read the report of the Oppenheimer group and then turned it over to the National Security Council for study. Early in this study Jackson and Cutler recommended to Eisenhower that he instruct Jackson, whose broad field was cold-war strategy, to work on a candid Presidential speech about nuclear weapons. In

April the President agreed. Jackson formed an interdepartmental committee and set to work. He called the task Operation Candor.

Month after month this operation turned out speech drafts, but no one particularly liked them, and they were deplored by the President because of their preoccupation with the single, gruesome theme of human destruction. One draft, largely inspired by Radford, was a completely grim recital of statistics about atomic weapons. For example: That the growing American stockpile exceeded by many times the explosive equivalent of the total of all bombs and all shells that came from every plane and every gun in every theater of war in World War II. And that atomic bombs were then more than twenty-five times as powerful as the bomb dropped on Hiroshima. Other drafts dwelt on what we could do to the Russians and what they could to do us.

But the President did not wish to be put in a position merely of horrifying the American people or of horrifying the Russian people. He wanted to tell the world of the awful consequences of nuclear warfare, but he did not want to leave the matter at that dead end. A way must be found, he felt, to raise the speech to a plane of sober understanding, combined with hope that the atom might serve man and not destroy him.

When he went to Denver on August 8, the problem was weighing on Eisenhower's mind, and the news that the Russians had exploded an H-bomb four days later added a grave dimension to it. As he groped for some practical way of kindling international cooperation to use the atom constructively, an idea began to take root in the President's mind. On a quick trip to Washington on September 10 for Chief Justice Vinson's funeral he told Cutler about it and asked him to pass it on to Operation Candor. After leaving the President's office, Cutler dictated a memorandum, which read, in part:

The White House
September 10, 1953

For Admiral Strauss and Mr.
C. D. Jackson:
In a discussion with the President this morning . . . he suggested

that you might consider the following proposal which he did not think anyone had yet thought of:

Suppose the United States and the Soviets were each to turn over to the United Nations for peaceful uses X kilograms of fissionable material. . . .

BOBBY

This was the first injection of this idea into Operation Candor. It was also the germ of the atoms-for-peace program, which, slow though it has been in gathering momentum, is one of the most constructive, original and appealing plans that Eisenhower has put forth.

Operation Candor had pretty nearly run out of steam by the time the President's idea arrived, but Cutler's memorandum reinvigorated it. Sometime after reading it Strauss called Jackson and said, "I think we have a way to work this out"—meaning to lift the Candor speech from horror into the realm of hope. On September 17 Strauss circulated among the President, Dulles, Jackson and Radford a memo of his own, which began, "The proposal is novel." He recommended that the idea be turned over for study by an N.S.C. *ad hoc* committee on disarmament.

On September 30 Cutler wrote Strauss again, saying that the President, who was back in Washington, had read his memorandum that morning. Eisenhower approved the suggestion of having the committee make a study of it, Cutler said, and hoped that the group would have a report ready by late October. Cutler told Strauss that the President's current thinking on the subject was that the United States and the Soviet Union should make annual gifts of fissionable material to the U.N.

All the top officials involved met with the President at breakfast on October 3, and that morning the project took on not only a new direction but a new name. Candor went out the window and was replaced by Operation Wheaties, a name inspired by its breakfast origin. The problem now was to translate the President's idea into a safe and practical plan and to revise the old Candor speech to put the proposal into words that would be appealing to the peoples of the world.

Strauss set to work on the first part of the task and in October he produced an undated six-page memorandum outlining a plan.

The basic assumption must be, he wrote, that "any agreement with the Soviets would be presently unenforceable by any known means." Nevertheless, he said, it was possible that "some concrete advantages can be had from an uneasy peace instead of an atomic war" and that "these concrete advantages can be bridgeheads that may be fortified and widened with the passage of time."

The problem, his memorandum said, was to find a formula for negotiation with Russia which would promote peace by total or partial atomic disarmament. Pointing out that such a formula would have to be consistent with our national interests, Strauss went on to list certain necessary criteria and conditions, as follows:

It must be safe, i.e., independent of reliance upon continued good faith or enforcement.

It must take into account the lapse of time since the Baruch plan and the progress of Russia in the atomic area meanwhile.

It must allow for the fact that absolute accountability for all fissionable material produced, down to the last kilogram, is impossible for either country, so that inspection cannot eliminate the possibility that weapons would to some extent be reserved.

It should avoid the issue of any sacrifice of sovereignty at this time by any requirement of international ownership, control, or operation of facilities within either country.

It should be attractive to other nations (the atomic "have nots") to the extent that it involves their self-interest, consequently enlists their sympathy and support, and will outrage them if rejected.

It should accord with the situation which assigns almost equal probability to the likelihood either that:

(1) Russia plans to attack us when she has reached some predetermined point in her armament; or

(2) That Russia is following the Stalin policy of adventitious absorption of pieces of geography while awaiting our economic collapse; or

(3) That Russia actually fears attack by us; or

(4) That Russia is substantially planless and that, like her attack on Finland and the Berlin blockade, her future actions will be similar improvisations; or

(5) A combination of any of these.

Then he outlined the plan, the underlying philosophy of which was "that with present conditions of mutual distrust, no sweeping, complete disarmament plan appears feasible and that the best hope lies in a gradual approach in which the goal is neared by stages."

The memorandum continued:

A PLAN—Recognizing that the possession and continued production of fissionable material and atomic weapons constitutes a threat to world peace, the United States proposes:

(a) That on ——, and at monthly intervals thereafter, each government shall deliver fissionable material to be defined as normal uranium and plutonium and in the amount of —— kilograms of each to a third party as described below. No disclosures need be required of either government at the outset as to the size of the total stockpile from which delivery is made. The delivery will be made in the form of metal or salt for convenient transportation.

(b) Delivery will be taken by the third party, an international body to be formed for the purpose, on which both the United States and the U.S.S.R. will have representation. The body will be called "The World Atomic Power Administration" or other suitable title. It will be composed predominately of neutral nations. It will have several functions. Among them:

(1) To receive and store the fissionable material.

(2) To treat it . . . to prevent its sudden seizure subsequently.

(3) To be the administrative channel through which the material in proper form is allocated to power uses throughout the world.

While it was to undergo many modifications, the proposal was now in clear and definite form. A copy of Strauss's memorandum was given to Jackson to work into the Wheaties speech, which went through some eleven drafts, including the one finally delivered by the President.

Taking form along with the speech was the idea that the President should deliver it before the U.N. General Assembly. Among others, Lodge discussed this with Eisenhower. He brought it up on the train on the way to Ottawa for Eisenhower's state visit of November 13 and 14, and the President said that the suggestion suited him very well. Some time later it was agreed that Lodge would arrange with Dag Hammarskjold, U.N. Secretary General, for the invitation to the President. Since the British and the French were not aware of the President's plans, however, it was decided that the invitation should be held up until Eisenhower had spoken to them at Bermuda.

The first to read it after the President got to Tucker's Town was Eden. He liked it and gave it to Sir Winston, who, in turn, passed it to Lord Cherwell, whom he had brought to Bermuda as his scientific adviser. Strauss had accompanied Eisenhower, and the President asked him to give Cherwell the necessary technical details about the proposed atomic pool so that the British scientist could make a report to Sir Winston. The Americans were somewhat apprehensive that Cherwell would object to the proposal, but he did not, though he felt it would have little chance of acceptance.

After studying a typed report from Cherwell, Sir Winston sent a personal note to the President praising the speech and venturing the hope that it would help ease international tensions and strike a note of encouragement throughout the world. He objected to two parts of the speech.

One was a reference, carried over from an earlier draft, to the "obsolete, colonial mold" in Southeast Asia. After reading the letter the President agreed to have it stricken.

The other was a passage, also a remnant of an earlier draft, to the effect that American forces in Europe were equipped with atomic weapons ready to be hurled at enemy forces in event of aggression. Sir Winston thought this statement was too belligerent for a speech of its kind.

"Winston doesn't like that," the President told Jackson.

"I think he is right," Jackson replied.

This passage also was deleted. These changes thus were the sum of Churchill's influence upon the speech. It was true, however, that while praising it as he did in his letter, he had doubts about the wisdom of the President's delivering it immediately after leaving Bermuda. He felt with good reason that the publicity would divert attention from the decision at Bermuda to accept a Russian proposal for a Big Four Foreign Ministers' conference in Berlin in January.

Careful preparations had been made to try to impress upon the Soviets the sincerity of the President's proposal. Since the Russians customarily deliver speeches for propaganda and make their serious offers in private, American officials were concerned that they would apply this standard to Eisenhower's speech. Before leaving Washington, therefore, Dulles had made arrangements with Bohlen to call on Molotov when notified by code.

The message was flashed to Bohlen from Bermuda after Churchill's letter. Bohlen cabled back asking if he could be told what the President was going to talk about so that he would not have to be too cryptic with Molotov. The group in Bermuda decided against this and Bohlen had to go to Molotov without it.

With Hammarskjold's invitation in hand, the President took off from Bermuda on the morning of December 8. The speech was still not in final form, and on that memorable flight to New York the passengers aboard the *Columbine* worked harder than the propellers. Immediately after the take-off Dulles, Strauss, Jackson and Hagerty gathered in the President's cabin and went over the speech line by line, reading, editing, rewriting, polishing. As each page was finished, it was handed to Marie McCrum, Jackson's secretary, who hurried forward and read it aloud, crouched between Mrs. Ann C. Whitman, the President's personal secretary, who was batting it out in the jumbo type Eisenhower uses for reading a speech, and Mary Caffrey, Hagerty's secretary, who was typing on stencils. One by one, as they were ready, the stencils were rushed to the rear luggage compartment, where Army Staff Sergeant Joseph Giordano cranked them out by hand on a duplicating machine. Once when Dulles wandered into the compartment where the secretaries were working, Mrs. Whitman shooed him out, saying, "You can't sit here, Mr. Secretary. We're busy."

When all the pages were assembled, the Secretary of State and the rest of the high officials of the United States who were aboard pitched in and stapled them together. The job was completed at about the moment the *Columbine* soared over LaGuardia Field.

Eisenhower's televised appearance before the General Assembly that afternoon was impressive, undoubtedly one of his best public performances as President. The first part of his speech was the old Operation Candor business about the annihilating power of nuclear weapons, coupled with a warning that "should such an atomic attack be launched against the United States, our reactions would be swift and resolute." Halfway through, the speech began to shade into a more hopeful tone, and this grew steadily stronger until the President reached his climax.

I therefore [he said] make the following proposals:

The Governments principally involved, to the extent permitted by elementary prudence, to begin now and continue to make joint contributions from their stockpiles of normal uranium and fissionable materials to an International Atomic Energy Agency. We would expect that such an agency would be set up under the aegis of the United Nations. . . .

Undoubtedly initial and early contributions to this plan would be small in quantity. However, the proposal has the great virtue that it can be undertaken without the irritations and mutual suspicions incident to any attempt to set up a completely acceptable system of world-wide inspection and control. . . .

The more important responsibility of this Atomic Energy Agency would be to devise methods whereby this fissionable material would be allocated to serve the peaceful pursuits of mankind. Experts would be mobilized to apply atomic energy to the needs of agriculture, medicine and other peaceful activities. A special purpose would be to provide abundant electrical energy in the power-starved areas of the world. Thus the contributing powers would be dedicating some of their strength to serve the needs rather than the fears of mankind.

The United States would be more than willing—it would be proud to take up with others "principally involved" the development of plans whereby such peaceful use of atomic energy would be expedited.

Of those "principally involved" the Soviet Union must, of course, be one.

When he concluded, pledging that the United States would "devote its entire heart and mind to find the way by which the miraculous inventiveness of man shall not be dedicated to his death, but consecrated to his life," even the delegates from the Communist countries applauded. The late Andrei Y. Vishinsky, Soviet Deputy Foreign Minister, called the speech "important"—a verdict that was echoed in much more enthusiastic terms around the world.

The idea blazed, then sputtered, at home and abroad. The Russians fished for facts in secret talks in Washington and again in

Berlin during the Big Four Foreign Ministers' meeting in January, 1954, but then turned away from it. In Denver the following Labor Day the President finally announced that the free nations would proceed without the Soviets to develop a "new atomic technology for peaceful use."

While abroad the Russians were holding aloof, at home suspicion, extreme caution, the inescapable public vs. private power issue, ponderous interdepartmental negotiation, and niggardliness all combined to stunt the program. Billions for bombs, but what soul-searching over a hundred kilograms or so for peaceful international experimentation! In Congress the extreme conservatives were alarmed and succeeded in limiting the President to bilateral agreements with individual nations rather than authorizing him to contribute fissionable material to an international pool. In fairness it must be noted that Congress did not have a specific international plan before it when it acted. When such a proposal with adequate safeguards is submitted, this restriction may very well be modified.

The President's idea dragged, but it did not die. On the contrary, the plan has recently taken on new life.

Between twenty and thirty bilateral agreements have been signed with friendly countries for co-operation in atomic research, with the United States leasing each a maximum of about thirteen pounds of atomic fuel.

At Pennsylvania State University on June 11, 1955, the President proposed "to offer research reactors to the people of free nations who can use them effectively for the acquisition of the skills and understanding essential to peaceful atomic progress," with the United States contributing half the cost. Although Strauss was not easily won over to this plan, some of Eisenhower's staff regarded it as so important that they suggested the President consider announcing it before a joint session of Congress.

Another notable development was the International Conference on the Peaceful Uses of Atomic Energy in Geneva in August, 1955, attended by delegates of seventy-three countries, including the Soviet Union. The conference had been proposed by the United States to further the atoms-for-peace program. The gathering aroused new interest around the world in peaceful applications of the atom.

And by demonstrating more effectively than ever before the impossibility of bottling up scientific knowledge behind national borders, it increased pressures for sharing information. With the blessings of Eisenhower and Soviet Premier Nikolai A. Bulganin another such conference is being planned a couple of years hence to carry forward the work begun in Geneva.

Even the Russians have been showing themselves a trifle more interested lately in the idea of international co-operation in peaceful use of atomic energy.

While vacationing at Thomasville, Georgia, in February, 1956, the President announced that over a period of years the United States would make available to non-Communist countries 44,000 pounds of Uranium 235, valued at some $500,000,000, for production of atomic power.

In April, 1956, the atoms-for-peace plan took an important step forward when twelve nations, including the United States and the Soviet Union, approved a charter for an International Atomic Energy Agency and agreed to submit it to a conference of eighty-four nations at the U.N. later in the year.

Not every tree reaches the sky, and there is no way of foretelling how far this one can rise in the atmosphere of the twentieth century. After two and a half years the atoms-for-peace program has barely attained the status of a major project. That nuclear weapons will get bigger and better no one doubts, but it remains to be seen whether the President's plan can make the deserts bloom. Still, the idea which he brought back from Denver on September 10, 1953, has survived. Its growth has been slow and sinuous, but its roots now reach into many parts of the world. The hopes that it has inspired will not be easily extinguished.

CHAPTER 14

White House Life Under the Eisenhowers

Family Christmas in Augusta – The President's Feeling About State Dinners – A Practical Joke on General Persons – Some Escapades of Tom Stephens – Golf – Camp David – Bridge – Eisenhower's Stag Dinners – The President as a Painter

After the speech at the U.N. the President returned to Washington for conferences on his legislative program for 1954. At Christmas, his first in office, he and his family went to Augusta for ten days. The weather looked unpromising for golf, but as they were leaving the White House Christmas morning, the President told Mrs. Eisenhower, "Nothing can get me mad today. Anything that will get me away from *this* place!"

Overlooking the Augusta National golf course a delightful white brick, split-level house, which the club members modestly call Mamie's Cabin, had been built for the Eisenhowers' use, and a lighted Christmas tree stood on the porch and a larger one in the living room. Young David Eisenhower had got a set of miniature golf clubs for Christmas, and the President, expressing himself as being "practically paralyzed" at the price of modern toys, gave his grandson lessons.

"A 3 wood is a spoon and a No. 1 wood is a driver," he explained. David nodded. The President took the irons out of the bag one at a time.

"Three, five, seven and nine, all odd numbers," he noted approvingly. "As a matter of fact," he commented to his son, John, "that's enough irons. No one needs a 2."

Nearly a year had passed since the inauguration, and the pattern of life in the White House under the Eisenhowers was now well established. The atmosphere was dignified rather than effervescent. Eisenhower had arrived in Washington with a feeling that there had been times of late when the dignity of the office had been let slip, and he brought somewhat more formality into White House affairs. While the President was to break with custom in some things, like holding occasional Cabinet meetings out of Washington and permitting filming of his press conferences, he has reverted to tradition in other ways. Some of them have been small things—restoration of the Easter egg roll in 1953, for example. This custom was begun by President Rutherford B. Hayes in 1878, but discontinued under Franklin Roosevelt in 1941 because of the war.

Formal White House functions change little from one administration to the next, and before the President's illness canceled them temporarily, the Eisenhowers carried them off valiantly and graciously, even though the President has never cared for them. During a discussion on foreign trade in the Cabinet on May 1, 1953, he suggested to Dulles with a chuckle that State Department personnel overseas drive Fiats instead of Cadillacs, and added, "Of course, you don't have to use them to take the wife to white-tie dinners, which you and I speak of *feelingly*."

At another meeting on October 9, 1953, he assured Cabinet members they needn't consider state dinners "command performances" but should feel free to accept or decline. The President is most at ease when he can round up eight or ten close friends, head for the solarium on the White House roof and broil steaks and roast corn in the husks on a portable charcoal grill. Presidents with such a bent do not have much chance to cook in the White House. But when Eisenhower gets to the Rockies in the summer, he spends hours in the kitchen in an apron cooking flapjacks made with cornmeal, chili as hot as the fire underneath it, beef stew lapping around great chunks of roast beef and thick vegetable soup that sometimes takes days in the making. After studying Eisenhower's qualification as a cook Merriman Smith, of The United Press, wrote that "the man is a walking recipe book."

The most notable of the social innovations under the Eisenhowers have been the President's small stag dinners, which have a sparkle and spontaneity rare in White House functions. Guests receive a personal invitation from the President, saying*:

> I wonder if it would be convenient for you to come to an informal stag dinner. I suggest that we meet at the White House about half past seven, have a reasonably early dinner and devote the evening to a general chat. While I am hopeful that you can attend, I realize that you already may have engagements which would interfere. If so, I assure you of my complete understanding. I shall probably wear a dinner coat, but a business suit will be entirely appropriate.
>
> *With warm personal regards,*
>
> DWIGHT D. EISENHOWER

While businessmen have predominated, the President has chosen his guests from many walks of life, and typical of the variety was the list for the first of these gatherings in 1953, which included Mac-Arthur, Francis Cardinal Spellman and former President Hoover.

Dinner, usually of pheasant, is served in the state dining room, but most of the evening is spent in Eisenhower's glowing white oval study on the second floor, which contains the magnificent trophies given him after the war by the governments of Europe. There he and his guests sit around in a large circle talking at random about subjects that may range from trout fishing to the most trying problems of foreign policy. Sometimes the President pauses to take his guests on a tour of the White House, explaining as he goes the history of the different rooms. In the Lincoln Room he points to the high bed where in 1941 the late Harry L. Hopkins, confined by illness, used to receive him on official business when Eisenhower was still Chief of War Plans Division of the War Department General Staff. Mention of this room brings to mind the statement that Mrs. Eisenhower once made to Hagerty that the only former President whose presence she could sense in the White House was Lincoln. Secret Service men and other employees who have spent long hours around the White House have experienced the same feeling.

Viewing Eisenhower's trophies, the costliest of which is the gold

*From *Newsweek*, November 29, 1954.

sword trimmed with pearls which Queen Wilhelmina of the Netherlands gave him, guests will sometimes remark upon the absence of
the Soviet award. One of several interesting stories about that is that
it is in the Eisenhower Museum in Abilene, where the President dispatched it without delay when he entered politics. Communist trophies were nothing for a candidate to be sporting in the 1952 campaign!

This platinum, star-shaped Soviet medal—the Order of Victory—
is three inches in diameter and contains ninety-one sixteen-carat
diamonds. The five large points of the inner star as well as the star
atop the Spaaskaya Tower depicted on blue enamel in the center are
rich red rubies. When Eisenhower came to have the medal appraised
so he could pay the insurance on it, none of the appraisers could
decide whether these six rubies were real or synthetic. They turned
for help to an expert at the Smithsonian Institution regarded as one
of America's two or three ultimate authorities on the subject, but
the quality of the Soviet rubies was such that he was as baffled as
the others. In the end he gave an opinion, not a conclusive finding,
that they were synthetic. What led him to this judgment was that
in all his experience he had never seen real rubies so flawless.

There is nothing taciturn about the President in company. He
loves to talk and to laugh. Once he gets started he can talk for
hours. He prefers the concrete to the abstract. The same is true in
official discussion. In a matter like the employee security program,
for example, Eisenhower's interest would warm up to the problems
of a particular man or woman involved much more readily than it
would to the theory and function of the whole program.

The President likes to reach his conclusions by talking out his
thoughts rather than brooding. His intimates are his sounding boards
almost as much as they are his advisers. His brother Milton usually
offers advice only in a few particular fields, but he listens to the
President and lets him work his thoughts out on him. Sometimes
when Milton is in Washington the two will sit together in the
President's bedroom for hours while the President grinds out his
ideas on different subjects. This is the process the President uses
habitually to clarify his thinking and plot the line from where he
is to where he wants to go.

Once he goes into action, however, Eisenhower does not relish having anyone else use this process on him. Nothing gets him out of sorts faster than for a subordinate to come in and start to hem and haw about a decision. He wants the decision and not the thinking out loud. One of the stratagems he employs is suddenly to throw a sharp challenge at any decision proposed to him to test the strength of conviction of the person offering it.

In spite of the earnest air, the Eisenhowers' White House has witnessed much gaiety, humor and sociability. The President brought to his staff a good many people who do not take themselves too seriously—not all the time, that is. It has never been unusual to find some of them cooking a Japanese meal for thirty on a four-burner stove at the Bon Air Hotel in Augusta or enjoying themselves around a barbecue on a ranch in the Rockies when the President is in Colorado.

In the first year or so of the administration Adams used to celebrate the birthday of each male member of the staff with a speech at luncheon in the mess in the basement of the West Wing. One such salute to the late Roger Steffan wound up in tumult when a brass band came crashing through the door. Adams admires Robert Frost's poetry and once brought Frost to this same mess to read his poems. Adams himself gave a reading of Frost on the President's train during the trip to Ottawa.

On General Persons's fifty-eighth birthday on January 19, 1954, Adams presided over a perfect practical joke on him. A Chinese-American Secret Service man named Alfred Wong, who was unknown to Persons, was brought into a staff meeting and introduced by Adams as General Chin Wee Lai, a visiting member of Chiang-Kai-shek's staff. General Chin explained that he did the same kind of work for Chiang that Persons did for Eisenhower, Persons having then been in charge of White House liaison with Congress. In a carefully rehearsed interview Wong-Chin discussed his own liaison methods in a way that made Persons's manner of doing business look preposterous. The line he was following was that if Persons kept on as he was, the Democrats would soon take over Eisenhower just as the Communists had taken over China. Completely fooled, Persons got redder and angrier until finally, his leg pulled hard enough, he hissed, "Is Adams crazy bringing this guy in here?" At just about this point Adams announced, "And with this we wish Jerry Persons a happy birthday." The doors popped open and three girls rushed in and showered Persons with roses while the President stood in the doorway laughing at Persons's sheepishness.

The joke had been plotted by Tom Stephens, who was, before he resigned as the President's appointment secretary in February, 1955, to resume law practice in New York, the rarest character in the administration. A native of Ireland who combines a cold shrewdness with a kindly disposition and an addiction to innocent mischief, he was always getting into funny situations with the President. Once when Eisenhower was putting on his golf shoes in the White House gymnasium, Stephens sat down on an electric exercising bicycle to talk to him. Suddenly the contraption started up with a bolt and Stephens had to grab hold for dear life while Eisenhower sat back and roared at him.

Another time, after a mess boy had brought him a pair of brown shoes he had shined for him, Stephens decided to put them on instead of the black ones he was wearing. Just as he had changed one shoe, the President sent for him in a hurry. With a shrug he walked into the President's office wearing one black and one brown shoe and wondering what effect *that* would have on "The Boss." To his relief Eisenhower paid no attention to how he was shod. The incident, however, set him speculating about how far one could go in the White House in a black and a brown shoe without being noticed. Determined to find out, he strolled in this office and out that, but one person after another failed to see anything amiss until he came to Colonel Robert L. Schulz, the President's military aide and a man who knows what's uniform and what isn't. After Schulz had caught him, Stephens went to Adams and told him, "A fine staff you've got here—they don't even wake up till ten-thirty."

In addition to his long vacations in Denver the President has made brief visits to Augusta in the spring and fall as well as at Christmas. An excellent golfer, he would play difficult courses in the eighties in his best form before his heart attack, and his golf and his work seem to have an effect upon each other.

Soon after he began his campaign in the fall of 1952 he dropped in at a Citizens-for-Eisenhower rally in New York which was so enthusiastic it heartened him. Some time afterward John Hay (Jock) Whitney handed Walter Williams, the co-chairman of the Citizens and now Under Secretary of Commerce, a note, saying, "Ike told Bill Robinson the meeting on Saturday 'made him feel the whole thing was worthwhile.' He shot an eighty-one!" (William E. Robinson is now president of the Coca-Cola Company.)

Once after Eisenhower became President and the farm problem was weighing on him, he was leaving for an afternoon of relaxation at Burning Tree when Shanley called to him to have a good game.

"My golf would be a lot better," the President replied, "if somebody would do something about the price of beef."

Golf has been the President's chief form of exercise. He has never liked to toss medicine balls like Hoover, or swim in the White House pool like Roosevelt (although he took it up on doctors' orders after his illness), or take long walks like Truman. Tramping over a golf course suits him because there is a definite purpose to it. Without a purpose he doesn't care much about walking.

In the winter he sometimes swings golf clubs in his high-ceilinged bedroom and putts in a disk on the carpet. In good weather he practices putting on a green installed for him out behind his office by the United States Golf Association and makes iron shots across the South Lawn. It has been a familiar sight late on pleasant afternoons to see the President, dressed in a white sport shirt, tan cap and gray slacks hoisting balls out from behind a clump of trees near the White House while his valet, Master Sergeant John Moaney, gathers them up in a yellow bag. Moaney was with Eisenhower in Europe. When Eisenhower was coming home to enter politics, he asked Moaney if he wished to accompany him, and Moaney said he did. Eisenhower warned him that he might lose the nomination or the election.

"Oh, that's all right, General," Moaney replied. "We'll make out somehow."

The President's golf has had a practical political side to it because members of both parties in Congress like to be invited to play with him. Nixon reported to the Cabinet on April 30, 1954, for example, that a game of golf with the President had seemed to have a very beneficial effect on a certain Republican Senator who was not always so co-operative as he might be.

When the President is on the golf course, affairs of state are not totally barred all the time. In their game at Augusta in April, 1953, he and Taft discussed F.H.A. interest rates. However, Eisenhower concentrates on his game and doesn't relish talking business.

He has a powerful drive—the first ball he hit off the tee at Augusta the day after he was elected soared nearly 250 yeards straight down the fairway. People who are supposed to know about such things say he does well with the 8 iron and the wedge. They also say his putting is erratic—better from far out than in close. As one who knows nothing about the game but has watched the President play many times, I must say I have never seen a man take up a golf club and whip it around with such sheer zest and affection as he does. Or heard a man live a game over with such gusto long after the last ball has been picked up!

As a rule shop talk is taboo at Burning Tree, but the ban hasn't always spared the President. Late on the afternoon of May 20, 1953, for instance, Cutler and General Carroll swooped down on him at the club with an urgent cable from C. Douglas Dillon, the United States Ambassador in Paris. The cable relayed a request from the then Premier of France, René Mayer, for an early Big Three meeting. Eisenhower, Carroll and Cutler piled into the President's car and drove back to the White House discussing the appeal on the way.

At a quarter after six they met in Eisenhower's office along with Jackson, Bedell Smith, H. Freeman Matthews, then Deputy Under Secretary of State, and—somewhat later—Hagerty. Deferring to Mayer's wishes, Eisenhower put in a call to Churchill. He told Sir Winston that he would agree to a meeting as a gesture to the French, but he felt it should be held in the United States.

At this point Sir Winston became a little deaf. His deafness seemed to increase when the President suggested that the three meet at Presque Isle, Maine.

"Winston, Presque Isle, *Presque Isle!*" the President fairly shouted. "In Maine. In the State of Maine, Winston."

By this time Churchill could hear nothing. The President sank back and let him talk. Presently Eisenhower clamped his hand over the mouthpiece and, turning to the Under Secretary of State, asked,

"Beedle, is Burmuda okay?" With Smith's nod, history passed Presque Isle by.

Unlike most of his predecessors of modern times Eisenhower has not maintained a yacht since his first few months in office. From Truman he had inherited the U.S.S. *Williamsburg*, and indeed in discussing with the Cabinet on February 25, 1953, the possibility of periodic long Cabinet round-table conferences, he suggested that these might be held aboard the *Williamsburg*. Two months later he informed the Cabinet that the cost of operating the ship was out of keeping with the administration's economy program and that he was laying the vessel up, which he did after one cruise to Annapolis and Williamsburg, Virginia, in May. Hagerty announced, "The White House believes the *Williamsburg* is a symbol of needless luxury in a budget which the administration is trying to cut as hard and as fast as it can."

About the same time, however, Eisenhower remarked somewhat ruefully to Colonel Schulz that he could understand why Presidents kept yachts. He said that he could scarcely step out of the White House without attracting attention and that when he did, those who were looking out for his comfort were so concerned about him they defeated their purpose. Even when he was trying to do some quiet fishing, he lamented, people always interrupted him with offers of new gadgets.

Instead of passing pleasant weekends on the water the President has spent them first at Camp David and then at Gettysburg after the completion of his farm in 1954. Camp David is the erstwhile Civilian Conservation Corps camp in the Catoctin Mountains of Maryland, north of Washington, which Franklin Roosevelt turned into a Presidential retreat and called it Shangri-la. Truman used it occasionally. When Eisenhower took it over, he renamed it Camp David for his father and his grandson. On August 13, 1954, he held his Cabinet meeting there and then turned the members loose to the trout streams, archery range and single-green golf course. Mrs. Hobby said that after some of her recent experiences with Congressmen, she would like to hang pictures of a few of them on the archery targets and let bow and arrow do the rest.

A couple of months previously the President had arranged, confidentially, he thought, to buy ice cream for the boys and girls at a nearby camp for crippled children. The next morning, June 29, it was all over the papers, and when the President met the legislative leaders that day, he apologized for the publicity he had received. He had gone to great lengths, he said, to avoid it.

"If that's the worst publicity you ever get," Representative Charles A. Halleck, Indiana, told him, "we won't disapprove."

The White House is amply supplied with television, but Eisenhower has never spent much time watching it, except for particular programs, like the Fred Waring hour, which he has enjoyed. It is the same with the movies shown in the basement. He goes to them occasionally but partly for the sake of being with Mrs. Eisenhower and Mrs. Doud, who is called "Min" by her family and friends. For months the President went around whistling the theme music of the Western *High Noon*, and on May 22, 1953, he opened a meeting of the Cabinet by recommending *The Life of Martin Luther*, which he had just seen. While it might seem controversial to persons of some religions, he said, he thought its merits were so high as to make criticism on such grounds unjustified.

The President likes to tell jokes about his family. At a luncheon during February of 1954 he told of the consequences of an erroneous item in a California gossip column that his daughter-in-law, Barbara, was then expecting another child. The column happened to be very much on Barbara's mind when Mrs. Eisenhower, knowing nothing about it, called her one day and asked how she was. The First Lady was flabbergasted when Barbara replied, "Are you calling about the new baby?"

"That columnist," the President laughed as he told the story, "was just about far enough away to have had a very good knowledge of the subject."

In the evenings, when he has a chance, the President loves to play bridge with friends like Bill Robinson, Clifford Roberts, a New York investment banker, who handles some of Eisenhower's personal affairs, and, when he is in town, General Alfred M. Gruenther, commander of the NATO forces. People who play bridge with the President are struck by the power of his memory, his mathematical alertness and his skill in figuring percentages. Like most of us, he doesn't relish mistakes by his partner. The late Ely Culbertson, an expert on the subject, said several years ago that he considered Eisenhower one of the best bridge players in America.

Increasingly the President has been devoting his spare time to painting, an avocation he did not take up until after he became Chief of Staff in 1945. One day at Fort Myer, near the Pentagon, he was sitting for the artist Thomas E. Stephens, whose name is identical with that of the man who later became the President's appointment secretary. After a time Eisenhower said that he would like to see how Stephens painted, so the artist obligingly did a sketch of Major General Howard McC. Snyder, the President's physician, while Eisenhower watched.

"I would like to try that," Eisenhower said, and he started in with Stephens's paints and brushes. Moaney made a canvas for him out of a soiled pillowcase. As Mrs. Eisenhower happened to be confined to the house with a cold, her husband chose her for his first subject, and with Stephens at his side urging him, "Put on more paint," he set to work. He kept at it until Mrs. Eisenhower sent him to bed at midnight. The painting, which is still in existence, is almost primitive in its effect. A green mist surrounds Mrs. Eisenhower's head. Her bangs come down to her eyebrows. The colors throughout are garish and her complexion, therefore, appears very red and her eyes a bright blue.

Eisenhower's interest in painting grew, and the next Christmas his wife gave him a box of paints. By the time he moved into the White House the hobby had become such a serious one that a room across the hall from his bedroom was converted into a studio.

The President has a facility for painting rather than an artistic talent, and he enjoys working with paint more than he does drawing. He has become proficient at drawing, but it takes more time than he can give to it. Hence in some of his work, like the Lincoln he did in 1953 and the portrait of Washington he did the next year, he has taken canvases with the outlines of the faces already drawn lightly on them by someone else and then has gone vigorously to work on the color. When he has more time to spend on a portrait, he both draws and paints and some of these efforts have come out very creditably. On a single canvas he once did a trio of Dulles, Wilson and Humphrey. He has painted all his family, including the grand-children, and one of his best works has been a portrait of Sir Winston on which he did the drawing as well as the painting.

At Christmas, in 1953, Eisenhower had copies made of his Lincoln portrait and gave them to his staff and friends. With that a painting became his traditional Christmas gift. In 1954 the Washington portrait was his Christmas picture. The next year he gave copies of his painting of St. Louis Creek, his favorite trout stream in the Rockies, on Byers Peak Ranch, near Fraser, Colorado. He had begun the painting at the ranch the week before his heart attack and finished it while convalescing in Fitzsimons General Hospital in Denver.

Once the President is ready to paint he goes at it with a dash that can't be halted even when Stephens stands by pleading vainly with him to pause and contemplate before putting the brush to the canvas. Unheeding, he simply plunges in and immerses himself in the work. One summer evening in 1954 Cutler had to see him on a rather urgent matter involving a message to the king of Saudi Arabia relating to the oil dispute between that country and Britain. The usher took him to the studio where Eisenhower, dressed in a sport shirt, slacks and a white linen cap, was walking around from one painting to another trying different kinds of retouching varnish.

"Hello, Bobby," he said, going right on with what he was doing, "which one of these do you think is best?"

After dabbling some more with the varnish he returned to work on a portrait of Mrs. G. Gordon Moore, who is Mrs. Eisenhower's sister, and talked of nothing but painting for fifteen minutes. Then he asked Cutler, "What did you come over for?"

Cutler explained the problem. Scarcely missing a stroke of the brush, the President picked up the threads of the matter and discussed it for more than a half-hour with his eyes on the canvas. Finally, he said that a proposed message which Cutler had brought from Henry A. Byroade, then Assistant Secretary of State, was the best way to handle the business. That decided it, and the President buried himself again in his painting.

Only one of the President's paintings hangs in his office. This is a green Colorado mountain scene. On his desk are small colored photographs of Mrs. Eisenhower and his mother, the late Mrs. Ida

Elizabeth Stover Eisenhower. Characteristic of his Army background, Eisenhower is a "clean-desk man"—no ivory G.O.P. elephants roaming around bumping into the gavel from the Republican convention or tripping over a replica of SHAPE headquarters. Four pens, two telephones, a blotter and a small silver tray set with a stone from each place the President has lived are its sparse furnishings. These and a small black piece of wood inscribed:

Suaviter in modo fortiter in re

Claudio Aquaviva

The inscription, translated on the back as "Gentle in manner, strongly in deed," was given to the President by Hauge, who came across the line somewhere and thought it caught the Eisenhower spirit.

On a table behind his red leather desk chair stands a black-and-green marble pyramidal clock, which the White House acquired during the Grant administration for four hundred dollars. In the center, below the face of the clock, is a barometer, and every morning when the President comes in, or later in the day if he forgets, he sets it.

There are mornings when the Presidential mood is not one for trifling with barometers—nor one to be trifled with either. Tom Stephens, who applies a science of his own to such matters, once discovered that Eisenhower's temper in the morning was most fearsome when he wore a brown suit. For months Stephens used to keep a watch out the window for the President and Colonel Schulz walking over to the office from the White House through the connecting colonnade, and whenever he spotted Eisenhower in a brown suit, he would flash the warning to the Presidential secretaries, Ann Whitman and Helen Weaver: "Brown suit today!"

One day when the President was safely dressed in blue, Stephens confided his theory to him. Stephens got the distinct impression thereafter that the President wore brown less frequently.

The President keeps a Bible in his desk and occasionally when he has a few minutes to spare he will take a volume of the works of Lincoln or Jefferson from the shelves in his office and read in it. While Eisenhower is not a heavy reader, he does a considerable amount of random reading. Each morning he pages through a half-dozen morning newspapers in the White House (he recently dropped the Chicago *Tribune* for the *Wall Street Journal*), but only one paper—the New York *Herald Tribune*—is regularly placed in his office. In the evening he sometimes relaxes with 25-cent paperback Westerns, his favorite Western authors being Luke Short, who wrote *Vengeance Valley*, and Bliss Lomax, best known for *Colt Comrades* and *The Fight for the Sweetwater*. On other nights he tackles something more serious. When it came out in 1954, for example, he read himself to sleep a couple of nights with Chester Bowles's *Ambassador's Report*. Recently considerable publicity was given to the discovery that the President had recommended *The True Believer* to Secretary Wilson. This study of political fanaticism by Eric Hoffer, a member of Harry Bridges's longshoreman's union, contains a number of passages which prompted Eisenhower, when he was NATO commander, to scribble such marginal notes as "Nuts" and "This, I think, is demonstrably false."

As becomes a resident of Gettysburg he is fond of Civil War literature and has read all three of Bruce Catton's series—*Mr. Lincoln's Army*, *Glory Road*, and *A Stillness at Appomattox*. He waded into MacKinlay Kantor's massive Pulitzer Prize novel *Andersonville*, a story of the notorious Confederate prison in Georgia, but lost interest in it. One of his favorite books about World War II is *Dark December*, a story of the Battle of the Bulge by Robert E. Merriam, now Deputy Director of the Bureau of the Budget.

The walls and bookshelves of Eisenhower's office reflect the President's great admiration for Lincoln. During a discussion of the business recession in the Cabinet on November 4, 1954, Eisenhower spoke of the need for facing facts as they are, and he urged members of the Cabinet to read more about Lincoln as a way of sharpening their own political insights. One of the first objects to strike a visitor entering Eisenhower's office is a Hesler photograph of Lincoln taken in 1860. *The Collected Works of Abraham Lincoln* line the topmost shelf of the bookcase inset in the office wall. Kevin McCann and other of the President's speech writers have figuratively at least beat a path to Volume II, 1848-1858. In it is a fragment of Lincoln's writing which Eisenhower uses time and again in describing his own philosophy of government. One version contained in the volume reads:

The legitimate object of government, is to do for a community of people, whatever they need to have done, but can not do *at all*, or can not, so *well do*, for themselves—in their separate, and individual capacities.

In all that the people can individually do as well for themselves, government ought not to interfere.

This fragment, to which Nicolay and Hay assign the date of July 1, 1854, does not specifically refer to the Federal government. Eisenhower assumes that this is what Lincoln meant.

CHAPTER 15

No More 1929's

The Onset of the "Recession" – The President's Reaction – Soul-Searching in the Cabinet – Humphrey's Calm – Unemployment Rises – The President Demands Action – Readying a Public Works Program – Eisenhower Gives the Cabinet His Views on Truman's Fiscal Policies – The Picture Brightens – Peace and Prosperity

President Eisenhower's immediate reaction to the warning in the Cabinet on September 25, 1953, of an economic decline was that the Republican Party must be ready to use the full power of the government, if necessary, to prevent "another 1929."

The situation described by Arthur Burns that morning was one which would have disturbed any administration but which struck a particularly sensitive nerve among members of the party that was just beginning to live down the depression of twenty-five years ago. No one in the White House needed to be reminded that a worse domestic calamity could scarcely befall the United States than a great dislocation of business, finance and farming. This was true not alone because of the personal hardships and political upheaval it would bring but because of the torpedo that economic disaster in America would ram under the free world's defenses against Communism.

By late September it was obvious that the economy was going downhill. The decline was blamed chiefly on excessive inventories, an imbalance of production and sales and the drop in military spending after the truce in Korea.

The administration had taken office during the economic boom of the Korean war. Inflation was then the bugaboo, and in April, 1953, the Secretary of the Treasury moved to tighten credit through the issuance of long-term bonds, which soaked up money that otherwise would have gone into corporate issues or mortgages. This was part of what was popularly called the "hard money" policy. The tightening process was so effective that within a couple of months it brought about, according to the President's Economic Report of January, 1954, an "incipient and possibly dangerous scramble" for cash.

The administration soon discovered that the trouble ahead lay in deflation rather than inflation, and the Treasury turned around and, with the Federal Reserve System, took steps to ease credit and make more money available. The fight against deflation was carried a step farther when Humphrey told the convention of the American Bankers Association in Washington on September 22 that the administration would make no effort to prevent the tax changes scheduled for December 31 from taking effect. Indeed, it would have been well nigh politically impossible to have done so. The changes were the expiration of the excess-profits tax and the lapsing of the 10 per cent Korea-emergency increase in personal income taxes. Together with the forthcoming reductions in excise taxes, as well as the revisions in the tax law itself, these were expected, when in force a full year, to release $7,400,000,000 in private spending power.

Confronted by signs of deflation, Burns, a pipe-smoking former professor of economics at Columbia University and an authority on the business cycle, told the Cabinet on September 25 that planning was called for as a precaution against further decline.

He said the situation was not critical. The strength of the economy was reflected in such things as its ability to withstand the recent "hard money" credit squeeze, the favorable distribution of income among the people and the basic soundness of the inventory situation.

The Council of Economic Advisers, he added, was thinking less in terms of increased government spending and more in terms of monetary policy, the activities of private business, tax reduction and government programs emphasizing loans rather than construction undertaken by the government itself. Legislation for these purposes, he said, was under study.

Humphrey approved. He pointed out that the credit-easing operations of the Treasury and the Federal Reserve would continue to "release" more money for several months.

The President reminded the Cabinet that in the 1952 campaign the Republicans had promised to use the authority of the government to the maximum to avert a repetition of 1929. The only thing now in question, he stated, was the Republicans' desire to assure the greatest possible economic activity by the individual.

Humphrey observed that because of recent record-breaking high levels, the only way for the economy to go was down. A few readjustments were not to be feared—employment could decline for six or seven months without becoming critical.

The administration, Eisenhower declared, was sensitive because of the number of "big businessmen" among its officials. He did not believe, he said, that there was any group more concerned about the welfare of the people than this Cabinet.

The Vice-President noted the psychological reactions of businessmen and suggested that the business community be kept well informed on the stable condition of the economy and on the administration's determination to maintain stability. Dulles seconded this suggestion. He said that he had sensed a "near panic" sentiment among people in New York City.

The President received favorably a suggestion by Benson and Mrs. Hobby that he make a speech on television emphasizing the stability of the economy.

By November, alarm was widespread not only in the United States but abroad. In the Manchester *Guardian*, an Oxford economist, Dr. Colin Clark, forecast a serious depression in America with unemployment possibly reaching seven million unless the government stepped in with a large spending program. At the turn of the year a persistent clamor for government action was rising from labor and from a number of Democrats, notably Senator Paul H. Douglas, of Illinois, who is an economist.

On January 13, 1954, Reuther wrote the President urging him to call a national conference on employment.

In the past six months [he wrote] the growth of our economy has been halted. . . . Claims for unemployment compensation, which are the most current index to the unemployment situation, have been rising at an alarming rate in recent weeks. . . . In the Detroit area . . . 107,000 workers—7 per cent of the area's labor force—are already unemployed with more layoffs expected in the weeks ahead. . . . Clearly a recession has set in. . . .

Failing to persuade the President to his proposal, Reuther himself called such a conference in the spring.

Week after week meanwhile Republican legislative leaders were reporting to Eisenhower that Congress and the country were worried about the recession. With a Congressional election only several months away, the Republican leadership had special cause for worry.

While certain elements of the economy, such as stock prices, had shown signs of improvement, unemployment was rising discouragingly. A new jolt was in store when the Bureau of the Census applied to the month of January an improved method of reporting unemployment, based on a larger sample. This registered an apparent rise in unemployment of 774,000 in one month, bringing the total to 3,087,000. Weeks, convinced that much of this increase was due to the new reporting, asked the President what he should do about it. If the figures were true, Eisenhower told him, let them be made public.

The President came under increasingly heavy pressure, especially from labor, to launch a large Federal public works program, and these dismaying statistics added force to it. Reuther demanded action leading toward a "bigger and more prosperous America," and Meany insisted upon "measures essential to bolster consumer buying and check the present recession before it gains momentum."

Weighing these appeals, Eisenhower spurred plans for an emergency public-works program. But until worst came to worst he continued to ride the squall as his fiscal and economic advisers urged, relying on the economy to right itself with the stimulus of tax reductions, freer credit, liberalized social welfare measures and, above all, confidence by businessmen, home builders, investors and consumers. During this whole period from January through July, 1954, Cabinet meetings and other White House discussions provide a striking picture of a President and his government grappling with trouble in a vast, complicated economy. It is a picture of deep concern but not fright, of urgency but not rashness, of patience but not complacence, of a willingness to act if necessary but a determination not to be stampeded.

Cabinet, January 15, 1954

Humphrey stated his opinion that prosperity depended more upon the confidence of all the people than upon any particular government measures other than removal of impediments to individual initiative. The President replied that he wished to avoid false expressions of confidence such as were proclaimed in 1929. He wanted to refrain from any suggestion that the government was unable to act positively to strengthen the economy. Dulles agreed that it was necessary to create public confidence by making it clear that the administration knew where it was and where it was going.

Cabinet, February 5, 1954

The President informed the Cabinet that he had asked Burns to co-ordinate reports from the various departments and agencies on their plans for public-works projects. It would be essential, he said, to have planning advanced sufficiently to insure that men would be put to work quickly. Too often, he added, preliminary planning, testing and surveys delay start on work. Projects planned for an emergency program, he insisted, must be intrinsically valuable to national development and must not be merely "made work."

He designated July 1 as a tentative date for the government to be prepared to act.

This was not the end of the matter. Eisenhower said that he was ready then and there to ask Congress for supplemental appropriations for a few immediate projects if any member of the Cabinet recommended it. Projects actually under way, he noted, gave the government flexibility in speeding them up or stretching them out, as conditions required.

McKay spoke up and said that it might be a good idea to initiate several power projects. He mentioned in particular that local government and private interests were prepared to undertake hydro-electric power development at Cougar Dam, a proposed flood-control project on the McKenzie River in Oregon. The government, he said, should not lag behind on a "partnership" project like this. Adams noted that such an arrangement would square with Eisenhower's power philosophy expressed in the 1952 campaign.

The President, who was to place increasing stress on a vast highway construction program, suggested building new toll roads with the government guaranteeing the bonds. Mitchell expressed his eagerness to have something done to check the rise of unemployment in the Pacific Northwest.

Humphrey then made his position known. He said that a broad public-works program would be desirable if operations then in progress should fail to turn the tide. He felt, however, that they might very well succeed.

McKay brought up the point that it was important to get adequate funds to carry through existing projects so that there would be no layoffs of workers.

To cap the discussion Lodge praised the care that was being taken by the administration to master the economic setback. He said that this attitude refuted charges that Republicans were bound to the "trickle down" theory of economics—the theory of helping the few at the top in expectation that the benefits will then seep down to the rest of the people.

(An interesting aspect of this discussion, as well as of similar discussions in the next few months, was the muting of emphasis on balancing the budget. This goal had been emphasized before and was to be emphasized very strongly again. But with the fate of the economy in the balance, it was submerged under the determination of the President and of the Cabinet generally to undertake an expensive public-works program if necessary and to prevent a serious depression at any cost.)

Confidential White House Briefing
February 11, 1954

Burns said the last chapter of the President's Economic Report definitely expressed Eisenhower's thinking on the threat of depression. These were some of the points to which he referred:

The first and foremost principle is to take preventive action. . . .

The second principle is to avoid a doctrinaire position, work simultaneously on several fronts, and make sure that the actions . . . harmonize and reinforce one another.

The third basic principle is to pursue measures that will foster the expansion of private activity by stimulating consumers to spend more money and businessmen to create more jobs. . . .

The fourth principle is to act promptly and vigorously if economic conditions require it.

On the basis of facts then available, Burns said, the government was justified in taking action to strengthen the economy, but not in launching a program to fight a real depression.

Cabinet, March 12, 1954

The President was in a deadly serious mood. The unemployment situation had worsened. In March the number of jobless reached the peak of 3,725,000, or 5.8 per cent of the entire civilian labor force. The fact that unemployment was then at the crest, however, was not known on this date.

Eisenhower said that, of course, the manner of presentation of unemployment statistics had to be discussed. However, he asserted the immediate need was to determine what to do about unemployment and when to do it. He said that plans had been prepared for countering a decline in the business cycle, but that when one came to look for recommendations as to when these plans should be put into effect, one looked in vain.

Humphrey told the President that Senator Douglas had warned that drastic action should not be taken before unemployment reached the level of 6 or 8 per cent of the labor force.

Timely action, the President retorted, would forestall the need for drastic action. Again he insisted at least upon preparedness to act at any moment.

Stassen proposed an immediate start on several lesser measures, such as lowering the interest rate on new housing. These measures could be slowed, he said, if employment drifted back to normal.

Humphrey, calm as a cucumber, as usual, advised the President against any radical action that could not easily be cut off. Uncertainty as to the fate of the tax-revision bill in Congress, he said, was retarding business, and before any extraordinary action was taken he preferred to wait until April or May to give the picture a chance to clarify. He pointed out that in a period of reduced government expenditures, unemployment was inevitable. As far as he could see, he added, the adverse reaction to the current readjustment was being kept to a minimum.

Flemming expressed his general agreement with Humphrey, but suggested that one helpful measure might be the initiation of a program of building tankers—a suggestion that Weeks agreed might be a good one.

The President concluded by asking Burns to appear at every subsequent meeting of the Cabinet until further notice to summarize each week's developments and keep all the members alert to the problem.

Cabinet, March 19, 1954

Burns reported that some favorable trends were appearing, but he urged that judgment be suspended for a while. The Council of Economic Advisers, he said, was moving ahead rapidly with projects that might be started if need should arise.

Stassen suggested that the general confidence of financial circles, evidenced by the steadiness of the stock market, was founded upon a feeling that the administration would take timely action if it was warranted. In his opinion the moment had come for some action, such as increased government purchasing. Burns agreed with his analysis of the reason for confidence in the financial community. Humphrey disagreed. Confidence, he argued, was based on a belief that the government would follow sound fiscal policies and would not act prematurely.

The Democrats were calling for even more spending power in the hands of the people to remedy the recession. A Democratic group, including Senator Walter F. George, of Georgia, had introduced a bill in February to increase the individual income-tax exemptions from $600 to $1,000 in two stages—$200 in 1954 and $200 in 1955. On February 19 Senator Douglas had written the President asking him to back this proposal to head off a possible depression.

So far as my being a prophet is concerned [he wrote], I have not predicted a depression. But I have, as emphatically as I could, tried to keep our Nation on its toes and ready to act to stop a worsening of the economic picture.

A look at the present economic situation indicates, in my judgment, that the time for action is here. At least we should take some initial effective steps to counteract the downward trend.

The administration, however, did not withdraw its opposition to the tax bill. At this same meeting of March 19 Humphrey and others remarked that economic trends would play a large part in the fate of the measure (which in amended form was defeated finally).

All the more reason, Eisenhower argued, for the administration to take immediate action to counter the decline and head off the Democrats. Nixon, too, suggested that anything constructive should be done then rather than several months later. Humphrey agreed that projects which the administration would undertake eventually might well be started immediately.

The President urged Burns to have the Council expedite its studies and determine what actions should be taken forthwith.

Presidential Press Conference,
March 24, 1954
Eisenhower said that the time had not yet arrived when a slam-bang emergency program was needed.

Cabinet, March 26, 1954
The sense of mounting urgency continued. Burns had made a list of actions that could be taken, such as modifying Federal Reserve requirements, liberalizing mortgage requirements, altering tax-depreciation policy and hastening domestic procurement. The President asked him to prepare an outline of useful legislation. Humphrey agreed that the administration ought to get additional measures started. Weeks urged faster action on the tanker program, and the President indorsed his suggestion.

Cabinet, April 2, 1954
Burns declared that continuing economic troubles called for the

actions he had suggested the previous week. To the extent that the executive branch had authority over them, the President said, these things should be done without delay. He cautioned, however, that the announcements should be carefully handled to avoid a jolt to public confidence.

Wilson noted the upturn in the automobile industry—a factor that was to prove extremely important.

Burns then called attention to another encouraging and unusual situation: Plant expansion and building contracts had been continuing at a very high rate through nine months of general decline.

He attributed this to confidence in the administration's ability to maintain a stable economy. Pointing out that public confidence was a precarious thing, he said that he could only fear what the outcome might be if the administration should betray signs of timidity or impotence.

On April 8 David McDonald called on the President and on behalf of the United Steelworkers urged a $5,000,000,000 public works program, a $5,000,000,000 home-building and slum-clearance program, $3,000,000,000 in increased unemployment benefits and pensions and a $4,000,000,000 cut in income taxes. He brought a union report showing that 189,334 of its members were idle and 257,026 more were working short weeks. The Steelworkers' convention subsequently passed a resolution calling upon Eisenhower "to act vigorously now."

Cabinet, April 9, 1954

Burns reported a sharp division between the industrial situation, which was poor, and the financial situation, which was strong. One way or another, he said, the two trends must be reconciled, either in a general decline or in a general advance. Cautiously, he predicted the latter.

Humphrey read the Cabinet some of his testimony before the Senate Finance Committee two days earlier on what the administration had done to cope with the recession. This included proposals for enlarging the highway program, expanding Social Security and unemployment insurance, revising the income-tax law and altering the terms of government-insured loans and mortgages. The list, Humphrey said, should effectively counter charges that the administration was awaiting further decline before acting.

The President said that the position of the administration should be that it would resolve uncertainties in accordance with the principle that there is more risk in doing nothing than in doing something.

Cabinet, April 30, 1954

Burns came armed with hopeful omens again. Among other things, he noted that contrary to expectations, the economies of foreign countries had remained strong during the sag in the American economy.

The President told the Cabinet that public works, such as highways, contributed to the future economic strength of the country and should be regarded as investments rather than expenditures.

The National Full Employment Conference of C.I.O. leaders met in Washington on May 11 and heard Reuther assail the administration for "doing nothing" to relieve unemployment. Two days later Truman told the C.I.O. Amalgamated Clothing Workers in Atlantic City that the economy was suffering from "creeping McKinleyism." He proposed a three-billion-dollar increase for public works and welfare. The A.F.L. Executive Council charged on May 17 that Eisenhower had failed to keep a promise to act at the first sign of a recession.

Cabinet, May 14, 1954

Humphrey read a letter from the manager of a retail chain voicing pessimism about the future. The Secretary said that it was vital to get Congress to act soon on such measures as tax revision, housing and Social Security extension so that the effects would be felt within the next six months.

Burns informed the Cabinet that even without new legislation, funds were probably available for military purchases, repair and modernization of Federal buildings and for construction of atomic energy installations, small bridges and forest roads. The President replied that departments which had money available for worthwhile projects should start them then rather than later.

True, the President said, the administration had come into office devoted to saving every dollar possible in order to balance the budget. But he said that savings should be limited to nonessential things. Humphrey maintained that the government should go ahead rapidly with necessary projects but that the economy program should not be discarded.

Cabinet, May 21, 1954

Rowland R. Hughes, who had recently succeeded Dodge as Budget Director, said that little further reduction was possible in spending on nonsecurity programs. Any substantial cut in the anticipated deficits, he said, would have to come out of security programs. The President then warned sharply against any loose political thinking on budget-balancing. He had refused to promise a balanced budget, he said, by any given date. In toting up its own achievements the administration ought to compare its record with the spending estimates left over by Truman. The administration was moving in the right direction. It should, he urged, cut out all unnecessary expenditures and thereafter fight for adequate and, if necessary, higher taxes to meet necessary expenses.

Burns suggested that the Democrats might make campaign material out of Truman's fiscal policies on the grounds that the economy had expanded during Truman's administration while the size of the national debt had remained relatively unchanged.

Eisenhower seemed astonished. While some people might wish to make a virtue out of the Democratic record, he replied, the fact remained that the Truman administration had improved the debt situation by a period of virtually complete neglect of national security. Then it undertook a belated preparedness program without any provision for financing it. The result, he added, was first to create a national security crisis and then to pass the bill on to the Eisenhower administration.

Coming up with still more hopeful news, Burns reported that for the third consecutive month the number of increases in orders and production had surpassed the decreases. He said that the economy might be swinging into an upturn.

Cabinet, June 4, 1954

Again Burns had an optimistic report, this time that the length of the work week had increased slightly in May over April.

The President, however, was still concerned about whether the administration was doing enough. Even though it jarred the logic of some members of the Cabinet, he insisted, everything possible must be done to restore vigor to the economy. It was important, he said, to produce results and to err on the side of doing too much rather than too little. He directed Burns to prepare a complete presentation for the Cabinet on additional actions the administration could take.

Cabinet, June 11, 1954

Burns made his presentation. He noted definite evidence that recovery was under way, but said the possibility remained that it would fizzle out. He recommended a number of measures, again stressing housing, building, interest rates and highway construction.

"Arthur, you'd have made a fine chief of staff during the war," the President told him.

Eisenhower said there was a limit to how fast and how far Congress could be pushed. But he ventured the opinion that influential members would recognize the political if not the economic benefits of the housing program if Burns should outline these at a luncheon that might be arranged by Persons. The President repeatedly urged that whatever needed to be done should be done quickly, and he asked heads of departments which would be affected by Burns's recommendations to report at the next meeting on what steps might be taken.

This marked the end of the urgency in the Cabinet over the recession. By July the dark clouds were blowing rapidly away in the gusts of new prosperity. The causes for this triumph of the economy were varied, as the President's Economic Report of January, 1955, noted:

Consumers [it said] not only maintained their spending at a consistently high level, but reduced their rate of saving. . . . Businessmen kept up their capital expenditures at a high rate, increased the flow of dividends to stockholders . . . Builders and real estate developers stepped up their operations. Trade unions conducted their affairs with an eye to basic conditions and with a sense of responsibility. . . . Commercial banks and other financial institutions made ample supplies of credit available on liberal terms. States and localities carried out large and expanding programs of school, hospital and road construction . . . the continuing recovery of Western Europe helped to augment our exports. . . .

Clearly, many people had a part in stemming the economic decline. . . . The Federal Government also . . . influenced the economy in two principal ways: first, through the automatic workings of the fiscal system; second, by deliberately pursuing monetary, tax and expenditure policies that inspired widespread confidence on the part of the people. . . .

There was a note of elation in the Cabinet on July 23 when Burns announced that the midyear economic indicators showed definitely that the decline had come to an end. To have passed from the Korean war economy to a peacetime economy without a far more serious drop, he said, was a tremendous accomplishment.

With the Congressional elections approaching, the Cabinet cheerfully discussed various opportunities for making all this clear to the public, especially the now favorable comparison between 1954 and 1952, the last year of Democratic rule.

CHAPTER 16

The President Fights for a Program

Legislative Program for an Election Year – "Liberal in Human Relations, Conservative in Economic Affairs" – Eisenhower Tells Leaders the Republicans Must Face Up to Their Responsibilities – He Recalls the One Difference He Had with General Marshall – The President Threatens to Carry His Fight for the Program into the Open

As his conversations at the Commodore before the inauguration revealed, Eisenhower had his eye on the 1954 elections even before he took office himself. Throughout the early months of 1954 —a period filled with the distractions of the debate on the Bricker amendment, the Army-McCarthy hearings and the Indo-China crisis—he strove to put through Congress a program that might carry the Republican Congressional candidates to victory in November. He likened it to a political "umbrella" for Republicans who would support it.

At a press conference on January 27, 1954, he described the philosophy behind it in these terms: "When it comes down to dealing with the relationships between the human in this country and his government, the people in this administration believe in being what I think we would normally call liberal, and when we deal with the economic affairs of this country, we believe in being conservative."

In the preceding December the President held a three-day conference with Republican Congressional leaders and committee chairmen to acquaint them with his recommendations and enlist their support.

His opening remarks revealed privately what was soon to be remarked publicly, and that was that his attitude toward his relationship with Congress was hardening.

During the first session he had made a great point of deferring to Congressional prerogatives. Eisenhower proposed, but he almost went out of his way to insist upon the right of Congress to dispose. He relied heavily on his faculty for charming and persuading by words, and was extremely sparing in the use of his immense prestige and power as President and party leader to try to compel Congress to follow him.

Now with the bitter discouragements and frustrations of the previous spring and summer behind him, he spoke with the new and firmer tone of one taking a more resolute view of his role as a leader. It was obvious, he said, that the administration must offer a definitive program which would command the respect of the majority of the people. The leaders, he asserted, must help him get it enacted.

The President told them flatly that the time had arrived when the Republican administration must face up to its responsibilities. He insisted that regardless of how many intraparty differences had to be thrashed out, there were minimum limits of achievement below which the administration must not fall.

Substantially all of his program, with a few exceptions such as the addition of housing legislation and extension of unemployment insurance, he said, was embodied in the 1952 Republican platform. The story of this program must be told to the people. He remarked that during the first year in office he had talked a great deal about foreign affairs. Now with a sizable speaking schedule ahead of him in 1954, he said, he was going to concentrate on domestic problems.

Some of the most conservative leaders at the conference criticized the housing program. One felt that the existing authorization for new public housing units should be spread out rather than having new units authorized; another feared the public reaction against the whole bill.

From start to finish the President defended the housing legislation, maintaining that it would help fulfill one of the basic needs of the people. He would not agree to hold it back.

When it came his turn, Humphrey recommended that the reduction in excises and corporation income taxes scheduled for April 1, 1954, should be postponed for a year. Digressing, he said that the United States was too dependent on income taxes in case of a depression. Greater stability, he thought, could be achieved by increased reliance on excises. He noted that in this respect the United States lagged far behind all other large countries. While no excises should be higher than 10 per cent, in his personal opinion a good case could be made for a 5 per cent excise on virtually all items except food.

Some of the leaders threw up their hands. There was no chance that such a proposal could pass the Senate, one of them said. A House leader ventured that while revision of excises could be made selectively, a general excise tax was out of the question.

The President observed that the forthcoming rise in Social Security taxes would offset for many workers the drop in income taxes on January 1. Some might have even less take-home pay than before. He suggested, therefore, that it might be possible to increase the exemptions of low-income families. (The administration never adopted this policy. On the contrary, when the Democrats proposed increasing exemptions, Humphrey fought the measure.)

The Secretary of the Treasury raised with the leaders the question of eliminating tax privileges for co-operatives, but Eisenhower said that no such action would be feasible at least until 1955.

The President brought up the proposal he would make in his State of the Union message on January 7, 1954, for a Constitutional amendment to lower the voting age from twenty-one to eighteen. Some leaders asked if this might not produce more votes for the Democrats than for the Republicans. Both Brownell and Dodge expressed the opinion that it would favor the Republicans.

The President, as he had done on a previous occasion, alluded to the possible need for an Official Secrets Act. One of the Senate leaders urged caution on this, reminding the President that such a law might be regarded as an infringement of freedom of the press. Great care, he said, would have to be given to the timing of such a proposal.

On the second day of the conference there was considerable discussion about Dulles's statement in Paris on December 14 that continued delay in establishment of "political, economic and military unity" in Western Europe would "compel an agonizing reappraisal of basic United States policy."

The President told the leaders that he had gone over Dulles's speech to the NATO Council in advance and that he was in complete agreement with the Secretary of State on this remark. The "facts of life" in the European situation made it necessary for the United States to be firm but not truculent. Rejection of the European Defense Community would be a serious blow to the United States, the President declared.

The fate of the E.D.C. was causing him grave concern at that time. At Bermuda a fortnight earlier he had reacted sharply to lukewarm talk by the British and French about it. He hammered away at the point that the E.D.C. was vital to the defense of the West and urged the French to end their hesitation and ratify it. He and Dulles returned from Bermuda, however, only too well aware that the current deadlock in the Paris government made the going all the more difficult for the E.D.C. treaty in the French Parliament.

Eisenhower spoke of this at a bipartisan meeting in the White House on January 5, 1954, at which he went over with Republican and Democratic Congressional leaders the parts of his State of the Union message dealing with foreign and military policy. While the economies of our European allies were growing stronger and the peoples were acquiring new confidence, he said, these gains were being offset by the instability of the French government, a condition which he felt was accentuated by France's distrust of Germany. The President cited as one of the great problems of American policy the finding of some means of bringing Germany and France together and of persuading France that Communist Russia and not Germany posed the worst threat to her freedom.

The President opened this meeting by turning his full charm on the Democratic leaders. He hoped, he said, that the faces of all those present would continue to be as relaxed throughout the year as they were that day. While the Republican Party was responsible for the conduct of the government generally, he went on, matters like foreign and military policy were of concern to both parties and found both parties in agreement to a great extent. Speaking particularly to the Democrats, he said that he wanted the leaders to feel free to call upon him directly or upon members of the Cabinet whenever they had the slightest feeling that the spirit of foreign or military policy was being violated.

One of the Democratic leaders inquired whether our allies understood American intentions in the Far East. Dulles assured him that they did. Another Democrat said that it was important for the administration to make it clear in the Senate that the United States was not bound to support Syngman Rhee under all circumstances.

In a discussion on Korea the President referred to his decision in December to recall two American divisions and said that the United States could not allow Communist threats to keep American forces too widely dispersed. He did not believe, he continued, that the withdrawal would have a poor effect on our allies. The United States had made it clear that it would take the offensive if hostilities should break out again. Dulles expressed the view that Rhee would be less likely to upset the truce if the prospect of embroiling the United States was lessened by the withdrawal of troops.

When the discussion turned to the problem of military reserves, Eisenhower said that the only disagreement between General of the Army George C. Marshall and himself that he could remember was on this subject. The President said that he had favored Universal Military Service whereas Marshall had advocated Universal Military Training. (The distinction between the two has now become blurred. Originally, the difference was this: Under U.M.S. all young men would have served a hitch in the regular active armed forces. Under U.M.T. they would first have gone into a separate corps and, after a period of training, been put on reserve status subject to call to the regular forces if needed.)

The President concluded the meeting by acknowledging that under American political traditions he and other Republican officials were legitimate targets for Democratic criticism. But there would be problems, he said, on which Democrats and Republicans must work together for the good of the country.

The President himself viewed his program as exemplifying what he meant by political moderation. Conserving many of the social

reforms of the 1930's it sought progress by modifying, by moderniz-
ing, by strengthening programs whose worth had been demonstrated by long usage. He proposed, for example, to:

Extend Social Security to about 10,000,000 more persons and in-
crease the benefits.
Continue public housing at a rate of 35,000 new units annually for
the next four years.
Bring 4,000,000 more persons under unemployment insurance coverage.
Increase grants for building hospitals and clinics.

Sensing no great public demand for innovation and experimentation, the President followed his inclination to conserve and strenthen.
The essence of his proposals was revision rather than radical change.
The fundamentals of the Taft-Hartley Act were to be kept intact;
its application in certain respects was what he would change. The
revision of farm policy was more drastic, but it was a course between
extremes and not an extreme change itself. The principle of price
supports for basic commodities was retained, but supports were to
become flexible, ranging from 75 to 90 per cent of parity, rather
than remain rigid at 90 per cent. Flexibility was not a new concept.
Indeed, it would have taken effect under an earlier law if Congress
had not intervened to extend 90 per cent supports. Powerful farm
interests wished to do so again in 1954, and it took some fortitude
by Eisenhower and Benson to oppose them. The idea behind flexibility, which unfortunately does not seem to have been much more
effective yet in this respect than the old system, was to check the
accumulation of surpluses.

The President's health program probably demonstrated as well
as any other his efforts to go down the middle, threading his way
between the poles of Truman's comprehensive government health
program and the American Medical Association, which viewed almost
any government venture into this field, including Eisenhower's,
as a possible opening wedge for "socialized medicine." On the one
hand the legislation avoided doing nothing to help the people, or
some of them, with their medical bills. On the other it steered
clear of national medical insurance. What Eisenhower proposed
was a plan under which the Federal government would set up a

fund of $25,000,000 to reinsure private voluntary health insurance plans for 75 per cent of any "abnormal losses" so that the cost of such insurance could be lowered and thus brought within reach of more people. This program was so squarely in the middle of the road that it got hit by traffic going in both directions. "The concentration and delegation of such potential power and control over a vital branch of American industry in a department of the executive branch of the government without clear and convincing evidence of need is extremely difficult to justify," declared the A.M.A. spokesman. The Americans for Democratic Action said, "A $10,000,000,000 problem cannot be solved by an advance of $25,000,000."

When this very point was made at a legislative leaders' meeting on May 10, the President observed, "I feel pretty good when I'm attacked from both sides. It makes me more certain that I'm on the right track."

It was not only the nature of Eisenhower's program for 1954 that was striking, but the scope. *Congressional Quarterly* listed 232 separate Presidential requests to Congress, ranging all the way from extension of the Reciprocal Trade Agreements Act to stripping of citizenship from those convicted of conspiring to advocate the overthrow of the government by force or violence.

The President was proud of this program. He said that he would fight for it, and he kept a steady pressure on the leaders to enact it. Everyone around the President reflected his seriousness about it.

At a meeting of the Cabinet on January 20, for example, the Vice-President suggested that the time might be approaching when patronage should be used to help force the program through, especially in cases where individual members voted against the administration on important issues without a good reason. He cited one Senator's desertion from the Republican ranks on a recent vote in committee. Nixon also suggested that administration officials might exercise their influence by accepting or not accepting speaking engagements in the districts of Republican Congressmen depending on whether these members supported the program.

The President indicated that an effort should be made then to let members know that this might happen in hope that the administration would not have to resort to such a course later.

Time and again in conferences with the legislative leaders Eisenhower prodded for action. Several times later in the session he suggested that they try to have one major item approved without fail each week not only to create a good record but to avoid a last-minute logjam that would obscure the record by burying one item under another.

As the session moved along, the administration ran into strong opposition, not only from the Democrats on measures like the tax bill but from Republicans on farm and housing legislation and from both on the health program. Five Republican members of the House Agriculture Committee, including the chairman, Representative Clifford R. Hope, of Kansas, held out for rigid price supports in the face of the President's fight for flexible supports. And on the House Banking and Currency Committee, which handled the housing bill, two Republican members from California, Representatives Edgar W. Hiestand and Gordon L. McDonough, denounced the measure in such terms as "socialistic" and "demoralizing."

Once at a leaders' meeting when the President was pressing very hard for results, one of the Republican hierarchy ventured a comment about the undesirability of pushing an independent Congress too far.

This remark stung Eisenhower. He shot back that he had no pride of authorship in the program. In the drafting of it, he said, he had sought every possible bit of legislative advice. He was intent solely on doing what was good for the country. He said that so far he had been fighting quietly under cover. But if he had to, he asserted, he would carry the fight into the open.

CHAPTER 17

Showdown with Bricker

Senator Bricker Proposes to Safeguard the Constitution Against Treaty-Made Law — Eisenhower First Sees Amendment and Sympathizes with Its General Aim — Dulles Warns the Cabinet the Amendment Would Fetter the President in Conducting Foreign Affairs — Eisenhower Opposes the Amendment — The Efforts to Get a Compromise — The Final Battle in the Senate

Almost before Congress could get started on the President's big 1954 program the session was convulsed by two of the most emotional and vexing domestic issues that have faced Eisenhower during his years in the White House.

One was the Bricker amendment, the controversy over which has been called "our greatest debate about the Constitutional ordering of our foreign relations since 1788." The other was the loud, lurid, acrimonious and often venomous quarrel that raged over the person and conduct of Senator McCarthy.

Both issues had swirled around Eisenhower off and on since he became President and indeed even before. Both issues aroused deep political passions in America and set right against left, Old Guard against the new, liberal against conservative, internationalist against isolationist. In the final analysis both issues bore a threat to the Presidential power and prerogative.

A difference between the two problems was that in the case of the Bricker amendment no grievous personal conflict developed between the President and the senior Senator from Ohio. Between

Eisenhower and McCarthy, on the other hand, there was intense dislike, to which McCarthy but not Eisenhower gave voice in public with ever-increasing harshness.

The showdown on the Bricker amendment came on February 26, 1954, but the issue had dogged Eisenhower since the days in the Commodore in January, 1953. It was there that he first saw the amendment, which would have had the effect of limiting the President's powers to make treaties and thus of augmenting Congressional authority over foreign relations.

The proposal stemmed from resentment over such executive agreements as Yalta and, as Bricker had said in a speech, from a fear that "American sovereignty and the American Constitution . . . are threatened by treaty law."

Its ostensible purpose was to provide protection against the possibility that a President, aided by an unwary Senate, would impose on the country through a treaty legal obligations which would deprive the people of Constitutional rights or would invade the domain of power reserved to the states. In particular its proponents regarded it as a bulwark against international agreements drafted by the U.N. or its specialized agencies, which might, as these proponents feared, deny or abridge fundamental rights of United States citizens or interfere in purely local matters. In a nutshell Bricker was telling the American people that their Constitution was in danger of being contravened or superseded by treaty and by executive agreements and that they had better close the door against this menace.

His announced aim of protecting the Constitution and American liberties looked plausible and appealing to a great many people, and when the amendment was first presented to Eisenhower, he felt sympathetic toward its general purpose. He himself believed that the Constitution should not be changed by other than the Constitutional process. He recognized furthermore that there was widespread anxiety over the possibilities Bricker warned of, and he was concerned that this feeling might turn American opinion against the U.N.

Before introducing the amendment on January 7, 1953, Bricker called the Commodore and solicited the support of Eisenhower and

Dulles. Since Eisenhower had not studied the problem, the request was turned over to Herman Phleger, an attorney, who was to become Legal Adviser to the State Department. After looking at the complexities of the question, Phleger advised Eisenhower against taking a position until the new administration had had a chance to study the amendment. This was the course the President-elect followed.

The first report on this study was made to the Cabinet by Dulles on February 20, 1953. If it was adopted, Dulles said, the Bricker amendment would seriously curtail executive authority and make it impossible to conduct foreign affairs effectively. Brownell and Wilson both concurred in this. The President did not commit himself, although he did refer to his feeling that the Constitution should be changed only by regular procedures.

On March 13 Dulles gave a further report. This time he warned that the administration and the Bricker movement might clash head-on and urged that every possible effort be made to find a safe and acceptable substitute. He characterized the amendment as "impossible" and did not see how mere revision could change matters. He said he thought that Bricker and his supporters already had achieved their purpose in large part by calling attention to the possible danger of law made by treaty. Nixon suggested that a substitute proposal might be worked out which would express the sense of Bricker's argument without tying the President's hands in foreign relations.

Eisenhower, who was now coming around toward positive opposition to the amendment, remarked on the difficulty of lining up Republican Senators against it. To him, he said, this seemed to indicate that these Senators were not concentrating on writing a record of co-operation with the administration. Concern over the outcome of the Congressional elections a year and a half away did not appear to be nearly so strong among Republicans on Capitol Hill, he observed, as it was in the White House. Later he commented that while some Senators might feel secure in their six-year terms, committee chairmanships would be at stake in 1954, and a good Republican record would be essential to keep them from being lost.

On March 20 the President and the Secretary of State reported that they had talked to Bricker. The conversation, they said, indicated that the Senator would not insist on the exact content of his amendment as it stood, but that he was very desirous of having Congress enact some amendment to this general purpose, and one which bore his name.

Dulles cautioned, however, against the administration's agreeing even to an apparently harmless amendment, especially, he said, since American history did not show that treaties had had a detrimental effect inside the country. The President said that giving Congress control over treaties would jeopardize the permanence of treaties because one Congress could nullify the action of a preceding Congress.

A way to solve the conflict over the Bricker amendment, the Attorney General suggested, might be to create a commission headed by Bricker to make a new study of the problem. If any such group was appointed, Nixon interposed, the administration should make two things clear. One was that the administration could not support the Bricker amendment as it stood, and the other that the objective of the commission would be to find a substitute.

Despite the Vice-President's statement, the administration had still not taken a formal position on the amendment.

At a meeting of the Cabinet two weeks later, on April 3, it was decided that any members who were called upon to testify on the amendment were to state their views as individuals. Any member who wished to do so was free to support the amendment, but the President asked that he first check with the State Department as to the facts of the case. Which way the wind was blowing, however, was shown very clearly by the President's remark that he believed that the amendment was unnecessary and would be damaging to the United States. To try to protect against a possible harmful treaty by such means, he said, would only compound the difficulty of the problem. Within a few days both Dulles and Brownell testified strongly against the amendment.

When the Cabinet met on May 8, Dulles said that the increasingly emotional nature of the controversy had been demonstrated the day before by Bricker's attack in the Senate on Phleger and Under Secretary of State Smith. The Senator's criticism of these two State Department officials was directed not at their opposition to his amendment but at their support of the NATO Status of Forces agreement then before the Senate. This agreement concerned the jurisdiction over crimes committed in one NATO country by personnel of another, and Bricker was very hostile to it. He proposed a reservation which would have given the United States exclusive jurisdiction over crimes committed by American troops stationed abroad. It was finally defeated by the Senate on July 14.

The Status of Forces agreement, as it happened, had a part in turning Eisenhower strongly against the Bricker amendment. As Commander of the NATO forces he had become thoroughly familiar with the problems the agreement dealt with, and he wanted it ratified. The meaning of the Bricker amendment, therefore, struck him adversely and with great force when his legal advisers explained that if the amendment were then in effect, the Senate could not ratify the NATO agreement because it dealt with a matter outside the powers delegated to Congress by the Constitution. This seemed to give the President a sharper picture than he had had before of what was involved in Bricker's proposal.

At this same meeting on May 8 the Cabinet talked about the hopes of the administration in preventing a debate on the amendment in the Senate, which would have opened a deep new split in the already divided Republican ranks. This was something the President and the Cabinet were very anxious to avert. Brownell suggested that the problem be brought up at the next legislative leaders' meeting. Thinking it over, the President replied that perhaps the administration was not making the best use of these meetings to achieve its ends in Congress. Nixon cautioned him, however, against expecting too much from such conferences. No one can "deliver" the Senate, the Vice-President told him.

On June 5 the President, reporting to the Cabinet on his meeting with the Republican leaders the day before, said there was strong sentiment in the Senate for the Bricker amendment.

The Secretary of State responded by saying that this change in Constitutional principles, if it went through, would have a disastrous effect. He defended Phleger against criticism that had been directed against him by some of the leaders, and he said that these leaders were looking for a compromise on principle on a point on which no compromise was possible.

A good deal of "salesmanship" would be needed to bring the Senate around to the administration's viewpoint, the President said.

The Cabinet agreed that Brownell and Phleger should set out to arrange for some substitute proposal which would offer a way out for Senators supporting Bricker but which would avoid compromising the principle of Presidential authority over foreign relations. General Persons was to work closely with members of the Cabinet to determine how their personal influence could be used most effectively in swinging support away from the Bricker amendment and to the substitute.

Benson and others in the Cabinet said that the reason the Bricker amendment had gained such widespread backing was that its dangers had not been adequately explained to the people.

A mention had been made earlier in another connection of small atom bombs. Philip Young facetiously recalled it during the discussion on the Bricker amendment, saying that maybe some of these bombs could be used now to good effect. The President took him to task for this. He said sharply that he did not wish to hear any talk of a "Pride's Purge."

(Before a vote on bringing the king of England to trial in the seventeenth century, Colonel Thomas Pride stood outside the House of Commons with his regiment and excluded all Presbyterian and Royalist members, whose names appeared on a written list given him by the army council.)

On June 15 the Senate Judiciary Committee reported out a new version of the amendment, redrafted along the lines proposed by the American Bar Association through its Committee on Peace and Law Through the United Nations. Bricker espoused this version, but to the administration it was fully as objectionable as the original.

It gave Congress the power to regulate all executive and other agreements with foreign powers and the U.N. Furthermore it provided that a treaty would become effective as internal law only if Congress passed implementing legislation, "which would be valid in the absence of treaty." This clause went to the heart of the controversy.

Simply, the administration's objection may be summarized as follows:

Under the law as it stood, and still stands, the President may negotiate and the Senate may ratify a treaty on a subject not within the delegated powers of Congress and the President. Congress may then pass laws to implement it. The "which" clause would have prohibited Congress from passing implementing laws in areas beyond its delegated powers. Thus whether the treaty was effective in the United States would depend upon whether it conformed to the laws of the respective states or, if it did not, whether the states would pass laws that conformed to it. The President contended that this would return the country to the situation that existed under the Articles of Confederation, in which each state had a right to repudiate treaties.* Thus, he maintained, in dealing with foreign nations the President and the Secretary of State, instead of speaking for one government, would be saddled with the "impossible task of representing forty-eight governments."

The President said at his press conference on July 1 that while he did not believe a treaty could contravene or supersede the Constitution, he was willing to support a Constitutional amendment containing a simple statement to that effect. Meanwhile Brownell was working with Knowland and others to write a substitute that would fit this prescription.

At the meeting of the Cabinet on July 3 Eisenhower took note of charges that he had compromised his stand on the Bricker amendment. He told the Cabinet that he did not feel that he had been inconsistent. He said that he had always felt that treaties should not supersede the Constitution, that it was not necesary to amend the Constitution to insure this, but that a statement reaffirming that the Constitution was paramount would be perfectly acceptable.

In the Cabinet on July 17 Dulles suggested either that action on the Bricker amendment be put over to another session of Congress or else, if a showdown was to come, that every Senator be acquainted in the most unequivocal terms with the President's views. Dulles and Stassen both believed that Bricker's defeat three days earlier on his reservation to the Status of Forces agreement indicated that

* Bricker called this interpretation "erroneous."

the Bricker amendment could be defeated. They felt that its total defeat was preferable to enactment of a watered-down substitute.

On this point the President said that public opinion had to be taken into account, and he questioned whether the fears raised by Bricker could be quieted by the complete defeat of his amendment.

Brownell and Nixon suggested that as a result of the vote on the Status of Forces reservation, Bricker would probably be willing to accept the language of the substitute which the administration was preparing. Brownell warned that to defeat the Bricker amendment outright and without any substitute measure would cause a serious split in the Republican Party. In the end the Cabinet agreed that he should continue working with the Senate leaders to draft a satisfactory substitute, which he did.

On July 22 Knowland finally introduced it, and Eisenhower issued a public statement saying that it had his "unqualified support."

The Knowland amendment provided that a treaty or international agreement which conflicts with the Constitution would have no force. It also provided that a treaty could be ratified only by recorded vote. This meant that all Senators would be notified when the vote was to be taken and that a treaty could not be shouted through, as once happened on a minor protocol, for instance, with only two Senators on the floor.

While the President said in his statement that "the reassurances contained in the Knowland amendment meet all legitimate demands that have been made in this field of foreign relations," Bricker flatly rejected it, and that left the issue at a dead end for the 1953 session.

This was only a respite. The full power of the Bricker movement bore down upon Congress when it reconvened in January, 1954. This time it was clear that the Senate would have to act. It was also clear that the President was in for a hard fight to defend his powers against limitation of one sort or another by Constitutional amendment.

The political pressure that had been built up behind the amendment and powerfully applied by heavy lobbying was immense. Arrayed in support of the amendment were the American Medical Association, the Daughters of the American Revolution, the Chicago Tribune, the American Bar Association's Committee on Peace and

Law Through the United Nations, the Committee for Constitutional Government, Frank E. Holman, former president of the American Bar Association, and the Vigilant Women for the Bricker Amendment, a "volunteer organization of housewives and mothers of boys overseas." This last group alone presented petitions to the Senate bearing an estimated 500,000 signatures.

When the original amendment was introduced in the Senate in 1953, it had sixty-four cosponsors—the two thirds of the Senate needed to approve a Constitutional amendment. Even within the administration, as was mentioned earlier, the Bricker amendment had the ardent support of Clarence Manion.

Opposed to the amendment were the American Bar Association's Section of International and Comparative Law, the Association of the Bar of the City of New York, the American Association for the United Nations, the League of Women Voters and many liberal organizations and independent newspapers.

Fully aroused to the danger that the amendment might be forced through the Senate under this heavy pressure, the President sent a strong letter to Knowland on January 25, 1954, in which he said, in part:

I am unalterably opposed to the Bricker amendment. . . . It would so restrict the conduct of foreign affairs that our country could not negotiate the agreements necessary for the handling of our business with the rest of the world. Such an amendment would make it impossible for us to deal effectively with friendly nations for our mutual defense and common interests.

These matters are fundamental. We cannot hope to achieve and maintain peace if we shackle the Federal Government so that it is no longer sovereign in foreign affairs. The President must not be deprived of his historic position as the spokesman for the nation in its relations with other countries.

Adoption of the Bricker amendment in its present form by the Senate would be notice to our friends as well as our enemies abroad that our country intends to withdraw from its leadership in world affairs. The inevitable reaction would be of major proportion. It would impair our hopes and plans for peace and for the successful achievement of the important international matters now under discussion. . . .

Formal debate on the issue began in the Senate on January 27 and for nearly a month the battle went on. Everyone was a Constitutional authority for a day. Legalisms beat down like hail. Personalities were berated. The Secretary of State was accused by Bricker of turning legal summersaults. Jenner linked the opposition to the amendment with a "secret revolutionary corps" aligned with such figures as Harry Hopkins and Harry Dexter White, who had been dead for years, as well as with Henry A. Wallace, Owen Lattimore and Alger Hiss. It was all that many could do to keep up with the flood of amendments offered from the floor, and far more than most could do to grasp their possible consequences. Before the debate reached a climax the Bricker amendment had been modified in a half-dozen ways, but was still unacceptable to the administration.

The President, of course, had to sit through one session after another with his advisers to try to keep abreast of the confused developments, and the endless hauling, hairsplitting and negotiation wearied and irked him. One such meeting with Smith and Phleger on January 29, 1954, ended just before the Cabinet meeting. The President went into the Cabinet room and took his chair. After the silent prayer he said that he welcomed that quiet moment because it gave him a welcome opportunity to remove himself from the wear and tear and tugging and pulling that went on in his own office. In that minute of prayer, he remarked, he could recapture a frame of mind appropriate to a meeting around the Cabinet table where all were friends.

When the subject of the continuing Senate debate came up, Eisenhower said that it was vitally important that the administration act simultaneously to protect the President's right, authority and responsibility in the conduct of foreign affairs and to relieve the legitimate fears of those who were supporting the Bricker amendment. The amendment, he believed, could be beaten. If this proved to be the case, he said, the next thing for the administration to do would be to take steps to keep this spurious issue, as he called it, from flaring up in the Congressional election campaign. He took pride, he said, in the efforts the administration had made to be decent and reasonable throughout the controversy without having surrendered one iota on the essential points.

Wilson said that he shared the feeling of the Bricker supporters that treaties should not be allowed to take away fundamental rights and that agreements such as those reached at Yalta and Potsdam should in the future be prevented by law if possible.

Of itself, the President replied, the Bricker amendment could not serve as a guarantee against either of these circumstances.

(Eisenhower had been assured by his legal advisers that the Bricker amendment would not have applied to Yalta and Potsdam because they were political agreements and not treaties or executive agreements.)

Two days later, on February 1, the President met with the legislative leaders and told them he would have no part in upsetting the balance established between the different branches of the government by the framers of the Constitution. His disgust with the whole business showing through, he said that something struck him as ironical. This was the way he put it: For twenty years the Republicans had been accusing the Democrats of unconstitutional actions. Then what did the Republicans do as soon as they came to power but begin trying to alter the Constitution without even being in complete agreement as to the meaning of the changes proposed.

At his meeting with the leaders the next week, February 8, Eisenhower found some amusement in the subject by repeating a quip he had heard that the Constitution was being demolished "brick by brick by Bricker."

When at last it came, the showdown was not over the Bricker amendment but over a substitute introduced by Senator George. The oft-revised Bricker amendment was rejected on February 25, forty-two to fifty. For all practical purposes this narrowed the fight to the George amendment and the revised administration amendment sponsored by Knowland and others.

George's amendment eliminated the "which" clause and was milder than the Bricker amendment, but still the administration feared the limitations it might place on the President's powers. When Brownell sent a letter to the Senate opposing the George amendment, George, a man of massive dignity and voice to match, said, "I would resign my seat before I would let my vote be governed by such an odd Attorney General."

On February 26 the Senate chose the George amendment in preference to the Republican leaders' proposal and proceeded to vote on it. Bricker and his followers threw their full weight behind the George amendment. In spite of the administration's opposition, even Knowland, the Republican leader of the Senate, voted for it. (He explained that he could not ignore "a dangerous tendency toward executive encroachment on legislative powers.") As the roll call progressed, sixty votes piled up for the amendment. Thirty-one were cast against it, and that thirty-first nay saved Eisenhower from a severe political defeat. Had that vote gone yea, it would have given George sixty-one, which would have been the two thirds needed for a Constitutional amendment. The amendment would then have taken effect if approved by two thirds of the House and by the legislatures of three fourths of the states.

While the defeat of the Bricker amendment brought victory and relief to the President, any hopes he may have had that it would free Congress to concentrate on his program were quickly dispelled. Even before the final vote on it an uproar was brewing between McCarthy and Secretary of the Army Robert Stevens over McCarthy's treatment of Brigadier General Ralph W. Zwicker. The troubles between the junior Senator from Wisconsin and the Pentagon were soon to explode into the political brawl and television extravaganza of the Army-McCarthy hearings.

CHAPTER 18

Eisenhower and McCarthy

The President Reads a Letter About His Attitude Toward Senator McCarthy – Trying to Get Along with McCarthy – McCarthy Attacks – The White House Staff Is Split on Strategy – Eisenhower Refuses to Attack McCarthy Personally – Zwicker, Stevens and the Peress Case – The Army-McCarthy Hearings – Censure – Eisenhower's Feelings About McCarthy

The President opened a meeting of the Cabinet on March 27, 1953, by reading a letter he had received on the subject of his attitude toward Senator McCarthy. Eisenhower said he believed that the letter reflected the consensus of public opinion. This fell within the period in which McCarthy was investigating the Voice of America, fighting the President on the Bohlen nomination and launching sorties of one kind or another, such as his negotiation with some Greek shipowners to halt trade with Communist ports in Asia.

The writer of the letter was severely critical of McCarthy's activities. He implied at least that McCarthy had usurped the national leadership from Eisenhower, and he urged the President to wrest it away from him.

Laying the letter aside, the President told the Cabinet that he thought it would be altogether wrong for him to challenge a single individual. McCarthy's activities, he felt, were the responsibility of the constituted leadership of Congress. What he and the executive branch could and should do, he said, was to give all encouragement possible to established leaders like Taft, Millikin and Saltonstall to help them in the exercise of their responsibilities and to strengthen them in their dealings with extremists.

The President said that he did not consider it his function to battle Congressional figures in the arena of the press conference. The thing that was needed in coping with the problem raised by McCarthy, he concluded, was patience.

This attitude, however much his liberal critics deplored it, was a key to his approach to McCarthy, at least during his first several months in the White House. While at SHAPE Eisenhower had observed the effect McCarthy was having on our European allies. And during his campaign in 1952 he had come up against the Mc-Carthy problem directly, especially in Wisconsin. There Governor Walter J. Kohler, Jr., had persuaded Eisenhower through his staff to delete from Eisenhower's speech in Milwaukee a passage praising General Marshall, one of McCarthy's targets.

In Wisconsin, Eisenhower gave McCarthy's candidacy an indorsement, though a cool one, by announcing his blanket support for all Republican candidates. He said that he and McCarthy agreed that subversives should be eliminated from the government and that the differences between himself and the Senator "apply to method."

When Eisenhower came to office, he was well aware that Mc-Carthy was going to be a headache for him. As his early Presidential press conferences showed, however, he resolutely set himself against feuding with the Senator. He refused then, as he did consistently thereafter, to discuss McCarthy personally in public. He took the position that as chairman of the Senate Permanent Investigations Subcommittee, McCarthy had a right to investigate and that public opinion would serve to keep investigations within the bounds of propriety and justice.

The President's aim in approaching this problem was not to alienate any wing of the Republican Party beyond hope of reconciliation. Whenever Eisenhower finds himself in conflict with another man, it is his practice not to say anything, if he can avoid it, that will make it impossible for the other fellow to come around to his way without an embarrassing loss of face. This consideration was present in his relations with McCarthy that first year. He hoped that with a con-servative Republican administration in power and obviously determined to deal with any internal Communist problem it encountered, McCarthy would forget the tactics he had used against Truman and Acheson and go along on a live-and-let-live basis.

Trying to get on reasonably with McCarthy, therefore, became one of the rules of the administration. Harold Stassen, to name one person, learned this in March, 1953, when he pitched into McCarthy over the Greek ship deal, testifying that McCarthy's negotiators had in reality "harmed" and "undermined" the government's efforts to curb strategic trade with the Communists. Almost before the echoes of his testimony had died away, he was cut off from the rear. At Nixon's suggestion Dulles received McCarthy at the State Department and assured the Senator that he had acted in the national interest, though he hoped that McCarthy's subcommittee would not barge into foreign relations. And the next day, April 2, 1953, the President said at a press conference that in the nature of things McCarthy could not have negotiated an agreement in the field of foreign policy. Thus, he said, he did not think McCarthy had undermined the government's efforts. "Infringe," he thought, was probably the right word. Thereupon Stassen changed his statement from "undermined" to "infringed."

From Greek ships McCarthy went on to all Western trade with Communist China. At the prompting of a Democratic colleague on the subcommittee, Senator Stuart Symington, of Missouri, McCarthy sent a letter to Eisenhower on May 20 asking for a Presidential explanation of why the administration did not try to halt such trade.

On the basis of press reports that the letter was on the way the White House staff took up the matter at a meeting on May 22. Hagerty said that McCarthy's information apparently was based on false reports about this trade. The State Department had the correct facts, the press secretary said, but because the material was classified, the department could not publicly put the matter to rights. Cutler warned that the letter would have a dangerous effect upon the relations between the United States and its allies. If this kind of thing went on, he said, the United States would have no allies left. At this point the Vice-President stepped into the situation and persuaded McCarthy to recall the letter, which he did, evidently before it had reached Eisenhower's desk.

The "don't join the book-burners" episode and the J. B. Matthews affair followed. Then McCarthy's name came up again in the Cabinet on August 27 when Nixon was presiding in the President's absence. McCarthy's subcommittee had been investigating security regulations in the Government Printing Office. Presently McCarthy and G.P.O. officials got into a dispute as to whether the F.B.I. file on a certain bookbinder listed forty informants as having reported that the man had engaged in Communist activities. McCarthy maintained it did, but G.P.O. officials issued statements saying that it contained nothing like this number.

The Vice-President told the Cabinet that he considered these statements unwise. The administration should go in fighting, he said, only when McCarthy's facts were quite wrong and McCarthy was clearly out of line. He emphasized, and Benson signified his agreement, that the administration could display a co-operative spirit even in showing up errors of Congressional committees. Nixon urged that whenever any Communist infiltration was discovered, it should be admitted forthwith and the Communists expelled.

McCarthy opened the first of his major offensives against the Eisenhower administration in a national radio and television broadcast on November 24, 1953. The networks had given him free time to answer Truman's use of the word "McCarthyism" in the former President's speech eight days earlier defending his conduct in the Harry Dexter White case. McCarthy first fired some salvos back at Independence, Missouri, and then swung his guns around toward the White House and the State Department. While the Eisenhower administration was doing "infinitely" better than Truman and Acheson, he said, there were "a few cases where our batting average is zero—we struck out."

He singled out two examples. One was that John Paton Davies, Jr., a controversial career diplomat, who had been cleared seven times by State Department loyalty boards and once by the old Loyalty Review Board, was still in the department as counselor at the United States Embassy in Lima, Peru. The other was that the Eisenhower administration had failed to liquidate the "foulest bankruptcy" of the Truman administration. McCarthy listed this as the continuance of mutual assistance to Britain while the British traded with Red

China, the jailer of American flyers and soldiers captured during the Korean war.

Are we going to continue to send perfumed notes? [McCarthy demanded] . . . it is time that we, the Republican Party, liquidate this blood-stained blunder . . . we promised the American people something different. Let us deliver—not next year or next month—let us deliver now. . . . We can do this by merely saying to our allies and alleged allies, "If you continue to ship to Red China . . . you will not get one cent of American money."

McCarthy also took direct issue with Eisenhower, who at his press conference the preceding week, as it happened, had protested that he did not know what the term McCarthyism meant. At that same press conference the President had said he was confident that the administration's routing of subversives would prove so thorough that the Communists-in-government issue would have no place in the 1954 campaign.

McCarthy gruffly disagreed. The "raw, harsh, unpleasant fact" was, he told his national audience, that "Communism is an issue and will be an issue in 1954."

In public Eisenhower continued to hold himself aloof from McCarthy. In private he could go up in an utter blaze over him. McCarthy's tactics disgusted and infuriated him. On the one hand, he was frustrated by McCarthy's impregnability—a President cannot remove a Senator. On the other, he was torn by conflicting advice. His friend and former political lieutenant, Paul G. Hoffman, chairman of the board of the Studebaker-Packard Corporation, for instance, was urging him to let McCarthy have it with both barrels. Contrary advice came from the Vice-President, who warned Eisenhower that a personal frontal attack on McCarthy might lead the President into the vicious situation that had embroiled Truman and Acheson. The White House staff itself had been split right down the middle on the question, and McCarthy's speech revived and rather bitterly intensified the difference.

On November 27 Jackson sent a memorandum to Adams saying that watching the McCarthy telecast had been an "exceptionally horrible experience." Here, he said, was an open declaration of war by a Republican Senator upon a Republican President. This opinion expressed privately by Jackson was widely held in public. *The Commonweal,* for example, commented that the speech "actually contained Senator McCarthy's public declaration of war upon the present administration." Jackson wanted the President to repudiate McCarthy as a Republican. He wanted him to do so at his very next press conference, which was to be held on December 2.

On the same side as Jackson in this dispute, actively or passively, were such members of the staff as Hagerty, Bryce N. Harlow, Charles F. Willis, Jr., Tom Stephens, Cutler and Stanley M. Rumbough, Jr. A man of strong opinions with a strong personality behind them, Jackson had argued that the President was morally involved in the McCarthy issue and no longer could stand aside. He maintained that McCarthy was an irresponsible politician with whom it was impossible to come to terms in any case. "Appeasing" McCarthy, he argued, was useless. Sooner or later McCarthy was going to war on the administration, he said, and when that day came, it would be better for the administration to have been on the offensive than suddenly to have to dig a defensive position.

On the opposite side were members of the staff who, by and large had had a great deal of previous experience on Capitol Hill and whose jobs in the White House involved the handling of relations with Congress. This group included General Persons, Shanley, Gerald D. Morgan, I. Jack Martin, Earle D. Chesney, Lodge and Homer H. Gruenther, brother of General Gruenther, and siding with them usually was Adams.

Their contention was that it would only make matters worse for the President in Congress if he engaged in a personal quarrel with McCarthy. They could foresee no end to such a row. Neither could they see how the President could out-brawl McCarthy. Once a personal Eisenhower-McCarthy fight began, they feared, it would sunder the Republican ranks and thereby jeopardize the President's leadership and his program.

While this debate churned on in the White House, Dulles made the administration's first formal reply to McCarthy in his press conference on December 1. His statement, answering McCarthy's denunciation of mutual assistance to Britain, had been approved by the President earlier that morning.

Without mentioning McCarthy by name, Dulles said that the Senator's criticism "attacks the very heart of U.S. foreign policy." It was the "clear and firm purpose" of the administration, the Secretary said, to treat other free nations as sovereign equals, helping them but not assuming that this help gave the United States the right to dictate their trade policies or "make them our satellites." To deter the Soviets from atomic attack, he continued, the United States must always be ready "to retaliate with a devastating blow against the vitals of Russia." The potentiality for such retaliation existed, he said, "only because we share the well-located bases of other friendly countries."

Before Eisenhower's press conference the next morning, his staff met with the President to draw up a statement he intended to read to the reporters. Jackson came with a proposed Presidential statement he had drafted, attacking McCarthy by name. The President put on his spectacles, took a look at it and banged it down on the desk.

"I will not get in the gutter with *that* guy," he told Jackson angrily.

Many times in those days Eisenhower made this same point: To fight McCarthy, either he would have to descend to McCarthy's level or else bring McCarthy up to the President's level, and he would not do either one.

Instead of Jackson's statement, the President and his staff, with Jackson helping, prepared a restrained reply to McCarthy's attacks on assistance to Britain and to his assertion that the Communists-in-government issue would blossom again in the 1954 campaign. The statement did not mention McCarthy by name.

To coerce our allies on their trade policies, Eisenhower said at the press conference, "would be a mark of the imperialist rather than of the leader." As for the Communist issue, he said, in part:

The best way to keep subversives out of the government is not to employ them in the first place. The administration will continue to hunt for any that are present and, of course, any subversives located by a Congressional Committee will be removed just as promptly as any others.

In all that we do to combat subversion, it is imperative that we protect the basic rights of loyal American citizens. I am determined to protect those rights to the limit of the powers of the office with which I have been entrusted by the American people.

The very next day, December 3, McCarthy struck back by calling upon "every American who feels as I do about this blood trade with a mortal enemy to write or wire the President . . . so he can be properly guided." This denunciation of Britain's "blood trade" with China was made by McCarthy on a filmed television appearance on the eve of the President's meeting with Churchill and Laniel at Bermuda. By the time the conference opened, letters and telegrams were pouring down on the White House. By December 9 the White House said it had received some fifty thousand messages, with McCarthy having the edge among the letter writers and Eisenhower winning with the telegram senders.

A brief lull ensued, and then the storm broke again in all its fury in February, 1954, while the President was vacationing in Palm Springs, California. During an investigation of alleged espionage at Fort Monmouth, New Jersey, McCarthy's staff had come upon the case of an Army dentist named Major Irving Peress, who had been accused of Communist activities. At a hearing of the subcommittee on January 30, 1954, Peress invoked the Fifth Amendment in refusing to answer these charges. McCarthy thereupon sent a demand to Secretary Stevens that Peress be court-martialed. Instead the major was honorably discharged at Camp Kilmer, New Jersey, on February 2. On February 18 McCarthy called as a witness at a closed hearing in New York the commandant of Camp Kilmer, General Zwicker, an officer with a fine combat record, and questioned him about the Peress discharge.

McCarthy had taken up the cry that the Army was "coddling Communists," but this was mild compared to what he had to say to Zwicker. When the record of the hearing was published four days later, it showed that McCarthy had told Zwicker that he was "not fit to wear that uniform" and that he should "be removed from any command." McCarthy impugned "either your [Zwicker's] honesty or your intelligence," and he implied that the general did not have "the brains of a five-year-old child."

Stevens denounced this "humiliating treatment" and "abuse" of

Zwicker and ordered the general not to answer McCarthy's call to appear again. The Army issued a statement that McCarthy would not be given, as he had demanded, the names of others involved in the discharge of Peress. Stevens declared that he would testify himself. McCarthy retorted that Stevens was a "dupe."

The dispute was at this impasse when Stevens agreed to attend a fried chicken luncheon with McCarthy and other Republican members of the subcommittee on February 24, which had been arranged by Senator Dirksen. Stevens had not made this known to the President, who had returned that morning from Palm Springs. By and large the White House had been taking a hands-off attitude toward the dispute up to this time on the grounds that it was the Army's affair, and there was little co-ordination between the White House and Stevens on it.

The luncheon was held in Dirksen's office in the Capitol. Nixon was in an adjoining office (but said later he had had nothing to do with the affair). When the luncheon was over, the Senators made public a "memorandum of understanding" with Stevens, in which the Secretary of the Army conceded to McCarthy practically everything that McCarthy could have hoped for. Contrary to the Army's announcement of five days before, Stevens agreed to give McCarthy the names of those who had had a hand in the discharge of Peress. Instead of insisting upon testifying himself as the civilian head of the Army, he agreed that McCarthy had a right to question Zwicker and other officers.

Public reaction, viewing this as a capitulation, was so bad that the day after the luncheon the White House made Hagerty's office available to Stevens to read a press statement, which the President had approved. Denying that he had retreated, Stevens said, in part:

I shall never accede to the abuse of Army personnel under any circumstances, including committee hearings. I shall never accede to their being browbeaten and humiliated. . . . From assurances I have received from members of the subcommittee, I am confident that they will not permit such conditions to develop in the future. . . . If it had not been for those assurances, I would never have entered into any agreement whatsoever. . . .

McCarthy immediately called this interpretation of the agreement "completely false."

On March 1 the President took up the situation at his weekly meeting with the Republican legislative leaders, saying that he hoped the administration could get help from Congress in improving the handling of investigations.

He said that he was going to make a statement at his press conference the next day, acknowledging the right of Congress to investigate but declaring that Communism could not be defeated by destroying the standards of fair play.

The President told the leaders that Stevens was a fine and an honest man and that he had endeavored to co-operate with the Republican Senators. Stevens had agreed to attend the luncheon, Eisenhower continued, on the assurance that it would be a secret affair and thus he had not even informed the President. When he reached the Capitol, however, Eisenhower said, Stevens found a large number of reporters already assembled and during the luncheon agreed to a statement, the public effect of which was terrible.

Upon his return from Palm Springs, the President said, his staff had acquainted him with the situation. He directed that Stevens should be advised to admit a mistake in the handling of the Peress case and then stand his ground. Eisenhower told the leaders he had not known that Stevens had already, on February 16, written to McCarthy that while "defects" in the draft procedures for medical personnel had made it impossible to halt Peress's honorable discharge, "corrective changes" would be made to prevent similar cases in the future.

The President told the leaders that how to treat medical personnel in a situation like the Peress case had been an unsettled question, complicated by court rulings. Nevertheless, he said, the fact that a blunder had been made in the Peress case did not by any means excuse some of the things that had happened since.

At his press conference on March 3 Eisenhower said that the Army had "made serious errors in handling the Peress case" and, therefore, was changing its procedures. Never, he said, had the administration suggested that any official must "submit to any kind of personal humiliation when testifying before Congressional committees or elsewhere." He praised the loyalty and courage of Zwicker, and added:

Officials in the Executive Branch of the government will have my unqualified support in insisting that employees . . . who appear before any type of executive or Congressional investigating body be treated fairly. . . . Obviously, it is the responsibility of the Congress to see to it that its procedures are proper and fair. Of course, I expect the Republican membership . . . to assume the primary responsibility in this respect, since they are the majority party and, therefore, control the committees. . . .

Then the President sent the following memorandum to all members of the Cabinet:

The White House
Washington

March 5, 1954

PERSONAL AND CONFIDENTIAL
SUBJECT: Treatment of Government Personnel.

During the course of the past year, I have frequently expressed to the chief officers of the Executive Branch certain views pertaining to the handling of governmental personnel. A particular phase of this subject, often discussed among us, involves the security problem; we have proceeded on the theory that working for the government is a privilege and not a right. Adherence to this principle gives great initiative and authority to each responsible officer in proceeding against individuals whose records have created doubt as to their security in positions of trust and confidence.

I summarize below the views I have often before expressed on these matters:

(a)   In these critical times, it is important that we have subordinates in whom we place the utmost confidence as to security and loyalty. We must be vigilant in discovering those in whom there is reason to have little or no confidence and to see that they are removed from positions in which they could possibly do any harm.

(b)   Fairness, justice, and decency must characterize all the procedures that are set up to handle personnel; we cannot defeat Communism by destroying Americanism. We must observe every requirement of law and of ethics.

(c) Having assured ourselves of the efficiency and dedication of subordinates (a process that should continue all down the line), each superior, including me, must remember the obligations he has to his own subordinates. These obligations comprise, among other things, the protection of those subordinates, through all legal and proper means available, against attacks of a character under which they otherwise might be helpless.

(d) No hope of any kind of political advantage, no threat from any source, should lead anyone to foresake these principles of organizational leadership.

The above may be something of an oversimplification, but my purpose is merely to make record of certain essentials that have long been understood among us.

I realize that individual cases sometimes arise that may become subjects for Cabinet discussion or for consultation with me personally. In such instances, I know you feel the utmost freedom in bringing the matter to my attention.

DWIGHT D. EISENHOWER

cc: Gov. Adams

Tawdry as the Peress affair was, it was but a sideshow in the circus that moved into Washington in mid-March in the form of the Senate investigation of the Army-McCarthy dispute. This new rumpus began after the Army gave each member of McCarthy's subcommittee on March 11 a copy of a report charging that McCarthy and Roy Cohn, chief counsel to the group, had made many threats to Army officials to get a commission and other favored treatment for Private David Schine. Schine, who had been Cohn's sidekick on the seriocomic junket across Europe investigating the overseas information service a year before, was a subcommittee consultant, who had been drafted into the Army in November, 1953.

The report, which the Army had prepared at the suggestion of Sherman Adams, was in the form of a chronology of alleged threats and intrusions by McCarthy and Cohn on behalf of Schine. It alleged, for example, that upon learning that Schine might be sent overseas, Cohn had warned that this would "wreck the Army" and undo Stevens as Secretary; that Cohn had threatened to "expose the Army in its worst light"; that Cohn had tried to get Schine relieved from Sunday KP, and that McCarthy had asked Stevens to give Schine the military assignment of studying the "pro-Communist leanings in West Point textbooks."

McCarthy countercharged that the report was "blackmail" to force the subcommittee to end its investigation of the Army. He said that Stevens had tried to shake the subcommittee off the Army's trail by urging the investigators to go after the Navy and the Air Force instead, a statement Stevens hotly denied.

In the Cabinet on March 12 Nixon reviewed the background of the Army's charges. If the report was correct, he said, his own personal conviction was that the Republicans should take the initiative in dismissing Cohn as counsel.

On April 2 the Cabinet was discussing the wire-tapping bill and other measures on the President's program to combat subversion.

"Bad thing about McCarthy," Eisenhower said, "is that he is impeding this work."

In view of this, the President added, but more in jest than seriously, it might be a good idea for the Kremlin to put McCarthy on its payroll.

The White House did what it could to throw the investigation from McCarthy's subcommittee into the Senate Armed Services Committee where McCarthy's influence would have been much less strong. The efforts failed, however, partly because Saltonstall, who was chairman of Armed Services, wanted nothing to do with this hot potato. He was facing a fight for re-election in Massachusetts the following November, and he could see nothing but trouble with the Irish Catholic vote if he got entangled with McCarthy. The Permanent Investigations Subcommittee retained jurisdiction, but with McCarthy temporarily relinquishing the chairmanship to his friend, Senator Karl E. Mundt, Republican, of South Dakota.

The televised hearings began on April 22 with an ineffable cast of characters that included McCarthy and Stevens, Cohn and Schine, Francis P. Carr, the pudgy director of the subcommittee staff; John G. Adams, the gaunt counselor of the Army; Ray H. Jenkins, long-jawed Tennessee trial lawyer, who was counsel to the subcommittee, and Joseph N. Welch, a witty and polished Boston attorney, who was counsel to the Army.

For thirty-six days the hearings were the national business, the national pastime and, as some said, the national disgrace. For Eisenhower these five weeks were a period of acute embarrassment, anger, impatience and frustration. Until he came to the White House he had lived a lifetime in the Army. Pride, loyalty and devotion to the Army are second nature with him. The Army has a strong emotional hold on him. One small insight into his sentiment shows up in the fact that while in office he has never attended an Army-Navy football game, as his predecessors did, because he has felt physically incapable of displaying the impartiality between the teams that is expected of the Commander-in-Chief.

A lot of Army men were hurt inside their hearts, he had remarked during the Peress case. The same could be said of his own feelings during the televised hearings. That in his administration Army officers and Army affairs should have been dragged before the public eye in the tumultuous, disorderly and acrimonious manner of these proceedings galled him. His resentment over the airing of haggles involving the Secretary of the Army and a private was boundless. A President seldom speaks with more revealing contempt in public than Eisenhower did at his press conference on April 29 when he referred to Schine as "*this private.*"

When a reporter asked him that day how, as a former commanding general of the Army, he felt about the privileges that had been accorded to Schine, he was almost overpowered by emotion. He asked to be excused from answering. The whole business, he pleaded, was nothing to talk about.

"I just hope it is all concluded very quickly—that's all," he said, starting out of the room even before the conference had been formally ended.

"Our only hope now," the President said at his next press conference, "is that America may derive from this incident advantages that are at least comparable to what we have suffered in loss of international prestige, and, I venture to say, judging from my correspondence, national respect—self-respect. Now that is just about the way I look at it. . . ."

So far no one has ever discovered any such advantages, but one very important result, indirect yet bound up inextricably with the Army-McCarthy hearings, was that the following December the Senate voted to condemn McCarthy for conduct unbecoming a Senator. This grave action, rare in American history, all but obliterated McCarthy's power to offer further serious challenge to President Eisenhower under foreseeable circumstances.

Two days after the vote was cast the President offered his warm congratulations to Senator Arthur V. Watkins, Republican, of Utah, chairman of the special Senate committee which heard the charges against McCarthy and recommended censure. The President told Watkins at a White House meeting that he had done a "splendid" job. Three days later McCarthy apologized to the American people for having advocated Eisenhower's election.

An assumption that many observers have made is that Eisenhower pursued a conscious strategy of giving McCarthy enough rope to let him hang himself. If true, McCarthy's downfall in December, 1954, proved the President's course a very shrewd and canny one.

Very shrewd it may have been. The fact is, however, that most, although not all, of those who were closest to this problem in the White House do not believe that the President followed any carefully planned, deliberate strategy toward McCarthy. In their opinion it was an attitude rather than a strategy that guided him. If there is any single word that can epitomize this attitude, it is disdain.

The President felt that McCarthy's motives were neither sincere nor inspired by the national interest. He considered his tirades and his reckless charges against individuals despicable in a United States Senator.

During the most exasperating moments that McCarthy inflicted upon him, Eisenhower never believed that McCarthy represented a lasting sentiment of the American people. Even in January, 1954, when a Gallup poll showed that public approval of McCarthy had climbed sixteen points in six months, the President was convinced that this popularity had been fanned by emotionalism and would give way in the end to American common sense. He did not share the concern of many persons that McCarthy could usurp executive powers.

In the face of this high emotion, he believed, the President should act to calm public opinion and not to excite it further by rowing with McCarthy. The national state of mind being what it was at the time, he also saw the further danger that an Eisenhower attack on McCarthy might play straight into McCarthy's hands, putting McCarthy in the role of an underdog being kicked by the President while he was in the very act of saving America from Communism.

The public, of course, could not be privy to Eisenhower's thoughts at that time, and while the Senator was riding high, the President's aloofness left a discouraging void in the movement against McCarthy. To the people—and there were many—who believed that the most important problem in America then was to flatten McCarthy, the President's attitude was so unsatisfying as to be almost unendurable. Yet in view of the fate that overtook the Senator from Wisconsin, a very strong case can be made for it.

Perhaps the President's true feelings on the whole subject were best expressed at a meeting of the Cabinet on July 29, 1954. The censure motion introduced by Senator Ralph E. Flanders, Republican, of Vermont, came up in a discussion of the adjournment date.

The President remarked that he had never believed that a mere censure resolution lacking specifications, as the original Flanders motion did, was in order. But he added that certain situations do develop at times when men finally see themselves compelled to speak out without regard for any technical limitations that may stand in the way.

CHAPTER 19

Dilemma Over Indo-China

Eisenhower, Dulles and Radford Ponder United Action – The "Falling Domino" Theory – The United States Rejects French Pleas for Air Support at Dienbienphu – The Eisenhower-Dulles Terms for American Intervention – United Action Fails to Materialize – The French Agree to Partition of Vietnam – SEATO

On Sunday evening, April 4, 1954, Eisenhower, Dulles and Admiral Radford met in the President's cheerfully lighted study upstairs in the White House to discuss the crisis in Indo-China. While the Army-McCarthy squabble was monopolizing attention at home, the world struggle against Communism had been undergoing a damaging setback in Indo-China in the deterioration of the French position and the Red siege of the French garrison at Dienbienphu. The threat of imminent military disaster to our allies, the French, confronted the President with the hard question of whether, and on what conditions, the United States should take the momentous step of intervening with its own armed forces to halt the Communists in Indo-China as it had in Korea.

Six days before this meeting Dulles, in a speech to the Overseas Press Club of America, in New York, the text of which had been approved word by word by the President, said:

Under the conditions of today, the imposition on Southeast Asia of the political system of Communist Russia and its Chinese Communist ally, by whatever means, would be a grave threat to the whole free community. The United States feels that the possibility should not be

passively accepted, but should be met by united action. This might
have serious risks, but these risks are far less than would face us a few
years from now if we dare not be resolute today.

This whole question of organizing united action among the
United States and its allies was taken up by the President that
Sunday night in his talk with Dulles and Radford. In the end he
agreed that if a collective defense in Indo-China could be arranged,
he would recommend to Congress that the United States take part
in it. He dispatched a cable to this effect to Sir Winston.

The Indo-China war was a problem the Eisenhower administration
had inherited, and the difficulty in dealing with it from Washington
was compounded by the fact that the war and the political negotiation
with the anti-Communist nationalist authorities were being conducted
not by the United States but by France. Yet while it was in this respect
a French war, in a broader sense it was America's war, too, because the
United States was the leader in the struggle against Communism, and
after the Korean truce Indo-China became the only active battlefield
in this struggle. Furthermore, although the French were in command,
the United States in 1954 was paying more than a third of the cost
of French operations and was supplying matériel and technical
assistance.

Eight months after the Eisenhower administration took office it
agreed to increase financial aid to bolster the French. At the same
time the French, with American approval, set in motion the Navarre
plan, named for the French commanding general in Indo-China.
The plan contemplated a small increase in French and French Union
forces and a major increase in the strength of the Vietnamese army
and in American aid in arms and money. With this increased
strength the French proposed to create mobile combat teams for
offensive operations. The objective, as Dulles stated it, was to smash
"the organized body of Communist aggression by the end of the
1955 fighting season and thereby [reduce] the fighting to guerrilla
warfare, which could in 1956 be met for the most part" by the
native Indo-China forces.

The plan failed. The French, as Acheson had intimated to Eisenhower in the postelection briefing in the White House, were as fed

up with the war in Indo-China as the Americans had been with the Korean war. The offensive spirit needed for success was lacking. Much of the native population simply refused to take sides with the French. In France, meanwhile, increasing political pressure was piling up on the government to negotiate an end to the unpopular war, with its drain on French resources and French man power.

In spite of the fact that so much of the material on the subject remains highly classified, it is possible to give some account of the evolution that occurred in American policy toward Indo-China in 1954. The picture that emerges from available facts is one of painful and perhaps tardy groping and negotiation among the allies, which began with the assumption that Indo-China was vital to the free world but which could never quite achieve agreement on what to do to prevent an important part of it from falling under Communist rule.

As the crisis came on, American policy was based upon the "falling domino" concept, which the President described at his press conference on April 7, 1954.

"You have a row of dominoes set up, and you knock over the first one," Eisenhower said, "and what will happen to the last one is the certainty that it will go over very quickly. So you have a beginning of a disintegration that would have the most profound influences."

Indo-China was the first domino, and if the Communists knocked it over, the next to collapse might be Burma, Thailand, Malaya, and Indonesia. Also, Eisenhower noted, the falling dominoes could topple into America's island defense chain of Japan, Formosa, the Philippines and then on southward, threatening Australia and New Zealand. The many consequences of this would include, the President pointed out, not only the loss of an irreplaceable source of raw materials but the extension of Communist hegemony over additional tens of millions of people.

These would have been the consequences, that is, in the unlikely event that the United States did not finally move in to prevent such a disaster. Indeed the fact that American strategic planning did contemplate checking the wholesale collapse of the Western position in Southeast Asia made the Joint Chiefs and the Pentagon unhappy over the President's use of the domino analogy.

As the Vietminh pushed the French back, the key domino began to totter. Still Washington continued to rely on the effectiveness of American dollars and American supplies in keeping the anti-Communist forces in action. Certainly, up to January of 1954, the Eisenhower administration did not contemplate committing American military power to Indo-China, barring possibly some unusual development such as overt intervention by the Chinese Communists. The idea of unilateral intervention by the United States was out of line with the whole drift of the administration's peaceful course of agreeing to a truce in Korea, reducing military spending and withdrawing some of its troops from Asia into strategic reserve to avoid overextension.

At the joint meeting of the Cabinet and Republican Congressional leaders on January 4, 1954, to review the President's forthcoming State of the Union message Eisenhower read the passage asking Congress to authorize continued military assistance to France. A Senator inquired if this could mean sending men to Indo-China.

"No," the President assured him, "I can write in 'material assistance.' " That is the way the passage was worded in the final draft.

Superimposed on the whole picture of the development of American policy in 1954 is the impression one gets that the problem came before the President piece by piece and not altogether at the same pace as events on the battlefield. The climax arrived sooner than some of the very highest American officials had expected in the beginning, although toward the end certain officers in the Pentagon were making book on when Dienbienphu would fall. Washington's appraisal of the situation in Indo-China seems to have been distorted also by conflicting intelligence, for which much blame was placed upon the French.

By February the situation was so critical that, regardless of previous policy, the possibility of American intervention by one means or another became the subject of serious deliberation within the government. The problem was one that troubled Eisenhower very deeply, and his public statements at that time all revealed an abhorrence of the idea of America's being sucked into a war in Indo-China.

"No one," he said at his press conference on February 10, "could be more bitterly opposed to ever getting the United States involved in a hot war in that region than I am. Consequently, every move that I authorize is calculated, so far as humans can do it, to make certain that that does not happen."

"Mr. President," a reporter asked, "should your remarks be construed as meaning that you are determined not to become involved or, perhaps, more deeply involved in the war in Indo-China regardless of how that war may go?"

Eisenhower drew away from this question, saying that he would not try to predict the course of events.

"I say," he emphasized, "that I cannot conceive of a greater tragedy for America than to get heavily involved now in an all-out war in any of those regions, particularly with large units."

At a press conference on March 10 a reporter reminded the President of a warning by Senator John Stennis, Democrat, of Mississippi, that the United States might become involved in the war as a result of the presence of two hundred Air Force technicians in Indo-China. America was not going to become involved, the President replied forcefully, unless Congress exercised its Constitutional right to declare war. Let that be clear, he said.

The question of intervention came up in two distinct forms. One was intervention through united action with our allies in Europe and Asia to deal with the broad assault by the Reds in Indo-China. The other was swift intervention by the United States alone in an effort to save Dienbienphu.

The first intimation from the French that they would welcome an American air strike to relieve the pressure on Dienbienphu came through diplomatic channels from Paris just before the visit to Washington of the French Chief of Staff, General Paul Ely, in the third week of March, 1954.

During this general period Admiral Radford also favored limited intervention by American air power. General Matthew B. Ridgway, the Army Chief of Staff, was profoundly opposed. Believing that ground troops sooner or later would have to be committed, he felt —as he says in his memoirs, *Soldier*—that the jungles, rice paddies, and poor roads, harbors and communications would have made it a "tragic adventure" for the United States. He says that he forwarded this view to Eisenhower and that "to a man of his military experience its implications were immediately clear."

Sometime after Ely's visit the French again urged an air attack to relieve Dienbienphu, this time the overture being made by French Foreign Minister Georges Bidault to Ambassador Dillon in Paris. Dillon cabled Dulles, but Dulles rejected the suggestion without consulting the President, knowing that Eisenhower was dead set against intervention of any kind without Congressional approval.

These appeals from the French caused diplomatic commotion in Washington, often centering in Dulles's home on week ends. Through the Secretary's library, a deep, comfortable room with beams, book shelves to the ceiling, a stone fireplace and high windows looking upon a garden, members of the State Department staff came and went. Sometimes Radford was there talking to Dulles as the Secretary paced slowly back and forth in front of the fireplace wearing a tweed suit and chewing on a pencil. Throughout the crisis there was a chronic shortage of pencils in the Dulles home. Everybody was borrowing from everyone else.

Now and then Dulles would pick up the phone and talk to the President. This would start a fresh spurt of activity, with Dulles jotting things down on a large yellow pad. Although it is customary to use yellow pads in the State Department, there seemed to be a shortage of these also, and members of the staff had to use white pads. Once during a lull a subordinate remarked to Dulles that he was the only one with yellow pads.

"I bought these myself," the Secretary informed him.

A third approach was made by the French late in April while Dulles and Radford were in Paris for the session of the NATO Council. Bidault took the Secretary of State aside and pleaded for air support, saying the situation at Dienbienphu was desperate. Dulles weighed the request overnight, but again turned the French down, this time not only in consideration of the President's insistence on prior action by Congress but for the further reason that the situation at Dienbienphu had deteriorated too far to be saved by air attack. This opinion was then shared by Radford, who felt that the battle lines were becoming so indistinguishable as to make an air attack ineffective. Two weeks later, on May 7, Dienbienphu fell.

While the French failed to get the United States to intervene with air power at Dienbienphu, the United States enjoyed little more success in organizing united action in time to save the military situation.

On April 3, five days after his speech in New York proposing united action, Dulles met with Republican and Democratic Congressional leaders at the State Department and outlined what would be involved in establishing a collective defense in Indo-China. No formal understanding was reached, but the Secretary departed feeling assured that the leaders would go along if the conditions on which united action was based were satisfactory. His discussion with the President and Radford took place the following evening.

In agreeing to submit the proposal for united action to Churchill, the President laid down certain conditions that would have to be met before the United States would move into Indo-China with its allies. Prominent among them was that Congress must first authorize American participation in any military action.

The other conditions were these:

1. Britain must participate. Implicit in this, in the American view, was participation also by Australia and New Zealand.
2. France and the Associated States—Vietnam, Cambodia and Laos —must invite the United States and the allies to join them in their struggle.
3. France must agree to stay in the war and see it through.
4. France must go beyond her previous efforts in granting unequivocal independence to Vietnam, Laos and Cambodia so that American entry into Indo-China would not have the taint of colonialism.

In addition the President and Dulles were desirous that Thailand and the Philippine Republic should participate to demonstrate that East and West were joined in opposing Communist aggression.

Following the exchange of cables between Eisenhower and Churchill on united action, Dulles went within the week to London and then to Paris. When he returned to Washington, it was with a sense of confidence that he had achieved at least a generalized agreement on organizing united action. Instead, he found that he had on his hands a serious misunderstanding as to the nature and timing of united action. Rather than being ready to enter immediately into a collective defense of Indo-China, both the British and French were determined to see first what could be accomplished through negotiation at the nineteen-nation conference on Asian problems which was opening in Geneva in the last week of April.

At about the same time, the lack of zeal among the American people for intervention was reflected by the adverse reaction to a supposedly off-the-record remark by the Vice-President on April 16 at the convention of the American Society of Newspaper Editors in Washington. If France should withdraw its troops from Indo-China, he was asked, should American troops be sent to replace them if that were necessary to prevent the loss of Indo-China to the Reds? Nixon replied that the free world could not afford further retreat in Asia. He hoped and believed that this could be avoided without intervention.

But under the circumstances [he continued] if in order to avoid further Communist expansion in Asia and particularly in Indo-China— if in order to avoid it we must take the risk now by putting American boys in, I believe that the Executive Branch has to take the politically unpopular position of facing up to it and doing it, and I personally would support such a decision.

This suggestion was shot down quickly by a barrage of Congressional disapproval. Three days later, after visiting the President in Augusta, Dulles said that the possibility of American troops being sent to Indo-China was "unlikely."

United action, based upon the conditions set forth by Eisenhower and Dulles, was the only course that had the President's approval. He never consented to unilateral intervention. An air strike was ruled out by his personal decision. On a large body of world opinion, obviously, American bombing of the Vietminh forces would have had a flagrant effect. It might have thrown the United States into war with the Chinese Reds. Moreover, it would have been less than consistent for the President, who a year before had refused to enlarge one war against the Communists, to have ordered American planes into action now in one battle in Indo-China where allied strength was infinitely less than it has been in Korea.

Only a united defense offered the military and moral premises.
Eisenhower was willing to accept. Even then all of the several conditions he prescribed were most unlikely to be fulfilled. The sum of
his influence, therefore, tended away from rather than toward military intervention of any kind.

Public opinion had never been prepared for accepting intervention.
Influential leaders of the Republican Party—and of the Democratic
Party, too, for that matter—would have looked with dread upon
the prospect of a new Korea, with fresh casualty lists, higher defense
spending, larger draft calls and revived economic controls.

Yet if by chance agreement had somehow been reached with our
allies on the President's terms and Congress had approved, the
United States would presumably have been at war again on the
mainland of Asia less than a year after the truce in Korea.

As the Geneva conference got under way the emphasis shifted to
seeking a *modus vivendi* with the Communists—a course, as Eisenhower put it, between the unacceptable (a total Communist victory
in Southeast Asia) and the unattainable (a settlement with the
Reds satisfactory to the West).

On July 21 the French agreed to a cease-fire and a partition of
Vietnam. The settlement gave the Communists the northern half
of Vietnam, including the Red River Delta and Hanoi. On the
other hand, it denied them the whole peninsula, which they might
have won by conquest.

The United States did not participate in the final declaration of the
conference but in the end it gave tacit support to the French in their
settlement. The statement by Under Secretary Smith that his country
would show "grave concern" over any renewal of aggression was taken
to mean that the United States would not stand by if the Reds violated
the cease-fire. By making this clear, Washington was helping materially, at least in the opinion of its diplomats, to get the best of a bad
bargain and thus played an important part in keeping the domino
from going all the way over with a crash. Another point of view held
by some is that the Reds stopped where they stopped because they
felt it to be in their own best interests at that particular time to do so,
hoping to take over the rest of the country by political means later on.

Meanwhile the plan for united action, which failed to bear fruit

during the war, materialized in somewhat different form afterward
in the Southeast Asia Treaty, signed at Manila in September, 1954.
This collective-security arrangement was an old concept which new
events and new Communist threats throughout Asia brought to
life. A collective-security treaty covering Southeast Asia had been
an aspiration of Eisenhower and Dulles for a long time. "United
action" was no new expression when Dulles used it in March, 1954.
As far back as his speech to the editors in April, 1953, the President
had said that "the free world . . . knows that aggressions in Korea
and Southeast Asia were threats to the whole free community to be
met only through united action. . . ."

Joined with the United States in SEATO are Britain, France,
Australia, New Zealand, the Philippines, Pakistan and Thailand. Each
is committed, subject to its own constitutional process, to act against
armed attack upon the area of Southeast Asia and the Southwest
Pacific covered by the treaty. A separate protocol extends the protection to Laos, Cambodia and Vietnam.

One of the chief criticisms of SEATO has been, especially since
the signs of new Soviet influence in Asia in 1955 and 1956, that it
attempts to deal militarily with a problem that has become essentially political and economic. At the meeting of the SEATO Council
early in 1956 Dulles sought a start toward correcting this weakness.
The Council agreed to appoint an economic officer and pledged to
"press forward with national and international programs to raise
standards of living in the treaty area."

The President addressed himself not to SEATO but to this whole
problem when the collapsing of the French position in Indo-China
was under discussion in the Cabinet on May 14, 1954.

There would have to be, he said, a far greater popular understanding that, although expensive, mutual security, technical assistance and other programs for helping friendly nations realize their
aspirations were in reality insurance against catastrophe for the
United States.

The United States and its allies had a long and hard road to travel
in the conflict that was dividing the world, he declared, but the only
alternative was simply giving in to the Communists.

CHAPTER 20

Eisenhower, Nixon
and the '54 Elections

*The Cabinet Discusses the Political Problems of the Campaign – What
Part Shall the President Take? – Congress Delivers on the President's
Program – Eisenhower Takes to the Hustings – Nixon's Role in the
Administration – The Vice-President's Campaign Infuriates the Demo-
crats – The Democrats Win Control of Congress – The Cabinet Holds a
Post-mortem.*

As the Congressional election campaign neared its climax in the
fall of 1954, the big question facing the Republican Party was
summed up by Postmaster General Summerfield in the Cabinet on
October 19. How could Eisenhower's popularity be imparted to
individual Republican candidates in the forty-eight states? The
voters, Summerfield said, simply did not look upon Republican
Congressional candidates with the same enthusiasm as they regarded
Eisenhower.

Various members of the Cabinet offered suggestions. Summerfield,
for example, recommended that more stress be laid upon the F.H.A.
scandals of Democratic origin. Mrs. Hobby urged that Republican
candidates play up the new Social Security benefits. Stassen wished
to see more attention given to the facts about the Republican support
in Congress for the President's program.

Arthur Burns quoted a letter to Eisenhower from a prominent
conservative Democrat urging that Republican campaign speakers

keep .epeating current employment statistics to show that the Democratic and not the Republican Party was the party of unemployment.

The President agreed emphatically with this proposal, and suggested that every campaign speech ought to include a brief paragraph at least about how the Republicans had reduced unemployment. So much publicity had been given to the economic decline, he added, that he was afraid people were accepting the idea that the country was threatened with a depression. He was very anxious to advertise the fact that 1954 was the most prosperous peacetime year this country had ever enjoyed. He asked Burns to get up a brief summary of statistics that would show this.

The President told the Cabinet that in domestic legislation and foreign policy the administration had accomplished a great deal. The administration, he said, had done a good job in changing the economy from a wartime to a peace time basis, but he lamented that it seemed impossible to get that story across to the people.

Neither these issues, however, nor others raised by the Republicans that summer and fall succeeded in providing candidates with a satisfactory substitute for Eisenhower's popularity. As time passed, therefore, the President came under immense pressure from his party to get out and campaign personally.

For more than a year political strategy and the part Eisenhower should play in the campaign had been discussed by the President and his advisers in public and in private. In the Cabinet on April 3, 1953, the President took note of comment that the administration was losing the confidence of Democrats and independents who had voted for him in 1952. He urged his associates to demonstrate to these voters that the Republican administration was anxious to satisfy their desire for honest, efficient, middle-of-the-road government.

At the meeting of the Cabinet on April 17, 1953, Nixon, presiding in the absence of the President, observed that the ultimate success of the Eisenhower administration might depend on the outcome of the 1954 election. The reason he gave was that if the Democrats got control of Congress, they might not be so co-operative as they were while they were in the minority. The election could be won or lost then, in the 1953 session of Congress, and he added that a good public relations program was the key to success. He suggested that Cabinet members could make their most effective contribution by concentrating their speaking in critical areas.

Summerfield reminded the Cabinet of the help needed by Senator Homer E. Ferguson of Michigan because of the powerful opposition that might come from Michigan's popular Democratic Governor, G. Mennen Williams.

On another political topic the Vice-President urged the Cabinet to proceed cautiously and in consultation with the legislative leaders. Higher postal rates were a hot issue, he warned, and the additional revenue proposed (Summerfield later estimated it at $240,625,000) might not be sufficient to justify the political disadvantages entailed.

On May 8, 1953, Hall indicated to the Cabinet that after a discussion of the 1954 campaign, he and the President had agreed that Eisenhower would not campaign across the country.

The President discussed this same point on May 20, 1953, at a conference with Hauge, Emmet Hughes and other members of his staff. Again he said that he would not stump the country, but would make several televised speeches to tell the people what the administration had accomplished.

At his press conferences during the remainder of 1953 Eisenhower clung to the position that he was not going to take part in local campaigns. For one thing, he said, voters resent such intrusion. For another, the occupant of the White House is "President of all the people" and, he insisted, he did not "intend to make of the Presidency an agency to use in partisan elections." As a practical matter, events were to demonstrate, this position was an untenable one for the leader of a great political party.

With the arrival of the election year the subject became more and more pressing. On February 16, 1954, Nixon, reporting to the Cabinet on recent tours of New England and the West Coast, said that Eisenhower's popularity seemed higher than it had been in 1952. The reaction toward the administration generally, he said, was surprisingly favorable.

Issues like the Bricker amendment and "the 2,200"—in his 1954 State of the Union message Eisenhower had announced that the administration had dismissed 2,200 persons under the new employee security program—aroused only mild interest beyond the Eastern seaboard, the Vice-President said. Most people, Nixon concluded, felt that the Eisenhower program had given the whole government the "new look" which the Republicans had promised in 1952.

The President said that he personally had made a survey of the views of nineteen editors on the political situation and was gratified by the result.

The relationship of patronage to the campaign was discussed in the Cabinet on March 5, 1954. The Cabinet received a report from a Republican Senator that there was considerable distress throughout the party over the continuance of Democrats in the postmasterships of many small towns and villages. As he almost invariably does when patronage is mentioned, the President urged attention to specific cases rather than trying to deal with the subject in generalities.

The Cabinet was told that many complaints were coming in from Republican organizations over the retention in office of persons allegedly trying to undermine the policies of the Eisenhower administration. It was mentioned, for example that a Republican Representative from Maryland had been embarrassed by anti-administration speeches by an employee of the Department of Interior.

The President agreed that measures should be taken to insure that public servants, regardless of party, make no political talks.

On April 9, 1954, James Murphy, chairman of the National Citizens-for-Eisenhower Congressional Committee, told the Cabinet about the activities of this organization and said that very few who worked for the Citizens' group in 1952 were reluctant to pitch in again in 1954. The President cautioned against an overly partisan approach. He remarked also that he himself must take care to be completely nonpartisan in using the national radio and television networks except on programs paid for by the party.

Farm prices and the administration's controversial program for replacing rigid 90 per cent price supports with a flexible scale were already a serious political issue. Benson mentioned it in the Cabinet on June 4, 1954. On a recent trip through the Midwest, he said, he had found farm sentiment for the administration's program remarkably strong. He noted that several Republican organizations in Minnesota had gone on record supporting the administration and opposing the stand taken by their Representatives in Congress against flexible supports.

Nixon hailed this as evidence that the administration by aggressive support of sound principles could turn popular dislike of a program into popular approval. Foreshadowing a line he was to take in the fall, he urged members of the Cabinet to repeat frequently the facts and figures Eisenhower had cited at his press conference two days before on the administration's handling of subversion. Among other things, the President had credited the administration with eighty-four deportations of alien subversives, one conviction for treason, two convictions for espionage and forty-one for Communist Party leadership.

Eisenhower opened the Cabinet meeting on July 2, 1954, by voicing his gratification that the press had treated passage of the farm program by the House as an administration victory. Later Stassen brought up the question of the possible effects unemployment might have on Republican chances. He presented charts showing areas suffering from industrial decline. To the possible disadvantage of the Republicans, he noted that a number of these areas corresponded with Congressional districts where the election contests promised to be very close.

During a White House conference with the Republican legislative leaders on July 19 Mrs. Hobby urged action on several items, including health reinsurance legislation. A Senate leader replied that because of the heavy load of work still confronting Congress before adjournment, it would be extremely difficult to pass the reinsurance bill.

This brought a quick reaction from Eisenhower. If this bill was not passed, what could be said, he asked, to satisfy the American people in their deep concern over the costs of prolonged illness? The President recalled that he had spoken out many times against socialized medicine. But he felt he had a duty to show not only what the administration was *against* but what it was *for*.

This was typical of the attitude he kept impressing on the leaders that summer to get action on a program that would give the people a reason for voting Republican in the fall. For a time in the spring, while the Army-McCarthy hearings were diverting the Senate from legislative problems, he had even given some thought to the possibility of calling a special session if the regular session failed to act on his program. This had been discussed in the Cabinet on May 21, with Nixon suggesting that a Presidential hint of a special session, dropped at the right moment, might have a persuasive effect upon Congress.

In the end it proved unnecessary. Despite the sideshows, Congress managed to turn out a large volume of legislation. Social Security and unemployment insurance were broadened, as the President had requested. The new farm program was adopted. The St. Lawrence Seaway was approved. Nearly two billion dollars was voted for highways. The atomic energy act was liberalized to give industry a role in the commercial development of nuclear power. The housing program was extended for another year, but with Eisenhower's request for new public housing units sharply trimmed. The reciprocal trade agreements act was extended for a year, though the President had originally asked for a three-year extension. The long-needed customs simplification bill was passed.

Congress voted an extensive antisubversive program. As the President had proposed, it provided for loss of citizenship by those convicted of conspiracy to advocate violent overthrow of the government. It made peacetime as well as wartime espionage punishable by death and broadened the sabotage laws. To facilitate obtaining information about subversion it granted immunity from prosecution to certain suspected persons testifying before Congressional committees and the courts. It also included a bill, of Democratic origin, to outlaw the Communist Party. The administration had originally opposed such a ban on the grounds that it would drive the Communist movement underground, but after the bill had been toned down, Eisenhower approved it as a measure that might prove helpful in strengthening internal security.

Passed also was the administration's comprehensive but controversial tax-revision bill, which gave more than a billion dollars in tax relief to individuals and corporations. A noisy argument had raged over its provisions for more liberal treatment of corporate taxation of depreciation allowances and research and development outlays and for some relief for the double taxation on dividends. The Democrats argued favoritism to the rich, pay-off to large Republican campaign contributors. These changes were needed, the Republicans retorted, to keep the economy growing.

Among the measures that fell by the wayside were the Taft-Hartley amendments, health reinsurance, the wire-tapping bill, Hawaiian statehood and the proposal for eighteen-year-old voting.

After adjournment Eisenhower jubilantly posted his "batting average for the session as .830. (On the basis of a more detailed tabulation *Congressional Quarterly* put it at .646.)

There is no doubt that the President viewed the record of the 1954 session, in which he received crucial Democratic as well as Republican support, as one of the bright spots of his years in the White House. The Democrats called his elation exaggerated and said the program was largely an extension of their laws. This did not change the fact, however, that in 1954 it bore the Eisenhower label, that its success filled him with new hope and confidence and helped blot out the memory of his earlier frustration and despair of accomplishment.

It was perfectly obvious that it gave him a feeling that he had been able to lead his party along the road of doing something constructive for the welfare of the people and that it was a factor in changing his mind about participating in the campaign. This was by no means the only factor. As the signs of Democratic resurgence grew, pressure increased greatly on Eisenhower to campaign. Putting aside his earlier reservations about keeping the Presidency out of political contests, he threw himself into the most active role, in all probability, that a President has ever undertaken in an off-year election.

In return for a pledge of support of the Eisenhower program, the President indorsed Joseph T. Meek, a conservative Republican and McCarthy supporter, who was opposing Paul Douglas in Illinois. Then Eisenhower began his active campaigning in mid-August with a speech at the Illinois State Fair. In Denver following the adjournment of Congress he went before a nation-wide television audience to salute the record of the session and paint an optimistic picture of affairs at home and abroad.

In September Eisenhower made a 2,764-mile campaign trip by air from Colorado to the Pacific Northwest and Los Angeles, where he made an effective speech in the Hollywood Bowl. Even more interesting was his talk the next morning to a barely cordial A.F.L. convention, in which he told the A.F.L. leaders he thought they were in the wrong occasionally. His important political speech at McNary Dam on the Oregon-Washington border received about as negative a response as reporters who travel with him had ever seen accorded an Eisenhower campaign talk.

The President propounded his conservative "partnership" concept of power development to an audience that seemed far more interested in when the Federal government was going to give the region some "starts" on new hydroelectric projects. A "partnership" man, Senator Guy Cordon, Republican, of Oregon, sat on the platform with the President. On election day he was defeated by a public power advocate, Richard L. Neuberger. (In addition to the power issue Neuberger had much more skill and enthusiasm as a campaigner than Cordon. His victory was an important factor in giving the Democrats control of the Senate.)

Back in Denver, the President resumed campaigning with a speech that contained the most celebrated line in any of his talks that fall and one that he was to retract after the election. If the Democrats should win control of Congress while the Republicans held the executive branch, he said, the result would be "a cold war of partisan politics." "History shows, that when the Executive and Legislative Branches are politically in conflict, politics in Washington runs riot."

Running riot at that particular moment were bird dogs in Michigan, where Homer Ferguson and Pat McNamara, the Democratic candidate, were waging a close fight for the Senate. At a press conference in Detroit, Secretary Wilson, never a man to put a semaphore in front of a metaphor, made a remark which, the allied Democratic and labor forces protested, likened working men to dogs. Wilson had been discussing unemployment. Someone asked about the possibility of assigning defense contracts to distressed areas. Defense work was too important to treat as "made work," Wilson said. He made the point that people without work should go to where there were jobs available, and added:

"I've got a lot of sympathy for people where a sudden change catches 'em—but I've always liked bird dogs better than kennel-fed dogs myself. You know, one who'll get out and hunt for food rather than sit on his fanny and yell."

Although Eisenhower and Nixon came to his defense and Wilson himself apologized for "inept remarks," his words became one of the big weapons of McNamara's successful campaign.

While the furor was still going on, Eisenhower headed back to Washington in mid-October. Leonard Hall had made plans for a modified "whistle stop" tour by the President, with platform appearances from the rear of a regularly scheduled train between Denver and Washington. The President agreed, but when Adams heard of it in Washington, he moved in to stop it. He considered it impractical and rather silly. Eisenhower later substituted a whirlwind campaign trip by air which took him in one day to Cleveland, Detroit, Louisville and Wilmington. Although Republican Senate candidates lost in three out of four of the states the President visited that day, political observers generally felt that his campaigning kept Republicans throughout the country from a more severe setback than had been forecast.

One of the events during the campaign that most exasperated the Democrats was the first meeting of the Cabinet ever put on television. With the announced purpose of hearing a report from the Secretary of State on the signing of the Paris accords, the Cabinet met in the evening. The session bore little resemblance to a regular Cabinet meeting. Almost entirely a Dulles show, the whole tenor of the performance was that things were going splendidly abroad. He was confident, Dulles told the Cabinet, that Russia "doesn't like what is going on." He assured Humphrey, whom he addressed as "Mr. Secretary of the Treasury," that the Paris accords would not "cost us a nickel" more than the E.D.C., which, to the administration's great distress, the French had rejected in September.

"I am sure that is a relief to you," he told Humphrey.

"Well, Foster," the President said at the end, "I feel like we almost ought to give you a standing ovation."

The President continued his campaign efforts right up to the election. Leaving the broadcasting studio after his final get-out-the-vote appeal on election eve, he said to Hagerty, "By golly, sometimes you sure get tired of all this clackety-clack."

While Eisenhower had been capturing the largest headlines, the brunt of the day-to-day, grass-roots campaigning was borne by Nixon. In this century only Henry A. Wallace has been as controversial a Vice-President as Richard Nixon was by the time he emerged from that campaign.

Nixon's role in the administration has always been primarily political. Not exclusively so, to be sure. More than any other Vice-President he has participated in the highest discussions of military and foreign policy through his membership in the National Security Council. In the inner circles of the government he has pressed his opinions on foreign affairs, particularly Far Eastern policy, his views on which have often coincided with the strong line advocated by Radford.

From the beginning it was Eisenhower's policy that Nixon should be kept fully informed on what was going on in the administration in case he might suddenly have to assume the Presidency. Eisenhower established a historic precedent by designating Nixon to preside in the President's absence over the N.S.C. and the Cabinet. (Nixon insists on presiding from the Vice-President's chair; he never sits in the President's place.) As the President's emissary he has made good-will tours of the Far East and Central America.

It is in the political field, however, particularly in the area of political maneuver involving Congress, that Nixon's help has been most sought by the President and his associates. At the second meeting of the Cabinet, on January 30, 1953, Nixon offered his services in trying to overcome difficulties between the White House and the Republicans in Congress arising out of investigations. Ever since, that has been one of his important concerns. Until his own break with McCarthy following McCarthy's repeated attacks on the President, Nixon labored to prevent the wide-open split that finally occurred.

Nixon has never been an intimate friend of Eisenhower's. There has not been the kind of companionship between them that has existed between, say, Eisenhower and Humphrey or Eisenhower and

Bill Robinson and Cliff Roberts. Eisenhower and Nixon are twenty-two years apart in age. They have different backgrounds, different interests, different friends. Nevertheless their cordial relationship has been much more than merely official. The President likes Nixon and trusts him. He appreciates his loyalty. In addition to seeing him regularly at Cabinet, N.S.C. and legislative leaders' meetings, he invites him to the White House for breakfast every month or so. He talks freely to him and throws out ideas for his reaction.

The President welcomes Nixon's judgment on how certain proposals will be received in Congress. Occasionally someone at the White House will telephone Nixon at the Capitol and say that the President would like to know what he thinks about a measure under consideration. In the Cabinet and the N.S.C. the President looks to Nixon to reflect the Congressional viewpoint and raise a red flag whenever he thinks something will breed political trouble. Nixon's role has been described as that of political broker between the conflicting wings of the Republican Party.

His frequent contact with the President enables Nixon to play an important part as salesman of Eisenhower's policies in the cloakrooms. He does so with a knack for interpreting the President's proposals in terms of a Congressman's self-interest.

"I go in and lay it right on the line," he has said.

He has served the President well in dissuading individual Republicans from deserting him on tough issues. A typical example was the provision written into the tax bill by House Democrats over administration objections in 1955, granting a twenty-dollar tax reduction to everyone entitled to a personal exemption.

"But how can we vote *against* it?" Republicans would ask Nixon.

"You will not be defeated at election time by being for or against this particular cut," he would argue. "What will count is whether you were for or against the President. This is the big test on that. People will be watching this one, so you had better vote right if you want to have a record of supporting Eisenhower."

Nixon has handled difficult assignments of a political nature for the President outside Congress as well. In September of 1953, for example, Eisenhower telephoned the Vice-President from Denver and asked if he would represent him in speaking to the A.F.L. convention in St. Louis. Durkin had just resigned as Secretary of Labor. The A.F.L. was bitter about it, and the convention gave Nixon a cold and at times a derisive reception.

After a Cabinet meeting some weeks later the Vice-President was lingering in the room with Dodge. He thought Eisenhower had departed. Suddenly he felt a tap on his shoulder and heard the President say in a slightly gruff voice, "I just wanted to thank you for that job you did out there."

Nixon's political activity in the first three years of the administration reached its zenith in the 1954 campaign, in which he flew 26,000 miles, visited 95 cities in 31 states, delivered 204 speeches and held more than a hundred press conferences.

He aroused the passionate antagonism of the Democrats by his prolific use of the Communist issue against them. In the Truman administration, he alleged, "some misguided officials . . . were blind or indifferent to the danger." He started an angry "numbers game" by saying that the Eisenhower administration had been "kicking Communists and fellow travelers and security risks out of the government . . . by the thousands." This figure was based overwhelmingly, of course, on the dismissal of security risks, who can be anything under the sun but Reds. By lumping Communists and security risks (drunks, perverts, unreliables as well as subversives) together in this way, the Democrats charged, Nixon was implanting the false notion that hosts of Democratic-appointed Reds had been discovered in the government.

The Vice-President labeled Senate candidates like Neuberger in Oregon, Joseph C. O'Mahoney in Wyoming and John A. Carroll in Colorado as "left wing" Democrats and declared at another time that the Communist Party "has determined to conduct its program within the Democratic Party." The Democrats later made a "chamber of horrors" exhibit out of such of Nixon's charges as that a Democratic Congress would be dominated by a "left wing" clique and that if a Congress of Adlai Stevenson's choosing was elected, "the security risks which have been fired by the Eisenhower administration will all be hired back."

The Democratic view of all this was that Nixon had hit below the belt, reviving by innuendo smears long ago discredited. "McCarthyism in a white collar," Stevenson said.

In most Republican eyes Nixon had a legitimate issue and an effective one. Since political campaigns are played for keeps, a campaigner does not soft-pedal a good issue just because it offends the opposition. The very fact that the Democrats were screaming, Nixon's supporters argued, only went to prove that Nixon had hit them in a vulnerable spot.

From a nonpartisan view, one would have to say that the issue of whether the Truman administration was sufficiently alert to the danger of Communist infiltration was unquestionably a legitimate one if stated fairly. Unquestionably Nixon stated it in a way he considered effective. Unquestionably it was an issue that he relished and felt at home in. But either he grossly exaggerated it or else Eisenhower was guilty of burying an urgent, significant and pertinent issue, because the President paid scant attention to it. His speeches dwelt on unemployment, the farm problem, the danger of split government and the administration's accomplishments abroad, among which he included the favorable settlements in Iran and Trieste and the squelching of the Communist uprising in Guatemala.

Toward the end of the campaign the President complimented Nixon on his labors. He wrote him from Denver:

Dear Dick:
Whenever my burdens tend to feel unduly heavy, I admire all the more the tremendous job you have done since the opening of the present campaign. You have personally carried a back-breaking load of hard, tedious, day by day and state by state campaigning. And in doing so you have been undismayed by problems of time, distance, and physical effort.

I know we share the urgent hope that there may be returned to the Congress a Republican majority that will work with the Executive Branch in completing the program that we believe is in the best interests of all America. No man could have done more effective work than you to further that hope. Whatever the outcome next Tuesday, I can find no words to express my deep appreciation of the contribution you have made toward that goal.

Please tell Pat, too, that she has aroused my admiration as an able campaigner; there is no question but that she is the most charming of the lot.

With warm regard,

As ever,

D. E.

Historically, the party in power loses ground in midterm elections. With the Republican control of Congress as slim as it was in 1954, the Republican strength in both houses was expected to take a big dip. Instead the party showed surprising power in an extremely close election, in which the outcome of some contests remained in doubt for two or three days. The Democrats barely won control of the Senate through a net gain of two seats. Their margin in the House was twenty-nine seats.

For the Democrats this was a modest victory in terms of total gains, but it was a highly important one in terms of morale, prestige, power and promise of a comeback from the 1952 defeat. It was a jolt to the Republicans to lose control of Congress. The Democrats also scored an important victory in the gubernatorial elections, picking up seven governorships previously held by Republicans and losing none of those with which they had gone into the elections.

(Months before the election Eisenhower had questioned the desirability of continuing the two-year term for Representatives. He brought the subject up during a meeting of the Cabinet on July 23, 1954, after commenting on the heavy pressures exerted upon Congressmen in election years to vote more money. He asked the Cabinet to consider whether the administration should recommend a Constitutional amendment extending the term of Representative from two to four years, coinciding with the President's term.)

When the Cabinet met on November 4, 1954, the President, Nixon and the other members held a post-mortem on the election.

Eisenhower began by saying that a great deal of thought would have to be given to specific means of co-operating with the new Democratic majority. Until the administration had time to consider the various suggestions that were being made, he went on, the best course would be to refrain from public discussion, except to indorse bipartisanship in foreign policy. He told the Cabinet he was planning to announce almost immediately an invitation to Congressional leaders of both parties to attend a White House briefing on foreign affairs. He read a draft of the announcement of the meeting to be held on November 17. He did not see how there could be any question of the need for the White House to work with the Democratic leadership because of the problem of scheduling legislation, hearings and so forth.

The discussion then turned to historical precedents. Weeks recalled the relations between Truman and the Republican Eightieth Congress. Eisenhower went back to the early 1930's when Hoover was in the White House and the Democrats controlled Congress. Hoover, he said, had been subject to vicious partisan attacks and his program stymied.

Wilson commented that the situation was different in 1954 because television enabled the President more effectively to take his case to the people. Eisenhower interposed to say that the administration must conduct itself in a way that would convince the people that it was doing its best to co-operate with Congress.

The Vice-President analyzed the results of the election. The outcome, he said, was "really a dead heat" and thus made it unlikely that Eisenhower would be subject to the difficulties that had beset Truman and Hoover. Nixon rejected the idea that the Democrats had been given a mandate to change the course of policy. He took up Republican defeats in particular districts and checked off the reasons for them—here an ineffective candidate, there a regional economic problem, somewhere else a weak local organization. The party, he emphasized, must continue to follow Eisenhower's "middle road" course. The credit for the showing the Republicans made in the election, he said, was due to the President's program and to the campaigning of top administration officials, particularly Eisenhower.

The party losing one election has a natural advantage in the next, he philosophized, since, having been acquainted with its weaknesses, it reorganizes and strengthens itself with new blood and new enthusiasm. He spoke of the desirability of casting about at once for strong candidates for the Senate in 1956. Looking ahead to relations with the new Congress, the Vice-President predicted that in matters of foreign policy the administration would get on better than it had under the Republican Congress. He forecast also that Democratic investigations of the administration would be rife. On that score Eisenhower said that department heads should immediately step forward and offer to co-operate. In cases where information might have to be withheld for national security, he said, administration officials should be very sure of their ground in doing so.

Wilson, who had so recently had a taste of the Michigan campaign, said that a veritable labor party was forming in that state as a result of C.I.O. influence in the Democratic organization. Benson warned that in the new Congress the administration might encounter difficulties in the House and Senate Agricultural Committees. Stassen declared that the President's greatness in history could depend on his success in the next two years.

Eisenhower observed that a serious split existed in the Democratic Party and that it would become more visible as the Democrats took on the responsibility of running Congress. The next two years, he said, would be extremely critical ones for the administration's policy of moderation. This was so, he explained, because the case for moderation still remained to be proved to the people to the extent necessary to attract them away from political ideas fostered during wartime emergencies.

Following up this point, Humphrey cautioned that it would be difficult always to maintain current high levels of prosperity. He predicted that the Democrats would press for higher Federal spending along with further tax reductions. He pleaded with the Cabinet to fight such pressures, whether from Democrats or Republicans.

To demonstrate what the Republicans must do to retrieve their defeat Nixon took a mechanical toy drummer from his pocket and sent it marching across the polished table beating its little drum before the eyes of the President and the Cabinet.

"Just keep beating that gol-darned drum," the Vice-President said.

CHAPTER 21

Ups and Downs
of the Security Program

*The Administration Revises the Employee Security Program – Executive
Order 10450 – The Bungling of the Ladejinsky and Chasanow Cases –
The President Tells the Cabinet the Program Must Be Fair – He Opposes
"Star Chamber" Proceedings – Eisenhower Orders a "Blank Wall" Be-
tween Oppenheimer and Government Data – Strauss Tells Oppenheimer
– Agitation for Reform*

I

Following the dismissal of John Paton Davies, Jr., a discussion in
the Cabinet on November 19, 1954, produced expressions of
opinion that the employee security program was a case of the administration's having done the right thing only to come off second
best in publicity. "Second best" was putting it mildly considering
the storm that the Department of Agriculture was to raise a month
later when it ruled Wolf I. Ladejinsky a security risk and for that
and other reasons barred him as agricultural attaché at the United
States Embassy in Tokyo. Ladejinsky had a long history as an anti-
Communist and a distinguished record as a land-reform expert. His
work with the Japanese under MacArthur was regarded by some as
an important contribution to the retarding of Communism in rural
Japan. Under the sharp eye of Scott McLeod the State Department
several months previously had cleared Ladejinsky. On the basis of
the same information Benson said that he did not meet security
requirements. Two weeks later Stassen, giving him full clearance,

hired him with Eisenhower's approval to supervise the American-supported land-reform program in South Vietnam.

The sheer inconsistency of the case, to say nothing of the injustice done Ladejinsky and the effect on public opinion abroad, caused more than unfavorable publicity. It renewed deep and widespread doubts about the security program itself and a clamor, often from unexpected sources, for reform. Yet to the extent that was true of certain other cases, the program itself was never fully put to the test in the Ladejinsky affair by the Department of Agriculture. No charges were filed; no hearing was held. It was more a case of poor judgment and nonprofessional handling of the matter by Benson and his staff. As a result of it, however, Benson himself was one of those who urged the President to institute a bipartisan study of the whole security system.

The question of what the new administration should do about the employee security program was considered by the Cabinet at its first meeting in the White House on January 23, 1953. As it then stood, the program promulgated by Truman in 1947 denied Federal employment when reasonable doubt existed as to one's loyalty. The discussion in the Cabinet centered on the desirability of changing this to make the interests of national security rather than, specifically, loyalty the precondition of employment. This change was finally instituted by the President in his Executive Order 10450 issued on April 27, 1953, embodying the administration's security program.

Under the new standard a person was to be barred from employment if he was found to be a security risk—that is, if his employment was not clearly consistent with the national security. This was a more comprehensive yardstick. It included not only disloyalty but such traits as untrustworthiness, criminal, immoral or disgraceful conduct, sexual perversion, drug addiction, drunkenness and mental disease. The program applied to all departments. The old Loyalty Review Board was abolished, and the head of each agency was made responsible for determining under the terms of the order whether his employees came up to standard. The order specifically stated that government employment is a privilege rather than a right. (This declaration is not accepted without reservation by some critics who consider it a "cliché" under which employees could be treated unfairly.)

The administration had a number of reasons for changing the program. It was felt that the Truman program failed to eliminate some dangerous subversives and that, in the case of William Remington, for example, they had continued in their jobs until Congressional committees dug them out. Truman had had both a general loyalty program and a security program limited to sensitive departments. The Republicans believed the problem could be better administered through a single program. Also, loyalty was more difficult to judge than the question of whether one was a security risk, and the label of security risk was thought to carry less stigma than loyalty risk.

The changes, motivated by these and many other technical considerations, were mainly procedural. Obviously, the President wanted the system to operate fairly, and he has from time to time exerted his personal influence to this end. But there was no disposition to alter the system so fundamentally as to meet some of the most serious criticisms that have been directed against it, as it has functioned under both Truman and Eisenhower.

In the Godkin Lectures at Harvard in 1955 John Lord O'Brian summarized some of these criticisms: ". . . imputing guilt because of association. . . . Adjudging men to be untrustworthy, not because of wrongful acts, but because of their ideas, because of motives attributed to them or because of suspicion as to their future conduct . . . the use of [the Attorney General's List of Subversive Organizations] in determining qualifications for employment . . . The use of secret information contributed by anonymous accusers . . . the lack of any Constitutional protection which might be given through judicial review. . . ." These circumstances, O'Brian concluded, "in some degree invade or threaten invasion of the Constitutional liberties of the citizen. . . ." This view is generally disputed by the men who administer the program.

One of the first cases to go through the mill of the new procedure was that of Abraham Chasanow, who had been employed for twenty-three years in the Navy's Hydrographic Office. On July 29, 1953, Chasanow was summoned to the personnel director's office and handed letters informing him that he was suspected of being a security risk and was being suspended without pay.

Late in September a board met to consider the charges. One was that he had associated with known Communists. Another was that he had been a leader of a radical group in Greenbelt, Maryland, where he lived. A third was that he had been a member of the National Lawyers' Guild in 1939. And so on. The board found unanimously that the charges were without merit and recommended that Chasanow be restored to his job. Months passed, however, and Chasanow, still suspended and having run through his own savings, was living on loans from his wife's family. On April 7, 1954, he was notified that he was dismissed. A special Security Appeal Board had overruled the findings of the hearing board, and Assistant Secretary of the Navy James H. Smith, Jr., had thereupon ordered dismissal. Even before the dismissal, Anthony Lewis, then a reporter for the Washington *Daily News*, had begun digging into the case. His articles, which were to win a Pulitzer Prize, and other news stories following the dismissal, resulted in another hearing and clearance for Chasanow. Smith apologized on behalf of the Navy, admitting that Chasanow had suffered "grave injustice." He blamed Chasanow's accusers—two agents of the Office of Naval Intelligence—for having failed to "corroborate their testimony or . . . produce specifics of earlier allegations." The Navy, Smith said, was revising its security procedures.

The Chasanow case was a glaring example of the miscarriages that could occur under the revised program, but no one could fairly say that it was typical of the way the program has been administered.

The question of a public announcement of the number of actions taken up to that time under 10450 was raised in the Cabinet by Summerfield and Brownell on September 25, 1953. The President said he felt that the program should be conducted as openly as possible and not as a "Star Chamber" proceeding. Nixon argued that public reports were necessary because the issue was one that had given the people concern in the 1952 election. Mrs. Hobby's suggestion was to treat the announcements as routine. Wilson thought that any announcements should be disposed of as quickly and as inconspicuously as possible.

In October the Cabinet approved publication of the results of the program to date. One who participated in the discussions recalls that the general feeling in the Cabinet was that the figures were evidence of progress by the administration in eliminating undesirables from government jobs. On October 23 the White House announced that in the first four months of the program 1,456 persons had been dropped from the Federal payroll. Of these, 863 were dismissed, and 593 resigned when notified of "unfavorable" reports about them. All but five of the 1,456 were holdovers from the Truman administration, it was said.

Publication of these figures, making no distinction between cases of subversion and cases of otherwise unreliable conduct, gave rise to the long and heated political controversy of the "numbers game." Some Republicans boasted that they were evidence that the party was cleaning up the government at long last, while Democrats charged that the figures were a hoax to deceive the people into thinking that the Truman administration had left the government honeycombed with spies and Communists. In time the reporting system was changed to insure that cases involving only untrustworthiness should not be included. The only exceptions were cases in which employees held such important jobs that untrustworthiness itself constituted a security risk.

When the program was next discussed in the Cabinet on November 12, 1953, Mrs. Hobby complained that too much trivia sometimes appeared in the case reports of security officers. She proposed that these officers be directed not to include petty material of a kind that would not enter into a final judgment of a case. In particular she cited statements such as that the person under investigation read the *Daily Worker.* Many people had to read the *Worker* as part of their jobs, she said.

One of the frequent and basic criticisms of the program was brought up by Dulles in the Cabinet on January 15, 1954, when he said that a clear understanding had not been reached as to the nature of a security risk. Cases had been sent to him, for example, he said, just because a file had contained such items as instances of drunkenness, the presence of a pacifist in the family or membership in the United World Federalists.

The President commented that if such cases were carried to the secretary of a department, it was a sign that the department needed a new security officer. Security officers, Dulles replied, tended to protect themselves by passing the buck on up the line.

Nixon suggested that the conduct of the security program in the United States Information Agency should be reviewed because the number of security risks reported was very small in comparison with the size of the agency.

In the Cabinet on July 2, 1954, the President deplored the recriminations of the "numbers game" and said it was important to bring the program up to date so that the emphasis could be placed on care in employing new government personnel rather than on firing those already on the job.

(For all practical purposes the review under 10450 of persons already in the government has been completed. Henceforth the program will apply mainly to applicants, except where new information comes to light about persons on the payroll.)

On July 16, 1954, the Cabinet again discussed the problems of administering the program fairly. Dulles renewed his complaint about trivia and unsupported charges in personnel files, and he asked, in effect: What is derogatory information? He suggested that it might be wise to ease the provisions of the order requiring suspension, which means cutting off salary. In the face of this hardship, he pointed out, officials were loathe to act on any basis other than well-substantiated information.

Eisenhower agreed that premature suspension should be avoided. He suggested recourse to transferring an employee from a sensitive to a nonsensitive job. (As a result of the President's continuing concern over hardships of suspension pending investigation, procedures were relaxed so that while a final judgment was awaited, a person could be transferred to a nonsensitive job. This does not apply in cases involving subversion.)

The Secretary of State cautioned that capable employees might resign rather than go through the experience of formal hearings required in their cases to arrive at a security clearance.

The President said—and repeated it more than once—that a procedure must be worked out for assuring justice to the individual in such cases. He told the Cabinet that he would take the responsibility personally for establishing whatever method might be necessary.

He was very insistent that no official of the government should take the easy way out by dismissing an employee if that official was convinced the employee met the standards of the program. Under these circumstances, he said, an official must have sufficient courage to defend the individual.

One possible solution, which was supported by Nixon, Brownell and Flemming, was the use of written interrogations under oath and the holding of preliminary hearings, which could be done without requiring suspension. On the other hand, both Nixon and Dulles pointed to the Hiss and Oppenheimer cases as exemplifying the difficulty of forming correct judgments before having all the information which can be developed through sworn testimony.

One of the many dilemmas of this problem was illustrated in an exchange between Dulles and Humphrey. The administration, Humphrey said, ought to be able to find enough men and women above a shadow of suspicion to fill all the posts that needed to be filled.

Did this mean, Dulles inquired, the dismissal of all people against whom there were unproved charges, such as that they had associated with Hiss in the State Department or Harry Dexter White in the Treasury?

Humphrey was quick to say that it did not. In such cases, he acknowledged, investigation and a full review would be needed.

On November 5, 1954, Dulles dismissed John Paton Davies, Jr. The Secretary of State agreed with the unanimous finding of a special hearing board that "Mr. Davies' lack of judgment, discretion and reliability raises a reasonable doubt that his continued employment in the Foreign Service of the United States is clearly consistent with the interests of national security." The board said that Davies was "frequently less than forthright in his response to questions." Dulles's action climaxed years of controversy over Davies. Critics, led by George F. Kennan, former Ambassador to the Soviet Union, charged that the dismissal of the career diplomat would undermine the Foreign Service.

While the controversy was still going on, Dulles told the Cabinet on November 19 that the case had been very thoroughly investigated and that the hearing board had been chosen with particular concern for disinterestedness. There could be no grounds, he insisted, for disagreement with its conclusions.

A good deal of thought, he continued, had been given to publishing the record of the hearing. However, he said, this could not have been done in full without danger to the work of security agencies, and to have published it in part would have been unfair to Davies and to the administration.

The President reiterated that everything possible must be done to assure fairness to persons involved in security procedures. Referring to Arthur Krock's column in the *Times* of November 16 discussing the rigidity of the program, Eisenhower again urged the practice of transferring certain doubtful cases from sensitive to nonsensitive positions. Philip Young assured him that this was now being done.

The President told the Cabinet that the administration could not undertake the task of expurgating records for publication. Possibly, he said, the reasons for dismissing persons in some cases could be stated and specific evidence cited in the public announcement. By all means, he concluded, he wished to avoid creating the impression that the program was being conducted as a "Star Chamber" proceeding.

Giving the accused the right to counsel and the opportunity to cross-examine provided a guarantee against this, Dulles said.

Secretary Weeks then made the comment that the program was a case in which the administration had done the right thing but had come off second best in publicity. Secretary Mitchell concurred fervently. He said that the administration ought to put on a campaign to spread understanding about its handling of the security program so that it would not be placed on the defensive after the new Democratic Congress convened. Mrs. Hobby commented that this would have to be done in a way that would get beyond the Washington correspondents. The President mentioned the possibility of discussion of the program by an expert on TV or at a White House press conference. Mrs. Hobby said that the presentation should be by one who would command respect. The President suggested someone like

John W. Davis, the lawyer and 1924 Democratic candidate for President. (Davis died not long afterward.)

The discussion ended without a decision, but the President enjoined the Cabinet to examine the subject of improving and explaining security procedures and not just let the matter drift.

On January 7, 1955, Eisenhower opened the meeting of the Cabinet by commenting with a laugh that he had just heard a description of an immoderate progressive—"a man who believes in total unemployment with a guaranteed annual wage." Getting down to business, he said that the new Congress might ask for the names of persons discharged under the security program. Despite any demagogic outbursts, he continued, the administration under no circumstances should give out the names of these individuals. Stassen later made the point that the responsibility should be left to the individual to announce, if he desired, that he had been dismissed. The only reason the government was reluctant to give out names, Eisenhower replied, was to protect individuals. Dulles recalled that the Association of the Bar of the City of New York had received a $100,000 grant from the Fund for the Republic to study the security program. Brownell replied that this was a good thing and that the Justice Department had agreed to co-operate. Dulles remarked upon the difficulty of obtaining the right people to make up competent security review boards.

Wilson reported that the Annie Lee Moss case was nearing completion in the Defense Department.

(Mrs. Moss, an Army code-machine operator, who didn't understand the codes herself, was suspended in 1954 after testimony at the McCarthy-Army hearing that she had been a Communist. The Army said her case had been under study since before the hearing and that she already had been transferred to a nonsensitive job. After her suspension she testified that she had never been a Communist. She was reinstated as a supply-room clerk. In August, 1954, she was suspended again purportedly on the basis of new information.)

Eisenhower emphasized that Wilson was responsible for seeing to it that a just decision was reached.

(Three weeks later Wilson restored Mrs. Moss to an Army job outside the Pentagon. He said that the record "does not support a conclusion that she is actually subversive or disloyal" but that there was an indication of "certain derogatory information" pertaining to the period before 1946.)

On April 1, 1955, the President told the Cabinet that in security cases the welfare of the country must be paramount. By way of comparison he cited the authority that a military commander must have to replace subordinates for the sake of the safety of the men.

II

On November 7, 1953, William L. Borden, former executive secretary of the Joint Congressional Committee on Atomic Energy, sent a letter to J. Edgar Hoover saying that "more probably than not J. Robert Oppenheimer is an agent of the Soviet Union." With this letter Borden, who had long had access to facts about Oppenheimer's background, started the most celebrated of all the security cases that have arisen under the Eisenhower administration thus far.

Oppenheimer, a man of extraordinary intellect and personality, was, and is, the director of the Institute for Advanced Study in Princeton. A former professor at the University of California, Oppenheimer directed the laboratory at Los Alamos which produced the first atomic bomb. After the war he became chairman of the General Advisory Committee of the Atomic Energy Commission. In 1953 he was a consultant to the commission, although of late his services had been used practically not at all.

Borden's letter set forth a number of statements about Oppenheimer's background that had long been familiar to the government. For instance: ". . . He was contributing substantial monthly sums to the Communist Party [before April, 1942]. . . . His wife and younger brother were Communists. . . . He had no close friends except Communists. . . ." Among the many other statements in the letter was: "He has worked tirelessly from January, 31, 1950, onward, to retard the United States H-bomb program."

So much has been written on the Oppenheimer case that I am not going into it except to report some details of the origin of it, not all of which have come to light heretofore.

After Borden's letter arrived, the F.B.I. prepared an inch-thick summary report on Oppenheimer—the full Oppenheimer dossier, when stacked up, rises, it is said, four feet and six inches above the floor—and distributed it, along with copies of the letter, to the White House and interested government departments on November 30.

A copy, of course, went to Strauss, who has since been violently attacked by Oppenheimer's friends for his role in the case. Strauss had been generally familiar with this material since 1947. At that time, as a commissioner of the A.E.C., he had joined in the unanimous vote to clear Oppenheimer for the General Advisory Committee. Upon receipt of the report, therefore, he first circulated it among other members of the commission.

Simultaneously another copy had gone out from the F.B.I. to the Pentagon, where it caused a shock. Appalled by the summary, Wilson sought the President's permission to terminate Oppenheimer's clearance to military installations. Eisenhower himself said later that he had found the information "very disturbing."

On December 3 he called a meeting to consider the matter. Among those he summoned were Wilson, Brownell, Cutler and Strauss. Strauss was the last to arrive. The discussion was in progress when he got there. Eisenhower inquired whether a formal hearing had ever been held on the charges against Oppenheimer. He was told that none had. In that case, he said, a hearing ought to be ordered. In the meanwhile, Eisenhower continued, a "blank wall"—that was the expression he used at the meeting—should be placed between Oppenheimer and government secrets.

That same day the President sent a two-paragraph memorandum to Brownell, with a copy to Strauss, directing that "a blank wall be placed between Dr. Oppenheimer and any secret data" and that established procedures be followed. The memorandum concluded with the statement that Eisenhower was in no sense prejudging the case. On December 10 the A.E.C. voted unanimously to institute its regular procedure to determine the truth or falsehood of the charges. Soon after that, Strauss telephoned Oppenheimer, with whom, of course, he was well acquainted, and said that he had something to talk to him about.

On the afternoon of December 21 the atomic scientist appeared in Strauss's office, Room 236 of the Atomic Energy Building on Constitution Avenue. Strauss and Major General Kenneth D. Nichols, then general manager of the A.E.C., received him. The office is a large, paneled room with a fireplace and tall brass andirons, bookshelves, two leather sofas and Strauss's large desk with an American flag in a standard behind it. Along the windows facing Constitution Avenue is a conference table with ten chairs.

The three men sat down at this table. Strauss and Oppenheimer exchanged amenities. Briefly, they spoke of the recent death of their friend, Rear Admiral William S. Parsons, the atomic-bomb expert who had armed the Hiroshima bomb. Then Strauss told Oppenheimer about Eisenhower's order, about the determination of the President not to prejudge the case and about the procedures to be followed.

During the conversation the question arose as to whether Oppenheimer instead of facing a hearing on the charges might quiet the whole business by resigning. In a letter to Strauss the following day, which has since become part of the record Oppenheimer wrote:

> You put to me as a possibly desirable alternative that I request termination of my contract . . . and thereby avoid explicit consideration of the charges. . . . Under the circumstances this course of action would mean that I am not fit to serve this Government, that I have now served for some twelve years. This I cannot do. . . .

Not part of the record is certain hitherto unpublished material which sets forth that, on the contrary, it was Oppenheimer and not Strauss who first brought up the question of resignation. Immediately after Oppenheimer departed, Nichols prepared minutes of the meeting. They contain the following line: "Dr. Oppenheimer raised the question of resigning prior to Mr. Strauss discussing this alternative."

Oppenheimer did not resign. What happened thereafter is well known. His case was heard first by a three-man board headed by Gordon Gray. In contrast to Borden's letter, the Gray board said that "we have come to a clear conclusion . . . that he is a loyal citizen" and that "it must be said that Dr. Oppenheimer seems to have had a high degree of discretion reflecting an unusual ability to keep to himself vital secrets." In a two-to-one decision, however, it recommended against clearance on several grounds, the first of which was that Oppenheimer's "continuing conduct and associations have reflected a serious disregard for the requirements of the security system."

The A.E.C. then voted four to one against reinstating his clearance. The commission paid no attention to the charge that Oppenheimer had retarded H-bomb production. But the majority report written by Strauss and published one day before Oppenheimer's clearance would have ended in any case with the expiration of his contract was a severe indictment. It cited as reasons for rejection of Oppenheimer "proof of fundamental defects in his character" and the finding that "his associations with persons known to him to have been Communists have extended far beyond the tolerable limits" expected of one who had held government positions of such importance as Oppenheimer had occupied.

In a dissenting report Commissioner Henry D. Smyth wrote that Oppenheimer's "loyalty and trustworthiness emerge clearly" and that as a distinguished physicist, "his services could be of great value to the country in the future." He said: "The security system has . . . neither the responsibility nor the right to dictate every detail of a man's life."

The Oppenheimer case was one of those affairs that go to the root of human conflict. The two points of view remain unreconciled to this day. Scarcely a line in the whole record escapes controversy. Great as the public controversy has been, however, it pales by comparison with the impassioned bitterness below the surface. Few who were deeply involved in it on either side came out of this conflict without a mark, and some carry scars that will never heal in their lifetimes.

This was one of the few security cases that Eisenhower has been directly involved in. Ordinarily, he does not take a hand personally unless a case is dumped in his lap as the Oppenheimer case was.

In the Ladejinsky affair Benson thrust the details at him in a brief discussion and from the viewpoint formed by the Secretary himself. Thus the President was under the impression that Benson was hiring a new employee and not one who had been in the government for nineteen years and was trying to transfer back to the Department of Agriculture from the State Department. Neither did he know of Ladejinsky's anti-Communist writings. On the basis of what he was told, he recounted later, he said to Benson that the case would "scare" him. Once Ladejinsky had been barred and the controversy broke, revealing both sides of the case, the President publicly stood by Benson, saying it was a matter on which men could honestly disagree. Even the employment of Ladejinsky by Stassen, however, left the administration on the hook until Benson, to the relief of the White House, announced months later that he was expunging the security-risk label from the department's records on Ladejinsky. Later he testified that the finding had been "gratuitous and unnecessary."

(The story of Ladejinsky's career in the government has a strange denouement. Early in 1956 he was forced to resign because he had bought stock in a Formosa glass plant, thus violating a rule of the International Co-Operation Administration that its employees cannot invest in American-aided firms.)

Among the voices raised in criticism of the loyalty program after the Ladejinsky case was that of former Senator Harry P. Cain, Republican, of Washington, a member of the Subversive Activities Control Board. His criticism was the more surprising because in the Senate he had been identified with the extreme right wing. Cain blasted the handling of the Ladejinsky case and said the program had "swung too far on the side of injustice." Privately, the President was rather irked by Cain's speeches. He felt that as a Republican and government official, Cain should have discussed these issues privately with the administration before airing his views publicly.

Finally, Cain saw Adams and explained his objections to the program—that it sometimes harmed the innocent and produced insecurity instead of security. Adams reminded Cain that he was a member of a "team" and should play the game accordingly, supporting the fixed policy of the administration in handling the security problem.

To iron out one of the flaws disclosed by the Ladejinsky case the administration promptly revised procedures so that a person cleared by one agency should not be labeled a security risk by another without consultation to make sure all factors had been considered. In event of disagreement the Attorney General would review the case. Another effect of the Ladejinsky case was to arouse sufficient sentiment in Congress to establish a bipartisan commission to study the security problem.

Although he went along with this, the President never favored such a study. He feels the administration can work the flaws out of the program by keeping it constantly under review. He points to the many improvements that have been made since 10450 went into effect. Generally, he believes, the system is working fairly—that while cases like the Ladejinsky and Chasanow affairs arouse public disputes, thousands of others pass unnoticed because they have been handled with propriety and justice.

In May, 1956, the Atomic Energy Commission liberalized its procedures to permit security boards to use "common sense" in judging a person's left-wing associations. Thus when such association "is the result of, and is limited to, normal business or professional activity or chance or casual meetings," the boards would be free to decide whether or not this tended to make the person a security risk. The boards would not be bound to consider it derogatory information. "If possible," the accused is to be confronted by the accuser in security hearings—a step, though only a limited one, away from reliance on the word of anonymous informers.

One of the most encouraging developments of the last three years has been the waning of hysteria over the loyalty question, creating a more wholesome atmosphere for re-examining the program. However, the outlook is for gradual change through improved procedures rather than a broad and fundamental modification of the whole program, which some advocate but for which there is as yet no heavy popular pressure upon the administration.

CHAPTER 22

The Tightrope Over Formosa

Red China Bombards Quemoy – The President Is Urged to Intervene – He Refuses a Showdown – Chiang Is "Released" – Communists Invade the Tachens – Eisenhower Asks Congress for Authority to "Fight, If Necessary" – Congress Approves the Formosa Resolution – Eisenhower Says U. S. Would Use Atomic Weapons – Senate Ratifies Paris Accords – Dulles Credits Eden for E.D.C. Substitute

In Korea in 1953 and Indo-China in 1954 President Eisenhower had thrown his influence on the side of reducing the chances of American involvement in a war with Red China. In a more dramatic and urgent fashion he tried for a third time to avert war in Asia early in 1955, when months of tension erupted in a Communist thrust into the Nationalist-held Tachen Islands north of Formosa.

Serious trouble began to develop in the Formosa Strait in September of 1954 while the President was vacationing in Denver. The Chinese Communists, whose avowed objective is the capture of Formosa, opened heavy bombardment of Nationalist-held Quemoy off the China coast about the time the Southeast Asia Treaty was being signed in Manila, and dueling between the Reds and the Nationalists over offshore islands ensued.

There had never been any question of Eisenhower's determination to defend Formosa and the Pescadores (Penghus), which are part of the United States island defense chain in the western Pacific.

"Any invasion of Formosa," the President said at his press conference on August 17, 1954, "would have to run over the Seventh Fleet."

But the disturbing question thrust upon him by the Red bombardment was what the United States should do if the Chinese Communists invaded offshore islands like Quemoy and the Matsus,
opposite Formosa. The juridical status of those islands differed
from that of Formosa and the Pescadores. The United States had
captured Formosa and the Pescadores from Japan in World War II
and was within its rights under the peace treaty in defending them
pending their ultimate disposition. But the offshore islands had
always belonged to China and "were we," as Walter Lippmann
wrote, "to intervene in the offshore islands, we would be acting
on Chinese territory in a Chinese civil war."

As the crisis grew, the policy of the United States was to brandish
its determination to defend Formosa but to mask its intention
respecting the offshore islands. Thus the mutual defense treaty with
Chiang, signed on December 2, 1954, pledged the United States to
defend Formosa and the Pescadores. But supplementary notes exchanged between Dulles and George K. C. Yeh, Nationalist Chinese
Foreign Minister, said that by joint agreement the United States
could act in these other islands. Thus, the United States was not
bound to act in the other islands, but it left itself the option of
doing so if it chose.

A momentous debate went on around the President as to the
course the United States should take. Although the record of what
occurred in the councils of the government that fall and winter is
still wrapped in secrecy, it is clear from many signs, including the
writings of General Ridgway, that the President was being strongly
urged by some of his highest military advisers to commit the United
States to the defense of the offshore islands.

Pressed upon Eisenhower was the view long identified with Radford that a showdown between the United States and Red China
was inevitable. There were those "in high places," Ridgway makes
clear, who felt that "we should take a stand" against invasion of
Quemoy and the Matsus and thus, if challenged, bring on the
showdown then and there by going to war.

Ridgway's reference to the "interventionists" recalls reports that
Radford, General Nathan F. Twining, Air Force Chief of Staff, and
Admiral Robert B. Carney, Chief of Naval Operations, proposed to
the President in vain at an N.S.C. meeting in Denver on September

12, 1954, that American planes aid the Nationalists in bombing the mainland to prevent a Communist landing on Quemoy. Ridgway was deeply opposed to intervention, as he had been during the Indo-China crisis, and the opinion he expresses in his memoirs is doubtless the one he pressed upon the President at that time in opposition to Radford.

Such an action [Ridgway writes] would be almost impossible to limit. It would bring us into direct conflict with the Red Chinese. It could spread to full and all-out war, employing all the terrible weapons at our command.

And we could, by such an all-out effort, conquer China.

But I challenge any thesis that destroying the military might of Red China would be in our own long-range interest. We could create there, by military means, a great power vacuum. Then we would have to go in there with hundreds of thousands of men to fill that vacuum—which would bring us face to face with Russia along a seven-thousand-mile frontier. If we failed to go in, then Russia herself would fill it, and the threat to our own security would not have abated one iota.

As in the past, the President did not want war with China, and he felt that the course urged upon him by the "interventionists" was too great a risk to take. Rovere observed in his letter to The New Yorker:

Though the administration is seriously divided on China, with the President on one side and Senator Knowland, various members of the Joint Chiefs of Staff, and—some of the time—Secretary Dulles on the other, almost everybody believes that the President is determined to have his view prevail. His view appears to be that—in this area at any rate—we have more to gain from making an effective effort to reduce tensions than from merely exploiting them to our own advantage.

Instead of a commitment to make a stand on the offshore islands, the President and Dulles decided that whatever action the United States might take would depend upon what Eisenhower judged to be the aim of a Communist attack. If the attack was of a purely local or defensive character, in the President's opinion, that was one thing. But if the President decided that the attack was part of a grand assault on Formosa and the Pescadores, then the United States would be ready to use whatever measures would be needed to frustrate this offensive.

Meanwhile Chiang was "re-leashed" when, in connection with the mutual defense treaty, a promise was exacted from the Nationalists that they would not attack the mainland without first consulting the United States.

On January 18, 1955, the Communists finally challenged the American policy of deliberate ambiguity toward the offshore islands by moving into the Tachens and seizing the island of Yikiang. Dulles and Eisenhower at their respective press conferences promptly wrote off the barren Tachens, lying two hundred miles from Formosa, as not being an essential part of the defense of Chiang's bastion. The President welcomed efforts by the U.N. to arrange for a cease-fire in the Formosa Strait.

Nevertheless the invasion of Yikiang produced a sense of high emergency in Washington, the more so since it followed upon Chou En-lai's truculent plea to his people to liberate Formosa, banish Chiang and smash the mutual defense treaty. The atmosphere of crisis was heightened by the statement on the Peiping radio after the fall of Yikiang that the attack showed a "determined will to fight for the liberation of Taiwan. Our people will use all their strength to fulfill that task."

Eisenhower, Dulles and Radford conferred several times. During this period the President stood firm against any American reaction calculated to bring on hostilities. But he did agree with Dulles that the United States should take a dramatic step that might deter Red China from starting a war. It was in these talks that the idea of the Formosa Resolution evolved. After consultation with Congressional leaders of both parties, the President sent up his unprecedented message on January 24.

As was intended, his fight-if-we-must declaration hit with great impact.

The situation [he said] has become sufficiently critical to impel me, without awaiting action by the United Nations, to ask the Congress to participate now, by specific resolution, in measures designed to improve the prospects for peace. These measures would contemplate the use of the Armed Forces of the United States, if necessary to assure the security of Formosa and the Pescadores.

This would include the authority to use sea and air power to evacuate Nationalist forces from the Tachens.

As for Quemoy and Matsu, the policy of suspense, of keeping the Communists in doubt as to how the United States would react to attack, was continued. However, the President asked Congress for authority to act in these offshore islands if this should become necessary to the larger defense of the area. The effect of this request was openly and dramatically to put the Communists on notice that invasion of Quemoy and the Matsus would invite retaliation by the United States.

We must be alert [he continued] to any concentration or employment of Chinese Communist forces obviously undertaken to facilitate attack upon Formosa, and be prepared to take appropriate military action.

I do not suggest that the United States enlarge its defensive obligations beyond Formosa and the Pescadores. . . . But, unhappily, the danger of armed attack directed against that area compels us to take into account closely related localities and actions which, under current conditions, might determine the failure or the success of such an attack. The authority that may be accorded by the Congress would be used only in situations which are recognizable as parts of, or definite preliminaries to, an attack against the main positions of Formosa and the Pescadores.

As the Democrats were to point out in the debate that followed, the President had the Constitutional power as Commander-in-Chief to take many, if not all, of the measures which he was asking Congress to authorize in advance. But in his message Eisenhower said that by joining with him in the resolution Congress would be making clear the "unified and serious intentions" of the United States.

Thus [he said] it will reduce the possibility that the Chinese Communists, misjudging our firm purpose and national unity, might be disposed to challenge the position of the United States and precipitate a major crisis which even they neither anticipate nor desire.

In the interest of peace, therefore, the United States must remove any doubt regarding our readiness to fight, if necessary, to preserve the

vital stake of the free world in a free Formosa and to engage in whatever operations may be required to carry out that purpose.

To make this plain requires not only Presidential action but also
Congressional action. In a situation such as now confronts us, and under
modern conditions of warfare, it would not be prudent to await the
emergency before coming to Congress. Then it might be too late.
Already the warning signals are flying.

Obviously the President had other reasons beside this one of warning the Communists. He believed that Truman had made a serious
mistake in not going to Congress before committing American
forces in Korea in 1950. Truman's position was that the Communist
advance was so swift he had no time to consult Congress. But since
there had not been unity of action between Truman and Congress
to start with, the foundation was laid for the increasing disunity
that developed as the war became unpopular. This was a fate that
Eisenhower wished to escape if war broke out in the Formosa Strait.
Whether the members liked it or not—and despite the overwhelmingly favorable vote, many of them did not—the Formosa Resolution
saddled Congress with a share of the responsibility for the possible
dangers ahead. "Eisenhower is passing the buck," Senator Wayne
Morse, Democrat, of Oregon, complained. Others observed that in
seeking advance Congressional support for strategic actions he
might take as Commander-in-Chief, the President was setting a
precedent that could bedevil his successors in their conduct of
foreign affairs.

Criticism arose also over the failure of the resolution to draw a
precise line of defense between Formosa and the mainland. The
President's decision to make this line discretionary rather than fixed,
thus continuing his free hand to deal with an attack on the offshore
islands, was based, we may suppose, on a number of considerations
not explained in the message.

A line excluding Quemoy and the Matsus would have outraged
the Nationalists, and Washington was not indifferent to the problem of maintaining the morale of Chiang's forces. Knowland and his
colleagues in the Senate would have had little enthusiasm for a
resolution consigning these Nationalist-held islands to the Communists. On the other hand (Knowland would not have enthused

over this, either) the chance always remained that so long as Red China did not hold the islands they might be traded off to her later for a cease-fire. It was Dulles's view at that time, however, that the Communists had no interest in settling for Quemoy and the Matsus. Their interest, he felt, was in overthrowing the Nationalist government and thereby removing Chiang's army as an obstacle to further Communist expansion.

Critics in and out of Congress saw serious danger in giving the President authority to intervene, if he chose, in defense of the offshore islands. Their view was that the United States might get mouse-trapped into a war in the worst possible strategic circumstances over some puny islands which hadn't the remotest bearing on American security and to which we had no legal rights in any case. Republican Senator Flanders went even farther in his speech in the Senate.

"We have had intimations from the highest quarters," he said, "that it would be militarily advisable to prevent the massing of troops and equipment gathered for the purpose of making an assault on the islands. Put in plain English, this is preventive war. And it is seriously proposed as a possible action pursuant to the purposes of this resolution."

An amendment to restrict the use of the armed forces specifically to the defense of Formosa and the Pescadores was introduced by Senator Hubert H. Humphrey, Democrat, of Minnesota, but was defeated.

The most commanding figure in the debate was Walter George, then at the peak of his extraordinary influence in the Senate. When the Democrats took control of Congress that January, George, the dean of the Senate, was entitled by seniority to the chairmanship of the Finance or the Foreign Relations Committee. One day before the session began he was at the White House on other business when the President intimated to him that he would like to see him take over the Foreign Relations Committee. The next Democrat in line on the committee was Theodore Francis Green, of Rhode Island, who at eighty-seven was ten years George's senior. George saw the wisdom of having a spry seventy-seven-year-old directing the foreign-policy battles on the Senate floor. In this role he did much to carry bipartisan co-operation in foreign policy to its highest peak since Vandenberg had been the Republican chairman of the Foreign Relations Committee under a Democratic President. George had his doubts about some of the disputed points of the Formosa Resolution, but he considered a forthright stand the best course in a bad situation. He supported it with great force and eloquence in committee and on the Senate floor.

Before George spoke in the Senate the President strengthened the Senator's hand by moving to allay doubts which had arisen that the resolution might open the door for Chiang or Radford to maneuver the United States into war with Red China. Hagerty issued a statement saying:

"The President made it clear that these United States forces were designed purely for defensive purposes and that any decision to use United States forces other than in immediate self-defense or in direct defense of Formosa and the Pescadores would be a decision which he would take and the responsibility for which he has not delegated."

George put up a staunch defense of the President's decision not to draw a clear defense line and to seek Congressional approval of his course.

"I hope no Democrat will be heard to say," George concluded, "that because the President of the United States came to Congress, he is thereby subject to criticism. The President chose a courageous course, a course which would be taken only by a prudent, patient man, who knows the pitfalls along the course and who knows the horrors of war."

The resolution was passed by the House, 410 to 3, and by the Senate, 85 to 3. It was signed by the President on January 29, George's seventy-seventh birthday, and when the Senator went to the White House for the ceremony, Mrs. Eisenhower gave him a kiss.

The Communists spurned efforts by the United States, Britain and New Zealand to negotiate a cease-fire agreement in the U.N. High tension continued over the Formosa Strait for weeks. In February the Seventh Fleet evacuated fourteen thousand Nationalist regulars and guerrillas, and a like number of citizens, from the Tachens without incident. In public statements both the President and Dulles warned the Communists that the United States would use tactical atomic weapons on military targets in event of general war in Asia. Answering a question about these weapons at his press conference on March 16, 1955, Eisenhower said:

In any combat where these things can be used on strictly military targets and have strictly military purposes I see no reason why they shouldn't be used just exactly as you would use a bullet or anything else. I believe the great question about these things comes when you begin to get into those areas where you cannot make sure that you are operating merely against military targets. But with that qualification, I would say yes, of course they would be used.

Just as it seemed the crisis was subsiding late in March, a new scare was generated by the publication of off-the-record remarks to some Washington reporters by Admiral Carney, predicting that the Communists might attack Quemoy and the Matsus soon after April 15. In a statement of his own and through Hagerty the President contradicted Carney, saying that he had no information to support it.

(Nine months before, eyebrows had been raised in the Cabinet at its meeting on June 4, 1954, over a speech Carney had made the preceding week on Indo-China. Addressing the National Security Industrial Association in New York in words called grim by newspaper editorials, the admiral said that the free world faced "graver alternatives" in Indo-China than those that had led to the decision to intervene in Korea. This speech came after the emphasis here and abroad had shifted from consideration of intervention to seeking a *modus vivendi*. It had been submitted for clearance by the State Department but not enough time had been allowed for it to reach top officials. The President urged the Cabinet at that session to be very careful in using foreign-policy material in speeches. With each speech, Dulles suggested, the question should be raised as to whether a military man or a diplomat should deliver it. The President declined to set a firm rule. He preferred to trust the discretion of Cabinet officers. He reported, however, that he had told the Joint Chiefs that foreign-policy speeches by men in uniform were undesirable.)

The Formosa crisis eased, especially after Chou proposed at the African-Asian Conference in Bandung, Indonesia, in April that the United States and Red China discuss ways of relaxing tensions in the Far East. The talks, stretched out over months, were held in Geneva, but the situation in the Formosa Strait has not been altered fundamentally. The Nationalists are holding the offshore islands, the Reds are glaring at them from the mainland, and the President still holds the power of decision on American military action in case the Communists launch an invasion.

Soon after adoption of the Formosa Resolution the Senate put in place another stone in the administration's foreign policy by ratifying the Paris accords ending the occupation of West Germany and admitting Germany to NATO. This was a reasonably happy ending to a story that had given the President a bad jolt when the French rejected the European Defense Community.

His experiences in Europe had made Eisenhower a vigorous supporter of the E.D.C., a plan of French origin for forming a European army, including West Germany troops. Beginning with his inaugural address, Eisenhower had exerted pressure on behalf of ratification of the E.D.C. by the Western European members. Month after month he and Dulles maintained this pressure in the face of dwindling hope that the French, weakened by the Indo-China war and fearful of new German militarism, would adopt it.

Augmenting Dulles's threat of an "agonizing reappraisal" in December of 1953, the White House warned that the United States might have to review "its basic policies" if the E.D.C. was not soon established. To encourage French ratification the President on April 16, 1954, pledged that the United States would continue to maintain a "fair share" of forces in Europe and would regard any action threatening the "integrity or unity" of the E.D.C. as a threat to itself.

Notwithstanding, the French National Assembly rejected E.D.C. on August 30, 1954. At the Iowa State Fair in Des Moines that same day Eisenhower called the vote a "major setback" to United States foreign policy.

Anthony Eden reacted to this setback by proposing the solution that led finally to the Paris accords. After visiting the capitals of Western Europe, he took the initiative in a plan for making West Germany and Italy sovereign partners in the Brussels mutual defense treaty of 1948. In October representatives of the United States, Britain, France, Canada, West Germany, Italy, The Netherlands and Belgium signed an agreement in London creating a Western European Union under an enlarged and strengthened Brussels treaty to replace the E.D.C. A decisive step toward this agreement was taken by Eden in abandoning Britain's traditional policy against committing troops to the Continent and agreeing to keep four divisions and a tactical air force there for as long as a majority of the Brussels partners desired. Dulles also had pledged that if the Western European Union were established, he would recommend to the President that the United States make the same commitment on troops that it would have under the E.D.C. The agreement in London paved the way for the Paris accords on restoring German sovereignty and bringing the Bonn government into NATO.

After his return to Washington the Secretary of State told the Cabinet on October 19, 1954, that Eden's historic commitment on troops had been the fundamental reason for the success of the London conference.

CHAPTER 23

How to Handle
a Democratic Congress

The Democratic Professionals Take Over – Rayburn and Johnson Rule Out Obstructionism – Eisenhower Expects "Wedge-Driving" – A Rocky Legislative Road – Stevenson Angers Eisenhower – The President Accuses the Democrats of "Fiscal Irresponsibility" – Neely's Blockbuster – The Salk Vaccine Muddle and Mrs. Hobby

The prompt and overwhelming Congressional approval of the Formosa Resolution and the Paris accords were good omens in the budding relationship between Eisenhower and the Democrats controlling Congress.

At his press conference the day after Democratic victory in the 1954 election Eisenhower regretted having said that this outcome would precipitate a cold war in Washington. He set about immediately to bring the Democratic leaders in for a discussion on foreign policy.

Although the election returns disappointed him, they yielded certain political advantages to the President. For one thing Democratic control submerged the Republican right wing, which had given him such deep trouble during his first two years in office. McCarthy, for example, lost the chairmanship of the Permanent Investigations Sub-committee, a circumstance which, added to the censure vote, all but annihilated his power to harass the President. On the Republican side the pro-Eisenhower faction was able for the first time to seize a larger share of influence than the Old Guard.

On the Democratic side true professionals were in control—men of demonstrated breadth and ability, like Walter George, Senator Lyndon B. Johnson, of Texas, and Speaker of the House Sam Rayburn, a Texan also. The President was born in Denison, in the Fourth Congressional District of Texas, which Rayburn, eight years his senior, has represented in Congress since 1913. Once when Rayburn was taking the hide off the Republicans from the rear of a sound truck in Texas during the 1952 campaign, a heckler yelled, "What about Ike? Wasn't he born in the old Fourth?"

"Yes," Rayburn replied, "and he was a wonderful baby."

Eisenhower had come to the forefront in public life under Democratic administrations, and he and the older Democratic leaders knew each other well.

"I don't see any reason," he said at his postelection press conference, "why these people shouldn't be my friends, that have been my personal friends in the past."

Even when they were in the minority during his first two years, the Democrats gave Eisenhower support that was often the margin of victory for him. Leaders like Johnson and Rayburn never lived by the rule that the only business of the opposition is obstruction. Inasmuch as they took the position that a great deal of the President's program was simply an extension of Democratic reforms, they found no difficulty in backing these measures. In the Senate, Knowland and Johnson worked well together across the aisle, and the Democrats did not resort to clobbering every Eisenhower proposal, as the late Kenneth Wherry, of Nebraska, had when he was the Senate Republican leader in the Eightieth Congress during Truman's administration. Indeed a criticism sometimes directed at the Democratic leadership during the first three Eisenhower years was that it was too uncritical and overly willing to accept the President's recommendations.

Nevertheless the Democratic leaders are men with their own game to play, and one of the big goals of this game is retaining control of Congress. While, especially in the 1955 session, they collaborated with the President, notably in foreign policy, they have bided their time awaiting an issue. They seized upon the Dixon-Yates contract, but this was a complex subject in which there was little popular interest outside the T.V.A. region. One of their first sharp breaks with the President came over his veto of the natural-gas bill early in 1956. And when, in April of 1956, he vetoed the farm bill, a decision widely applauded by those without axes to grind, the Democrats felt that at last they had an issue that would pay off in votes, and they poured it on the President broadside.

The Cabinet met on December 3, 1954, a month before the new Congress convened. Eisenhower was eager for any ideas on how to get along with the Democrats. So far as foreign policy was concerned he did not think he would have any serious problem. But he believed that careful attention would have to be paid to differences on domestic issues if he was not to encounter the frustrations that gripped Presidents Wilson and Hoover. As in previous years, he questioned whether he should deliver the State of the Union message in person. Mrs. Hobby and Benson said that it was very important that he do so.

In the Cabinet on December 10, Jack Martin, Administrative Assistant to the President, who had for years been Taft's right-hand man, suggested that Democratic strategy might center on investigations of the administration.

The President replied that any individual or department—except an organization like the Central Intelligence Agency, which deals in secrets—should insist at once upon the airing of all the facts. It was folly, he said, to try to cover up administrative errors. Stassen observed that it was difficult to do business at all with McCarthy's subcommittee. (This was while McCarthy was still chairman.) In such case, the President advised him, the complete facts should be given to another committee. He recalled that in mid-1953 he had advised Stevens that it would be desirable to clear up difficulties at Fort Monmouth without any attempt to conceal the fact that this was being done.

On December 17 Eisenhower cautioned the Cabinet to be alert to the standard political tactic of wedge-driving when the Democrats took control of Congress. He said that he did not wish to do anything that would restrict a Cabinet officer's freedom to say what he wished, but he urged members to laugh off any efforts at creating differences among themselves. Thus far, he added, the Cabinet had been very successful in settling differences of opinion by friendly discussion.

At a joint meeting of the Cabinet and Republican legislative leaders on January 3, 1955, Bryce Harlow, Administrative Assistant to the President, read the latest draft of the State of the Union message, which Eisenhower again had decided to deliver in person. The President asked whether it would be wise for him to hold out hope of tax reduction in 1956. Humphrey came in with a very decided yes. Eisenhower ribbed him for this. Mostly, he said, the Secretary of the Treasury emphasized the necessity for balancing the budget, but when it came to tax reduction he liked to anticipate savings. The President cautioned that heavy reductions in government spending were not in sight. He agreed, however, to mention his hope that on the basis of increased revenue resulting from economic growth taxes could be cut eventually. He told Humphrey that he—the Secretary—would have to take the responsibility for the statement.

Budget Director Hughes thought that a cut would be possible if the administration continued its current policies. Dulles held that if taxes were going to be cut, the reduction must be made possible by growth in the economy. Wilson was for omitting the statement altogether because, he said, defense programs were becoming constantly more complex and thus more expensive.

Taking a political view, one of the Senate leaders argued against the statement. If taxes were cut in 1956, the administration would get credit in any event, he said. But if a hope was held out and failed to materialize, then the administration ran the risk of exploitation of the issue by the Democrats. A leader of the House disagreed.

The President's decision stood, but he admonished the Cabinet and the leaders not to suppose the statement was so important that it would shake the world.

In the State of the Union message he said:

> . . . It is now clear that defense and other essential government costs must remain at a level precluding further tax reductions this year. Although excise and corporation income taxes must, therefore, be continued at their present rates, further tax cuts will be possible when justified by lower expenditures and by revenue increases arising from

the nation's economic growth. I am hopeful that such reductions can be made next year. . . .

A House leader asked if the section of the message about water resources had been co-ordinated with the Hoover Commission task force on Water Resources and Power. Rowland Hughes replied that there had been some discussions—not with the former President himself—which indicated that Hoover could not support Eisenhower's position but would not oppose it publicly. In his message Eisenhower re-emphasized the willingness of the Federal government to develop water resources in partnership with state and private interests. And he went on to say that the Federal government must shoulder its obligation of "undertaking projects of such complexity and size that their success requires Federal development."

Eisenhower told the Cabinet and the leaders that continuing drought in parts of the country underscored the need for utilizing water resources fully. Nixon said that the administration must live up to all its previous commitments in this field. In answer to a question from a Senator as to what the administration's water policy was, the President replied that a Cabinet committee had this matter under study and was waiting to have a look at the Hoover Commission recommendations. The aim, he said, was to develop a broad, long-range policy to avoid the expenditure of billions on a piecemeal program.

The administration was committed to proposing an increase in the minimum wage above the prevailing level of 75 cents an hour. At this joint meeting one of the House leaders asked whether raising the rate to 90 cents would be disadvantageous to the farmers. The President said that there were compelling reasons for increasing the minimum wage and that the impact on the farmers would be largely psychological.

The subject had been before the Cabinet several times. In these discussions Secretary Mitchell said that an increase to 90 cents or $1 was justified. Humphrey agreed that the time was ripe for an increase but questioned going to $1. The President favored acting in moderation and felt that any figure under $1 would be moderate. Mitchell predicted that the administration sooner or later would have to go to $1 or higher, and Nixon felt that if the effect upon the economy would not be harmful, the $1 level was preferable from a political point of view. Subsequently the Treasury and the Labor Departments and the Council of Economic Advisers recommended 90 cents and the Department of Commerce 85 cents. The President decided to propose 90 cents and compromise on $1 if the Democrats tried to outbid him. That is the way it came about finally.

On January 14, 1955, Mrs. Hobby and Dr. Samuel M. Brownell, brother of the Attorney General, who is Commissioner of Education, outlined a program designed to stimulate school construction. Some of the President's advisers had felt that the administration should hold off a school bill until after the White House Conference on Education scheduled for November 28, 1955, but Eisenhower insisted at least on an interim measure for submission to the new Congress.

Mrs. Hobby's department came up with the complicated proposal presented to the Cabinet by Dr. Brownell. It provided, among other things, for Federal purchase of the school bonds of communities unable to market them at reasonable rates. With grants to be matched by the states, the Federal government would support a lease-purchase plan under which state school-building authorities would put up schools and lease them to school districts until principal and interest were paid, after which the districts would take title to the buildings. Federal grants of $200,000,000 over a three-year period would be made to impoverished school districts unable to issue bonds or participate in the lease-purchase plan. For the Federal government the long-term cost of the whole program would have been very modest.

Humphrey admired the theory of the program and said that schools had to be built, but he raised a number of technical questions about the issuance of bonds and so forth.

The President replied that the Treasury was within its rights in examining these matters. But he said that he was concerned that the program did not go far enough. To neglect education, he told the Cabinet, was as dangerous as to neglect national security. However, he liked the aspect of the program that left a large share of the responsibility in the hands of the states.

Vice-President Nixon praised the moderate character of the program, contrasting it with proposals for simply handing out Federal funds. He observed that Earl Warren's sponsorship of school and road building in California had enhanced his reputation as a liberal, and he thought it important that Eisenhower be identified with a school-building program. He cautioned, however, against Federal control of education.

When the measure reached Congress, it got caught in a political crossfire with the Democrats protesting that it was inadequate. A number of rival bills were introduced calling for larger Federal appropriations for schools. The upshot was that a school bill never reached the floor of either house.

The predicament of the school program was discussed from time to time in the Cabinet. On April 22, 1955, Mrs. Hobby spoke very gloomily about the prospects for all the legislative proposals submitted by the Department of Health, Education and Welfare. It looked, she said, as though the Democrats were out to see that the President received no glory in this field.

On July 8, 1955, the President was hopping mad over Adlai Stevenson's speech to the National Education Association in Chicago two days before. Stevenson had said that "nothing" had been done by the administration to solve the school problem, except to call the White House conference in the fall. This was pure demagoguery, the President fumed. He told the Cabinet that much more could and should be done to acquaint the people with what the administration was doing. He felt that Cabinet members should enlist the help of friends outside the administration to carry this effort forward. He said he was directing former Governor Howard Pyle, of Arizona, who was now one of his administrative assistants, to see how well it could be organized.

The housing program was discussed in the Cabinet on January 28, 1955. Rabb alluded to the lawsuit brought by the National Association for the Advancement of Colored People to end a ban on Negro purchases of homes with government-insured mortgages in Levittown, Pennsylvania. The President said that he was disturbed over rumblings of dissatisfaction against the housing program in general and was anxious to have it reviewed soon by disinterested people.

He expressed his determination that no act of the Federal government must discriminate against people because of their race or color. He recognized, however, that a subtler problem was raised by indirect government programs, such as guaranteeing loans for private housing. But he thought it was entirely improper for the Federal government to lend money under circumstances in which a single individual could bar members of a race from a whole community.

This problem was never dealt with in the housing bill passed that year. The bill authorized a start on forty-five thousand public housing units by July 31, 1956, but Eisenhower signed it with "serious objections" to some aspects, notably its failure to limit public-housing aid to those communities which had developed workable slum-clearance programs of their own.

At the request of the administration Congress passed bills raising the antitrust penalties and giving the government the right to sue for damages sustained as a result of antitrust violations. Brownell told the Cabinet on March 18 that by comparison with the Democrats, the Eisenhower administration had brought more antitrust cases into court, had completed more cases and had displayed greater impartiality of enforcement by acting against both business concerns and labor unions when there was evidence of collusion.

In advance of the President's special message on the Inter-American Highway appropriation the matter was discussed in the Cabinet on March 25. Nixon urged that the program be speeded up so that the highway could be completed in another three years instead of in fifteen or twenty. Eisenhower replied that the matter should be well handled because if there was one thing he detested, it was to talk big and do little. At the President's request Congress authorized $74,980,000 for this country's share of the cost of completing the highway in three years.

At the Cabinet meeting on April 22, Eisenhower bristled over the pressure being put on him in establishing higher wages for postal employees. He had proposed increases averaging 6.5 per cent. Deputy Postmaster General Charles R. Hook, Jr., reported to the Cabinet that Congress would approve a figure between the 8.2 increase voted by the House and the 10 per cent boost approved by the Senate. If the President should veto, Hook said, it might then be possible to get through a bill more to the administration's liking. Eisenhower said that it would be difficult to justify a veto of 8.2 per cent, which was so close to the administration figure, but he said he was convinced that he would be right in resisting the "blackjack efforts" of those trying to force through a higher scale.

At his weekly conference with Republican leaders on May 10, he let it be known that he was exasperated with the lobbying over postal pay. (Some of the heaviest pressure was being exerted by the A.F.L. National Association of Letter Carriers.) At least for the next twenty months, he snapped, he was not going to move out of the White House and let the lobbyists move in.

The following day a bill was passed raising wages by an average of 8.59 per cent. Eisenhower vetoed it. Then Congress passed another bill shaving the average down to 8 per cent, and he signed it.

In his State of the Union message the President had again urged Congress to approve the billion-dollar Federal project for water storage facilities in the Upper Colorado River Basin. Old controversies were renewed. Californians maintained that it jeopardized their interest in Colorado River water. Paul Douglas called it an economic "boondoggle," and some conservationists warned that it would invade the national park system. Those in favor of it argued the need for water for power and irrigation in that region.

When the Cabinet discussed it on April 22, Eisenhower said the project would be valuable as a "lifetime investment." He asked McKay what the Department of Interior was doing about the Fryingpan-Arkansas water power project. The Secretary replied that the department was working on it, that it was rather expensive but a good project. Then the President, who must have known about such things from observations around his Gettysburg farm, commented that there seemed to be little topsoil left in the East, and asked if any irrigation projects were being planned for the Eastern seaboard. Benson said that he thought one could be undertaken somewhere in this region.

Water resources came up again in the Cabinet on May 20, when McKay took exception to the agitation for public power carried on by Democratic Senators from Washington and Oregon. He spoke out against the idea that all power development in the Northwest should be the responsibility of the Federal government. The only two areas of the country currently short of power, he said, were those where Federal projects predominated—the T.V.A. region and the Northwest.

Stassen warned that the Democrats might challenge the Republicans on the adequacy of the government's part in the partnership program, and he urged the administration to initiate some of its own power projects. McKay said that some had been started, inadequate though they were to the need, but he acknowledged that while certain ones had been authorized during the Eisenhower administration, they were part of earlier Democratic programs.

The President cut through this talk to ask what was the status of the Upper Colorado at the moment and what was the administration doing to get the legislation through Congress. McKay said that the Department of Interior was putting up a fight on it. The President declared that he wanted to see a start made on some large multiple-purpose project for which there was a genuine need. The most desirable, Nixon said, was the Upper Colorado. Lodge hoped that there could be a "dirt-turning" ceremony before the year was out. This might be accomplished, Nixon replied, out of remaining planning funds in anticipation of appropriations for construction. Nixon and Stassen both urged that the administration cling to the middle way between the extremes represented by the public and private power lobbies.

In the end the Senate voted for the Upper Colorado, but the House, after a favorable committee report, laid it over until 1956.

Eisenhower did not press the Democratic Congress for amendment of the Taft-Hartley Act. In the Cabinet on May 13, Mitchell said that considering the attitude of Congress, little was to be gained by trying to force the matter. In his opinion, the issue had long been exaggerated, and it was just as well to have it deflated somewhat.

At an earlier meeting, on February 18, Mitchell had discussed the impending merger of the C.I.O. and the A.F.L. in a matter-of-fact way. Eisenhower asked if there was any reason for concern over the creation of such a large organization overshadowing every other in the same field. Mitchell replied that he did not regard the merger as a menace in any respect.

Congress gave the President the three-year extension of the basic reciprocal-trade program he had asked for, though not without certain concessions to protectionism, which some of his critics felt he should have fought. It also enacted at his request the first comprehensive peacetime military reserve program, though again the measure fell short of all he had sought. The President also won his fight to kill off the attempt by House Democrats to write in a twenty-dollar income-tax cut for all. Rayburn no longer considered Eisenhower a wonderful baby after the President said at his press conference on February 23 that the bill reached the "heights of fiscal irresponsibility." What kind of responsibility was it, Rayburn exclaimed, when the Republicans "didn't give the little folks anything last year and gave the dividend folks theirs?"

This manner of partisan sniping continued off and on through the session, but both sides held back the blockbusters—everyone, that is, but Senator Matthew M. Neely, Democrat, of West Virginia. Speaking before the C.I.O. United Auto Workers in Cleveland, on March 28, he accused the President of a hypocritical display of going to church on Sundays, saying, "Eisenhower never joined a church until after he became President."

At the legislative leaders' meeting the next day Eisenhower had an amusing comment on this attack. When he had awakened the preceding Sunday, he related, he was tired out and felt he ought to loaf around the White House. But Mrs. Eisenhower thought he should attend church and prodded him into that extra ounce of effort it took to get dressed and go. So what was his reward for this little sacrifice?

"Neely!"

It was Sherman Adams who supplied the comment officially uttered by Hagerty on the Neely speech: "What Peter says about Paul tells more about Peter than it does about Paul."

One of the principal setbacks to Eisenhower's program in the new Congress was the collapse of his huge highway bill in a disagreement between Republicans and Democrats over financing. The President proposed paying for highways out of a Federal bond issue, which would not show up, at least for many years, in the public debt. The Democrats charged that this was evasion and "legerdemain" —and a "bonanza" for the bankers.

As the President had been warned, the Democrats conducted

numerous investigations. For the first time in years the emphasis of Congressional inquiries turned away from a search for Reds and spies toward matters like the Dixon-Yates contract and Secretary Talbott's affairs, which will be discussed in later chapters, the stock market, the military cutbacks and the mix-up over the distribution of Salk vaccine.

The prodigious confusion for a time over the Salk vaccine gave the President one of his worst headaches during that spring of 1955. The mix-up was compounded of an extremely difficult technical problem, public excitement and inadequate preparation by Mrs. Hobby's department. The White House was dismayed when Mrs. Hobby testified during the uproar that the vaccine shortage was "tremendous" and that "no one could have foreseen the public demand."

A woman of exceptional ability who had done an excellent job in getting Congress and private organizations to approve the creation of her new department, Mrs. Hobby nevertheless ran into endless difficulties once it began functioning. Her conservative outlook jarred those who advocated more government aid for education, health and social welfare. Her temper led her into difficulties with her staff, and when Rockefeller departed as Under Secretary to go to the White House, the post was left open and organization within the department suffered. With the safety of so many millions of children involved, the Salk vaccine problem was a tough one, and at times Mrs. Hobby showed signs of being utterly frightened by it.

Although she was an editor and publisher in private life, she never mastered press relations in Washington. One of her first big meetings with the drug manufacturers to speed up distribution caused great friction with newspaper men. They were not admitted, and it took longer to get Mrs. Hobby's announcement drafted than it did to hold the morning and afternoon sessions combined, so that the news did not get out until midnight.

At the next Cabinet meeting on April 29, Mrs. Hobby explained that the press could not have been admitted because she could not ask the drug concerns publicly to discuss their trade secrets and plans for distribution. The meeting, she said, had been a complete success.

The President inquired how much it would cost to provide vaccine for children who could not afford to pay for it. He was told $4.20 for three shots. Mrs. Hobby said that five states already had voted funds for inoculation of such children and thirteen others were in the process of acting. Rather than announce immediately a Federal program of matching grants to states for this purpose, she preferred to wait to see how many states would provide such funds themselves. Thus the government's program might be limited to helping states which could not put up such funds.

Eisenhower insisted that the government must insure that Federal funds would be available, if necessary, to pay for vaccine for all children who could not afford it. No child must be denied the vaccine for lack of money, he said. Some source must be found—if necessary, he would use the President's emergency fund.

At the President's request Congress voted $30,000,000 for grants to the states and $4,500,000 for distribution of the vaccine.

Mrs. Hobby, whose husband was seriously ill, had been intending to resign for some time, and in July she finally left, with the President and the Cabinet providing unusual fanfare. At her last session she told the Cabinet she planned to open an administration "branch office" in Houston, her home, where she would work as hard as ever for Eisenhower's ideals. There were some in the administration who felt that the time was ripe for a change in her department, but so far as one can learn, the President did nothing to urge it and, on the contrary, was disappointed to see her go.

When the 1955 session ended in August, the President at a press conference commended the Democrats for their co-operation on foreign policy. But on domestic policy he criticized them for failure to enact a number of specific measures.

"And so it would be completely futile on my part," he concluded, "to say that in this field, in this domestic field, that I believe we have been as successful in this past Congress as we should have been."

The Democrats disputed this, and both sides were to have more and spicier things to say on the subject when the 1956 session rolled around.

CHAPTER 24

"New Look"—Later Phases

*The President Resents Charges That He Is Trying to "Wreck the Army"
— Nuclear Weapons Become Conventional — "Massive Retaliation" — The
Armed Forces Are Cut — The President's Philosophy of National Security
— Conflicts with Ridgway and Trevor Gardner — "Parochialism" vs. Per-
spective*

I get a little bit tired of having to defend myself against the charge
of being out to wreck the Army," the President told Republican
leaders at a White House conference shortly before the end of the
1955 session.

At this meeting on June 8 the discussion concerned the pending
military reserve bill and the possibility that a related move would be
made in Congress to increase the Army by 150,000 men. The President was opposed to this expansion, estimated to cost some $450,-
000,000. Where would all the additional men be stationed, he asked,
and, considering the character of modern warfare, what was the need
of this increased manpower?

"Do you want to make a fight on the issue?" a leader inquired.

"Indeed I do," Eisenhower replied. "There are much better uses
for that money if it has to be spent."

The great need, the President explained, was for a good reserve
program and for flexibility in the military establishment.

Nothing ever came of the proposal for increasing the Army. But
this conversation was illustrative of the considerations which came
before the President month in and month out as to what was required to make America secure.

During his early months in office, it will be recalled, the President argued that the economy was a basic element of national power, and to conserve it against excessive strain of prolonged military spending he approved a cut in the defense budget. Emphasis was placed upon air power and Continental defense, and plans were made for leveling out defense spending for the long haul, without building up to any specified period of crisis. In the summer of 1953 the Joint Chiefs of Staff appointed by Truman were replaced by the new quartet headed by Radford and selected with a nod of approval from the Republican leadership in Congress. Taft had publicly denounced the old Chiefs, and when a friend asked him if he had chosen the new J.C.S., he replied, according to White:

"I wouldn't say *that*. But I *will* say that before a single new appointment was announced Wilson had me out to his apartment in the Wardman Park Hotel and showed me the list. I found it entirely satisfactory."

The new Chiefs set to work reappraising military policy. The Korean war had ended, and by the beginning of 1954 the advanced phase of the "new look" approved by Eisenhower began to take form.

Nuclear weapons, large and small, became the mainstay of American military power, taking their place in the arsenal of conventional weapons of each branch of the armed forces. In time numbers of American troops overseas were redeployed to what was designated as a mobile reserve, in the United States or in bases like Okinawa and Hawaii. Redeployment from Europe has been slight—some of the troops stationed in Austria before the peace treaty, for example, have been brought home. But from Korea, Japan and elsewhere in the Far East it has been considerable.

Basic to the Eisenhower military policy was a decision that American ground strength would not be scattered everywhere it might be needed but that reliance would be placed primarily upon mobility and power to inflict swift and severe retaliation. There was nothing new about the threat of retaliation in the American military scheme; our atomic bombs had served as a deterrent against Soviet aggression since the end of World War II. But the Eisenhower administration dressed it up in Sunday clothes.

Reporting on a decision of the President and the N.S.C., Dulles told the Council on Foreign Relations in New York on January 12, 1954:

Local defense will always be important. But there is no local defense which alone will contain the mighty land power of the Communist world. Local defenses must be reinforced by the further deterrent of massive retaliatory power. A potential aggressor must know that he cannot always prescribe battle conditions that suit him. . . .

The basic decision [is] to depend primarily upon a great capacity to retaliate, instantly, by means and at places of our choosing. . . .

In his State of the Union message five days earlier the President had used similar language, telling Congress that "we shall not be the aggressors, but we and our allies have and will maintain a massive capability to strike back."

While no one doubted that the United States would retaliate against attack, the doctrine of "massive retaliation" aroused misunderstanding and controversy. Almost in the next breath after threatening instant retaliation Dulles declared, "I have said, in relation to Indo-China, that if there were open Red Chinese Army aggression there, that would have 'grave consequences which might not be confined to Indo-China.' " As no open Chinese aggression occurred, this threat was not tested. The objection some critics had to Dulles's words was that they created an impression that the United States was ready massively to shield Indo-China from Communist conquest in any form. In this light, the critics said, the subsequent fall of Dienbienphu and the partition of Vietnam made the words look like bluff. Another criticism was that if massive retaliation was our policy, we were clumsily equipped for dealing with small wars.

Dulles's associates say that the speech made it clear that massive retaliation would apply only to aggression on a major scale since he acknowledged that the free world might suffer temporary and local setbacks. The fact that he was not suggesting sending every small conflict up in a mushroom is apparent, they say, in the passage, "If we can deter such aggression as would mean general war, and that is our confident resolve, then we can let time and fundamentals work for us."

For obvious reasons of national security the President, even if he has worked out a formula of retaliation, massive or otherwise, has never revealed what it is.

"There is only one thing I can tell you about war and almost one only," he said at a press conference after the Dulles speech, "and that is this: No war ever shows the characteristics that were expected. It is always different. And what we are trying to say now is to express a generalization that would apply in an infinite variety of cases, on an infinite variety of provocations, and I just don't believe it is possible. I think that what has got to be decided is how deeply is the safety and security of America involved."

Along with relying heavily on atomic weapons for our own defense, the United States is providing its allies sufficient information about the characteristics and effects of these weapons to enable them to train their troops to team with ours in integrated air-ground warfare. The law does not permit the President to turn over nuclear weapons to other countries. But it is Eisenhower's view that eventually allies with modern air forces should be equipped so that in event of war they could use nuclear weapons in tactical support of ground forces. Once they had developed integrated air-ground forces trained and equipped for nuclear fighting, there would be a material increase in their contribution to the general deterrent and defense efforts and a diminishing need for stationing large numbers of American troops abroad.

On the theory that the greater power of modern weapons diminished the need for men, the President directed Wilson and the new Joint Chiefs to review the size of the armed forces and advise him on establishment of new levels.

Speaking with very great candor, he told them that they might have differences of opinion. And, as Ridgway's dissent was to prove, they did. Those who differed might come to him, he said. But he declared in no uncertain terms that as the Commander-in-Chief he expected the loyalty of all of them to his final decision.

His decision was set forth in a letter to Wilson on January 5, 1955, a fortnight before the Formosa crisis. The armed forces, then numbering about 3,200,000, were to be cut to about 2,850,000 by June of 1956.

Especially under the impact of the Soviets' rapid technical progress, concepts of national security are continuously changing. But the President's philosophy at the time of the Wilson letter may be summed in these general terms:

While no "danger date" was in sight, modern weapons were so devastating that unless the United States took the necessary precautions, it could be knocked out of action in thirty days of war. Thus the American people must maintain a capability to deter an enemy from attack and to blunt that attack if it should come. This required air-nuclear retaliatory power and a constantly improving continental defense system.

The initial phase of a general nuclear war would consist of exchanges of staggering blows at the homelands of the antagonists. The great test for the United States would be to survive this terrible period, knocking out in the meantime the enemy's capacity to inflict further damage on America. Once this point had been reached, the country could then proceed in the customary way of building up the resources needed to go on and win the war.

Since survival is everything, troops would be needed at home in the initial phase to cope with disorder and destruction. Vast overseas deployment would not come until later. Hence the United States need not maintain in peacetime large numbers of troops for this purpose. What it required were well-trained, modernized standing forces plus a trained and organized reserve and a strong mobilization base.

In smaller wars involving America's vital interests or the principle of collective security, the United States should be prepared with mobile forces to help indigenous troops. If necessary, American forces would use tactical atomic weapons.

It was the President's feeling at that time, finally, that if the United States kept itself adequately prepared to survive and retaliate, nuclear war would never come—no enemy would ever be so insane as to invite the destruction which the United States could inflict.

The dispute over the President's cut in defense spending in 1953 proved to be only a foretaste of controversy in the field of military policy. The reduction in forces in 1955 and guided-missile and jet-aircraft production in 1956 drew serious criticism, some of it partisan and some of it not. Was the administration more interested in balancing the budget than in winning the cold war? Was it going along in a business-as-usual attitude while the Soviets were turning out new types of jet fighters and bombers and surpassing the United States in certain types of guided and ballistic missiles? These questions were raised with increasing persistence not only in the press and in Congress but within the Pentagon itself.

While he was Army Chief of Staff, Ridgway testified before Congressional committees against the cuts in manpower, warning that they would "jeopardize" national security. After retiring on June 30, 1955, he declared unqualifiedly in his memoirs that the military budget "was not based so much on military requirements, or on what the economy of the country could stand, as on political considerations." He accused Wilson, in effect, of warning him not to oppose the President's wishes and of forcing a "directed verdict" on the Joint Chiefs in the matter of the size of the armed forces.

In February of 1956, more criticism hit the administration when Trevor Gardner resigned as Assistant Secretary of the Air Force for Research and Development in a dispute with Wilson, he said, "as to whether budget-balancing or air power was the more important." In an article in *Look*, Gardner asserted that the United States outnumbered the Soviets in only one class of airplane, the B-47 medium jet bomber. In all other categories, he said, "they either do or can outnumber us." Not only does the Air Force lag behind the Soviet air arm in quantity, but the American "quality lead is also slipping dangerously." "Short-sighted limitations," he charged, had held back research on guided missiles, which will probably be the decisive weapons of the future.

In the Senate two Democratic members of the Armed Services Committee, Henry M. Jackson, of Washington, and Symington, who was formerly Secretary of the Air Force under Truman, have kept up prolonged criticism. Their argument has been that in its eagerness to curtail government spending the administration has habitually underestimated Soviet progress in aircraft and missiles, with the result that future supremacy in air power is in doubt. Such charges led to a Senate investigation of United States air strength in April of 1956 by an Armed Services subcommittee headed by Symington.

In the face of this criticism the administration took steps to strengthen Air Force programs. After Gardner resigned, Wilson brought E. V. Murphree, president of the Esso Research and Engineering Company, into the Pentagon, as "czar" of missiles production. And shortly before the Symington hearings began, the President proposed to Congress a $547,000,000 increase in the new budget to hasten production of the intercontinental B-52 jet bombers and to extend the early-warning radar screen.

After Ridgway had opposed the manpower cuts in 1955, the President commented that the General had been speaking from a sense of responsibility which was "parochial"—limited to concern over only one branch of the service. The Army Chief of Staff was not responsible, as the President was, for the needs of all the services. Similarly, throughout the later controversy over aircraft and missiles Eisenhower felt that it was to some extent a case of champions of one phase of military power arguing with more zeal than perspective of the whole problem of developing the many sides of national strength. Furthermore he took a more optimistic view than they on the progress this country is making in developing guided missiles.

During the Symington hearings General Curtis E. LeMay, commander of the Strategic Air Command, created headlines with his testimony that under current programs the Soviet Union would have greater striking power in long-range bombers than the United States by 1958-60. Again the former five-star general in the White House disagreed with an erstwhile comrade-in-arms, as he had with Ridgway over manpower and Radford over military thrusts on the mainland of Asia. His response was that the problem was broader than one of how many of a particular kind of weapon—in this case the longe-range bomber—the United States has in relation to the Soviets.

Eisenhower's concept is that it is the sum of American power that counts. Whereas LeMay focused on intercontinental bombers, the President insisted on bringing into the picture also America's matchless naval air power, the air power of our allies and our overseas bases which bring the Soviet Union within the range of our medium bombers (B-47's) and thus lessen, in his opinion, our dependence upon the long-range plane.

"The most dangerous thing you can do in trying to evaluate military strength," he told his press conference on May 10, 1956, "is to get into what I call the numbers racket, just taking one particular item or kind of weapon and putting them on an arithmetical equation and saying, we can whip that fellow because we have more.

"There comes a time, particularly in these latter days when the destructiveness of weapons is so great as to be beyond human imagination, when enough is certainly aplenty, and you do no good, as I see it, by increasing those numbers except to get, say, an added factor of safety."

A statement he once made to the legislative leaders during the Ridgway controversy was typical of his attitude in the later disputes. Every branch of the service, he said, could make a good argument for increasing its own strength. The heart of the problem, however, was not to put all the eggs in one basket, but to take the many ingredients of national power—airplanes, ground forces, battleships, industry, the economy, the spirit of the people—and blend them in such a way as to insure essential security for the United States.

As he has discovered, of course, the more complex the technology of war becomes the more difficult it is going to be for Eisenhower or any other President to convince his critics that his blend is as good as theirs.

CHAPTER 25

Conflict of Interest

Wilson Brings Up the Hoover Commission Proposals on Conflict of Interest – Eisenhower Suggests Initiative for Revision Come from Congress – Secretary of the Air Force Talbott Resigns – The Strobel and Mansure Cases – Adolphe H. Wenzell and Dixon-Yates – Troubles with the Celler Committee over "WOC's" – Eisenhower Declares that He Will Not Cripple the Presidency

The troubles which had beset the administration off and on over the conflict-of-interest statutes brought fresh grief in the summer of 1955 when Secretary of the Air Force Talbott resigned after a Congressional investigation of his outside business activities.

Before the Talbott case broke, Wilson, who had been the first administration figure to tangle with the statutes, introduced the matter in another connection in the Cabinet on July 8, 1955. He called attention to the recommendation made by the Hoover Commission. A task-force report had said that requirements for disposal of personal holdings before taking a government post constituted a "particular obstacle to attracting competent men," and the commission recommended that the whole subject be reviewed. It suggested a study to ascertain whether the intent of the statutes could be "better achieved by other and more positive means which would encourage rather than discourage entry of competent men into public life."

Wilson recalled that the Defense Department had issued a directive requiring officials to disqualify themselves in any government transaction affecting their own outside private interests. The problem, however, was one that made it increasingly difficult, he said, to get men whose experience and training in private industry was valuable to the government.

The President told the Cabinet that a member of Congress had expressed to him the opinion that in existing form the conflict-of-interest laws were obsolete but that Congress, rather than the executive branch, should take the initiative in revising them. Eisenhower agreed that the initiative might better come from Congress. As a possible alternative, he suggested, the administration could bring up the subject in a routine fashion in any proposals it might make for carrying out recommendations of the Hoover Commission.

Brownell also felt that any attempt to modernize the statutes might better stem from the Hoover Commission report, with the impetus supplied either by members of Congress identified with the commission or by an organization like the Citizens Committee for the Hoover Report.

Conflict of interest has troubled both parties throughout their history; the Eisenhower administration had no monopoly. However, the large number of businessmen Eisenhower brought to Washington and the difficulties some of them had in being confirmed by the Senate made the issue conspicuous from the outset. Dramatized by the cases of Wilson, Stevens, Talbott and others, it fitted neatly into the traditional Democratic line that the Republicans are the party of special privilege.

The Talbott case was one that caused the President a good deal of personal dismay. Although he and Talbott were not close friends, they had come to know each other well and had played bridge together at the White House two or three times.

When Talbott came to Washington, he retained his partnership in the New York engineering firm of Paul B. Mulligan & Company. Within a matter of months he began writing letters on Air Force stationery and making telephone calls in the interest of getting business for the Mulligan firm. Some of the companies he approached had contracts with the Air Force.

The most damaging testimony against Talbott at the hearings before the Senate Permanent Investigations Subcommittee was given by Samuel E. Ewing, general counsel for the manufacturing and services division of the Radio Corporation of America, which held defense contracts. Late in 1954, he testified, he had felt it was unwise for R.C.A. to enter into a new contract with Mulligan because of Talbott's interest in the firm. Sometime after this feeling had been conveyed to the Mulligan firm, Ewing said, he received a call from the general counsel of the Air Force about it, and then a man who identified himself as Talbott came on the phone. This man listed a dozen other companies which had contracts with the Air Force and yet did business with Mulligan, and then demanded to know, "If all of these other companies could take contracts with Mulligan & Company, why was R.C.A. acting so high and mighty?" Talbott testified that he could not remember making such a call.

At one point in the hearing Talbott testified: "Now there is no question at any time in my mind about whether I have tried to be helpful to Mulligan. I have."

During his first two years in the Pentagon he received $132,032 in profits from Mulligan & Company. No violation of law was charged against Talbott, who was former chairman of the Republican National Finance Committee, and he denied that he had been guilty of any impropriety or wrongful use of influence.

At the close of the hearings on July 27 the President said that he personally would review the record and come to a decision.

I do not believe [Eisenhower said] that any man can properly hold public office merely because he is not guilty of any illegal act, and, of course, in this case there is no charge of any illegal act.

But I believe it was in [the fall of 1952] I tried to explain my conception of what a public servant owed to the government . . . that his actions had to be impeccable, both from the standpoint of law [and] from the standpoint of ethics. So what is now involved is: Was a proper standard of ethics violated?

Three days later Talbott resigned, saying that his actions had "been within the bounds of ethics" but that he did not wish to embarrass the President by staying on. Eisenhower replied that "under the circumstances your decision was the right one." In its report the subcommittee said that Talbott had "acted indiscreetly."

Another case was that of Peter A. Strobel, Commissioner of Public Buildings for the General Services Administration, who had retained a 90 per cent interest in the New York engineering firm of Strobel & Salzman. Under an old contract this company had a claim of $7,500 against the Corps of Engineers. Strobel went to see the Army engineers about it. Eventually the claim was settled for $3,000. He said that he had visited the engineers at lunchtime, not during working hours. He also testified that his bureau had awarded Federal contracts to two clients of Strobel & Salzman, but that this had resulted in no profits to his firm. Protesting his innocence, he submitted his resignation on November 9, 1955, to the administrator of the General Services Administration, Edmund F. Mansure.

Three months later Mansure resigned under fire after having admitted that he allowed political favoritism to enter into the award of certain contracts under the jurisdiction of the General Services Administration. "Practical politics," he testified, dictated that a large brokerage contract should not go to a firm which did "not help this administration get into office."

The most celebrated of all the conflict-of-interest cases was the double role of Adolphe H. Wenzell during the preparation of the Dixon-Yates contract. Wenzell was simultaneously a consultant to the Bureau of the Budget, participating in conferences which led up to the contract, and vice-president of the First Boston Corporation, which became the financial agent for Dixon-Yates.

Conflict of interest, however, was only part of the Dixon-Yates controversy. Politically it was overshadowed by the power issue in the background. It all began with the need for additional power in the Memphis area, which is served by the T.V.A. To supply this need the T.V.A. had asked for funds to build a new steam plant at nearby Fulton, Tennessee.

The Truman administration had first disallowed the request and then restored it to the Budget Truman left over for the Republicans. Eisenhower wanted to keep the government out of the power business as much as possible, and after discussions with Dodge and others he also rejected the Fulton plant.

In a conference with the President on May 11 Dodge outlined his own objections to the way things were shaping up in the T.V.A. He put the situation in these terms: The T.V.A. had been established to develop water resources. The resulting cheap power eliminated private competition. Hence the T.V.A. had taken to operating steam plants in areas formerly served by private utilities. The cheap power attracted industry, which created the need for more power. Finally, the T.V.A. wound up in the position of wanting to build more steam plants to supply more power, thus attracting more industry which in turn would require more power.

It was these ripples going out from the pebble that Eisenhower objected to and wanted to check.

In an off-the-cuff speech to Republican leaders at Custer State Park, in South Dakota, on June 11, 1953, he had said, "I believe that for the past twenty years there has been a creeping socialism spreading in the United States." At a press conference six days later he was asked what he had meant by "creeping socialism."

He replied: continued Federal expansion of the T.V.A. He reiterated for what he said was the thousandth time that he would not destroy the T.V.A., but he said that he thought it was socialistic to continue putting money paid by all the taxpayers into a single region which could then attract industry away from other areas.

(An impression got about that the President had called the T.V.A. itself "creeping socialism," and a good deal of criticism resulted. On June 22 Hauge sent him a memorandum cautioning him against using the expression "creeping socialism." Hauge pointed out that the phrase had been the "hallmark of the Old Guard Republicans for years against Roosevelt" and said that the Republican "new look" under Eisenhower should have its own idiom free of old connotation. After reading the memo, the President jotted at the bottom, "Yes, D.E.")

At a meeting of the legislative leaders on July 20, 1953, Eisenhower said he was "outraged" by T.V.A. plans for expansion around Memphis.

"That would require taxing the whole country to provide cheap power to the Tennessee Valley and allow it to siphon off industry from other areas," he said.

He told the leaders, however, that he had no intention of crippling the T.V.A.

Meanwhile Wenzell had been retained by Dodge to study T.V.A. In September of 1953 Wenzell recommended among other things that private steam-power companies be organized to sell power to the T.V.A. and that private companies serve cities on the rim of the Tennessee Valley. Dodge said later that the report did not influence the administration with respect to the Dixon-Yates contract, yet the approach suggested by Wenzell was similar to that adopted in the contract. In December of 1953 Gordon R. Clapp, whose term as chairman of the T.V.A. was nearing an end, suggested that if funds for T.V.A. steam plants again were to be disallowed, the administration might consider relieving the T.V.A. of some of its commitments to provide power to the Atomic Energy Commission. Following this recommendation Dodge went to see Strauss, and soon negotiations were begun with private utilities. This was not without precedent. The Truman administration had bought power from private utilities for A.E.C. installations at Paducah, Kentucky, and Portsmouth, Ohio.

The new A.E.C. negotiations led indirectly to Edgar H. Dixon, president of Middle South Utilities, Inc. He proposed building a plant near Memphis, which could serve both the T.V.A. and the city. Meanwhile Eugene A. Yates, president of the Southern Company, had approached the government with a plan to sell power in the T.V.A. area. Before long he got together with Middle South and the result was the Dixon-Yates combine.

On June 16, 1954, the President, acting on a recommendation of Rowland Hughes, ordered the A.E.C. to negotiate a contract with Dixon-Yates for a $107,250,000 privately owned plant at West Memphis. Among the criticism leveled at this arrangement was that it was between Dixon-Yates and the A.E.C. rather than the T.V.A., presumably because of T.V.A. opposition. Two commissioners of the A.E.C. complained that the contract "involves the A.E.C. in matters remote from its responsibilities."

The President meanwhile declined to reappoint Clapp. Eisenhower recognized his excellent record of public service but said privately that Clapp's approach to the whole power question in T.V.A. was too doctrinaire and that he had to have someone who would look at facts objectively. In his place he nominated Brigadier General Herbert D. Vogel, an Army engineer.

During a discussion of power policy in the Cabinet on July 9, 1954, the President alluded briefly to the T.V.A. He said that he was under much pressure to sponsor development of other river valleys, and it could well be argued, he indicated, that some other regions should have their needs met before more was done for the T.V.A. He reiterated his willingness that the government should build some dams too costly for states and local interests. He also brought up his favorite quotation from Lincoln to the effect that the function of government was to do for the people those things which they themselves could not do, or could not do so well. Eisenhower thought that the government should build some steam plants to supplement hydroelectric power. But he said that the process should not be perpetuated to extend the T.V.A. monopoly on power. Nixon said that it was necessary for the administration to stress the positive aspects of its policy on water resources—as represented, for example, by the St. Lawrence Seaway project.

The unpopularity of the Dixon-Yates contract in the T.V.A. area put the Democrats on the scent of an issue for the 1954 elections, and they opened up on the administration with charges that it was trying to "wreck" the T.V.A. and hand the development of power over to the bankers. A foretaste of the vehemence of the debate in Congressional committees and elsewhere was conveyed by the charge of Stephen A. Mitchell, Democratic Chairman, that the President had a close friend who was a director of the Southern Company (and, by implication, who thus stood to gain by the contract the President had ordered signed). The friend was later identified by Mitchell's office as Bobby Jones, the former British and American open and amateur golf champion, a frequent companion of the President's at Augusta.

At his press conference the next day, August 17, 1954, Eisenhower said that he had known upon entering public life that he would be subject to innuendo by many kinds of strange characters. But he said he was astonished that Mitchell's innuendo would touch a private citizen of the standing of Bobby Jones.

Then the President made an offer which was to have some sour results. The facts about his action, he said, were open to the public. He told the reporters that they could go to the A.E.C. and the Bureau of the Budget and get the complete record beginning with the inception of the idea of the Dixon-Yates contract. When the document was made public a week later, it contained no mention of Wenzell or the First Boston Corporation. Wenzell's attendance at conferences in which the financial structure of the Dixon-Yates contract was discussed remained hidden until Senator Lister Hill, Democrat, of Alabama, stumbled upon it by chance in February of 1955.

All the difficulties the administration was having with Dixon-Yates were compounded by this omission and Hill's discovery. Hughes's explanation that Wenzell's name was left out because he was a subordinate was no help in saving the situation. Hill announced his discovery in a speech in the Senate, in which he asserted there was evidence that Wenzell had participated in government conferences on the Dixon-Yates contract at the time the First Boston was arranging the financing. The President was informed of Hill's speech by Hughes, who testified that he had been told that Hill's account was untrue. This, of course, played squarely into the hands of critics who were alleging that the President was being kept in the dark about what was going on. Eisenhower did not help his own case by his answer about Wenzell's role at his press conference on June 29, 1955.

"Now as far as the Wenzell report," he said, "Mr. Wenzell was never called in or asked a single thing about the Dixon-Yates contract. He was brought in as a technical adviser in the very early days when none of us here knew about the bookkeeping methods of the T.V.A. or anything else. He was brought in as a technical adviser and nothing else, and before this contract was ever even proposed."

When a reporter asked the President if he had been informed that Wenzell had had "no connection at all" with Dixon-Yates, Eisenhower replied: "My understanding of it, and it may have been —that part of it there may have been—an overlap of a week or two— there I am not sure of."

Later Hagerty issued an amplifying statement—one of the few that have had to be made after an Eisenhower press conference—

that Wenzell had given the Bureau of the Budget technical advice while the contract was in preparation in the winter of 1954.

Three days before, Hughes had testified that Eisenhower knew Wenzell's name "and his connection and all about him. In fact, he approved him before we got him down here. . . ."

Things were mixed up for fair, and the general effect of White House handling of the case was not improved when in June of 1955, Adams asked J. Sinclair Armstrong, chairman of the Securities & Exchange Commission, to postpone a hearing scheduled for the day the House was to begin debate on funds for a transmission line to the Dixon-Yates site. The hearing was postponed, and the House later voted the funds. But when Adams's call to Armstrong came to light, the Democrats charged that the postponement was a plot to conceal from the House facts about Wenzell's role that might have come out at the S.E.C. hearing and, therefore, might have influenced votes on the transmission line. Adams said that he sought the adjournment so he could take up with Brownell and Gerald Morgan the question of whether the government should oppose the testimony of certain witnesses scheduled to testify at the S.E.C. hearing.

Ground had been broken for the Dixon-Yates plant when the city of Memphis lifted the unhappy issue off the President's shoulders by deciding to build its own power plant. Eisenhower said at his press conference on July 6 that in the very beginning he had suggested that this be done but was told by the Tennesseans that it was impossible because of the city's contract with the T.V.A.

On July 11, 1955, the President ordered the Dixon-Yates contract canceled. Dixon-Yates had already spent money on the project and wanted to recover it. In November, however, the A.E.C. held that the contract was invalid. The commission's counsel, William Mitchell, advised that "it appears that Wenzell, while having a conflicting private interest, acted as one of the principal advisers of the government" in negotiating the contract. He said that between January and April of 1954 Wenzell had not only attended meetings with government officials "but also met with Dixon eight or ten times during this period. . . ." Mitchell declared that "the matters on which Wenzell was advising the contractor (Dixon) were the

same on which he had been employed to advise the government."
Dixon and Yates crowned the affair by suing the government for
$3,534,788 for expenses.

While the Dixon-Yates contract was being buried in the summer
of 1955, the administration got into a brush with the House Judiciary,
Anti-trust and Monopoly Subcommittee on another phase of the conflict-of-interest issue—the employment of WOC's. Abbreviated from
"without compensation," WOC's are the modern dollar-a-year men.
While receiving their regular salaries from their companies, they
serve the government as unpaid consultants or advisers, and the
question raised by Democratic critics was whether such men influenced government policy to the advantage of their own firms.
Representative Emanuel Celler, Democrat, of New York, chairman
of the subcommittee, demanded the confidential files of the Business
Advisory Committee of the Department of Commerce. Philip A.
Ray, general counsel to the department, refused to turn them over,
and the matter was brought up in the Cabinet on July 29.

The President recalled his ukase at the Commodore before the
inauguration that anyone who sought a government position on the
strength of friendship with him should be turned away. He said he
had exactly the same feeling about anyone who claimed a preference
because of his support of Republican campaigns. He told the Cabinet
he hoped such claims would fall on deaf ears.

Stassen said that the administration must be careful not to take
a merely defensive position toward the investigation and that the
American people should be acquainted with the smear of American
business implicit in the conduct of the investigation. Mrs. Hobby,
who was attending her final Cabinet meeting, called it a new "ism"
which would undermine the freedom of a citizen to offer advice to
his government.

Discussing the background of the Celler investigation, Brownell
digressed into a situation he had uncovered in the General Accounting Office. When the Attorney General investigated the failure of
the G.A.O. to report to the F.B.I. on questionable activities by a
certain clothing manufacturer, he discovered that some of the G.A.O.
staff had been instructed by McCarthy to hold back such information until McCarthy felt the right time had come for producing it.

Sherman Adams remarked dryly that the G.A.O. staff situation was being corrected.

Ray said that Celler seemed bent on a "fishing expedition" into the files of the Department of Commerce. The department, he said, had reviewed many of its files and had found no evidence of unethical conduct. Ray felt that the administration should stand on the principle enunciated by the President in a letter to Wilson during the McCarthy-Army hearings. This was that while the executive branch should furnish information properly within the jurisdiction of a Congressional committee, information deemed confidential by the executive branch should be withheld.

The President agreed that the departments involved should draw a line between what should and should not be turned over to the committee. He insisted, however, that the demarcation should not be dictated by expediency. If some situation was found that was wrong, he said, it should promptly be exposed and corrected.

Remarking on the long history of efforts by Congress to encroach on the prerogatives of the President, Eisenhower philosophized that such conflict was inevitable in a government in which powers are divided among three co-equal branches. It was his wish, he said, to make public as many government papers as possible. As evidence, he pointed to the revisions he had made in 1953 in Truman's order on classification of information.

Eisenhower believed it was important to have guide lines laid out for all government departments to follow in this matter of making information available to Congress. But he told the Cabinet he wanted it clearly understood that he was never going to yield to the point where he would become known as a President who had practically crippled the Presidency.

CHAPTER 26

Geneva and the Open-Skies Plan

Aerial Inspection and Exchange of Blueprints with the Soviets – Origins of the Open-Skies Plan – Nelson Rockefeller and the Quantico Panel – Eisenhower Arrives at Geneva Undecided about It – Eisenhower and the Russians – Talks in Paris – The President Decides to Propose Open-Skies– An Eisenhower Triumph

The conference of the Big Four in Geneva in July, 1955, was in its fourth day. Soviet Premier Nikolai A. Bulganin, benign and grandfatherly in his white goatee and looking for all the world like an old-time opera star, was presiding in the conference room of the marble Palais des Nations. Up for consideration was disarmament. In his statement on the opening day of the conference Bulganin had taken a familiar Soviet disarmament proposal out of mothballs. The United States, the Soviet Union and China would each be limited to a maximum of 1,500,000 men under arms. The maximum for Britain and France would be 650,000 each. Once these levels had been achieved, atomic and hydrogen weapons would be banned. Timeworn though this was, it was specific at least and more eye-catching than anything yet proposed by the other three.

President Eisenhower began what seemed to be a routine speech. Not a greal deal was expected of it. The United States, he said, was "prepared to enter into a sound and reliable agreement making possible the reduction of armaments." Eisenhower was seated with his back to the high windows looking out over Lake Geneva. Across the hollow square of tables from him was the impeccable Eden.

The French delegation, headed by Premier Edgar Faure, was on the President's left. Bulganin and Nikita S. Khrushchev, the tough boss of the Communist Party, were on his right. Halfway through his speech the President suddenly took off his glasses, laid them on the table and turned to Bulganin and Khrushchev. Speaking from memory, he said:

I should address myself for a moment principally to the delegates from the Soviet Union, because our two great countries admittedly possess new and terrible weapons in quantities which do give rise in other parts of the world, or reciprocally, to the fears and dangers of surprise attack.

I propose, therefore, that we take a practical step, that we begin an arrangement, very quickly, as between ourselves—immediately. These steps would include:

To give each other a complete blueprint of our military establishments, from beginning to end, from one end of our countries to the other; lay out the establishments and provide the blueprints to each other.

Next, to provide within our countries facilities for aerial photography to the other country—we to provide the facilities within our country, ample facilities for aerial reconnaissance, where you can make all the pictures you choose and take them to your own country to study; you to provide exactly the same facilities for us and we to make these examinations, and by this step to convince the world that we are providing as between ourselves against the possibility of great surprise attack, thus lessening danger and relaxing tension.

Likewise we will make more easily attainable a comprehensive and effective system of inspection and disarmament, because what I propose, I assure you, would be but a beginning. . . .

The United States is ready to proceed in the study and testing of a reliable system of inspections and reporting, and when that system is proved, then to reduce armaments with all others to the extent that the system will provide assured results.

The successful working out of such a system would do much to develop the mutual confidence which will open wide the avenues of progress for all our peoples.

As the President paused for the translation, thunder crashed across Lake Geneva, and the electricity went off.

"I didn't mean to turn the lights out," he laughed in the gloom.

When the lights came on again, the Soviets had nothing to say.

"I wish," Faure observed, "the people of the world could have been in this conference room to hear the voice of a man speaking from great military experience. Had this been possible, they would believe that something had changed in the world in the handling of this question of disarmament. I am sure that this conference has scored its first victory over skepticism."

The open-skies plan was the single most dramatic proposal made at the conference. Yet the President had gone to Geneva with no certain intention of introducing it. The decision was made at the last minute.

International aerial inspection and disclosure of military information had had a fairly long history in U.N. disarmament negotiations. After the United States had introduced the Baruch plan for international control of atomic energy in 1946, a U.N. commission had reported that aerial surveys would be essential to its effectiveness. Later Acheson made a more general proposal for international "disclosure and verification" of all armed forces and weapons. By 1955, however, these plans were pretty well covered with dust and forgotten.

In preparation for the Big Four conference the State Department worked on proposals for disarmament, but the idea that finally blossomed in Geneva had its main roots in the hard soil of the United States Marine Base at Quantico. With the approval of the President, Nelson Rockefeller in line with his work in psychological strategy had set up a panel of governmental and outside experts to study various recommendations which the United States might submit at Geneva. The group held its meetings at the Marine base.

In approaching the problem the Quantico Panel, as it was known, gave careful study to trends of public opinion in Europe. Surveys showed a strong feeling in favor of banning nuclear weapons. There were also signs of increasing indifference to NATO and unenthusiasm for the continued maintenance of American bases in Europe. From the American point of view, of course, the seriousness of these attitudes lay in the fact that United States military power rested heavily on atomic weapons and overseas bases. One of the things the Quantico Panel had to consider, therefore, was how the

United States could retain its nuclear power but still make it clear for all to see that its purpose was peace. It was while groping for this formula that the panel hit upon the idea of the President's breathing new life into old plans for aerial inspection and exchange of military information, presenting them freshly and affirmatively at Geneva. The Quantico Panel felt that the Soviets would offer a concrete arms plan at Geneva and that the President must be ready with an equally positive proposal.

The Quantico report went to the President on June 10, and he read it with enthusiasm. Three weeks before they left for Switzerland he and Dulles had a long but inconclusive discussion about it and related State Department suggestions. When the President arrived in Geneva, however, he had still not reached a firm decision on proposing the open-skies plan. He first wished to see what developed at the conference.

Talk of a conference among heads of the big powers had been in the air ever since Eisenhower became President. For a long time he held off, mindful of some of the sorry consequences of earlier meetings, like Yalta and Potsdam, and doubtful of the chances of any fundamental accomplishments through diplomacy of this character. The President insisted that before he would meet the Soviet leaders, he must at least be shown by their deeds that they intended to co-operate in settling differences.

By the spring of 1955 many circumstances combined to put great pressure on him to agree to a meeting. At home Senator George had re-echoed Sir Winston's call for a conference "at the summit." Abroad French leaders had urged it in the course of ratification of the Paris accords, and the British leaders wanted it to dramatize their quest for peace in the eyes of their people, who were about to vote in a national election. Furthermore, Moscow's agreement to an Austrian peace treaty met one of the suggestions the President himself had made regarding steps the Soviets might take to demonstrate their peaceful intentions.

After all parties had agreed to meet, Eisenhower—and, to a greater degree, Dulles—put on an air of reserve to avoid filling the people with false hopes for an early end to the cold war. The President, however, could hold himself down only so long. The nearer the conference drew the more his natural optimism and good will surged to the surface, and even before he took off with Mrs. Eisenhower and John, he was exuding a spirit of hope and confidence. While he still cautioned against expecting too much, his true feelings were reflected in his parting words that, however slowly, "a new dawn may be coming." He arrived in Geneva with infectious enthusiasm.

As chairman of the opening session on Monday, July 18, he got the conference seventeen minutes off schedule by pausing to greet his wartime comrade, Marshal Georgi K. Zhukov, now Soviet Defense Minister.

"I want to let you in on a Zhukov family secret," Khrushchev told the President. Zhukov had passed up his daughter's wedding to come to Geneva to see the President, Khrushchev said. Eisenhower beamed, and that evening he gave Zhukov two wedding presents for his daughter—an American portable radio and a marble pen and ink stand, inscribed, "From the President of the United States, July, 1955."

Eisenhower opened the conference with a low-pitched, unpretentious speech calling for a new atmosphere of mutual respect and confidence among nations.

We are here in response to a universal urge [he said] . . . we can perhaps create a new spirit that will make possible future solutions of problems which are within our responsibilities.

He addressed the Soviets with great earnestness, saying:

The American people want to be friends with the Soviet peoples. There are no natural differences between our peoples or our nations. There are no territorial or commercial rivalries. Historically, our two countries have always been at peace.

The President set forth the main problems the United States wished to discuss, including unification of Germany on the basis of free elections, disarmament and freer communication between East and West.

Bulganin's speech was friendly, plugging "peaceful coexistence." But on Germany he was unyielding. The admission of a remilitarized

West Germany to NATO was an obstacle. The problem of unification should be solved step by step, he said. And as a first step Bulganin proposed a new European collective-security system contemplating eventual abolition of NATO, the Paris accords and the Warsaw treaty.

The President opened the second day's session appealing to the Soviets to recognize that NATO was a purely defensive arrangement, threatening aggression to no one. Turning to the delegation from Moscow, he said:

> I would particularly like my friend Marshal Zhukov to listen carefully to what I have now to say. I have known him for a long time and he knows that, speaking as soldier to soldier, I have never uttered a single word that I did not believe to be the truth. . . .
>
> If there is any tendency to delay urgent consideration of the problem of German reunification because of the unhappiness or fear of the united Germany in NATO, then so far as it is possible for the United States to give the assurance of its pledged word, I say here and now: There is no need to fear that situation.

While the speeches continued, a whirl of activity was going on behind the scenes of the American delegation in lining up a proposal on disarmament. Messages flashed back and forth between Geneva and Paris, where a group of high administration officials had been ordered to stand by on call from the President and the Secretary of State. The group consisted of Rockefeller, Radford, Deputy Secretary of Defense Anderson and Stassen, who had become Special Assistant to the President on disarmament.

On Sunday preceding the opening of the conference they had met in the French capital, and Rockefeller went over the recommendations of the Quantico Panel. At first the reception was cool, but presently sentiment began to change. Radford became enthusiastic about the plan. So did Anderson. Then on Monday Bulganin submitted his proposal for a limitation of forces—stale but nevertheless specific. On Tuesday, Rockefeller sent a message to the President at Geneva urging him to come forward with a strong proposal, seizing the initiative for the United States. Anderson and Radford jointly sent a message to Dulles on the subject. That same afternoon word arrived from Dulles asking Rockefeller and Stassen to hop to Geneva immediately. Before they arrived the President broached the open-skies plan to Eden, and Sir Anthony warmed up to it immediately.

Late Wednesday afternoon the President called a meeting at his residence, the fifteen-room Château du Creux de Genthod, which had been placed at his disposal by the wife of the Swiss perfume-maker Andre Firmenich. At the conference were Dulles, Stassen, Radford, Secretary Anderson, Dillon Anderson, the President's Special Assistant for National Security Affairs, General Gruenther, Rockefeller, Livingston T. Merchant, Assistant Secretary of State for European Affairs, and Colonel Andrew J. Goodpaster, secretary of the White House staff.

After two hours, agreement was reached on the presentation of the disarmament problem, with the President personally deciding to make the open-skies proposal. Stassen was assigned to draft the general statement on disarmament, but Eisenhower himself wrote out detailed notes on what he would say about the open-skies plan. When the meeting broke up, however, the question was left hanging whether the President would include the open-skies plan in his opening statement on Thursday or save it until after the first round of discussion, by which time Bulganin would have spoken.

Arriving at the Palais des Nations Thursday morning, Eisenhower was still undecided on when he would spring his proposal, and it was not until he had actually begun his opening statement at the conference table that he made up his mind to offer it then and there.

Like the atoms-for-peace plan, the open-skies idea took root and began precariously to put some shoots above the ground, struggling for life in a hard international climate. After Geneva the Soviets showed a willingness to consider it. In August, 1955, they proposed supplementing aerial inspection and exchange of military blueprints by stationing inspection teams in each country at control points like airfields, rail terminals and ports. The United States agreed to incorporate this feature in its plan. Moscow also asked about the right to photograph overseas bases. The United States has no objection to this if the countries in which those bases lay consented.

While the Soviets were critical of the open-skies plan, they did not trample it down until the spring of 1956, when negotiations reached another stalemate.

In a letter to Bulganin on March 1, 1956, the President proposed, in effect, a marriage between atoms-for-peace and open-skies. If the latter was adopted with adequate safeguards, he said, the United States would consider halting further production of atomic and hydrogen bombs and use the fissionable material for peaceful purposes.

Opinions may differ now as to whether Eisenhower did the wise thing in going to Geneva and opening his arms to the Soviets, though it is hard to see how he could have spurned the universal yearning for a new attempt to achieve peace. However, opinion is almost unanimous that Geneva was a personal triumph for the President. Even the anti-American *Le Monde*, of Paris, commented, "Eisenhower, whose personality has long been misunderstood, has emerged as the type of leader humanity needs today."

The strength of the President's performance was its friendliness and warmth, its spontaneity and naturalness—in and out of the conference room. When he was not tied up in official or social activities, he was swinging golf clubs in the garden of his villa or shopping for his grandchildren, selecting an Alpine horn for David and Swiss dolls for David's sisters. Without being effusive or over-acting, Eisenhower conveyed a sense of decency and dignity which mocked the picture of his country as an immature nation hell-bent for war.

Having lived for so long behind the Iron Curtain under Stalin's rule, the new Soviet leaders were men with false impressions of the United States and of those who guide its affairs. Through his acknowledgment of Soviet good faith and peaceful intentions the President tried to dispel some of these misconceptions. He told Bulganin and Khrushchev he was convinced that they were as sincere in their desire for peace as he was—a statement which these same leaders were to use later as propaganda.

Neither the German problem nor any other issue of substance was settled at the summit, or at the subsequent Foreign Ministers' meeting to which these matters were referred. For a period a new era seemed to be ahead, but it did not prove to be the kind of era many had hoped and prayed for. In his moderate report to the American people after the conference Eisenhower said about as much as one could say for it at the time:

Now there exists a better understanding, a closer unity among the nations of NATO. There seems to be a growing realization that nuclear warfare, pursued to the ultimate, could be practically race suicide. There is a realization that negotiations can be conducted without propaganda and threats and invective. Finally, there is a sharp realization by the world that the United States will go to any length consistent with our concepts of decency and justice and right to attain peace. For this purpose we will work co-operatively with the Soviets and any other people as long as there is sincerity of purpose and a genuine desire to go ahead.

CHAPTER 27

The Fateful Summer

The President Returns From Geneva – After the Big Four the Little Four – Eisenhower Says a Balanced Budget Is His Great Objective – He Proposes a General 3 Per Cent Cut in Government Spending – No Reductions in National Security Programs – Eisenhower on the Democratic Investigations – The President Goes to Denver – A Golf Game at Cherry Hills and Trouble from Raw Onions

A gentle summer rain splashed in the President's face and rumpled his brown suit as he stepped off the plane at National Airport on July 24, 1955, on his return from Geneva. It was early on Sunday morning, usually a dead hour in Washington, but hundreds of people had turned out at the airport and along the roads leading to the White House to welcome the President home.

Eisenhower was smiling and happy. His performance at the Big Four conference had won universal acclaim. Nearly everywhere he was being hailed as a soldier who had become one of the great peacemakers of his time. Indisputably he was the leader of the free world. The disillusionment over Geneva had not yet set in. In a word, it was a propitious time for Eisenhower, one of the peaks of his Presidency.

In a cheerful frame of mind he announced at his next press conference that he had returned from the Big Four to learn there was going to be a Little Four.

"I got home," he said, "to be greeted by my daughter-in-law with the statement that if all goes well, I will be a grandfather for the fourth time next Christmas, which, of course, was a happy ending to the week."

The reporters applauded him.

In the domestic field one of the President's chief interests that eventful summer was in driving his administration across the last white lines to the goal of a balanced budget for the fiscal year 1957, which begins on July 1, 1956.

Before Geneva—on May 13—the President had told the Cabinet he thought it was very important that the administration should present a balanced budget for 1957. His comment was occasioned by a warning from Rowland Hughes that the small surplus in prospect could be realized only by careful control over expenditures. Eisenhower recalled his campaign speech at Peoria listing his goal as elimination of the Federal deficit within four years. He considered this a commitment. He told the Cabinet, however, that balancing the budget must not take priority over national security or essential government programs, but it must come before tax cuts and nonessential programs. If a tax cut was proposed in 1956 at the expense of a balanced budget, he said, he would fight it.

He hoped that even a small surplus could be realized to apply against the national debt. He would very much like to see a tax cut, particularly for those with low incomes, he said, but so long as he was President there was not going to be one at the expense of a balanced budget.

The immense significance Eisenhower attached to wiping out the deficit was vividly revealed in the observation on which he concluded his statement. A balanced budget, he said, was now his great objective. If he won that battle, he told the Cabinet, he would consider his task in the White House largely accomplished.

Humphrey then stepped into the discussion with a view on taxes that differed from the President's. His thought was that the administration should aim at a greater margin than was then anticipated between receipts and expenditures. He argued that increased economic activity held the key to a surplus, and he believed that the stimulus of a tax cut would be necessary to achieve this. In brief, he was for a balanced budget and a tax cut. He felt that this would be possible if every department would strive to cut expenditures somewhat more. The President was agreeable to renewed efforts to cut spending in nonessential areas. But he insisted that he would have to see a surplus in black and white before he would give his consent to reducing taxes.

When the Cabinet met on August 5 after his return from Switzerland, fiscal policy was not on the agenda, but the President brought it up at the outset. He said that he had been re-examining his campaign pledges on the subject. While he had never promised an immediate balancing of the budget, he recalled, he had said that, barring a serious deterioration in international affairs, a balanced budget should be possible within four years. The President said that even without a balance, taxes already had been cut. But now that the administration was so close to a balanced budget he was eager to make a genuine attempt in the next eleven months to reach the goal.

Then he took out a brief statement and read it to the Cabinet. It said:

In two and a half years we have come far toward balancing the budget. When this administration was inaugurated it was faced with a planned deficit of $9.9 billions. We have cut that deficit by more than half. At the same time we have absorbed a $7.5 billion tax cut. This is excellent progress.

But we still haven't reached our goal, even in this year of unparalleled prosperity. A deficit of from $1.5 to $1.7 billion is still likely for this fiscal year.

This amounts to only 3 per cent of the Federal spending planned for this year.

That 3 per cent stands as a challenge to every one of us. Surely in this giant government there are still programs, administrative costs or wasteful practices of one sort or another that we can root out without damage to anything truly essential.

I think we can find at least that 3 per cent and balance the budget this year. To this end I am directing the Budget Director to deduct 3 per cent of the expenditures planned for this year. I am confident that with determined effort throughout our government we will save at least this amount.

If anyone finds, after earnest application, that a cut of this size is an impossibility, he is to come to me as soon as such impossibility becomes apparent. I shall talk it over with him and the Director of the Bureau of the Budget.

In the discussion that followed Eisenhower made it plain that this was more in the nature of a spur to get the departments to cut out waste and nonessentials than it was a hard-and-fast order. It was a goal rather than a definite projection.

Wilson pointed out, for example, the difficulties of trimming the defense budget. The President assured him that while he was economy-minded, he was not going to damage any important program.

Benson observed that if there was ever a chance to cut government spending, it was at this time of peace and prosperity. This brought the President back to the subject of defense spending. It was this very spending that made the country secure and brought such peace as there was, he said.

Dulles warmly concurred in this. In spite of its cordiality, he said, the Big Four conference had brought no real concessions from the Soviets. Peace was not yet assured. If the smiles and handshakes should lead to a relaxation of United States defense efforts and a disintegration of the defenses of Western Europe, the Secretary of State warned, Geneva could prove a worse tragedy than Yalta. The Soviets had not yet made a material contribution to peace, he continued. They were proceeding with their atomic tests and their work on missiles. Their hold on the satellites had not been relaxed. Nor had the Chinese Communists dropped their aggressive attitude. The Communists wanted nothing more than to see the United States and the rest of the free world drop its guard, Dulles said, and to do so would invite catastrophe.

The President told the Cabinet in so many words that his request had not been prompted by events at Geneva. What he was trying to do was to get department heads to exercise leadership in a way that would imbue subordinates with the feeling that the budget goal was near and must be reached—that would make them compete with one another in finding places where money could be saved. The President preferred this approach to the mere issuing of instructions about savings, which, he said, might only bring staff members running in crying, "It can't be done."

Eisenhower assured Wilson that he intended no damage to the Nike program, the Distant Early Warning line, aircraft procurement, work on the intercontinental ballistic missile or any such vital program. But he pointed out many places where the Defense Department might look for unnecessary luxuries and wasteful practices, mentioning among others military schools and warehouses. He reminisced about old days in the Army when only the Chief of Staff had an automobile and all other officers, even when they went to testify before Congressional committees, were given streetcar tokens for traveling expenses.

Wilson said that he was already trying to cut expenses by 5 per cent to avoid exceeding his current budget and that the superimposition of the President's request would bring his economy goal to 8 per cent.

He declined to make a commitment on it. He said that all he could do was his level best. Eisenhower and Humphrey assured him that his best was good enough for them.

When the subject turned to the 1956 State of the Union message, Lodge said that it should be an address with constructive and popular issues expressed with emotion and feeling. It should carry the political offensive to grounds on which the administration was prepared to fight. With an insight validated by events the President commented that he thought many members of Congress would return in January with one thought uppermost in their minds—aid to the farmers. This issue, he said, might overwhelm all others.

On the question of a public announcement of the drive to balance the budget a difference of opinion developed in the Cabinet. One view was that the 3 per cent cut should be announced in the Mid-Year Budget Review as an accomplished fact. Another view, held by the President, was that this was going too far because the 3 per cent was only an objective and not certain of achievement. Nixon suggested the course that was finally followed. When the Budget Review was published on August 25, the 3 per cent cut was not included. But Humphrey announced that there was hope of a

balanced budget for 1957 and that the deficit could be wiped out
by a cut of only 3 per cent in spending.

The President met only once more with the Cabinet before his
fateful trip to Denver. The meeting was on August 12. The Attorney
General told the Cabinet that appropriations for Congressional
investigations were at an all-time high—eighty investigations were in
progress or pending. The President said that in the face of these
the administration should keep an eye to wise public relations.
He asked the Cabinet officers always to consult him well in advance
if anything was coming up at one of these investigations that he
ought to know about so that he would not suddenly be caught in
an awkward position. If the administration should find an instance
of criminal conduct, he said, it should open it up and prosecute the
offenders.

The thought of eighty investigations got Eisenhower's back up. Be
affirmative, he bade the Cabinet. Put the burden on the opposition.
Take the position that it is no wonder that a Democratic Congress
wants to investigate after some of the ethics of 1933-'53. He told his
colleagues that whenever a time came when they felt he could
be helpful by issuing a statement they should let him know.

As the meeting ended, Burns lamented the failure of Congress to
approve the highway program, which, he said, would have been
an important economic lever in 1956. The administration, he said,
should ask for action early in the next session or even consider
calling a special session beforehand if necessary. The others looked
to the President for his reaction. He slowly twisted his head around
to Burns and told him painfully that the cost of a special session
might be the sanity and possibly the life of one Dwight D. Eisenhower.

At his last press conference before his vacation the President
was asked what he had had in mind when he told a group of Ohio
Republicans the previous day that he could disclose his political
plans for 1956 only if the future were revealed to him. What did he
mean?

"What I intended to imply," he answered, "was that if I now
were such an infallible prophet that I could understand all about
the world situation, the domestic situation and my own situation—

including the way I felt, and possibly with the health and everything else as of that moment—then there would be no great excuse for deferring the decision.

"I do not have that gift of prophecy."

Nor, as the President took off for Denver on August 14, was there anyone else who could prophesy what the days would bring before he returned to the capital.

After arriving in Colorado the President lost little time in heading for the Rockies. As he settled down in the fastness of Byers Peak Ranch on the Western slope of the Continental Divide, eighty-two miles from Denver, he was in as happy a mood as his friends had known him in years. He felt a contentment that had eluded him on earlier visits. His first summer in office he had been dejected and irritable. That was the time his relations with the Republican Congress had exasperated him to the point where he had begun thinking about a third party. He had reached Denver frustrated, discouraged and tense. Even his blood pressure was up. The following summer things were much better but he had had to take a good deal of work with him, and even when it was disposed of, the approach of the Congressional elections kept him under pressure. In the summer of 1955, however, Eisenhower's gnawing frustration was gone. His popularity was high. Geneva had been a warming experience. He was enjoying a feeling of accomplishment. The recession had been beaten and the country was at a new peak of prosperity. His relations with his party had never been better. There was no campaign in the fall to bother him, and he had little paper work to do.

The days passed pleasantly, with the President working for an hour or so in the morning and spending the rest of the time playing eighteen or twenty-seven holes of golf, fishing, painting, playing bridge or generally taking life easy. Later in the month he interrupted his vacation to fly over the New England floods and to address the American Bar Association in Independence Hall in Philadelphia. In a word of caution about the still glowing "spirit of Geneva" he said that sometimes eagerness to avert war "can produce outright or implicit agreement that injustices and wrongs of the present shall be perpetuated in the future." "We must not participate in any such false agreements," he declared.

On September 10 forty-eight Republican State Chairmen flew to Denver to have breakfast with the President at the Brown Palace after telegraphing him that they looked forward to supporting him again in 1956. Eisenhower made a brief speech, which was soon to be clothed in new significance. In part, he said:

We don't believe for a minute that the Republican Party is so lacking in inspiration, high-quality personnel and leadership that we are dependent on one man. We don't believe it for a minute. Now as long as we have a man in the leadership position why, of course, as a party we are going to be loyal. We are going to help in the fight.

But humans are frail and they are mortal. Finally you never pin your flag so tightly to one mast that if a ship sinks, you cannot rip it off and nail it to another. It is sometimes good to remember.

Shortly, the President returned to Byers Peak Ranch, which is owned by his friend Aksel Nielsen, a Denver banker. He was in fine health and high spirits. Because they rode horseback at the ranch, he called his friend George E. Allen and his personal physician, General Snyder, cavalrymen. One morning when they were all going fishing together, he shouted, "Now you cavalrymen, come over here." He ordered them to line up alongside the car.

"Prepare to mount," he commanded.

They fell in by the car.

"Mount!"

They scrambled in, and he piled in after them.

On the morning of September 23 the President was up at dawn and cooked his own breakfast of hot cakes, fried mush, pork sausage and beef bacon before heading for Denver.

"I had my best night's sleep in years," he told Murray Snyder, his Assistant Press Secretary.

Back in Denver, the President went to his office in the yellow stucco, red-roofed administration building at Lowry Air Force Base. In turn Snyder, Mrs. Whitman, and Wayne Hawks, White House chief of records, brought in work that kept him busy for more than two hours. When he had finished he drove out to the Cherry Hills

Country Club. It was still early for lunch so he changed his clothes and played eighteen holes with Rip Arnold, the club pro, riding in a motor cart between shots. Four cartloads of Secret Service men followed. Eisenhower had often remarked to Arnold in the past that without golf he would have found difficulty living the life of a President, because the game absorbed some of the pressures.

After the eighteenth hole he dropped into the clubhouse, toting up an eighty-four on his scorecard. In the locker room he and Arnold and some other friends, including George Allen and David Gordon, president of the club, had lunch together. Eisenhower munched down a hamburger with large slices of raw onions. Helping himself to some extra slices that Allen offered, the President remarked that he never could eat raw onions until he learned to put a little vinegar on them. After lunch he and Arnold went out for a nine-hole practice game. This time the President walked instead of riding in the cart. On the eighth hole he complained of heartburn.

"Maybe I can't take those onions any more," he told Arnold. "They seem to be backing up on me. I seem to have a little heartburn."

Twice during the twenty-seven holes he was called off the course to receive telephone calls. One was from Dulles, who was calling about the answer being prepared to the letter recently received from Bulganin on the open-skies plan. The President and Dulles agreed to talk about it on the phone again early the next morning, but events were to change all this.

His golf over for the day, the President returned to Mrs. Doud's house at 750 Lafayette Street, where he and Mrs. Eisenhower stay whenever they are in Denver. On the front porch of the unpretentious eight-room gray brick house Eisenhower as a young officer had courted Mamie Doud, and the place had been second home to them in the years when they were being shifted around from one Army post to another. As he still had an hour or so before dinner, the President went down to a den in the basement to paint. His subject was the anguished face of an Argentine woman praying in a shrine smashed by Juan Peron's vandals. He was painting it after a photograph by Hank Walker in the July 11, 1955, issue of *Life*.

George and Mary Allen came for dinner with the Eisenhowers

and Mrs. Doud. The President's indigestion had vanished, but he told Mrs. Eisenhower that he had been troubled by the onions during the afternoon. When he took a look at the roast lamb, potatoes and vegetables that were placed on the table, he was reminded of the good work he was engaged in those days of trying to get Allen to reduce. Believing that there is nothing like a good example, Eisenhower told Allen that he would not eat much if Allen wouldn't. Allen agreed, and each man lived up to his promise. The Allens left about nine and the President retired an hour later, feeling well.

CHAPTER 28

Heart Attack

Mrs. Eisenhower Awakens the President – He Is Seized by a Pain in His Chest – Dr. Snyder Makes a Diagnosis and Passes a Lonely Vigil with the President – Eisenhower Is Taken to the Hospital – Nixon's Busy Night – How the Government Ran – The Cabinet Discusses Procedures for Carrying On in the President's Absence – Convalescence.

I

Shortly after 2:30 on the morning of September 24 Mrs. Eisenhower, whose bedroom was across the hall from the President's on the second floor, heard her husband tossing about in bed. She went into his quarters to see what was disturbing him. The plain, comfortable room was familiar. On her left as she entered was a round table with a lamp. On one side of the table was a small straight chair and on the other a large overstuffed upholstered chair and ottoman. In the far wall opposite the door was a fireplace flanked by windows. To Mrs. Eisenhower's immediate right stood a shoulder-high chest of drawers and just beyond, parallel to the windows looking out on the elm-shaded street, was the large old-fashioned double bed her husband slept in. At the foot of it, completing the furnishings, was a low dresser.

Mrs. Eisenhower stepped over and found the Prsident asleep, but because he was very restless, she woke him up.

"What's the matter, Ike?" she asked. "Are you having a nightmare or something?"

Rousing himself, the President replied that he was feeling all right, and with this assurance Mrs. Eisenhower returned to her room. The

President did not drop right back to sleep, however, and within a very short time he was assailed by a pain in his chest of a kind he had never experienced before. He went into Mrs. Eisenhower's room and put his hand on his chest to show where he was suffering. On the assumption that it might be a recurrence of the indigestion of the afternoon before, she gave him a dose of milk of magnesia and sent him back to bed. But not satisfied that this was sufficient, she telephoned General Snyder, who was living at the bachelor officers' quarters at Lowry four miles away.

"Ike has a pain in his chest," she said, as her words have since been recalled. "You'd better come over."

Snyder called the air-base dispatcher for a car and instructed him also to pick up a medical kit in his office on the second floor of the administration building. Without wasting a minute, the handsome, seventy-four-year-old physician, who had been Eisenhower's doctor for ten years, slipped on his clothes over his pajamas and was waiting on the steps with his bag when the car arrived, driven by Airman 2/c Jacob Judis.

"Seven hundred fifty Lafayette Street and step on it," Snyder said.

Speeding through the overcast night without paying attention to traffic light, Judis wheeled Snyder up to the Doud house at 3:11 A.M., and the general went at once to the President's room. Eisenhower was lying in bed restless, tormented by the severe pain in his chest. He was perspiring and flushed, though the flush was slowly giving way to pallor.

Snyder listened to Eisenhower's chest with a stethoscope and took his pulse and tested his blood pressure with a band on his arm. The pressure had gone up and the pulse was rapid. It took only two or three minutes for Snyder to come to the grave conclusion that the President of the United States was suffering from a coronary thrombosis. The extent of damage to the heart he could not, of course, determine immediately.

Quickly Snyder broke an ampoule of amyl nitrate and told the President to sniff it. Following this he gave him an injection of papaverine hydrochloride to dilate the arteries in the heart and then a shot of morphine to ease the pain and shock. A little later he prepared a hypodermic of heparin, which tends to increase the liquidity of the blood and to prevent clotting, and injected it in his arm.

A tall, straight, gray-haired, bespectacled man with unbounded affection for Eisenhower, Snyder stood tensely by the bedside observing his patient. He did not tell him what his diagnosis was, but the President knew he was very ill. His pain continued. About 3:45 A.M. Snyder gave him a second shot of morphine. As it pried loose the grip of pain, the President began sliding into a deep sleep. This was a profound relief to Snyder. The President was passing through a crisis, and the physician believed that sleep was the best thing for him.

To avert shock to Mrs. Eisenhower, who has long suffered from valvular heart disease herself, Snyder sent her back to bed without telling her the President's true condition. Also, he put aside the idea of a public announcement because he feared that it would cause great excitement which inevitably would permeate the Doud house and might possibly kill the President. Sitting alone in the dead of night with his slumbering patient, therefore, Howard Snyder was the only man in the world who knew that the President was stricken with a damaged heart.

All night long and through the morning, Snyder remained in the room with the President. He left the band on Eisenhower's arm to keep check of the blood pressure. Gradually the pressure came down and his pulse slowed to a steady beat. Although the President's condition was precarious and the future inscrutable, these encouraging signs were the faint beginnings of a remarkable recovery.

Shortly before 7 A.M. when the Presidential staff began stirring at Lowry, Snyder called Mrs. Whitman, the President's secretary, and informed her that the President was not feeling well and would not come to his office for appointments. Still holding back the truth about Eisenhower's condition, he told her that he was suffering from digestive upset. Soon afterward Murray Snyder (no kin to the general) got him on the phone and the doctor repeated this description of the illness. At 10:30 A.M. Murray Snyder, whose handling of the story in the next twelve hours won the deep admiration of the reporters in Denver, announced the President's condition as it had been told to him by Dr. Snyder.

Meanwhile Dr. Snyder calmly informed Mrs. Eisenhower of her

husband's condition and telephoned Colonel Byron E. Pollock, chief of cardiology service at Fitzsimons General Hospital on the outskirts of Denver and told him to bring an electrocardiograph to the Doud house. The President began stirring about 11:45 A.M. When he was fully awake but still very weak, Dr. Snyder told him that he had summoned Dr. Pollock to take an electrocardiogram. Pollock arrived with Major General Martin E. Griffin, commanding general of the hospital, and they and Snyder made a tracing of the President's heart impulses.

The doctors took the tracing downstairs and laid it out on the dining-room table. It confirmed Snyder's diagnosis. A blood clot had blocked an artery in the front wall of the President's heart, cutting off the supply of blood from that part of the heart muscle. Snyder and Pollock returned to the President's bedroom. Snyder told Eisenhower that his heart had suffered an injury.

"We would like to take you to Fitzsimons," Snyder said.

The news did not seem to shock the President in the least, but, of course, he was still somewhat numbed from morphine.

"We're not going to get an ambulance," Snyder said.

"All right, Howard," the President replied, "call Jim"—James J. Rowley, chief of the White House Secret Service detail—"and get my car and let's go out."

Sergeant Moaney, his valet, helped the President into a bathrobe, and the three doctors supported him walking down the stairs, taking as much of his weight on their shoulders as they could manage. They had decided that it would be less of a strain on the President to walk down in this fashion than to be strapped to a stretcher and tipped in the air at the sharp angle that would have been required to carry him down the steep and narrow stairs, rounding the small halfway landing.

A limousine had been backed into the driveway, and on the porch two sturdy Secret Service men, Rowley and Deeter B. Flohr, Eisenhower's chauffeur, took over from the doctors and supported the President down the steps and into the rear of the car. Snyder sat on one side of the President and Pollock on the other. General Griffin slipped into a jump seat. With Flohr at the wheel and Rowley beside him they pulled away from the Doud house and made the nine-mile drive to the hospital at moderate speed. At Fitzsimons the car rolled up under a rear portico where a wheel chair was waiting to carry the President to the elevator. He smiled at the attendants in the corridor and had a friendly word for Charles Adams, the elevator operator who brought him up the eighth floor to a special suite with cream-colored walls, light-green furniture and green drapes. As soon as he slipped into bed, an oxygen tent was placed over the upper half of his body.

Then the news was broken to the world. Shortly after 2:30 P.M. Murray Snyder turned the press room at Lowry into bedlam with the announcement: "The President has just a mild anterior—let's cut out the word 'anterior'—the President has just had a mild coronary thrombosis. He has just been taken to Fitzsimons General Hospital. He was taken to the hospital in his own car and walked from the house to the car."

Dr. Snyder had notified him about 2 P.M. that the President was suffering from a mild anterior coronary thrombosis—after examination in the hospital "mild" was changed to "moderate"—but the assistant press secretary, who is an experienced newspaperman, felt that the word "anterior" in the initial announcement might cause confusion.

Before the announcement Snyder had called Hagerty, who was back in Washington on vacation, and told him what had happened.

"Jim, I intend to play this straight," he said, "and give the fellows everything as fast as we can get it."

"Right," Hagerty replied. "Give it to them absolutely straight. I'll catch a plane out as soon as I can."

Twelve hours had elapsed between the heart attack and the disclosure of his true condition, but from that moment on Murray Snyder, Hagerty and the doctors kept the people informed of the President's condition with thoroughness and candor.

When Hagerty learned of the attack shortly after 5 o'clock in the afternoon in Washington, he telephoned the Vice-President at the latter's white-brick house in the fashionable Spring Valley section of Washington. Nixon had read in the *Evening Star* that the President was suffering from a digestive upset, and accepted at face value the report that his condition was not serious.

"Dick, I've got some bad news for you," Hagerty told him. "I've had a call from Murray Snyder in Denver. The President has had a coronary."

"Oh, my God!" Nixon gasped.

When the Vice-President could catch his breath, he told Hagerty that often heart attacks were not severe and that many patients enjoyed a complete recovery. Hagerty informed him that he was flying to Denver. He urged Nixon always to let him know where he could be reached.

Earlier Dr. Snyder had sent to Washington for Colonel Thomas M. Mattingly, the leading heart specialist at Walter Reed Hospital, who had the records on Eisenhower's heart dating back to 1946. Hagerty got in touch with Dr. Mattingly, a man on whose judgment the President came to place great reliance, and together they flew to Denver in an Air Force Constellation, arriving at 11:46 P.M. At the hospital Dr. Snyder told Hagerty that the President was glad he had returned to Denver. Snyder also quoted Eisenhower as having said, "Tell Jim to take over and make the decisions—and handle the story." Hagerty does not agree with an interpretation that has been placed upon these words that the President was delegating to him the authority to run the executive branch of the government even temporarily. What Eisenhower meant, in his opinion, was that he should carry on his normal duties as press secretary. The fact remains, however, that as the senior White House official on the scene for several days and as the President's only authorized spokesman, he was in a position of authority far greater than is customarily exercised by the press secretary. Indeed it is difficult to think of anyone whose authority in those first couple of days exceeded that of Hagerty, a very sure-footed official with a large capacity and a readiness to make decisions.

II

Nixon went dead inside after receiving Hagerty's call, he said afterward. For several minutes the Vice-President sat alone in his living room numbed by the possible implications of the President's attack. Presently he returned to the telephone and called his intimate friend Deputy Attorney General William P. Rogers, who had already heard the news, and asked him to come over. Rogers joined the Nixons for dinner, but with the telephone ringing constantly and newspapermen massing outside clamoring for a word with the Vice-President, it was next to impossible to carry on a conversation. Nixon suggested that they go to Rogers's house in nearby Bethesda, Maryland. Mrs. Rogers drove over to pick them up. To give the slip to reporters the Vice-President and Rogers ducked out a side door and scampered along an alley to another street where, by prearrangment, Mrs. Rogers was waiting.

After reaching his house Rogers telephoned General Persons, who, since Adams was in Europe winding up a vacation, was the senior officer on the White House staff. Persons had been notified of the heart attack by Hagerty before the press secretary took off for Denver. Rogers suggested that Persons join him and Nixon, and when the three of them got together later in the evening they had a long discussion. Nixon took the lead in urging, for example, that the administration should show the world that the business of government was being carried on in the usual manner, with the members of the Cabinet and the White House staff going ahead with their normal duties within the framework of policies that had been laid out in the Cabinet and the N.S.C. After checking their opinion with Hagerty and other officials by telephone, the three agreed upon this course.

In a rather general way they speculated on the effect of Eisenhower's heart attack on national politics, particularly on the 1956 Presidential election. They agreed again after sounding out others, that it would be best for administration officials not to make any public comments on this subject whatever until it was known how well the President would recover.

Reflecting the judgment that had been reached, Nixon made a statement to reporters after church the next morning, a Sunday, saying, "The business of government will go on without delay. . . . Under the President's administration a team has been set up in Washington which will carry out his well-defined plans."

In line with this display of "business as usual," four administration officials, including Dulles and Humphrey, went to Ottawa, as planned, that Sunday to attend the United States—Canadian Joint

Economic Conference. By prearrangement with Nixon the two Secretaries issued statements that the administration would keep its stride in spite of the President's illness.

Late Sunday, Nixon, Persons and Rogers again met at Roger's house, and during their discussion Nixon leaned to the opinion that he ought to call a meeting of the Cabinet for the following Friday. (Although a meeting of the N.S.C. had previously been set for Thursday, no Cabinet meeting was scheduled for the week.) He made the point that the gathering of the Cabinet might have the effect of demonstrating the orderly functioning of the government. He felt, however, that other members of the Cabinet should be consulted for their opinion, and no final decision was made that night.

Meanwhile that same day in Denver Hagerty had indicated that the Attorney General's office would be asked for a legal opinion as to whether during his illness certain of the President's powers might be delegated to others. His remark was in answer to a question about the signing of papers that are ordinarily brought to the President. Speculation was rife at the time on the possibility of having an "acting President" who would exercise temporarily some of the Constitutional powers of the President. Actually, Hagerty never asked the Attorney General for an opinion, and none was ever given on this point of delegation of Constitutional powers.

On Monday, however, Rogers, as acting Attorney General while Brownell vacationed in Spain, ordered a study on a related but fundamentally different question. This was whether the President while laid up could delegate his ministerial or non-Constitutional powers to one or more of his subordinates by executive order. Under such an arrangement there would be no question of an "acting President" or of the President's transferring authority specifically reserved to him by law.

That Monday—a day the stock market took its worst plunge since the great Depression—Sherman Adams arrived from Europe aboard General Gruenther's plane. At noon he had luncheon at the White House with the Vice-President, Persons and Rogers. While they were together, word arrived from Denver on the result of the first examination of Eisenhower by the Boston heart specialist Dr. Paul

Dudley White, who in ensuing weeks was to become almost as famous as his patient. His verdict was that the President's condition was satisfactory and his morale high, that "conceivably" he could resume conferences within two weeks and should be ready to take up his normal activity after a couple of months. He even made the point under questioning that if Eisenhower enjoyed a good recovery, he would be physically able to run for President again if he wished. This news made it less likely that the question of delegation of non-Constitutional powers would have to be put up to the President.

The next day the idea of the executive order was dropped during a luncheon in the Secretary of the Treasury's office, attended by Humphrey, Nixon, Adams, Persons, Rogers and Brownell, who had cut short his vacation. It was unnecessary, Brownell explained later, because the news from Denver "is encouraging."

There was a further reason. This was that no papers of any great consequence awaited the President's signature. A key to the whole problem was the fact that his illness struck at the lowest period of government activity. Congress had adjourned. The President had acted on all bills requiring his attention. The Big Four Foreign Ministers' meeting was still nearly a month away. Many high officials had just got off on vacation. Preparation of the major messages to be submitted by the President to Congress in January was in the earliest stages. Even if he had been in the best of health, it was a time when the President's participation in the routine business of government would have been at a minimum.

While consideration of delegation of powers was dropped, the idea of a Cabinet session on September 30 was approved.

III

The meeting was historic. The President lay in the hospital in Denver 1,551 miles away, improving but still not out of danger. Nixon, wearing a dark double-breasted suit, walked slowly into the Cabinet room with a serious air and took his place in the Vice-President's chair between Humphrey on his right and Brownell on his left. Opposite Nixon was the empty chair of the President. As there was no agenda, the polished table was largely uncluttered with papers. The room, however, was cluttered with officials—

thirty-four of them in addition to the Cabinet had crowded in and were banked around the white walls and the windows facing the rose garden.

At 9:30 A.M. the Vice-President called the meeting to order and asked for silent prayer. After a minute or so he broke the hush to read the morning medical bulletin from Denver. It said that the President had had an "excellent" night, sleeping almost uninterruptedly for nine and a half hours. It had been his first night out of the oxygen tent.

Nixon then looked to the Secretary of State for a review of the problems which faced the United States in foreign relations while the President was ill.

Dulles said that the most critical situation at the moment was the Middle East. In Cyprus, he said, the situation was inflamed. The Cypriots were demonstrating against British rule in their movement for union with Greece, and the disorder carried a threat to the Mediterranean flank of NATO. Dulles explained the United States had decided to support the British in voting to keep the Cyprus question off the agenda of the U.N. General Assembly mainly to give tensions a chance to ease in hopes that a gradual settlement could be reached.

The Soviet Union's decision to furnish arms to Egypt was also causing a critical problem, Dulles continued. He warned that the Soviet move threatened the peace between Egypt and Israel. The flow of arms, he said, might carry into other areas of Africa. Without giving any details, he assured the Cabinet that the United States was not without plans for dealing with the situation.

Dulles said that the talks between the United States and Red Chinese ambassadors in Geneva were not going well at the moment because, for possibly ulterior motives, the Chinese seemed to be reneging on the release of American civilians.

On the bright side he reported that talks among Americans, British and French in New York in preparation for the Foreign Ministers' conference in Geneva had gone splendidly.

Nixon then directed the attention of the members to the heart of the matter before the Cabinet—the plans for running the government in the President's absence.

Government affairs, he said at the outset, should be carried on with dispatch. Routine matters must not get piled up in a logjam awaiting the President's return. Nixon said that actions taken by the government should be within the framework of policies established by the President. One important way of doing this, he pointed out, was to channel important measures through the Cabinet or the N.S.C.

The Vice-President reserved for future decision by the President the establishment of important new policies.

He made certain suggestions for the carrying out of existing policies. Departments and agencies should proceed as usual in conduct of business which was strictly in their jurisdiction. In the case of other actions which ordinarily are submitted in advance to the Cabinet as a matter of courtesy, this practice should continue. On the preceding day, he said, the N.S.C. had decided that those actions in the Council's field which customarily are taken only after discussion with the President should now, during his illness, be reviewed in the N.S.C. in lieu of or as preliminary to discussions with the President. The Cabinet, Nixon said, might wish to decide upon a procedure to be followed with respect to its actions.

No immediate problem of conducting the government presented itself, he continued, because it now appeared that the President would soon be allowed by his doctors to sign routine papers. He said it was fortunate that the President had established an effective team that could—he quoted Dulles's statement of the preceding Sunday—carry on "the policies and principles" of the administration without harm to "the steady prosecution of our national and international policies." Nixon said that it was very important to keep the public aware that this was the Eisenhower administration and not the administration of any other person or group.

Brownell said that he saw no legal barrier to prevent the Cabinet from following the procedure agreed upon by the N.S.C. He went on to say that he was sure that all members would wish to lean over backward to make sure that no actions by their respective agencies affecting other agencies or the general policy of the administration would be taken without prior discussion in the Cabinet or the N.S.C.

The Attorney General had been asked, he said, to determine how the burden of purely routine actions might be lightened for the President. (Evidently this was a reference to the study ordered by Rogers on Monday.) Brownell suggested that each Cabinet officer prepare a list of actions in his particular department requiring Presidential approval and of suggestions as to which types of action might be handled by someone other than the President. Brownell said that certain duties had often been delegated by Presidents in the past. More could be in the future, Rowland Hughes observed.

The Attorney General read the draft of a statement he had been asked by the N.S.C. to prepare on the conduct of the government in the weeks ahead. The Cabinet suggested several changes in wording and agreed that it should be issued after the meeting by Murray Snyder, who had returned from Denver. The statement, in part, read:

After full discussion of pending matters, it was concluded that there are no obstacles to the orderly and uninterrupted conduct of the foreign and domestic affairs of the nation during the period of rest ordered by the President's physicians.

Governor Sherman Adams, the Assistant to the President, will leave for Denver today and will be available there, in consultation with the President's physicians, whenever it may later become appropriate to present any matters to the President.

The policies and programs of the administration as determined and approved by the President are well established along definite lines and are well known. Co-ordination of the activities of the several departments of the government within the framework of these policies will be continued by full co-operation among the responsible officers of these departments so that the functions of the government will be carried forward in an effective manner during the absence of the President.

Brownell and Humphrey both said it would be a good idea for members to refrain from public comment on this statement. The Secretary of the Treasury appealed for co-operation among departments and for frank thrashing out of complicated problems in the Cabinet and the N.S.C. so that in the coming weeks there would be no appearance of controversy within the administration.

Adams said that he had talked to Dr. White the evening before and that it was agreed that the doctors should determine at any given time whether routine documents might be submitted to the President for his approval. In this early stage of convalescence, Adams added, it also was agreed that the President should not be handed controversial issues or papers requiring such close attention as to tax his strength.

Stassen told the Cabinet he thought that effective teamwork in the days ahead would offer the highest tribute the members could pay to the President's ability in organizing the government and selecting capable subordinates. Summerfield asked about keeping speaking engagements during the President's illness. Humphrey said that this did pose a problem, but he felt that members should live up to their speaking commitments. He considered it important that such speeches should be confined to the administration's record and not calculated to arouse partisan controversy. The Cabinet agreed with Humphrey's suggestions.

Nixon reminded the Cabinet that questions were bound to arise about the outlook for the Republican Party. He suggested that they should be brushed right off as unworthy of discussion when the national concern was for the President's recovery. He also suggested that speakers might comment upon Eisenhower's skill in having formed an effective administrative machine.

Adams said that Dr. White had heard someone suggest that the President issue a public statement and that the doctor offered no objection. Benson and Lodge remarked that if and when such a statement was issued, it should express thanks for the many prayers being offered throughout the world for the President's recovery.

Howard Pyle, one of the President's Administrative Assistants, interposed to urge again that speeches during this period avoid controversy and emphasize that business was going on as usual. The President's illness, he said, did not make it necessary for members of the administration to reject speaking engagements.

Dulles reminded the Cabinet that in Denver, Adams would be the channel for presentations to the President. The Secretary observed that some individuals outside government (he mentioned no names) might presume authoritatively to reflect the President's opinions. This was all the more reason, he continued, to strengthen the position of Adams, who was already a highly respected national figure. Nixon seconded this and noted that in Adams's absence Persons would be senior at the White House. Government business should be channeled through the White House staff in the usual manner, he added.

Persons urged Cabinet members to assume responsibility for holding in their departments papers not requiring early action rather than allowing them to pile up in the White House, making it appear that the President's absence was impeding routine business. Nixon agreed with this and said it did not conflict with the plans already discussed for routing policy matters through the Cabinet and the N.S.C. He said that the Attorney General would have to take on the additional task of keeping an eye on any special legal problems that might arise under current conditions.

The discussion on operations of the government in Eisenhower's absence ended with a word from Kevin McCann on the desirability of co-ordinating speeches.

A few items of minor business were discussed.

Approval was given to Adams's suggestion for forming a Cabinet committee on the highway program.

Mitchell reported on plans for the National Conference on Equal Economic Opportunity. He digressed to say that an expert on racial relations under the Truman administration had offered high praise privately for the manner in which the Eisenhower administration was dealing with this problem.

There was talk on implementing Hoover Commission recommendations and on the state of the economy. Humphrey observed that even if the highway program was approved at the 1956 session of Congress, the economy would not feel the effect for another year or two. Hughes said that a "fine spirit" of co-operation had been evident since the last session when the President had set a goal of reducing expenditures by 3 per cent. Even without any economies in the Defense Department, Hughes said, he was hopeful that spending would drop by $700,000,000.

Departments were preparing to submit material for inclusion in the State of the Union message. Adams recalled that the President had once voiced his hope that some day he could deliver a "twenty-minute message." Adams hoped that departments would be very concise in their submissions this year.

At noon the meeting ended. Noting that Nixon had been under immense strain during the last week, Dulles closed the discussion by expressing on behalf of the Cabinet appreciation for the manner in which the Vice-President had conducted himself.

IV

In Denver the President's recovery continued without complications. Letters and telegrams poured into the hospital by the tens of thousands. Bags of mail piled up in an auditorium, and on her visits to the President, Mrs. Eisenhower, who was living in the hospital, would drop by and scoop up an armful and take them into his room and read samples to him. The note that predominated was that people were praying for him. This seemed to have a deeply heartening effect on Eisenhower. Over and over again he kept telling his visitors how much he was moved by the prayers and sympathy of the people for a stricken President.

"It really does something for you to know that people all over the world are praying for you," he said to Mrs. Eisenhower one day after she had finished reading some messages.

A little thing that did a great deal for the President's morale was the uncharacteristically gaudy costume the newspapermen sent him on his sixty-fifth birthday on October 14. It consisted of bright-red pajamas with a general of the Army's five stars embroidered in gold on each collar tab and MUCH BETTER, THANKS embroidered over the breast pocket. Setting off the pajamas was a glossy black Western tie with silver sequins, which Merriman Smith and Laurence H. Burd, of the Chicago *Tribune*, bought for thirty-nine cents. Day in and day out, the President wore this getup around the hospital in a mood approaching hilarity, and the doctors encouraged him to wear it.

Mrs. Eisenhower and her son ordered records of the President's favorite music for reading and relaxation.*

---

* They included "*Clair de lune*," Drigo's "Serenade," "Greensleeves," "Festival," "Dream of Olwen," "Song of Love," "Flirtation Waltz," "*Matinata*," "*Amoureuse*," "To a Wild Rose," "Serenade in the Night," "Barcarole," "In

On September 30 the President resumed his official duties by initialing two lists of recess appointments of foreign-service officers. Two days later it was announced that the President was "a little tired," and the news shook the stock market, sending leading shares down by from one to five points and reducing the total value of stocks on the New York Stock Exchange by four billion dollars. But the President bounced back and so did the market, and little by little as the days passed Eisenhower devoted more attention to government business. One after another, Cabinet officers and other leading officials came to Denver.

Partly these visits were intended as demonstrations of the President's continuing authority and of his gradual resumption of active direction of the government. Also, it has been pointed out, the press conferences at which these official visitors reported on their talks with Eisenhower constituted a form of communication between the stricken President and the people. But there was also another important side to these calls, and that was their therapeutic purpose. A sense of participation, of being able to discharge his responsibilities, was increasingly important to the President's morale and health, as it would have been in the case of any coronary patient.

Dr. Snyder and Dr. White soon became aware that Eisenhower was lying in bed thinking about government problems. These thoughts often escaped in his talks with them. White told Adams and Hagerty that it would be beneficial for the President to receive Cabinet officers. In the early stages their talks dealt with less exacting problems, but as time went on the doctors would buttonhole visiting officials before they went into the President's room and tell them to speak to him straight from the shoulder and not act as if they were addressing someone on his deathbed.

---

the Still of the Night," "Stardust," "Moonlight and Roses," "Sleepy Lagoon," "Indian Summer," "Drink to Me Only With Thine Eyes." Also a melody from *Die Fledermaus*, "Caucasian Love Song," a melody from *Countess Maritza*, "Toujours l'amour," "Songs My Mother Taught Me," a melody from *The Gypsy Baron*, "The Old Refrain" and a medley from *The Student Prince*. There were also these songs played by Al Goodman and his orchestra: "One Alone," "Time on My Hands," the entra'acte and intermezzo from *The Chocolate Soldier*, "Deep in My Heart," Beethoven's Minuet Number 2 in G, "The Funeral March of a Marionette," Schumann's "Nocturne," "Will You Remember?" and a medley from *The Merry Widow*.

"Look," White told Hagerty, "he's not so much of an invalid as he is the President of the United States lying in there. He wants to do his job."

Indeed, Eisenhower himself began to cut down on his callers' glowing words of greeting and urge that they get down to business.

Toward the end of October the President was able to take hold of a problem for an hour without ill effect. Adams, as usual, was the channel through which work flowed to and from Eisenhower, and in this period the influence of the Assistant to the President upon the operations of the government was very considerable. Working in a plain office on the second floor of the administration building at Lowry overlooking a parking lot, Adams was on the phone to Washington from morning until night, giving instructions, arranging conferences, summoning officials to see the President and making innumerable administrative decisions. He would lay out areas of policy in which the President alone must make decisions and then see to it that decisions were reached on matters beyond these boundaries. In Denver, as in Washington, his authority was enhanced by his unique prerogative in speaking for the President—"It is the President's wish that . . ." or "The President hopes you will . . ." and so forth.

Each week Adams would fly to Washington to attend meetings of the Cabinet and N.S.C. These sessions reflected many of the problems and activities of the government during the President's convalescence.

Cabinet, October 7, 1955

Adams brought word that the President was making excellent progress and with each day was more eager to get back on the job. The medical experts believed, Adams continued, that Eisenhower could soon take part in government affairs. After Nixon had noted that the President's birthday was only a week off, it was agreed that Adams should arrange for a birthday present from the Cabinet.

Benson brought up the farm problem and remarked that it would be an issue in the 1956 campaign. The agricultural surplus which the administration had inherited, he said, was a "time bomb," and he urged all high officials to close ranks to support the farm policy in 1956, as they had done in the 1954 campaign.

The Secretary presented a paper on the problem, which said that the farm situation was not likely to improve in the next twelve months. Farm income had declined some 20 per cent from its peak in 1951, second year of the Korean war, although the per capita income of all farmers from all sources had dropped but 6 per cent. The billions of dollars' worth of government-held surpluses took the buoyancy out of the market. The surplus couldn't be dumped in the ocean or sold quickly at any price or given away soon, the report went on. The commodities must be disposed of gradually. In spite of hardships, the report said, the status of the farmer was fundamentally sound as measured by working capital, reserves, land values and the ratio of debts to assets.

The report discussed the political aspects of the problem. The fortunes of the farmer had waned during the years the administration had been in office. The report put the blame on the difficulty of readjusting from a wartime to a peacetime economy, on what it called the bad farm law which the Eisenhower administration had inherited and the "irresponsible" decisions of the Truman administration. The problem, it said, was to make the people see through the "demagoguery" being practiced by the Democrats over the farm situation. Republican leaders, recalling the disaster of the 1948 campaign, were uneasy, and Democrats were trying to arouse dissatisfaction in the Midwest, capitalizing on the decline in the price of hogs.

Finally, the report suggested these measures: appropriation of perhaps $200,000,000 to help farmers turn land unsuited to crops into grass or forest; approval for farmers to grow wheat for their own use without any restrictions; assistance to the cotton market; readiness to help the market for hogs, potatoes and perishable foods through a limited program of government purchases; support of farm prices at the highest level that would be possible without causing undue acquisition by the government of further surpluses. The paper urged strong support of the White House and the Republican National Committee for Benson's farm policy.

Summerfield asked if it would not be a good idea to begin

purchasing hogs immediately because of current low prices. Benson
replied that it was a matter of timing. (On October 24 he launched
an $85,000,000 program for purchase of pork and lard.) The Post-
master General said that on travels across the country he had found
respect for Benson and the farm program, but a feeling notwithstanding that the Department of Agriculture was not sympathetic to
the farmer in times of crisis.

Stassen recalled things the administration had done to restore
the economy in the recession of 1953-'54 and argued that the farm
problem should be tackled now with the same determination. While
approving the economic soundness of the steps outlined in Benson's
report, he suggested that, in addition, more dramatic strokes were
necessary to give the program political appeal. He also emphasized
that the price of hogs must be turned upward before it hit rock
bottom. For the problem as a whole, he urged measures to reduce
the number of farms and for selling commodities abroad. In short, he
favored a long-range program plus immediate "crisis" measures.

As the meeting progressed, the farm program came under increasing
questioning. Stassen suggested that the heavy sums used to store
surpluses might be put to better use retiring land from cultivation.
Wilson noted that irrigation and fertilizer programs were creating
more surpluses. Brownell observed that Benson's report led to the
conclusion that the farm situation would not have bettered by the
fall of 1956 (when the Presidential campaign would be on), and
he also contrasted this with the improvement that had been achieved
in the industrial situation in the preceding year. Benson said that at
least the farm situation would remain steady, but he warned that
no quick solution was in sight. Brownell reminded the Cabinet that
troubles on the farm were standing out in contrast to good times in
the city.

Humphrey questioned whether a great deal could be done about
the farm problem except to let natural processes do their work. As
for the recession, he said that the things the administration did
were without great effect. The important fact, he argued, was that
the administration had established confidence in the minds of
the people that it would not try all sorts of manipulations with the
economy. There was no panacea for the farm problem and the

administration should not panic in the face of the situation, Humphrey said. The Secretary was not sure that business would continue to be as good in 1956 as it was in 1955.

Dulles cautioned against any thought of dumping surpluses abroad because of the resentment this would cause among our allies.

Secretary McKay was convinced that planned economy does not work. The country, he said, would be in the best possible shape when it could return to private enterprise unfettered by bureaucratic interference. He cited, for example, the natural shift in usages of land to meet changes in the price of commodities. He advocated a return to the fundamentals of the Constitution.

As the presiding officer, Nixon summarized the discussion. It showed, he said, no disagreement on the soundness of the long-range program outlined in Benson's report and agreement on the necessity for seeking additional measures. The Vice-President said he was sure the Cabinet recognized the political implications of the problem and the significance of Brownell's points. It was important, Nixon concluded, that the administration should arouse hope for improvement among the farmers and publicize the actions it was taking to better conditions.

Adams said that before his illness Eisenhower had shown a deep interest in this problem.

Cabinet, October 14, 1955

At Nixon's suggestion the Cabinet tape-recorded a birthday greeting to the President.

Adams reported that the preceding day the President had told the doctors it was his best since becoming ill. The President was anxious to get back into the swing of things, and numerous matters were now being discussed with him. During one of these conferences the President said he believed that the number of Federal employees was still too high. He felt that the number of new employees being hired by the government could be cut by perhaps a hundred thousand, and he asked Adams to relay his views to the Cabinet.

Reporting on his twenty-five-minute call at the hospital, Dulles had found the President's mind fresh and vigorous and had come away feeling that Eisenhower was ready to apply himself to any problem that might become acute.

Arthur Burns presented a program for assistance to depressed areas. An Agency for Area Development would be established in the Department of Commerce to provide technical assistance and make loans to assist local rehabilitation plans. Federal participation would be modest and the states would co-operate as partners.

Weeks questioned the creation of a new lending agency, and Humphrey cautioned against loans to perpetuate or bring into existence industries that were uneconomic and could not withstand certain inevitable changes. This would amount to taxing thriving concerns to subsidize potential rivals at considerable risk to the government, he said. Wilson, recalling his "bird dog" remark, asked whether it was sound to attempt artificially to stimulate activity in a particular area when it served no natural purpose. Stassen said that something should be done, perhaps with experimentation first through a "pilot plant." Humphrey agreed, as did Nixon. The Vice-President summarized the discussion as producing agreement that some program was necessary but that further study was required. (In Denver on October 24 the President gave "strong approval" to plans for introducing the Burns program in the next Congress.)

Nixon said that on his recent visit to Denver the President had asked him to carry back word that he was proud of the manner in which the Cabinet was carrying on in his absence. Eisenhower told the Vice-President he was sure that in the whole of American history there had never been another Cabinet like this one.

(During the President's convalescence Rabb sent Eisenhower summaries of Cabinet proceedings.)

Cabinet, October 21, 1955

Adams said that the President's interest in government affairs and his activity continued to increase. Particularly, Adams recounted the President's air of confidence and his optimism about the future. Eisenhower wished to get started with his work on the State of the Union message, Adams reported.

Dulles discussed the agenda of the forthcoming Geneva meeting of the Big Four Foreign Ministers. He said the conference might be successful if it could undertake a discussion of the German question, which the Soviets were anxious to avoid. He reported that he had discussed the conference with the President and with Congressional leaders. The leaders, he said, had given him their support.

The Vice-President then read the following letter:

> Denver, Colorado
> October 19, 1955

Dear Dick:

I want to say a word to you, and through you to my Cabinet associates, about the task which Foster Dulles will be assuming at Geneva. As head of the American Delegation he will be carrying a heavy load of responsibility, not only as Secretary of State, but as my personal representative having my complete confidence and with whom I have continuous close understanding.

This second meeting at Geneva was one of the steps toward solving the world problems which Foster and I planned together and which we have talked over fully not only before my illness, but twice since.

I hope that each one in Government will do whatever he can to make Foster's task easier. The Secretary of State must have the discretionary authority which is needed if there is to be effective negotiation and the spirit of conciliation which I have called for at that meeting. He must be the one who both at the conference table and before the world speaks for me with authority for our country.

With warm regard,

> As ever,
> DWIGHT D. EISENHOWER

The Vice-President
Washington, D. C.

Cabinet, October 28, 1955

Reporting on the President's progress, Adams said that Eisenhower should be able to participate in Cabinet and N.S.C. meetings by the end of the year.

Mitchell outlined the proposed legislation the Department of Labor expected to submit to Congress and said, in answer to a question by Brownell, that it would not include any recommendation for making unions subject to the antitrust laws. It would include the amendments to the Taft-Hartley Act unsuccessfully proposed in

1954 and 1955. Mitchell talked of the possibility of extending greater recognition to unions of government employees. Summerfield did not think this was a good idea.

Nixon said that public opinion polls showed that increasingly workers felt that the Republican Party served their interest best in economic affairs. The Democrats had slipped slightly in these samplings, he told the Cabinet.

Weeks reviewed studies of the recently established Cabinet committee on the highway program. The administration's plan for financing new highways by bonds outside the debt limit had been dropped, he said, in favor of raising money by new or increased taxes on gasoline and tires and higher excises on trucks and buses. Weeks desired to present this program at the meeting of the highway committee of the governors' conference, scheduled for November 3.

Humphrey agreed with these recommendations. He felt very strongly, he said, that he had erred the previous spring in testifying in favor of the bond issue. He realized now, he went on, that Congress could not enter into an agreement to commit revenues from certain taxes to particular purposes over a future period and thus the proposed bonds would have been backed only by the good faith of the government and general revenues. Adams asked for assurances—and received them—that under the new plan revenues from the increased taxes would be devoted in entirety to the highway program to ward off opposition from the states. The Cabinet approved submission of the committee's recommendations to the governors' committee.

The Postmaster General presented the case for increased postal rates. Nixon was doubtful whether the administration should blow up a storm over this issue in the election-year session. As a possible course he suggested that Summerfield seek a way of getting action on this issue without incurring the sharp opposition of the Democratic leaders. Stassen said that perhaps Summerfield could obtain Democratic support for establishment of a bipartisan commission to fix rates and thus remove this business from the field of politics. Summerfield felt sure that Speaker Rayburn would not go along with this idea. The Cabinet agreed that further study should be given to the final position the administration would take on postal rates.

(On February 1, 1956, the President asked Congress to increase rates so as to bring in an additional $406,000,000. Three-cent stamps would go to four cents and airmail stamps from six to seven cents.)

After nearly seven weeks in the hospital the President was discharged on November 11 and headed back to Washington immediately. At the airport in Denver he made a brief speech thanking those who had sent him messages and prayed for him. "Misfortune, and particularly the misfortune of illness," he said, "brings to all of us an understanding of how good people are." That same afternoon thousands turned out in Washington to welcome him home. As he stepped off the plane in his familiar tan polo coat and brown snap-brim hat he was greeted by Nixon and former President Hoover. "I am happy the doctors have given me at least a parole, if not a pardon," Eisenhower said, "and I expect to be back at my accustomed duties, although they say I must ease my way into 'em and not bulldoze my way into them."

After a long weekend in the White House during which he began taking practice swings again with his golf clubs on the south lawn, he drove to Gettysburg with Mrs. Eisenhower on November 14 to resume convalescence at his farm on the edge of the battlefield. Lincoln Square was jammed with seven thousand people who sang and cheered the Eisenhowers when they arrived. The square was hung with banners and placards reading GLAD YOU'RE HOME, IKE and WELCOME HOME, IKE AND MAMIE.

The President attended his first Cabinet meeting since his illness on November 22. It was held in trim, rustic Laurel Cottage on the mountainside at Camp David. As the meeting was breaking up, the President asked all members to wait so that he could take this chance to thank them and his staff for the way they had conducted themselves in his absence. For five weeks after his attack, he recalled, he had not seen a newspaper. However, he was shown an editorial expressing surprise that the Cabinet and staff had worked so well together under the circumstances. Perhaps, the President laughed, there might even have been a few hints that the Cabinet did better without him.

The only thing that surprised him, he went on, was that the editorial writer should have expressed surprise that the Cabinet worked harmoniously and successfully in following the administration's familiar and practicable middle course between the extremes of too little and too much. He knew, he said, that the Cabinet could carry on because of the dedication of the members to this policy at home and abroad.

The events of recent weeks, Eisenhower said, gave him pride in the choices he had made for members of his Cabinet and staff. He expressed his gratitude for their conduct. This Cabinet, he thought, was unique. He recalled that as long ago as George Washington's administration strife had rent the Cabinet while Hamilton and Jefferson were both members of it. No other Cabinet, in his opinion, had ever been so completely dedicated to a set of broad principles upon which all could work together. He was glad of the chance for putting this to the test. He added, however, that he had not relished the particular circumstances that brought it about.

CHAPTER 29

Winter of Decision

Second Term or Retirement? – The President Faces Other Problems – The Soviet Economic Offensive – Threats in the Middle East – The "4-H Club" – Eisenhower Calls a Private Conference – J. Edgar Hoover Reports to the Cabinet on Racial Tensions in the South – Eisenhower's Liberal '56 Program – A Budget Miracle at Last – Will He Run?

When Dwight Eisenhower first learned in September that he had suffered a coronary thrombosis, neither he nor the rest of the world, by and large, supposed the question could ever be asked again seriously whether he would be a candidate for re-election in 1956. Interest soared in other potential Republican candidates—Warren, Dewey, Nixon, Knowland, Stassen, Lodge, Humphrey, Adams, Governor Herter of Massachusetts, and even Milton Eisenhower.

So strong was the President's recovery, however, that by the time he reached Gettysburg the question of his candidacy instead of being preposterous was monopolizing attention.

It tantalized the stock market. Foreign governments studied it. It held the Republican Party in a state of utter suspense and tormented the Democrats. Press, radio and television wore it threadbare. From one end of the country to the other it was a ceaseless topic of conversation. For the President the question not only was laden with deep personal considerations, such as his health and the happiness of his family, but it also placed upon him the responsibility for a decision the consequences of which would affect future history. But there were also other and very difficult questions bearing on decisions of a different sort waiting when he returned to active participation in the government in the winter of 1955-56.

The most vexing of these was the cause of a meeting in the President's study at 5 o'clock on the afternoon of January 19, 1956. Present were Dulles, Under Secretary of State Hoover, Adams, Hauge, Dodge—who, after resigning as Budget Director, had become Special Assistant to the President on trade policy—and John B. Hollister, chief of the State Department's International Co-operation Administration.

The session was held against a background of historic change in international relations. In November the Big Four Foreign Ministers' conference in Geneva had ended in failure. Issues, such as the reunification of Germany, which the conference at the summit had handed unresolved to the Foreign Ministers were no nearer settlement when they adjourned. In the meanwhile the Soviet Union, with Bulganin and Khrushchev as its globetrotting salesmen, reached into Asia and Africa and even Latin America to challenge the long supremacy of the Western nations in trade and economic influence. The so-called spirit of Geneva was submerged in Khrushchev's gaudy attacks on the West, catering to the surging nationalism of old colonial areas.

Within the administration there had been divided counsel on how to meet this challenge. Nixon, Rockefeller and Stassen favored a dramatic response by the United States through material increase in mutual assistance, particularly in the economic and technical spheres. An opposing group, dubbed the "4-H Club" because of its dominance by Humphrey, Hollister, Herbert Hoover, Jr., and Rowland Hughes, held that while mutual assistance should continue, no great increase was needed because there was a limit to how much could usefully be spent in underdeveloped areas. In the end the President struck a compromise, asking Congress to increase the next appropriation for foreign aid from the then current level of $2,700,000,000 to $4,900,-000,000. He asked for limited authority to help other countries undertake large projects like the Aswan Dam in Egypt. Partly because some of his recommendations did not make greater headway, Rockefeller resigned as Special Assistant to the President. Often during those months Rockefeller's liberal views and buoyant temperament had clashed with the deeply conservative outlook of Herbert Hoover, Jr.

During the winter the President and Dulles approved a number of measures for reducing the danger of war in the Middle East. Veering away from the Tripartite Declaration of 1950, in which we, the British and French agreed to act "both within and outside" the U.N., American policy shifted in favor of action through the U.N. The White House issued a statement that the United States was "determined to support and assist any nation" in the Middle East that was the victim of aggression. Following Eden's visit to Washington in February, Eisenhower authorized the strengthening of the United States Sixth Fleet in the Mediterranean. While still refraining from joining the Middle East Treaty Organization, formed to oppose Soviet expansion to the south, the United States entered into more active participation in some of its affairs and agreed to establish military liaison with it. The President declared it to be against the policy of the United States to participate in the arms race by making large shipments to Israel or other Middle Eastern countries after the Soviet-Egyptian arms deal. However, the United States offered no objection to Israel's buying arms, if she wished, from Canada, France or other NATO countries.

When, therefore, the President and his advisers met in the White House on January 19, they had before them a whole series of new Soviet moves. Congress and the press were asking whether the Soviet economic offensive, coupled with its progress in jet bombers and missiles, its thrust into the Middle East, its exploitation of the fierce anticolonial spirit around the world, the waning fortunes of pro-Western parties in many vital areas and the troubles in NATO, threatened to tilt the balance of power in favor of the Communist world.

In opening the meeting the President said that he had called the group together to consider the Soviet attempts at economic penetration of Asia and Africa. The subject, he said, was one that was giving him a good deal of concern.

During the discussion Dodge warned that the United States should not get into a contest of bidding against Soviet "shills."

"What is a shill?" Eisenhower inquired.

Dodge explained that a shill was a decoy employed by an auctioneer to make bogus offers to get the bidding up.

The upshot of the meeting was that the President directed Dodge to make an exhaustive study of the new Soviet foreign economic policy, as a basis for later revisions in American policy.

Another problem before the President was the rise of racial tension and disorders in the South. The Cabinet considered segregation at its meeting on March 9. J. Edgar Hoover was present and made a long report.

In discussing resistance to segregation he noted that Democratic Senator James O. Eastland of Mississippi, new chairman of the Senate Judiciary Committee, had urged resistance at a meeting in Birmingham, Alabama, on February 10, saying, "The Anglo-Saxon people have held steadfast to the belief that resistance to tyranny is obedience to God." Hoover informed the Cabinet, however, that Eastland had not advocated violence. He quoted the Senator as having said at the same meeting, "The fight we wage must be a just and legal fight. Acts of violence and lawlessness have no place in our organization." He reviewed the Negro boycott of buses in Montgomery, Alabama, in protest against segregation, and the disorders at the University of Alabama to bar the admission of a Negro student, Autherine Lucy. Hoover called the latter a "disgraceful incident."

He then reported that the Communist Party was trying to infiltrate the National Association for the Advancement of Colored People, but that the association remained anti-Communist.

"The Communists have decided now," he continued, "to concentrate their activities in Alabama, Georgia and Mississippi since these are the growing areas of industrial concentration where Communists think they have their best chance to infiltrate and expand the party strength. The party is now engaged in an active program to send party members from the New England States to these three states where they will concentrate in the textile industry.

"The Communists intend to inject the Negro question into every possible issue. They claim that the unfortunate and brutal killing of fourteen-year-old Emmett Till in Greenwood, Mississippi, in August, 1955, is the finest thing that has happened from their standpoint. For public consumption they claim that the Till case is an historic event and the turning point in the Negro struggle for liberation."

The antisegregation white Citizens Councils throughout the South, Hoover said, "either could control the rising tensions or become the medium through which tensions might manifest themselves." The F.B.I. knew of 127 of these which had come into existence since the Supreme Court decision on school segregation. Hoover told the

Cabinet: "The Councils' program in some areas in applying economic pressure already has begun to make itself felt."

He cited a number of cases. For example: "A Negro dentist was told by the local bank he would be given no more financial assistance. A Negro gas-station operator who refused to put up a sign FOR COLORED ONLY was notified by the gas distributor that he would have to pay cash for oil and gas in advance. The local bank fixed a short deadline on his repayment of a loan. A doctor who was a member of the N.A.A.C.P. was told by patients that their employers would not pay their doctor bills in the future.

"Calm, judicious judgment, public education and real understanding are needed to avert explosive incidents," Hoover concluded. "The area of danger lies in friction between extremists on both sides ready with violence."

During the ensuing discussion Hoover said that the sale of firearms had increased significantly in the South—by 400 per cent in one community, he said, citing an extreme case.

Eisenhower said that as President he had a sworn duty to uphold the decisions of the Supreme Court. Whatever was necessary and proper for carrying out this duty he would do, he said. But he recalled that for many years the doctrine of separate but equal facilities, springing from another Supreme Court decision, had prevailed in the South and had established a pattern of life there. Now that a new Supreme Court decision necessitated a different pattern, he said, it would take time for people to uproot the old traditions and live by the new.

It was also a winter of important decisions for the President in the field of domestic legislation. In his fourth State of the Union message, read to Congress by clerks while Eisenhower was vacationing in Key West, he leaned toward liberal Democratic traditions in measures like the health and education programs. Breaking away from the conservative proposals Mrs. Hobby had advanced in previous years, he recommended $2,020,000,000 in Federal aid to education over the ensuing five years and $40,000,000 for Federal assistance to medical research. In a special farm message he proposed a billion-dollar "soil bank," an idea of Democratic origins for reducing surpluses by paying farmers to take land out of cultivation.

In Congress the Democratic majority restored rigid 90 per cent price supports, which Eisenhower had rejected two years ago, and practically challenged him to veto the bill in an election year. He did. It was his sixty-seventh veto.

"Bad as some of the provisions of this bill are," he wrote, "I would have signed it if, in total, it could be interpreted as sound and good for the farmers and the nation."

After three years of striving toward this goal the President was able to announce in his State of the Union message that he expected that the current budget for the fiscal year ending June 30, 1956, would be balanced and that he would submit a balanced budget for the fiscal year 1957. A significant fact about the new budget was, however, that while, owing to increased revenues, it would be in balance, expenditures would go up. Not only that, but the trend toward future expenditures would rise also. This was a reversal of the earlier Eisenhower budgets, which had forecast decreases in spending. There were a number of reasons for the rise. The government planned to provide more services. The salaries of government employees, like those of other employees, had gone up. The heavy costs of national security were pushing higher all the time. The prices of goods the government had to buy had risen.

As was often observed early in January, the prospect of a balanced budget, expanded social services, new benefits to the farmer, peace in the world and prosperity at home to the tune of nearly $400,000,-000,000 a year in the gross national product all added up to pretty comfortable circumstances for a President seeking re-election. But still they did not answer the question that was on everyone's mind: Would Eisenhower run?

CHAPTER 30

"Positive—That Is, Affirmative"

*In the President's Study – The President Is Advised to Run – Milton
Eisenhower Sums Up the Arguments – Hopes for Being a One-Term
President – He Weighs His Decision – The Considerations – The Crucial
X-Ray Test – Thomasville – The Riddle of the Nixon Candidacy – "I
Shall Accept"*

The hour of decision was approaching on the night of Friday,
January 13, 1956. President Eisenhower took his seat at the head
of a circle of intimate friends in the White House and explained why
he had invited them to an extraordinary conference.

One hundred and eleven days had elapsed since his heart attack.
With almost every day that passed his health came steadily back to
him. Through months of convalescence in Denver, at his Gettysburg
farm and at Key West after Christmas, the pendulum began swinging
back toward the possibility that he might run again. By January 13
the pendulum was gaining momentum.

Glancing around the circle, the President said that soon he would
have a profound decision to make. He could not make it yet because
he still awaited decisive medical tests and the final word of his
doctors. But he said that he had called his friends in this evening
and would welcome their comments on the great problem confronting
him. One after another he went around the group calling upon his
guests by their familiar names—Foster, Cabot, Tom, Jim and so forth.
Each spoke in his turn.

The meeting was in the President's second-floor study—or trophy
room, as he calls it, because it houses his World War II trophies. On

the east wall hangs a full-length portrait of the President's mother and on the opposite wall a full-length portrait of his father, the late David J. Eisenhower, both by Thomas Stephens, the artist. (The President considers the painting of his mother the best that has been done of her. He does not think the one of his father is equally good, but then, he says, his father had a hard expression to catch.)

Eisenhower and his guests wore business suits. The President sat with his back to the fireplace. On his left was Brownell; on his right, Leonard Hall.

The others were Dulles, Lodge, Adams, Persons, Humphrey, Summerfield, Hagerty, Pyle, Tom Stephens, the New York attorney and former Appointment Secretary to the President, and Dr. Milton Eisenhower.

The gathering had been set originally for Tuesday, January 10, but cancelled when word of it leaked out. With the greatest secrecy it was rescheduled for Friday night, and the President went to such pains to keep any hint of it from escaping that he personally brought the place cards for dinner over from his office to the mansion in his pocket. What then transpired has never before been recorded.

As the thirteen men and Mrs. Eisenhower went into the state dining room on the ground floor, the President confided, "I arranged the order of seating so that some of you who don't see each other so often can be together."

When dinner was over, Mrs. Eisenhower departed and the men went upstairs to the study, where the President lost little time in beginning his canvass. As he went around the circle, familiar sentiment built up steadily in favor of his running again.

His place in the world was unique, he was told. No other American was in a position to exert such influence for peace—so long as he was in the White House. Eisenhower had made great strides toward unifying the Republican Party and the American people, but the goal was not yet reached. Among Republicans, only Eisenhower was sure of victory in November. If a Democrat was elected, the trend which Eisenhower had started toward moderation and decentralization would be reversed.

Dulles warned that nuclear war would threaten the very existence of mankind. The President had a God-given ability for reconciling differences among men and nations and, if his health permitted, he should go on using this talent.

Others, like Lodge, emphasized Eisenhower's role at home. Lodge spoke with high praise for the President's work in healing divisions among the American people. This accomplishment was largely responsible, Lodge ventured, for the unparalleled prosperity the country was enjoying. The President's "sensitivity" to world opinion and his experience in international affairs, he concluded, put him in a matchless position to lead the United States through the next four years.

Political considerations were advanced. Stephens, urging the President to run, proposed that his announcement be made as early as feasible to set other prospective Republican candidates straight and to encourage pro-Eisenhower Congressional candidates to enter primaries. Stephens drew a laugh from the President when he added, "This is important to other Presidential candidates, including me."

Summerfield told Eisenhower that his work was unfinished. He recalled that for twenty years Republicans had developed habits of thought which Eisenhower had been forced to reverse. He said the President had clarified the thinking of Republicans and had reestablished the party as one of constructive action.

The arrangement was that each guest would comment until it was Milton Eisenhower's turn. He would then sum up the pros and cons. If each of the guests, or most of them, had solemnly advised Eisenhower not to run again, the American political scene might have undergone a great change in 1956. But by the time the President came to his brother, pro opinion was unanimous. Later he remarked jokingly to some of his guests, "I didn't know you'd all be against me."

Dr. Eisenhower summarized the arguments on both sides. One of the most telling points he made in favor of a second term was that if Eisenhower was to work effectively for peace, it would have to be from the White House, not from retirement. A Democratic President, his brother pointed out, would resent intrusion into foreign affairs.

Dr. Eisenhower marshaled forcefully the arguments against running. His brother had already spent more than forty years in public service. Four more years in the Presidency would be a great burden. These were years Eisenhower might enjoy with his family, doing the things he had long wanted to do—reading, writing, playing, traveling extensively and using his influence as a distinguished private citizen for peace.

In the President's mind, obviously, the arguments for outweighed the arguments against. While he did not say so that night, his guests seemed to sense it. A remark Brownell made to Milton Eisenhower as they were leaving suggested as much.

"As one who has had the task many times of summing up before a court when there wasn't much to summarize on the other side," he said, "I know what a tough job you had."

Some of the guests took away with them the impression, however, that this comment did not exactly capture Dr. Eisenhower's feelings—that Milton had felt indeed that a very great deal was to be said on the other side, perhaps even more than was to be said in favor of the President's running. But this was only one impression.

From the time he entered the White House Eisenhower's deep desire was to be a one-term President. In the years that followed he expressed this wish many times in private, and those who know him most intimately are convinced that he meant it. Nevertheless this desire for a single term was not so tightly sealed that cross-currents could not flow through it. One such current, and a strong one, was flowing when the President went to Denver in August, 1955, soon after the Big Four meeting.

When the President left Geneva, he had a feeling that somehow he had got through to the Soviet leaders. In particular, he felt that Zhukov liked and respected him. He knew perfectly well that Zhukov was an old-time Communist Party member as well as soldier and that Soviet leadership had not abandoned its old objectives. Still, Eisenhower sensed that he enjoyed a relationship with Khrushchev, Bulganin and Zhukov such as no other American did. He believed that occasionally he could communicate with the Soviet leaders and that there might be times when this contact could be very important. He sensed furthermore that he had developed over a long period a special relationship with other European leaders, notably Eden, which would be valuable in dealing with international problems of the next few years.

Such considerations served as a counterweight to his desire to leave office on January 20, 1957, but not yet a decisive one. He was still grappling with the problem before his heart attack. Sometimes he was resolved to bow out; then again he would drop this categorical attitude and weigh reasons for running. However, the time when he would have to announce his intentions was still far enough away so that he did not have to reach a final decision, and the question was in the balance when he was stricken.

During the early weeks of convalescence in Fitzsimons General Hospital Eisenhower took it for granted that his illness barred a second term. Mrs. Eisenhower was dead set against it. But Adams did not count the President out, nor did the political professionals in his Cabinet like Brownell and Summerfield. From the beginning such associates managed to keep the question open. Of course, they would not march into the hospital room and urge the President to run in 1956. But what they did do, successfully, was to combat whatever feelings Eisenhower had—and he was not without them—that he was washed up as a public figure. They kept holding before him the thought that one way or another he still had a large role ahead of him. In public meanwhile Hall was going ahead audaciously on his own proclaiming that he knew of no change in the Republicans' plans in 1956 and that Eisenhower was still his candidate.

Not until the second stage of his convalescence at Gettysburg did the President begin seriously to discuss the problem of 1956. And this was a time when even the worst days in the White House looked rather appealing by contrast. For Eisenhower, Gettysburg came close to being five weeks of torment. In Denver he had escaped the depression that often follows a coronary thrombosis. At Gettysburg it struck. His morale slumped. His spirits were low. He fretted over government affairs. On top of this the weather turned bad, and he was confined as he had never been in his life except in the hospital. Sometimes he could not get out at all, and when he did, the putting green on the farm as likely as not was frozen stiff. Unable to walk a great deal, he was sometimes forced to ride in a jeep for something to do. Indoors he was tense and nervous and stalked about the house with a golf club for a cane.

His recovery continued, however, and by December he was able to devote more and more of each day to work. By the time he returned to the White House five days before Christmas, he was itching to do still more.

"Don't give me mush," he would tell his associates. "I want the hard ones now."

His candidacy was very much on his mind when he went to Key West after Christmas. With some of those who are closest to him, including his brother and General Gruenther, he discussed the arguments for and against a second term during his vacation. With the doctors allowing him an increase in physical activity, which enabled him to drive golf balls and take brisk walks, he began to feel better and more vigorous. This gave him confidence in his strength and brightened his spirits. By the time he left Key West early in January there is little doubt that he was tending toward a decision to run again.

Yet, as was to be the case throughout the next month and a half, his public utterances on the subject were permeated by a mood of skepticism. The arguments he listened to in private were predominantly in favor of his running, but he emphasized to the people, or so it seemed, the reasons why, possibly, he should not. Rather than diminish the significance of his heart attack, he rather solemnly held it up to view.

"It is a very critical thing to change governments in this country at a time that is unexpected," he said at a press conference in Key West on January 8, 1956, before returning to Washington. (He stressed the same point in private conversations.) "We accustom ourselves . . . [to] changing our government every four years. But always something happens that is untoward when a government is changed at other times. It is a rather startling thing."

By a margin of nearly five to one the reporters at that conference were of the opinion that Eisenhower would not run. But in less than a week he was sitting that historic evening in his study listening intently as his friends and advisers urged him, one after another, to seek a second term. From that time on he gravitated toward his ultimate decision. Six days later he wrote to Henry E. Jackson, Deputy Secretary of State of New Hampshire, saying that he had no objection to having his name filed in the state's primary but emphasizing that this was not to be interpreted as meaning that he had

decided to seek a second term. In this letter he again raised very
pointedly the question which was on everyone's mind.

It would be idle to pretend [he wrote] that my health can be wholly
restored to the excellent state in which the doctors believed me to be in
mid-September. At the same time, my doctors report to me that the
progress I am making toward a reasonable level of strength is normal and
satisfactory.

My future life must be carefully regulated to avoid excessive fatigue.
My reasons for obedience to medical authorities are not solely personal;
I must obey them out of respect for the responsibilities I carry.

Again at a press conference on January 25 he said:

Now I have to guess as to the next five years, and the problem is what
will be the effect on the Presidency, not on me, and that is the problem.
And you can yourself, without any long dissertation here, just lay out
all the factors of energy, the intensity with which you can attack your
problems, the zip and the zest that you can take into conferences when
you have to get something done for the good of the United States.

Now this morning maybe I feel very zestful, but I do know that I have
had an attack.

Because of his recovery, however, even then his heart attack was
diminishing—some who are in a unique position to judge say
vanishing—as a factor in his decision. He still awaited the final word
of his doctors, of course, but increasingly the coronary thrombosis
was taking on the character of merely an intervening incident so far
as his decision on 1956 was concerned.

The reason was that certain consequences of the illness canceled
each other out. On the one hand was the fact that a person who has
had a coronary is more likely to have another attack than one who
has not been stricken. On the other hand, there was the danger,
acknowledged by his doctors, that because the President had lived
a life of decision and activity, retirement could bring him frustrations that would be a greater strain on his heart than the burdens
of the Presidency. So far as his health was concerned, therefore, it
was six of one or half a dozen of another. Thus once the doctors
had satisfied the President that he had recovered fully and he had
satisfied himself that he could live up to the regimen they pre-

scribed, the heart attack was neutralized as an element in his decision.

In the end the considerations which led him to run again were the same ones which would have influenced him whether he had had a coronary thrombosis or whether he had not.

What were these considerations?

To begin with, when Eisenhower took office in 1953 he had hoped that in four years the Republican Party could be reformed from its role of an opposition party and invigorated with more progressive leaders. He had hoped for the rise of what he called "positive" Republicans as opposed to "negative" Republicans. He regarded the negative attitude of many Republicans in the preceding twenty years as the curse of the party. He spoke in exactly those terms. He had hoped also that from the ranks of these "positive" Republicans would emerge a leader with a chance of being elected to the Presidency. More precisely, he had hoped for the emergence of many leaders, who could carry the party to victory in Congress as well as in the White House.

To a degree the transformation came about. Some thirty-nine new Republican state chairmen had been elected, and on the whole he found them to be younger men who believed in something and were not merely against everything.

Nevertheless the extent of the party's reformation disappointed him. The comprehensive change never quite came off. He asked himself, therefore, whether if he was in office eight years, the transformation would be greater in the end than after four years. The answer seemed to be yes.

Another consideration which the President took very seriously was the opinion being voiced by the experts that he alone among the Republicans could win the election. In December, General Clay discussed this point with him. Clay told the President that he would soon be meeting privately with groups of Republicans. He said that he was going to tell these gatherings that, his health permitting, Eisenhower would run again if he believed it his duty to do so. And he would further say, Clay continued, that one of the things that would make the President consider it his duty would be the prospect that otherwise the "old crowd" would return to the White House.

After listening to Clay, the President did not ask him to refrain from saying these things. And Clay said them. He said them at a meeting of Republican businessmen and leaders at the Links Club on East Sixty-second Street in New York and at a series of meetings in Brownell's house in Washington. Attending the meetings at the Attorney General's were Thomas E. Dewey, former Governor Dan Thornton, of Colorado; Paul Hoffman, Under Secretary of Commerce Williams, William Robinson, Tom Stephens, W. Alton Jones, chairman of the board of the Cities Service Company; Charles S. Jones, president of the Richfield Oil Corporation, and Fred G. Gurley, president of the Atchison, Topeka & Sante Fe.

Eisenhower felt that to some extent he and his administration had been able to reverse a trend which had developed under the Democrats. He was well aware that so far the difference was only one of degree. He knew that he had not turned the government about in three years. But still he felt that he had edged it in a new direction: away from extremes, away from deficits, away from centralization and toward fiscal stability, renewed reliance on private enterprise and a new relationship between the Federal and state governments. Slow though it might be, he believed that the longer this trend could be maintained, the better chance it would have of permanence. He did not feel that the Republican Party itself was fully united behind his philosophy of moderation. Would it, he asked, be more likely to achieve such unity if he was in office another four years? Again the answer seemed to be yes.

With the return of his health the President came under increasingly great pressure from many sides to declare himself a candidate.

There is good authority for saying that with respect to these foregoing considerations—the rebuilding of the party and the perpetuation of the trend he believed he had begun—this pressure had little or no effect on him. Eisenhower did not feel that he owed the leaders of the Republican Party any obligation to run again, and he followed his own thoughts.

But when it came to a third major consideration, Eisenhower was responsive to pressure, and doubtless the advice and the appeals he received had a deep effect. This was the part he could play in preserving peace. Individually and collectively, as at the meeting in his study on January 13, his friends and advisers reminded him of the uniqueness of his position in this respect. Not only from all over the country but from all over the world he received appeals to run again in the interest of peace. It was a theme that ran through much of the American press and many public speeches. "Mr. Eisenhower has the capacity and the talent and the trust to make a unique contribution to the cause of peace which America needs and which the world needs at this crisis period of the hydrogen age," said the *Herald Tribune* in a front-page editorial on January 30, "He is the right man in the right place at the right time to deal with the one issue which towers above all others—the cause of peace or war."

Constantly Eisenhower heard this appeal repeated, sometimes expressed in terms of duty, to which he seemed peculiarly responsive.

"It was this advice," an intimate said later, "that he took to bed with him when he was making up his mind."

One of the critical moments leading up to the decision came on February 11 at Walter Reed Hospital when the President's doctors took two X-ray pictures and placed one upon the other. The one on the bottom was a picture of Eisenhower's heart before his attack. Superimposed upon it was an up-to-date picture. Everything hinged on whether the damaged heart had enlarged since he had resumed more or less normal activity in January. Because the President had been under a doctor's eye every day, this question was the only one on which his physicians needed to be reassured. With the X-rays in front of them they bent forward to see if the outlines of one heart were contiguous to those of the other. When the pictures were fitted together, the two hearts matched almost precisely. This was decisive. It was the green light to the President to run again.

On February 14 the doctors announced at a press conference that "the President's health continues to be satisfactory."

"Medically," Dr. White said in answer to a question, "I think we would agree that his present condition and the favorable chances in the future should enable him to be able to carry on his present active life satisfactorily for this period, as I have said, for five to ten years, knowing full well, as we have just emphasized, the hazards and uncertainties of the future."

When asked if he would vote for Eisenhower if he should run again, White said that he would.

From this day forward all signs pointed toward Eisenhower's running. The next day he went to Secretary Humphrey's plantation at Thomasville, Georgia, where he tested his strength playing golf and hunting.

"He plunged into it with what you might call an I'll-show-'em attitude," one of his companions recalled later.

After a strenuous walk through waist-high grass hunting quail one day, the President returned to the house, saying proudly, "Well, I'm feeling pretty good. I didn't get tired out. It didn't bother me."

The reassurance that this exercise at Thomasville gave him was the final brick that went into the making of his decision. He flew back to Washington on Saturday, February 25, and began preparing secretly with Hagerty for announcing on Wednesday, the 29th, first at a press conference and later on a broadcast, that he would run. Mrs. Eisenhower, it appears, did not try to influence his decision one way or another. Some of those best acquainted with the family believe that in the gloomy November and December days at Gettysburg she had come to the conclusion that her husband was not ready for retirement.

At his celebrated press conference on Wednesday Eisenhower said that he had still been arguing with himself the day before as to whether he should run. But he was speaking in the sense that since his decision had not yet been announced, he could still change his mind. By the time he had returned from Thomasville on Saturday he was clear as to his decision.

On Tuesday afternoon he began passing the word to a few close associates like Nixon, Hall, Adams and Persons, who saw him individually (for Adams and Persons this was a formality because they knew what he had decided almost as soon as he had made up his mind), and he telephoned his brother at Penn State and invited him to Washington for the broadcast Wednesday evening. But even on Wednesday before the press conference, which was scheduled for 10:30 A.M., most of the White House staff did not know for sure that he was going to run. They did not know, but they sensed it as Hagerty, presiding as he always does at staff meetings on the mornings of press conferences, went through the order of business without saying a word about the question that was on everyone's mind. All knew that Hagerty was privy to the secret, but no one could quite get up nerve to ask him. Many of the staff felt, however, that if the President had decided not to run, Hagerty would have dropped a hint at this last minute. When he did not, they were confident that Eisenhower was going to announce his candidacy. One of the chief reasons the secret was held so tightly was that the President wanted to ward off any charges that the administration was a party to manipulation of the stock market.

Early in the morning, reporters had begun lining up for the press conference outside the Indian Treaty Room on the fourth floor of the Executive Offices Building, across the street from the west wing of the White House. Three hundred and eleven of them had jammed into the ornate room when at 10:31 the President walked in, dressed in a tan suit and vest, white shirt and brown tie. His head was bowed slightly as if in thought.

Great suspense filled the high-ceilinged room as he began to speak. In a circumstance like this, Presidents seem to experience an irresistible temptation to tantalize reporters. Eisenhower began by calling upon the people to support the Red Cross drive. Next he told of his pleasure over the visit of President Giovanni Gronchi, of Italy, who had just arrived in Washington. Then he voiced his opposition to the rigid price supports which had been written into the farm bill pending in the Senate. From there he dragged his impatient audience into the subject of the Upper Colorado River Basin project, which was then up for consideration before the House. He hoped it would be approved. Seven minutes had passed. Unconsciously he unbuttoned his coat. He thrust his left hand into the pocket of his trousers.

"Now my next announcement," he said, "involves something more personal, but I think it will be of interest to you because you have asked me so many questions about it.

"I have promised this body that when I reached a decision as to my own attitude toward my own personal future, I would let you know as soon as I reached such a decision. Now I have reached a decision. But I have found, as I did so, that there were so many factors and considerations involved that I saw the answer could not be expressed just in the simple terms of yes and no. Some full explanation to the American people is not only necessary, but I would never consent to go before them unless I were assured that they did understand these things, these influences, these possibilities."

The reporters groped for the meaning of all this. Was the President saying that he was or was not going to run? He continued:

"Moreover, I would not allow my name to go before the Republican convention unless they, all the Republicans, understood, so that they would not be nominating some individual other than they thought they were nominating."

This could only have one meaning—yes. But the President went on talking. He said:

"So for both reasons, because I don't know, certainly for certain, that the Republican convention, after hearing the entire story, want me, I don't know whether the people want me, but I am—I will say this:

"I am asking as quickly as this conference is over, I am asking for time on television and radio. I am going directly to the American people and tell them the full facts and my answer within the limits I have so sketchily observed; but which I will explain in detail tonight so as to get the story out in one continuous narrative—my answer will be positive; that is, affirmative."

Meanwhile another important question was to be left open. Neither then nor for some weeks would Eisenhower say whether he wanted Nixon again as Vice-Presidential candidate. The President repeatedly said he liked Nixon, and, at his press conference on March 7, 1956, he recounted that he had asked the Vice-President to "chart his own course and tell me what he would like to do." He resented speculation that he was trying to "dump" Nixon. But it was not until April 27 that he signified his desire or his willingness, whichever the case may be, to have Nixon as his running mate in 1956.

After a call on the President that day Nixon told reporters: "I informed the President that in the event the President and the delegates to the convention reached the decision that it was their desire for me to serve as the nominee of the Republican Party for their Vice-President, I would be honored to accept that nomination again . . . as I did in 1952."

Hagerty broke into the interview at this point to say to reporters: "The President has asked me to tell you gentlemen that he was delighted to hear of the Vice-President's decision."

To practical politicians that statement meant another Eisenhower-Nixon ticket. There are those who still believe that the President and his associates tried, but failed, to maneuver Nixon out of the nomination in favor of someone more mature and more acceptable to Democratic and independent voters. This would have been in keeping with the wishes of some of the President's staunch Republican supporters. On the other hand, certain political lieutenants in close touch with the President's thinking during those months do not believe this.

The truth may lie somewhere along the line that Eisenhower was trying to keep the Vice-Presidential nomination open until Nixon's standing with the party could be tested, but that by April it was clear that his strength among regular Republicans was so firm that leaving him off the ticket would have been a difficult business.

But having arrived, by February 29, at his own decision to run, the President's immediate task was to address himself to the people. Twelve hours after his press conference the President spoke by television from his office. While he was waiting to go on the air, someone called attention to the motto on his desk: *Suaviter in modo fortiter in re.*

"That proves I'm an egghead," he chuckled.

Launching into his speech, he said:

I have decided that if the Republican Party chooses to renominate me, I shall accept. Thereafter, if the people of this country should elect me, I shall continue to serve them in the office I now hold.

He discussed the problem of his health very frankly. He said:

Aside from all other considerations, I have been faced with the fact that I am classed as a recovered heart patient. This means that to some undetermined extent, I may possibly be a greater risk than is the normal person of my age. My doctors assure me that this increased percentage of risk is not great.

So far as my own personal sense of well being is concerned, I am as well as before the attack occurred. It is, however, true that the opinions and conclusions of the doctors that I can continue to carry the burdens of the Presidency contemplate for me a regime of ordered work activity, interspersed with regular amounts of exercise, recreation and rest. . . .

But let me make one thing clear. As of this moment, there is not the slightest doubt that I can now perform as well as I ever have all of the important duties of the Presidency. . . .

He said that he would have to eliminate many of the social and ceremonial functions of his office and that he would not stump the country during the campaign.

He then cited his political reasons for running again, concluding:

The work that I set out four years ago to do has not yet reached the state of development and fruition that I then hoped could be accomplished within the period of a single term in this office.

When his half-hour talk was ended, the President joined his wife and Major and Mrs. Eisenhower and other members of his family who had come into the office for the broadcast. Throughout the day he had not shown any of the elation that was sweeping through the Republican ranks all over the country as a result of his decision. Rather, his feeling seemed to be one of profound relief that he had at last made up his mind and had put the matter behind him. Before leaving his office he bade members of his staff good night.

"I'm glad to get that off my chest," he told them.

The Eisenhowers strolled back to the White House proper and took an elevator to the second floor. It had been a long day for the President and in a little while he went to bed.

INDEX

Acheson, Dean, 14, 260; outlines foreign problems facing new administration, 15
Adams, Charles, 366
Adams, Sherman, 12, 96, 156, 214, 248, 254, 321, 342, 369, 374-375, 378, 387, 394 ff., 403; responsibilities of and power wielded by, 69-72; Eisenhower's great faith in, 71-72
Adenauer, Konrad, 16
Advertising agency, coaching by, on TV round-table discussion, 146
Aerial inspection plan, 343-345
African-Asian Conference, 309
Agency for Area Development, 382
"Agonizing reappraisal," 309
Air Force, lag behind Soviet Union, 329
Air Force budget, cuts in, 52-54
Alabama, University of, protest against segregation in, 390
Allen, George E., 359
Amalgamated Clothing Workers Union, 219
American Association for the United Nations, 239
American Bar Association, 236, 238-239, 358
American Federation of Labor, 219
American Medical Association, 228, 238
American Retail Federation, 160
American Society of Newspaper Editors speech, 72-74, 266
Americans for Democratic Action, 229
Anderson, Dillon, 69
Anderson, Robert B., 158, 348
Andersonville, 207
Antisegregationists, 390

Antisubversive program, 274
Appointments, White House control over, 99; see also Patronage
Arab-Israeli policy, 67
Arms race, 389
Armstrong, J. Sinclair, 340
Army manpower cuts, opposed by Gen. Ridgway, 330
Army manpower problems, 324 ff.
Asia, as pivot in cold war, 18
Associated Negro Press, 155
Astor, Lady Nancy, 108
Aswan Dam, Egypt, 388
Atchison, Topeka & Santa Fe Railroad, 401
Atom bomb, Russian, 2, 51
Atomic arms race, 184
Atomic energy, international control of, 74
Atomic Energy Act of 1946, 44
Atomic Energy Commission, 43, 160, 166, 294, 357
Atomic Energy Conference, Geneva, 192
Atoms-for-peace plan, 164, 187 ff., 349-350
Augusta, Ga., summer home, 194
Augusta National Golf Club, 12-13
Austin, Warren R., 99
Automobile industry, unemployment in, 218

Balanced budget, see Budget
Baldwin, Hanson W., 126
Baruch plan for international control of atomic energy, 345
Batten, Barton, Durstine & Osborn, 146

409

259, 301, 325; performance on Korean trip, 19
Radio Corporation of America, 334
Randall, Clarence B., 168
Rankin, J. Lee, 161
Ray, Philip A., 341
Rayburn, Sam, 312, 321
Reactors, research, for free world, 192
Recession, onset of, 208 ff.; warning signals of, 165
Reciprocal Trade Agreements Act, 16
Red China, see Communist China
Reed, Daniel A., 59-60, 172
Reed-Curtis plan for social security extension, 173
Reinsurance bill, 273
Republican administration, 25-35
Republican National Committee, 62, 96; Finance Committee, 152, 334
Republican Party, interparty strife, 143-144; loses control of Congress, 282 ff.; 1954 Congressional election campaign, 269 ff.; Old Guard elements, 84; split over mutual security appropriations, 151; suspense over question of Eisenhower candidacy, 387
Republicans, "positive" vs. "negative," 400
Reuther, Walter P., 33, 160, 212, 219
Rhee, Syngman, 45, 61; releases anti-Communist North Korean prisoners, 120-123; threat to pull out ROK forces, 124-125
Richfield Oil Corporation, 401
Ridgway, Gen. Matthew B., 263, 301-302; clash with Secretary Wilson, 327-329
Roberts, C. Wesley, 96, 203
Robertson, Walter S., 123-124
Robinson, William E., 200, 401
Rockefeller, Nelson A., 67, 173, 345, 348, 388
Rogers, William P., 367-368
Roosevelt, Franklin Delano, 8, 12, 48; court-packing proposal, 162
Roosevelt, John A., 160
Roosevelt, Theodore, 152

Rosenberg, Ethel and Julius, 42; guilt corroborated, 45-50; Presidential clemency sought, 43
Rovere, Richard H., 74
Rowley, James J., 365
Rumbough, Stanley M., Jr., 348
Russia, Eisenhower speech on "peace offensive" aims of, 72-74; quest for improved relations with, 72 ff.; progress in jet plant production, 56; see also Soviet, Soviet Union

St. Lawrence Seaway Development Corporation, 76
St. Lawrence Seaway project, 65, 76-78, 143, 338; passage of bill, 78
Salk polio vaccine problems, 322-323
Saltonstall, Leverett, 110, 255
Sands Point Naval Station, 19
Schine, G. David, 90, 254-255
School construction, Hobby-Brownell plan, 316
Schulz, Col. Robert L., 199, 202
Schuman, Robert, 16
Second term, reasons for running, 400 ff.
Securities and Exchange Commission, 340
Security, vs. people's wants, 62
Security risks, 80, 286
Segregated schools, Army posts, 155 ff.
Segregation, Autherine Lucy incident, 390; problems of, 155-160; unconstitutional, 161
Senate Appropriations Committee, 133
Senate Armed Services Committee, 255, 329
Senate Committee on Labor and Public Welfare, 26
Senate Democratic Policy Committee, 49
Senate Finance Committee, 218
Senate Foreign Relations Committee, 87, 306
Senate Judiciary Committee, 390
Senate Permanent Investigations Subcommittee, 94, 244, 333-334
Seventh Fleet, U.S. Navy, defense of

Set in Linotype Electra
Format by Robert Cheney
Manufactured by The Haddon Craftsmen, Inc.
Published by HARPER & BROTHERS, New York